£13.99

To BRian with
fRom brother.

CW00971238

NO DOGS

AND

NOT MANY

CHINESE

NO DOGS
AND
NOT MANY
CHINESE

TREATY PORT LIFE IN CHINA
1843–1943

FRANCES WOOD

JOHN MURRAY
Albemarle Street, London

First published in 1998
by John Murray (Publishers) Ltd,
50 Albemarle Street, London W1X 4BD

A catalogue record for this book is available from the British Library

ISBN 0-7195-5758 5

Typeset in Adobe Garamond by Servis Filmsetting Ltd
Printed and bound in Great Britain by The University Press, Cambridge

Contents

Contents

Illustrations

The author and publishers with to thank the following for permission to reproduce illustrations: Plates 1 and 6, Trustees of the National Museums of Scotland; 2, 3, and 4, Martyn Gregory; 8, 10, 31, 33 and 43, HSBC Group Archives; 9, Miss P.B. Hawkings; 12 and 50, Education Board of the Merchant Company of Edinburgh and the School Governing Council of George Watson's College; 13, John S. Service; 15 and 22, Mrs N. Newman; 16, 19 and 47, Trustees of the British Library; 21, Special Collections, American Museum of Natural History, New York; 23, Mr B.J.N. Ogden; 24 and 26, ICI Archives; 25, Mission Photograph Album Collection, United Methodist Church Archives, Madison NJ; 30 and 52, Hulton Getty; 34, Daphne Robson; 36, Brian Power; 37 and 39, Katy Talati; 38, *Mervyn Peake: Writings and Drawings* ed. Maeve Gilmore & Sheelagh Johnson (Academy Editions, London/David Higham Associates); 40, Rena Rabinovich Krasno; 42 and 55, MacQuitty International Collection; 44, 45, and 56, Erh Dongqiang; 51, L'Illustration/Sygma.

Acknowledgements

My principal debt is to the thousands of ex-treaty port inhabitants and visitors who wrote their memoirs. In a random way, though much helped by Truong Buu Khanh, I have collected many volumes of China memoirs over the years, although I have also relied upon the Library of the School of Oriental and African Studies and the British Library. I have quoted from many at length, where my editor has let me, for various reasons. Visiting former treaty ports in recent years, I have greatly enjoyed finding sites described in old books. Eating ice cream with chocolate sauce in Kiessling's in Tientsin (during the Cultural Revolution, when it was temporarily renamed 'the Tianjin Canteen') was the more enjoyable for thinking of all those who had done so over the decades. And we took cold winter picnics to the terrace at Tan-che ssu, above pine-covered and frosty mountains, because this was the setting of Ann Bridge's *Peking Picnic*.

These reminiscences also remind us of how long ago it all was. Jokes about servants, and complaints about odd-tasting food and strange habits were part of life then and are perhaps less amusing when retold. It can be hard, writing about the treaty ports, not to begin to see all their foreign inhabitants as blimpish: using their own words was one way of trying not to judge them.

I am grateful to Katy Talati for showing me her memoirs and to my uncle Adrian for telling me about Chefoo School, its aubergine diet and the extraordinarily complex travel arrangements necessary to get home to his medical missionary parents for the holidays. And also to Rosemary Seton and Anne-Marie Erlich who made helpful suggestions about illustrations, and to Val Phillips of the Archive of the Royal Commission for the Exhibition of 1851. I am very grateful, as always, to my parents for so much help. It was Gail Pirkis of John Murray who commissioned the book and I have been conscious throughout, in the best possible way, of her knowledge of the subject. She has been very patient and extremely helpful.

The author and publishers would like to thank all those responsible for giving permission to reprint copyright material. Unless otherwise stated, all sources were published in London: Harold Acton, *Memoirs of an Aesthete* (Hamish Hamilton, 1984). Reprinted by permission of David Higham Associates Ltd; Fay Angus, *White Pagoda* (Illinois, Tyndale House Publishers Inc., 1978). Reprinted by permission of the author; W. H. Auden and Christopher Isherwood, *Journey to a War* (Faber & Faber Ltd, 1939); J.G. Ballard, *Empire of the Sun* (Victor Gollancz, 1984); J.G. Ballard, *The Times*. Quotation reproduced by permission of the author care of Margaret Hanbury, 27 Walcot Square, London SE11 4UB; Ann Bridge, *Four Part Setting* (1941). Reprinted by permission of Peters Fraser & Dunlop Group Ltd; Ann Bridge, *Peking Picnic* (Chatto & Windus, 1938). Reprinted by permission of the Peters Fraser & Dunlop Group Ltd; Robert Byron, ed. Lucy Butler, *Letters Home* (John Murray, 1991); Tsai Chin, *Daughter of Shanghai* (Chatto & Windus, 1988); Christopher Cook, *The Lion and the Dragon* (Elm Tree Books, 1985); Hope Danby, *My Boy Chang* (Victor Gollancz, 1955); John Espey, *Minor Heresies, Major Departures: A China Mission Boyhood* (California, University of California Press, 1994) © The Regents of the University of California; Peter Fleming, *News from Tartary* (Jonathan Cape, 1936) © the estate of Peter Fleming; Joy Grant, *Stella Benson* (Macmillan, 1987); Theodore Harris, *Pearl Buck* (Methuen, 1970), Harol Ober Associates, Inc., New York; Charles Higham, *Wallis* (Pan/Macmillan, 1989); Bernard Llewellyn, *The Chinese Puzzle* (Allen & Unwin, 1953), courtesy of HarperCollins Publishers Ltd; S.J. Perelman, *Crazy Like a Fox* (New York, Random House, c. 1944); Arthur Ransome, *The Chinese Puzzle* (Allen & Unwin, 1927); The Royal Archives © Her Majesty the Queen; John S. Service, *Golden Inches: The China Memoir of Grace Service* (California, University of California Press, 1989), © The Regents of the University of California; Osbert Sitwell, *Escape With Me* (Macmillan, 1949). Reprinted by permission of David Higham Associates Ltd; Stead Sisters, *Stone-Paper-Scissors* (Deddington, Oxford Publishing, 1991). Reprinted by permission of the authors; and Adeline Yen Mah, *Falling Leaves* (Michael Joseph, 1997).

Every effort has been made to trace copyright holders. In a few cases this has proved impossible. The author and publishers of this book would be pleased to hear from any copyright holders not acknowledged.

Transliteration

Romanization systems were invented by foreigners: the Chinese were and are quite happy with characters. When English-language newspapers changed from the Wade-Giles system to *pinyin* in 1976, many people got the mistaken impression that the Chinese had suddenly started calling their cities by different names. Nothing of the sort had occurred: it was simply that foreigners had adopted yet another spelling system.

Because I have used so many antiquated sources and because I describe an antiquated system, I have chosen to give the names of the treaty ports in the romanization system used (not always accurately) by most English-speaking foreigners of the period, sometimes described as the 'Post Office system' (meaning, of course, the foreign-run Chinese Post Office). I am not entirely happy with this choice and apologize to those whom it confuses. At the time of which I am writing, the Germans and the French also used their own romanization systems, and some English writers preferred yet another system followed in Morrison's *Dictionary* (1819). To this confusing mixture was added the (English) Wade-Giles system, considered slightly more 'scientific' than that of the Post Office.

The first time a place is referred to in the text, the current *pinyin* romanization is given in brackets: a full list is supplied in the Glossary. People's names are given in Wade-Giles romanization in the text; the *pinyin* equivalent is supplied in the Index.

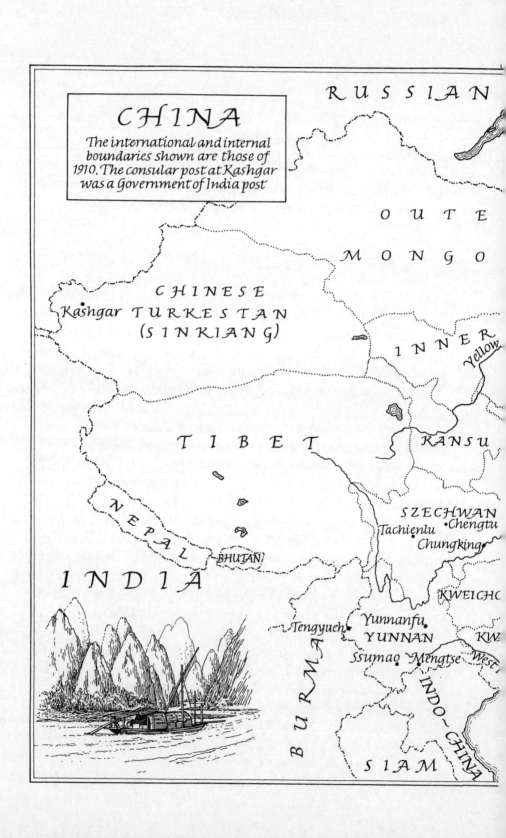

CHINA

The international and internal
boundaries shown are those of
1910. The consular post at Kashgar
was a Government of India post

RUSSIAN

OUTE

MONGO

CHINESE
Kashgar TURKESTAN
(SINKIANG)

INNER

Yellow

TIBET

KANSU

NEPAL

BHUTAN

SZECHWAN
Tachienlu •Chengtu
Chungking

INDIA

KWEICHC

Tengyueh• •Yunnanfu•
YUNNAN

KW

Ssumao •Mengtse •West

BURMA

INDO-CHINA

SIAM

EMPIRE

Lake
Baikal

R

L I A

MONGOLIA

HEILUNGKIANG

Harbin

MANCHURIA

Mukden

CHIHLI
(HOPEH)

Newchwang
Antung

Peking

KOREA

Peitaiho

Port
Arthur

Tokyo

Tientsin Taku
Taiyuan

Chefoo

Tsinan

Weihaiwei

SHANTUNG

Tsingtao
Kiaochow Bay

J
A
P
A
N

SHENSI

KIANGSU

HONAN

Nanking Chinkiang
Wuhu Soochow
Mokanshan Shanghai
HUPEH ANHWEI Hangchow
Yangtze Ichang Hankow Ningpo Chusan
R. Shasi archipelago
Kiukiang CHEKIANG
Yochow Kuling Wenchow
Changsha

HUNAN

KIANGSI

Foochow Pagoda Island
FUKIEN Tamsui Keelung

FORMOSA

ANGSI KWANGTUNG Amoy Tainan
Wuchow Samshui Swatow
Kongmoon Canton Hong Kong
Pakhoi Macao

Hoihow

HAINAN

Miles Kms.
0 ⫘ 0
100 ⫘ 200
200 ⫘ 400
300 ⫘ 600
400 ⫘ 800
500 ⫘

INTRODUCTION
Definitions

For a hundred years, between 1843 and 1943, there existed in China a series of treaty ports, created to serve as a vehicle for British and other Western interests in trade, diplomacy and evangelism, and established in the face of Chinese opposition. Dictionary definitions simply state that the treaty ports were 'opened' to foreign trade by 'treaty' and that there were treaty ports not only in China but also in other countries such as Japan and Korea. Nonetheless, it was in China that the treaty ports lasted longest, and there that they developed to a point where many foreign residents, born and brought up in them, sometimes over several generations, considered them their home.

From the beginning, the form they took varied, so that no single definition can serve to cover them all. The earliest treaty ports, opened in 1843, were indeed ports, whether coastal or up-river. Yet some of the places opened to foreign trade and residence by 1924 had never been the subject of a treaty and were hundreds of miles from the sea or navigable rivers. In most of the first treaty ports, 'concessions' or areas of land were marked out and 'rented' by foreign governments, who 'sub-let' to their nationals. In others, there were 'settlements' where foreign residents rented land and property directly from Chinese landlords. In still others, like Nanking (Nanjing), there was neither a concession nor a settlement: foreign residents lived side by side with Chinese. Some treaty ports, such as Shanghai, developed into great cities. Others, such as Ichang (Yichang) or Pakhoi (Beihai), were small and difficult of access, and never fulfilled the hopes invested in them.

To the Chinese, the existence of the treaty ports on Chinese territory, of whatever kind, was deemed a form of 'semi-colonialism'. It was imposed by force and deprived the Chinese government of authority over settlements in many cities and towns within China. Not only the Chinese government felt aggrieved. Many Chinese writers mention the public gardens laid out in the concessions, with bandstands, flower-beds and notice-boards inscribed with regulations. 'No dogs or Chinese' has become a stock phrase denoting the insulting existence of these municipal parks. Whilst it is not true that there was ever a sign bearing that bald prohibition – municipal councils in China were as long-winded as anywhere else – the hundreds of rules and regulations governing these tiny scraps of park did indeed exclude most Chinese people and all dogs, ball games, the riding of bicycles and the picking of flowers.

One Western author has defined the system as 'informal empire' for though the treaty ports and concessions were, in effect, ruled by foreigners, there was only a limited measure of foreign financial support and direction.[1] An imperial possession like India was ruled from home: though a colonial civil service was established under governors-general, ultimate responsibility rested in London. In China, the British (and the French and Americans who were close on Britain's tail) did not establish a colonial government: in the treaty ports there gradually developed a system of local government in the municipal councils, established by foreign residents for their own convenience and security. These were dependent upon the concept of 'extraterritoriality' (which exempted the foreigner from local, Chinese laws) first enunciated in the Treaty of Nanking and more fully defined in the Convention of Chefoo of 1876.[2]

Municipal councils were only part of a developing system of self-government which also saw the establishment of local courts of law to protect extraterritorials. A British Supreme Court was established in Shanghai in 1865 to exercise full civil, criminal and Admiralty jurisdiction over British subjects in China and Korea, though it was not empowered to grant divorce.[3] There was also a 'Mixed Court' in Shanghai from 1863, a police court where a Chinese magistrate presided in cases involving foreign interests. Consular assessors (British and American consular officers sitting twice a week, a German once a week) attended the court and could overrule the Chinese magistrate (although the exercise of this privilege frequently caused riots).

2

There were, however, representatives of the foreign powers in China in all the treaty ports: the consuls. They were answerable to their foreign ministries at home but could not always control the municipal councils as they might have wished. Foreign regiments were also stationed in China for the protection of foreign nationals and their property, and foreign naval gunboats anchored at the coastal ports and inland, on China's rivers, to the same end.

As the treaty ports developed, both in number and size, more and more foreign residents began to arrive. Along with the merchants and their families came lawyers and doctors, captains in charge of the Yangtze trading ships, dressmakers, architects and builders, policemen and churchmen – all the professions necessary to maintain a life away from home. Missionaries, too, from America and all over Europe reached China in increasing numbers, intent on converting the Chinese to their faith. In time the treaty ports grew into self-contained Western enclaves where foreign families did their best to live their lives as they might have done back home.

The most famous of the treaty ports – perhaps also the most infamous – was Shanghai, long a byword for lawlessness, where East and West co-existed in great wealth and extreme poverty. It was there that Maurice Dekobra, author of *Confucius en pull-over*, encountered taxi-girls clad only in skimpy silk dresses, absconders from justice, gun-runners and the 'electrical consul' of a small Latin American state who allowed the installation of a roulette wheel in his apartment in the French Concession. Gambling was forbidden but the consular residence enjoyed extraterritorial privileges. The consul went further, fixing a powerful magnet under the roulette wheel, and did very well until he played with a Canadian engineer who wore hob-nailed boots.[4]

Yet accounts of exotic low life in Shanghai have tended to obscure a very different aspect of foreign residence in China. For many of those who lived in the treaty ports attempted, above all, to maintain a Western way of life, albeit with exotic ingredients. The domestic concerns of Hope Danby, who lived in China for over twenty years and left only when the Japanese threatened to intern all enemy aliens after Pearl Harbor, were perhaps more representative than any account of Shanghai's *demi-monde*. In 1925 she decided to hire a new servant. A young man named Chang appeared with a sheaf of references, one of which, warmly commendatory, had been written in 1886. Another dated 1901 praised his courage during the Boxer rebellion; others, incomprehensible to Chang, were less complimentary: 'If you value the contents of your purse, kick him out as soon as you read this'; 'Chang, my pony-boy, is a rascal. He has cheated me every day during the past year.' Nevertheless, Mrs Danby hired Chang and grew very fond of both him and his family. There were irritations, as when she found him 'washing his feet in the largest saucepan with a cake of my best French soap floating in the grimy water' and ironing 'in a time-honoured Chinese way. This was by filling their mouths with water until their cheeks bulged; then blowing out a great spray on to the clothes.' His cooking was good but his menus were difficult to interpret: 'Rost Turk . . . Befe Stank . . . Snakes on Tost'; the last turned out to be snipe. However, Chang was brave and loyal. When Mrs Danby found herself surrounded by wild and hungry warlord soldiers on a weekend trip, Chang, clutching a cage containing his precious lark, announced that Mrs Danby was a very important person and that harming her would bring enormous misfortune on the soldiers. He then supervised the distribution of money so that they could buy food.[5]

The consequence of attempting to live life as it was lived back home was remarked upon by Harry Franck, an American journalist who visited Shanghai in 1925. The typical Shanghai businessman, he observed,

> makes it almost a point of honor to come into the least possible contact with the Chinese, with the subordinates in his office only professionally, with his house and club servants, his grooms, caddies, tennis-ball chasers – no self-respecting foreigner in China would any more dream of pursuing his tennis-balls beyond the foul line than of driving his own car – in the same superficial, impersonal way that he does with . . . a rickshaw man . . . I have met adult children . . . who were born and have spent most of their lives in Shanghai yet have never been in China . . . they have never set foot in the Chinese city, just across the street from the foreign settlement; when they have gone to the foreign school at this or that treaty port, to Kuling . . . or to some other foreign resort, they have travelled by foreign steamers.[6]

Though Shanghai has come to stand for treaty port China, it was not necessarily typical. It was easier there, and in Tientsin (Tianjin), to live as if China hardly existed, but in many of the treaty ports and foreign settlements life was difficult. Milk for babies and young children was hard to find, meat and vegetables were strange and exotic, unknown ailments struck fast and fatally, and clothing and houses were eaten by white ants. The only Chinese that many foreigners came into contact with were their servants. They may have been affordable in far greater numbers than at home, but they were difficult to understand and to train in Western ways. At times, the smaller treaty ports, inhabited by no more than a handful of beleaguered foreigners, seemed frighteningly distant from the comforts and security of Shanghai. In these small communities, there were constant frictions between French and British, between Catholic priests and Protestant missionaries. In tiny Chinkiang (Zhenjiang), the local consul watched helplessly as warring British merchants set up rival municipal councils. In isolated Pakhoi, never attractive to British trade and residence, consul after consul suffered a nervous breakdown.

And even in Shanghai, throughout the hundred years of the treaty port, external events impinged on the city's foreign residents. Stones were thrown with regularity, rebellious armies interrupted commerce and anti-foreign riots were quick to break out. In the twentieth century, when warlord armies made travel difficult, some of the treaty ports were besieged, banditry was prevalent and from 1937 onwards the Japanese threatened.

Though life in the treaty ports was not always easy, by the time they came to an end there were many families who had lived in China for three generations, for whom treaty port life was all they knew. Though driven out of China in the 1940s, after extraterritoriality had for practical and political reasons been abandoned and the concessions had been returned to a China that was itself changing, they retained fond memories of the life they had left behind.

Between 1843 and 1943, Russia, Germany, France, Italy, America and Japan all held territorial concessions in China. In this polyglot community Britain, however, dominated numerically and led the way in the administration of the treaty ports. It is British sources and British lives therefore which form the focus of this book. In describing their experiences I have taken treaty port life to be virtually synonymous with 'foreign' life in China during the hundred-year period. The portmanteau term also corresponds with the treaty port 'mind', a mentality castigated by Arthur Ransome in the 1920s for its blinkered self-interest. I hope, however, that I have been able to place more emphasis on the variety of foreign experiences in the very different settlements in different parts of China and to broaden somewhat Arthur Ransome's narrow view of narrow minds, for life in China between 1843 and 1943 was by no means static and residence in the treaty ports deeply affected many people.

Paradoxically, the treaty ports never really fulfilled the ends of those who fought to establish them. Their very existence contradicted the principle of free trade upon which they had been founded. Traders lobbying for the opening of China to foreign trade may have envisaged them as secure bases from which to conquer undreamt-of markets, but the Chinese saw them as areas of confinement. These opposing views were to dominate their history.

PART I

The Founding of the Treaty Ports
1750–1860

I

The China Trade

The earliest treaty ports in China were a product of the first war between Britain and China, a war whose immediate cause was opium but whose origins lay in a conflict of cultures.

The Chinese traditionally regarded those beyond the Chinese pale

> as barbarians, sometimes formidable in a barbarous way but by definition morally and intellectually inferior. Through a mist of ignorance and cultural arrogance, they saw in Western civilization, fatefully advancing towards them in a shrinking world, no more than further barbarism, and met it with their traditional airs of lordly superiority.[1]

The British East India Company, holding a monopoly from the Crown on trade with China, had since the early eighteenth century conducted a profitable business. But it did so on humiliating and frustrating terms. Though the Portuguese were able to maintain their foothold in Macao, on the southern coast of China, where they had been established since the sixteenth century, the British and other foreign merchants were restricted by the Chinese authorities to the southern city of Canton (Guangzhou). The restrictions did not end there. Increasingly, foreign traders calling at Canton found themselves bound by imperial decrees, such as that of March 1760 which stipulated that they could trade only with a group of named merchants, known as the Hong or Cohong merchants.[2] Hong was derived from the Chinese *hang*, meaning company or firm; the term was applied to both foreign firms and their buildings. All such trade was controlled by the Hoppo,[3] the Controller of Customs appointed by the court in Peking (Beijing)

9

who himself controlled the licensed group of Cohong merchants. This monopoly denied foreign traders free access to raw materials and led to price-fixing and considerable corruption as the Hoppo tried to make as much money as he could for himself and his associates during his brief period of office.

Foreigners were not allowed to deal directly with shopkeepers, nor to learn Chinese or keep Chinese servants. They were not permitted to stay throughout the year in Canton but could arrive only in the autumn and were required to depart in January or early February. As well as being forbidden permanent residence, they were also denied access to the city itself and were allowed to live and move only on a small area of the shoreline. Lastly, no foreign women were allowed at Canton. Such restrictions caused inevitable frustration with the Chinese authorities.

Nevertheless, the East India Company built a handsome mansion and godown (warehouse) on the Canton shore. In 1769, William Hickey, libertine, diarist and temporarily a member of the East India Company's armed forces in Madras, left India to return home via Canton. Between mid-August and early December, he stayed in the East India Company factory (the term used for what was effectively a trade centre) which stood on the riverside between the French and the Swedish factories and which he described in some detail.

> The English being far more numerous than any other nation trading with China, their range of buildings is much the most extensive. Each supercargo [company agent] has four handsome rooms; the public apartments are in front looking to the river; the others go inland to a depth of two or three hundred feet, in broad courts, having the sets of rooms on each side, every set having a distinct and separate entrance with a small garden and every sort of convenience.

The factory, with its covered veranda, its rooms opening on to a court with windows back and front for a cooling draught and its association of storage facilities and living quarters, was built in a style that was to dominate European architecture in the Far East for nearly two hundred years. Hickey and his travelling companion Maclintock were allotted 'two spacious bedchambers with dressing-room adjoining each, two large sitting-rooms and one for eating – the whole neatly furnished and having a complete small library'. They were free to join the other eleven supercargoes for dinner in the great hall at two o'clock unless they preferred to eat in their rooms. Every evening, they drank coffee or tea at seven, then played cards or billiards or 'sat chatting on the terrace which projected from the hall and went several feet over the river, being supported by large piles; the situation was cool and refreshing'. At ten they ate supper and then retired to find their servants waiting with 'candles, slippers and all the etceteras of the night'. When they dined with a Mr Carvalho, a band played throughout the meal; dining with Pankeequa, a Cohong merchant, they were served *à l'anglaise* with knives and forks and entertained with a play, and on the following day there were fireworks, conjuring tricks and acrobatic shows, and 'everything was Chinese, all the European guests eating, or endeavouring to eat, with chopsticks'. Hickey was sick after a frog fricassee and, with slightly more frequency, 'from having swallowed so enormous a quantity as I had of a rich, luscious wine'.

The ship's surgeon on the East Indiaman *Ashburnham*, Denil Court, amused himself by enticing pickpockets with a handkerchief (securely tied to a coat button) dangling from his pocket. When anyone tried to take the handkerchief 'he suddenly turned upon the thief whom he began to thrash with a stout but pliant bamboo he carried in his hand for the purpose'. He also encouraged the visitors to break the local laws by taking 'a view of the interior of the city'. As soon as they passed beyond the limits allowed by the Chinese authorities, children pelted them with bricks and stones. Undeterred, they pushed past the guards at the gate and walked through the city, accompanied by 'hooting, pelting and ... dogs which followed us barking'. The city was a disappointment, lacking 'a single object of any kind that could in any way compensate for the ill-treatment we received', and Hickey counselled, 'Let no stranger ... ever think of forcing his way into Canton in the expectation of his being gratified by handsome buildings, or in any respect whatsoever.'[4]

Hickey was a visitor: whilst he forced his way into the forbidden city of Canton or took a boat to meet the prostitutes of Lob Lob Creek, the supercargoes were making their daily reports to London on the progress of trade, hampered by restrictions as to where and with whom they

could deal and who they could employ as interpreters or pilots or compradors (their Chinese agents).

The East India Company also had problems at home where a series
of Acts of Parliament, designed to protect British textile manufacturers
from imported silks and calicoes, left them with tea as 'the only article
which could be forced into universal consumption without competing
against home manufacture';[5] in 1783 alone, nearly six million pounds of
it were sold in London. It provided the whole profit of the East India
Company and government-imposed duties on tea raised 10 per cent of
the total revenue of England. Such success, however, left the Company
with an increasing imbalance in trade. Only gold and silver bullion were
accepted in China. Yet between 1792 and 1807, while Company exports
from England to China were worth only £16,602,338, imports from
China were valued at £27,157,006.[6]

To redress this imbalance, two significant measures were taken. The
first was to make use of the 'country trade', in other words licensing
private traders to export Indian goods that were, unlike British textiles,
in demand in China; the second was to make political representations
to the Chinese government in Peking.

In 1787, the consumptive Lieutenant-Colonel Charles Cathcart
embarked on an official British embassy to China. He was furnished
with royal letters of accreditation, but the embassy was financed by the
East India Company. Cathcart died at sea off Sumatra in 1788 without
ever reaching China.[7] Owing to a failure of communication between
Canton and London, the opportunity to send another mission on the
occasion of the Ch'ien-lung emperor's auspicious eightieth birthday (25
September 1791) when the emperor might be assumed to be in a warm
and welcoming mood, was missed, and it was not until 1792 that Lord
Macartney of Lissanoure was dispatched by the East India Company at
the head of a second embassy. His aims were

> first, to negotiate a treaty of commerce and friendship; second, to estab-
> lish an ambassador at the Court of Peking; third, to improve trading
> conditions at Canton; fourth, to extend British trade by opening new
> ports; fifth, to persuade the Chinese to cede an island base to Britain ...
> probably on the Chusan [Zhoushan] archipelago, closer to the tea and
> silk-producing areas, thus reducing transport costs and provincial taxes;
> and sixth, to create new markets in China, especially Peking.[8]

In some respects the mission was very successful. Macartney's entourage included a young but skilful artist, William Alexander, whose massive sketchbooks and finished watercolours present a unique, almost photographic view of China and the Chinese; a self-taught astronomer and 'mechanic', Dr Dinwiddie, who brought an air balloon and a diving bell to demonstrate to the Chinese and collected plants for Kew; and Lieutenant Henry William Parish who produced maps and elevations of the Chusan archipelago, the Great Wall and the imperial temples at Jehol (Chengde). The wealth of information thus acquired became greatly in demand throughout Europe, for apart from the official report on the embassy produced by Macartney's Vice-Minister Plenipotentiary, Sir George Leonard Staunton,[9] many other accounts were published (and translated into Polish, French, German and Dutch). They included those of Huttner (the German tutor to Staunton's son, Macartney's page-boy), the Comptroller Sir John Barrow and even Macartney's valet, Aeneas Anderson, whose ghost-written book went into two editions in London and Dublin and was translated into French, to the disgust of Sir John Barrow.

Literary success came later. In China each of Macartney's diplomatic requests was refused. There has been much discussion as to why the embassy failed, often emphasizing Macartney's refusal to kowtow (kneel and knock his head three times on the ground before the emperor),[10] but the fact was that the Chinese government was not prepared to accept the European idea of free trade.

The East India Company's second measure to improve its trade balance was more successful. Two Indian products, raw cotton and opium, shipped on licensed 'country ships' – 'small pinnaces and galleys ... Malay prahus and Chinese junks, often commanded but rarely crewed by Europeans' – found ready buyers in Canton. Opium, the product of the opium poppy, was known in China as a medicine and cultivated there though not widely used. However, the Chinese were quick to adopt the drug for recreational as well as medicinal purposes, as the East India Company soon discovered.

An imperial edict banning the import of opium was issued at the end of the eighteenth century but little effort was made to enforce it.[11] As the number of shipments of opium in privately licensed ships grew – from 600 chests in 1750 to 5,106 in 1816 and 23,570 in 1832[12] – a further

British embassy was sent to China in 1816 under Lord Amherst. He took with him Sir George Staunton who had accompanied Lord Macartney as his page in 1792 when he was only 11 years old. He had learned Chinese on the voyage from two Chinese Jesuit converts, and by addressing the elderly Ch'ien-lung emperor in Chinese he had succeeded in charming him. When he accompanied Lord Amherst to Peking in 1816, he was serving as the Chief of the East India Company factory in Canton. Sir John Davis, a long-time servant of the East India Company and later Governor of Hong Kong, also accompanied the ill-fated embassy. This time, the British refusal to kowtow loomed large and Amherst stayed only one day in Peking, having been summoned to the imperial presence a day early and before he could get his baggage and 'appear decently before the emperor'.[13]

Western traders were well aware of the illegality of shipping opium, as was illustrated in the case of the *Emily*, an American ship which arrived at Canton in 1821. When a crew member accidentally dropped a pot overboard, hitting a fruit-seller in a small boat below who fell into the water and drowned, the captain at first refused to hand him over to the local authorities for punishment. However, fearing that his illegal cargo would be seized and that this would be followed by a blanket ban on all American trade at Canton, he eventually gave up the sailor who was tried in secret and executed. Such cases, which were increasingly common, added another item to the list of grievances against the Canton authorities and led to calls for foreigners to be allowed to conduct their own trials of their own people. Yet whilst calling for legal independence, ships of all nations continued to import illegal opium, avoiding the local authorities by unloading at the fortified hulks moored near Lintin (Lingding) Island below Canton. The opium was then carried away in small, fast local boats.

By 1825, the balance of trade, once so unfavourable to the East India Company, had swung in the other direction, thanks to opium, and the amount of Chinese silver required to buy the drug was beginning to threaten the national economy.[14] In 1834, in the interests of free trade, the East India Company's monopoly on trade with the Far East was ended by Parliament. There followed a predictable increase in the number of private traders calling at Canton with cargoes of opium. Aware that the increasing outflow of silver in payment for imported opium was endangering the economy, in 1838, the Tao-kuang emperor appointed Lin Tse-hsu, an official from Foochow (Fuzhou) in Fukien (Fujian) province, to take decisive action to stop the opium trade. He tried to do so through public appeals for all smokers to hand over their pipes and opium, and by instructing the Cohong merchants to deal with the Lintin hulks and enforce pledges from the foreign traders that they would not trade in the drug. He even addressed a letter to Queen Victoria in August 1839 begging her to stop the immoral trade and implying a threat to halt the export of tea and rhubarb to Britain, in the belief that withholding the latter laxative might bring a constipated nation to reason. The letter, not acknowledged, perhaps never received, had no effect.[15]

The foreign traders refused to give up their opium, claiming that since they traded on behalf of others it was not theirs to surrender. In March 1839 Lin tried to arrest Lancelot Dent of Dent & Co., one of the larger opium concerns, but finding Dent shielded by the foreign community, he then ordered the cessation of all trade and the withdrawal of all Chinese working in the factories. Next he proceeded to blockade the factories. After six weeks, 20,000 or more chests of opium were given up to Lin who then had to contrive the destruction of nearly three million pounds of raw opium: 500 labourers, under the supervision of 60 officials, broke up the balls of raw opium, mixed them with water and washed the residue into the sea.[16]

Furious at this destruction of foreign property, the Superintendent of Trade in China, Charles Elliot, a servant of the Crown since the abolition of the East India Company monopoly, appealed to the Foreign Secretary, Lord Palmerston. Palmerston wrote to 'The Minister of the Emperor of China' protesting at 'violent outrages' against British residents, and a considerable lobby for action against the Chinese grew in England, organized by the China merchants and led by the most prominent of them, William Jardine. In late May 1839, Elliot removed himself to the small island of Hong Kong and 16 warships, 4 armed steamships (amongst the first ever made), 28 transports and 4,000 troops (many of these stationed in India) were dispatched to China to reinforce Palmerston's protest. In June 1840, the flotilla blockaded the entrance to Canton's harbour. As this, the First Opium War, proceeded, Chusan was taken and the remainder of the

British fleet sailed to Taku (Dagu), the port of Tientsin, not far from Peking.

There, in January 1841, Ch'i-shan, governor-general of the region, negotiated the retreat of British troops from the north of China, an indemnity, direct official contact for the British with the Chinese government and the reopening of Canton – concessions for which he was sentenced to death (though the sentence was commuted to banishment).

Palmerston was angry that better terms had not been exacted from the Chinese and now dispatched Sir Henry Pottinger, Charles Elliot's successor as British Trade Superintendent, to negotiate directly with the emperor. By the time Pottinger arrived in the summer of 1841, the British had destroyed the Bogue forts near Canton and much else, and had occupied part of the city. Pottinger pushed inland up the Yangtze to Nanking and there concluded the treaty that was to open an unwilling China to foreign residence and trade.

The Treaty of Nanking, signed on 29 August 1842 and ratified the following year, stipulated the opening of Canton, Foochow, Amoy (Xiamen), Ningpo (Ningbo) and Shanghai to foreign residence and trade and the establishment of consulates. It also ceded the island of Hong Kong 'to be possessed in perpetuity' by Queen Victoria and her successors. The Canton Cohong system was abolished in favour of 'mercantile transactions with whatever persons they please'. Indemnities were agreed to pay for the opium that had been destroyed and to settle 'expenses incurred', and it was agreed that the debts owed by the frequently insolvent Cohong merchants should be met by the Chinese government. British subjects taken prisoner were to be immediately released and all Chinese who had worked for foreigners were granted an amnesty. British troops were to withdraw from Nanking but continue to hold Chusan until all the indemnities had been paid and the treaty ports opened. Opium, still an illegal drug, was not mentioned.

The treaty was of interest to other nations trading in China who had not been directly involved in the war. In early 1844, Caleb Cushing, a Congressman from Massachusetts, home of the American China traders, negotiated a supplementary treaty in Macao. Some of its provisions considerably extended the terms of the Treaty of Nanking, allowing Americans to acquire sites for the construction of Protestant missionary hospitals, churches and cemeteries, to employ freely any Chinese they wanted and to learn Chinese. The question of legal procedures was addressed in Article 21 which stipulated that Americans committing crimes in China should be tried by their consuls 'according to the laws of the United States', although Americans trading in opium would still be dealt with by the Chinese authorities.

The French further extended these treaty provisions in October 1844, reinforcing the right of extraterritoriality – by which foreigners were judged according to their own laws – by extending authority to the consuls of any friendly power if a French consul was unavailable. They also achieved the overturning of the Yung-cheng emperor's edict of 1724 which had ordered the closure of all Christian (at the time, Catholic) churches and the renunciation of the faith.[17] The protection given to Catholics in China was soon extended to cover Protestant missionaries as well. In a flurry of supplementary legislation, the British had also renegotiated terms. By the inappropriately named 'most favoured nation' clause of 1843 any 'additional privileges' granted to foreign countries were to be 'extended to and enjoyed by British subjects', thus limiting the Chinese government's ability to play one nation off against another.[18]

The treaty ports were created by Western governments mindful of the need to avoid the enormous expense of imperial administration, as experienced by the East India Company in India. Yet though the East India Company had been behind the earliest attempts to open China to trade, its final influence was more indirect. In the end, pressure on Palmerston to act against the Chinese government had been largely organized by the private opium trader William Jardine, on his own behalf and that of his fellow-merchants. They now turned their attention to establishing their headquarters in the new treaty ports.

2

Early Days in Shanghai

Of the five new treaty ports, Shanghai was the fastest to expand. In 1843 it had a foreign population of 100 of whom 7 were women. In 1850 this had grown to 175, not counting sailors. Far greater than the increase in population, however, was the growth in the number of ships calling at the port: 44 foreign ships arrived in 1844; a decade later, 437 dropped anchor in the muddy waters of the Whangpoo River in a single year.[1]

The rapid growth of Shanghai had much to do with its position. Situated within the delta of the Yangtze River, which flows through the major silk- and tea-producing areas of China, it was nevertheless far enough from the sea to be protected from coastal typhoons. Such advantageous conditions had been noted as early as 1756 in an East India Company report. That year an exploratory East India Company ship, the *Lord Amherst*, sailed up the Whangpoo tributary of the Yangtze with a Mr H.H. Lindsay on board. Unable to get anywhere in negotiations with the local superintendent of trade, instead he counted the junks on the busy river and felt hopeful of an opening for British woollen textiles in the cooler western provinces accessible via the Yangtze: 'Considering the extraordinary advantages which this place possesses for foreign trade,' he noted prematurely, 'it is wonderful that it has not attracted more observation.'[2]

He was not alone in his assessment. Nearly eighty years later the missionary Dr Walter Medhurst visited Shanghai to 'ascertain the facilities for tract distribution and preaching',[3] and described it as 'one of the greatest emporiums of commerce on the east coast of China ... receiving silk brocades from the Arcadia of China ... The trade of this place is equal if not superior to that of Canton.'[4]

The city had first grown as a result of agricultural improvements during the T'ang dynasty (618–907) when drainage canals left much of what is now Shanghai above sea level, and during the Sung (960–1280) when sea transportation northwards of essential rice from the middle Yangtze made Shanghai a significant entrepôt. It was also important in the growing overseas trade in silk and tea, especially to Japan. Incursions by Japanese pirates in the early sixteenth century led to the walling of the town in 1554: the circular form of the walls and their gates (which were demolished in 1912) can still be seen in the street patterns and street names of Shanghai.

Robert Fortune, the Scottish superintendent of the hot-house department of the Royal Horticultural Society at Kew, was sent on a collecting trip to China shortly before the opening of the treaty ports in 1843. On that first visit, he called at all five ports and also made illegal forays beyond treaty port limits into Anhwei (Anhui) up the Yangtze, and into Chekiang (Zhejiang) and Fukien provinces.

Fortune described Shanghai, surrounded by rich agricultural country, as 'one vast garden'. The town was walled and the gates closed at night although the inhabitants could re-enter from the extensive suburbs by payment of a few cash, or not, according to his description of the process. 'When the gate is opened to one, a whole crowd are ready to rush through along with him, the first only paying the cash.' The walled city was filled with joss houses or temples where theatrical performances were held, and the streets and squares with jugglers, fortune-tellers and a 'jolly crew' of beggars.

> The streets are generally very narrow and in the day time are crowded with people actively engaged in business [selling] cotton goods, porcelain, ready-made clothes of all kinds beautifully lined with skins and fur, bamboo pipes six feet long ... pictures, bronzes ... But articles of food form of course the most extensive trade of all; and it is sometimes a difficult matter to get through the streets for the immense quantities of fish, pork, fruit and vegetables.[5]

Into this crowded city, the first British consul ventured in November 1843, bringing with him Walter Medhurst junior (who had accompanied his missionary father to the city in 1835). The consul, George Balfour, had served with the Madras forces in China, acting as receiver for the indemnity debts settled at the Treaty of Nanking. He established the first British consulate in the house of a wealthy local merchant. Robert Fortune was lodged in a similarly temporary manner,

> in a kind of bank or government shroff establishment, in company with two or three gentlemen who were here for purposes of trade. [A shroff was a silver expert employed to examine dollars and other forms of silver; in later use, a debt collector.] As none of us carried a cooking establishment with us, our meals were necessarily of the roughest description, neither exactly Chinese nor English but something between the two. Our bedrooms were miserably cold; often in the mornings we would find ourselves drenched in bed with the rain; and if snow fell it was blown through the windows and formed 'wreaths' on the floor . . . Whenever we moved out of the house, hundreds of people crowded the streets and followed in our wake, as anxious to catch a glimpse of us as crowds in London are to see the Queen.[6]

One of Balfour's first duties was to settle arrangements for the land allocated for foreign residence, a marshy waste which lay to the north of the circular walled city. The problem of the ownership of the land was settled by arranging leases with foreign governments for this concession land to be held 'in perpetuity'. Thus, whilst ultimate ownership of the land was Chinese, foreign investment in land and buildings was protected by payment of a nominal land rent. Land-renters contributed to the upkeep of roads and jetties, the income and expenditure of their contributions being organized by a small group appointed by the consul, the Committee on Roads and Jetties.[7]

The area given over to the British lay between the walled city with its dirty narrow streets and Soochow Creek to the north. Like most of the land allocated for foreign residents in the new treaty ports, it was vacant ground, given over to mulberry trees, cotton fields and ancestral graves. In Foochow, the area of foreign settlement was similarly situated in an old burial ground, a choice of location which, according to Paul Claudel, a later French vice-consul, made it difficult to keep servants who were frightened of ghosts. Pearl Buck's missionary parents' home in Chinkiang was also set amongst grave mounds. Though such sites were conveniently empty of other buildings, it is tempting to suspect that they were also selected as a deliberate challenge to unwelcome foreign residents.

In Shanghai, the Americans quickly acquired rights to land in Hongkew (Hongkou), north of Soochow Creek, and the French settled in an area south-west of the British concession. In 1849, Monsieur de Montigny, the first French consul, made a similar arrangement to that of Balfour with the senior Chinese official in Shanghai, establishing the French Concession.

Municipal government, however, was not the first consideration of the early settlers and it was not until 1854 that the British, French and American consuls proposed new land regulations and new municipal arrangements. The French Concession remained consul-run, but in the British concession an annual meeting of land-renters, of whom there were then about 300, fixed the rate to be paid for services and appointed a sub-committee to levy the rates and disburse funds. This committee marked the beginning of the Shanghai Municipal Council. Initially there were few Chinese residents within the British concession, but as a result of the Small Sword rebellion in the early 1850s, their numbers soon swelled with an influx of refugees. By July 1854 there were about 20,000 and it was decided that they should pay a house tax in order to enjoy the benefits of policing and street lighting, though they were not, of course, entitled to vote.[8]

The main preoccupation of foreign firms in Shanghai in the early days, however, was to establish trade and erect their headquarters. These bore a striking resemblance to the early 'factory' buildings of Canton and Macao, described by William Hickey nearly a hundred years before.

Though varying to a certain extent in details and in size, all foreign 'hongs' were very similar, because they were built to supply the same purposes. They all stood in their own compounds, enclosed by a wall; and varied in extent from one acre to two or three.

The important building was the dwelling house, which usually stood to the front part of the compound. It was built in a very solid fashion, with thick walls, and usually with a veranda running all round it both on the ground floor and the storey above. The number of rooms varied. As a rule the mercantile offices were all in this building, the spacious verandas being often enclosed and utilized as offices. The rest of the house was taken up with dwelling-rooms and bedrooms. The kitchen and servants' quarters were always quite apart in a building behind, but connected with the house by a covered way. At the sides of the compound, but generally thrown back a little, were the godowns . . .

The offices and dwellings of the Comprador and Shroffs . . . and all the Chinese mercantile assistants, were arranged around about the godowns. In most of the hongs . . . there were . . . also stables and mafoos' [grooms'] quarters. In the case of the large firms, in addition to the main dwelling house, there was an annexe, quite separate from it, with a separate entrance. In this building the assistants would live and have their mess, which was styled the junior mess, the partners occupying the main building, and being called the senior mess, both being served by the same kitchen.

When these buildings were erected, in the early days of Shanghai . . . there were no foreign architects; and the plans had to be drawn by the merchants themselves, with the assistance presumably of the Chinese architect or contractor. Probably the whole thing was managed by the comprador. This style of architecture . . . was christened by some wag the *compradoric* style . . .

There were usually two gates, with a carriage drive to the front door, one gate for entry and the other for exit. There was a flower-garden, with roses and many varieties of English flowers which grow well in Shanghai. In addition to these there were many of the semi-tropical plants and flowers such as flowering aloes, yuccas, and various palms; and wisteria in great abundance. The magnolia and tulip tree were generally found there, and occasionally a salisburia, so that the approach to the houses in spring was very picturesque.[9]

Within these walls, the merchants lived. Young men, selected in London to work for the great trading firms, spent the best part of every morning in the metropolis examining the different varieties of silk. Once they had mastered the difference between *taysaam* (of which there were at least five varieties) and *tsatlee* (of which there were also five varieties), they were sent off to China on a P&O steamer with other silk 'griffins' and the tea-men or *cha-sees*. 'Griffin' was the name applied to the wild ponies driven from Mongolia to Peking and Shanghai for foreigners to ride and race: their 'semi-wild, unkempt and ragged state' was assumed to be similar to the mental condition of new arrivals in the Far East.[10]

It was hardly surprising if the new arrivals were ragged for they had been on board ship for anything from three to five months or more.[11]

Once in Shanghai, a griffin was assigned to a room in the company mess, whereupon he might join his fellow-workers for a breakfast of boiled shad with cucumber, followed by roast spring snipe and beef-steak. After an afternoon in the silk-room, it was common to take a walk 'to shake up our livers' before dressing for a dinner of six or more courses, followed by cards and cigars.

Work followed a seasonal pattern and office hours were elastic. Though some of the big firms or hongs specialized in tea or silk or opium, most had multiple departments in the early days, covering tea, silk, Manchester cotton goods, shipping and insurance, and including possibly a land agency. Smaller firms might deal in 'muck and truck'; that is buffalo hide, horn, horsehair, bristles, Chinese grass and other items. The fastest form of communication with London was the telegraph, which took three weeks (as it involved some steamer transport beyond land lines), whereas letters took at least seven. Tea-men, pursuing what they called 'the blasted vegetable', spent more time out of Shanghai, travelling in late spring to Hankow (Hankou), Kiukiang (Jiujiang) or Foochow, near the tea-producing areas from which they were still, to their increasing fury, excluded. The tea all had to be tasted and inspected since the substitution of a lesser quality or, worse, adulteration was not uncommon. The tea might be coloured with Prussian blue or gypsum or it might contain, as Dr Herbert Giles, a former consular official and later Professor of Chinese at Cambridge University, noted, 'a medley of used tea-leaves, the leaves of various other plants, and rubbish of all kinds'.

Yet such difficulties with the raw materials were as nothing compared to the hideous complications with money. Hosea Ballou Morse, who served in the Chinese Imperial Maritime Customs for over thirty years, noted that 'In China, every one of the hundreds of commercial centres not only has its own [silver] tael-weight [a foreign term for an ounce], but in many cases has several standards side by side; and these taels of money will be weighed out in silver which, even in one place, will be of several degrees of fineness.' He continued with a baffling set of sums and equivalents:

> The weight of the Shanghai tael is made up of three elements – the weight, the quantity of silver, and a convention. The weight on the scale is the Tsaoping tael of 565.65 grains, the silver is reduced to a standard of 944 fine on the Kuping basis of 1,000 fine, and the convention is that

98 taels of this weight and this silver settle a liability of 100 taels 'Shanghai convention currency'. All official payments at Shanghai are made in this local currency, and the rate of exchange between the Government Treasury, or Kuping, tael is thus calculated:

Kuping taels 100 weight = Tsaoping taels	101.800
Add for touch of pure silver on two shoes	5.600
	107.400
Divide by the 'convention' 0.98	109.592
Add for meltage fee	.008
	109.600

There results, in consequence, the fixed rate: Tls. 100 Kuping are equivalent to Tls. 109.600 Shanghai, and in the same way, for Customs duties, merchants pay Shanghai Tls. 11.40 as the equivalent of Hai-kwan or Customs Tls. 100.[12]

Add to this crystal-clear set of figures the use of foreign silver dollars (Spanish Carolus III, Bolivian, Peruvian, Mexican and French) which varied in value against the tael from 110.622 to 113.150, and 'broken money' or chipped dollars from Hong Kong on which a loss of 5–8 per cent was reported in 1847, and it is no surprise that there were difficulties.

In the early days, the major hongs had banking departments or agency houses which largely financed the China trade. For smaller businesses, this could pose problems, for the agency houses were also their business competitors and were therefore not always ready to finance them.[13] Eventually, banking houses were established, beginning with the Oriental Banking Corporation, the Mercantile Bank of London, India and China, and the Agra Bank, all founded in 1854, and followed by the Hongkong and Shanghai Bank, founded in Hong Kong in 1864.

Despite the advent of modern banking, exchange problems persisted and it is hardly surprising that the residents of Shanghai and other treaty ports resorted to a system of 'chits' in their daily transactions.

It was not the custom in those days for foreigners to carry money, the only coinage available being of a clumsy and non-portable character. They paid their way by 'chits' or orders upon their comprador and it was not uncommon for them in those early days to pay for supplies during their excursions into the interior by a few hieroglyphics pencilled on a scrap of paper, which the confiding peasant accepted in perfect good faith and with so little apprehension that sometimes a considerable interval would elapse before presentation of these primitive cheques.[14]

The early arrivals in Shanghai who wrote of their experiences dwelt long on their pastimes. By 1850, there were two amateur (and entirely male) theatrical groups which performed in tea godowns. The first ever event featured a double bill of *Diamond cut Diamond* followed by *Roof-scrambler* (an operatic burlesque extravaganza based on the recent performance of a pony of that name), and subsequent evenings saw performances of *Love, Law and Physic, Bombastes Furioso, The Heir at Law, High Life below Stairs, Used Up, Ye Dragon of Wantley* and *Turned Down*.[15] Some firms were concerned that their griffins might spend too much time in amateur dramatics and they were only allowed to participate with the permission of the senior partners. Such was the scarcity of entertainment that even the audience might spend much time at the theatre: the future Inspector-General of the Chinese Customs, Robert Hart, reported from Tientsin, 'In the evening I went again to see the Minstrels of whom I now think I have had enough.' A month later he was complaining of an evening in Canton spent watching *Birth at the Swan, Canton Minstrels* and *Taming of the Tiger*, 'Acting very poor and the theatre terribly cold and full of draughts.'[16]

Music was scarce. In 1855, Mr Gibson of Gibb's & Co. presented a Gray & Davidson organ to Trinity Church, though there was some fear that the organ was too powerful for the building (its roof had collapsed in 1850). The organ survived. By 1920, it was housed in the Masonic Hall, a testimony, as one contemporary observed, to the musical standard, 'which at that date considered this instrument "splendid" '.[17] A home-made organ with bamboo pipes was installed in the Roman Catholic Cathedral in 1857. Its local origins notwithstanding, it apparently compared favourably with Mr Gibson's gift.

Of far greater interest to the average Shanghai inhabitant of the early decades was riding 'to shake up the liver', though as foreigners were not allowed far outside the city and as the foreign settlement in Shanghai slowly became urbanized, 'galloping horses in narrow lanes gradually became an installed hazard, not least to shoppers and shopkeepers. When carriages were introduced it was even worse … Frequent pleas appeared in the press begging that ponies, whether ridden or driven, be debarred from various parts of the town.'[18]

The merchants' ponies provided the inspiration for the sport of horse-racing which began in Shanghai before 1848, though it was not until 1851 that the first racecourse, described in a Chinese account as 'a big gambling den', held its inaugural meeting.[19] The year before, a Mr Hogg, manager of the trading firm Lindsay & Co., which mainly trafficked in opium, and four other people had formed the Race Club. Their first racecourse was just east of 'Muddy Flat', not far from the river bank and Soochow Creek, with its grandstand at the corner of present-day Jiangxi Road and Nanjing Road. Willows and flowers were planted beside the track. With the increase in Shanghai's population, the racecourse was twice moved further out into the suburbs. In 1863, the Shanghai Recreation Fund bought land in the centre of the racecourse for a cricket ground. In 1865, a piece of ground adjacent to the cricket pitch was 'conceded' after 'levelling, sodding, ditching and fencing ... for the purpose of the game of baseball'.[20] The Recreation Fund also supported a rowing club with a boat house on Soochow Creek, a skating club and the Lyceum Theatre. Nowhere in its history is there mention of the fact that some sixty Chinese families were displaced from their homes and ancestral tombs by the acquisition of land for the racecourse and cricket and baseball pitches.

Despite these expanding facilities, horse-riding remained the favourite sport. Shanghai was rather better suited to horse-ownership than Canton or Macao for the Yangtze marked the traditional southernmost limit of the Mongolian horse-dealers driving their hundreds of wild horses, 'shaggy, furry little creatures looking as much like large dogs or bears as horses', to the annual horse fairs. The horses were not expensive to buy or maintain but their features and potential were almost impossible to judge in their wild and furry state so their acquisition was a gamble in itself. In March, they were clipped, revealing their shapely legs, powerful bodies with strong backs and short necks. 'The first month with one's China pony was one long tussle, marked by many bruises and some bites' and, 'since they invariably locked the bit behind their teeth, controlling their speed was far from easy'.[21] After the bruising and biting and daily riding, owners rode their own horses in all the races at meets in spring and autumn, except the 'Native Purse' which was for Chinese grooms, and betting was keen.

Hunting was difficult in the early days at Shanghai since there were no foxes and sorties into the countryside were extremely dangerous. A sort of point-to-point began in 1855, and in 1863 some residents and officers of regiments stationed in Shanghai began to go paper-hunting as had been done in the Crimea and India, where it was made a substitute for fox-hunting. A trail of paper was laid across the countryside by one member as the fox who was then followed and chased by all the others. The first recorded 'Hunt' in December 1863 was won 'by Mr Augustus Broom on a pony named Mud . . . the second was won by Mr E.H. Gore-Booth on Bogtrotter'.[22] In 1866, the *North China Daily Herald* noted that whilst snipe and pheasant shooting were 'proofs of madness which Chinese have daily opportunity of noting amongst the Anglo-Saxon race ... when both these birds may be bought in the Market', paper-hunting was 'rank madness'. Weekend observers could watch 'two men ... gallop frantically over field and creek, at imminent risk of life and limb, with a dead certainty of innumerable spills and a grave probability of manifold duckings – for the mere purpose of scattering bits of paper which others take delight in following up under similar difficulties'.

Local farmers did not simply regard these activities as 'madness'. The historian of the Shanghai Paper Hunt branded its opponents 'a group of extremists', maintaining the implausible defence that no crops were damaged without compensation.[23] Endless stories were told of Chinese farmers making false claims for damage, just as those who shot over the local farms told stories of Chinese claiming to have been peppered with pellets and demanding financial recompense.

Social events in Shanghai during the early years were largely masculine affairs: there were at first very few women in the treaty ports and such as there were were mostly married to missionaries. The first Bachelors' Ball was given in November 1850, followed five years later by the first Race Ball. As late as 1864, when the Freemasons held their first ball, 'there were present ten gentlemen to every lady'. Nevertheless, the first dressmakers seem to have arrived in Shanghai in about 1859, and by 1861 Mrs Clifton, the wife of an ex-Superintendent of Police, was running a millinery business.[24]

Finding an eligible single lady may not have been easy but marriages did take place: the daughter of Trinity Church's first organist, Mr

Mackrill Smith, married Mr E. Jenner Hogg; Mr (later Sir) Rutherford Alcock, second consul in Shanghai, married (as his second wife) the widow of the first British chaplain to Shanghai, the Reverend John Lowder, who was drowned in 1849. Such unions between the bereaved were quite common.[25]

Churches mushroomed in Shanghai. At Siccawei (Xujiahui), some distance inland and on ground belonging to the descendants of China's most famous Catholic convert Paul Hsu Kuang-ch'i, a pupil of Matteo Ricci, the sixteenth-century founder of the Jesuit missions in China, the Catholic cathedral of St Ignatius was built in 1848 (the cathedral that survives was erected in 1906). The first Protestant service was held in the British consulate in 1843, conducted by Dr Medhurst, but in 1848 the rickety Protestant Episcopal Trinity Church was put up on land presented by Mr T.C. Beale of Dent & Co., which specialized in 'shipping, opium clippers, etc.' Trinity Church was so cheaply built that it required constant repairs and was pulled down in 1866. In the same year, Gilbert Scott, then a young architect, drew up plans in England for a new church, in the style of the 'Gothic of the early thirteenth century', but funds were insufficient and the design was modified by a local architect, William Kidner (and the tower was not added until 1893).[26] Even less flush with funds were the Nonconformists who put up a chapel in 1853 near the Shantung Road Hospital, opened in 1846 and run by Dr William Lockhart of the London Missionary Society.

Some early foreign residents achieved considerable longevity: Consul Alcock died at the age of 88; Consul McGregor of Canton, though retiring because of ill-health at 62, lived to the age of 93; F. Parish, senior consular assistant at Amoy, retiring on similar grounds, survived until he was 81; and the first consul in Shanghai, George Balfour, who resigned at the age of 35 to become an MP, lived to 83. However, the vast majority died young. As with the consular lists, which record the premature deaths of so many of the Consular Service's early employees, Wylie's collection of obituaries of Protestant missionaries (1867) shows that of those who did not drown, get killed by pirates or leave early when their wives 'broke down', the majority suffered from chronic, if not terminal, ill-health after a couple of years' residence. A sad number seem to have died near St Helena on the voyage home, frequently made in a desperate attempt to escape tropically induced sickness.

An early work on local medical conditions illustrates some of the problems encountered, particularly by the over-indulgent merchant class. Dr James Henderson, author of *Shanghai Hygiene or Hints for the Preservation of Health in China* (1863), himself suffered from 'indications of failing health' and prostrating sickness after a mere four years at the Chinese Hospital in Shanghai and left for Japan 'as a last resource', only to die in Nagasaki.[27] A few weeks later, his widow also lost her small child.

Henderson acknowledged 'the general relaxation and debility which unavoidably supervene during a *protracted residence in sultry climates* [his italics]' and considered that conditions on the voyage out started the rot: 'The condition of an Englishman arriving by P&O Steamer in Shanghai is, what many would call bordering on a state of disease from over repletion', for he had been 'subjected to a hot atmosphere, supplied with food of a highly stimulating and nutritious nature; while exercise is almost, in many cases is altogether suspended . . . and alcoholic beverages of all sorts are supplied *ad libitum*, and freely partaken of'.

Henderson's strictures give some idea of the meals enjoyed by Shanghai business residents. He advised against the ingestion of fruit or vegetables in the summer and was 'fully convinced that were people to confine themselves to a plain joint of mutton, beef or fowl, with rice, or rice and curry for dinner, with two or three glassfuls of claret, or Rhenish wine, there would be very little diarrhoea, dysentery, or disordered liver during the summer months in the East'.

Unfortunately, most of his patients

> begin dinner with a rich soup, and a glass of sherry; then they partake of one or two side dishes with champagne; then some beef, mutton, or fowls and bacon, with more champagne, or beer; then rice and curry and ham; afterwards game, then pudding, pastry, jelly, custard, or blancmange, and more champagne; then cheese and salad, and bread and butter, and a glass of port wine; then in many cases, oranges, figs, raisins and walnuts are eaten with two or three glasses of claret or some other wine; and this AWFUL repast is finished at last with a cup of strong coffee and cigars.

As the water in Shanghai was too dangerous to drink, the ingestion of liquid presented a problem. Since in his view the principal agent in the action of tea was sufficient to 'kill a full-grown frog', Henderson concluded that 'a man's health is more secure with a moderate quantity of wine in such a climate as this … by which I mean from 3 to 5 or 6 glasses per day of port or sherry, or from half to a bottle of French or German wine'. Champagne he regarded as safe in hot weather but he warned against an excessive intake of soda water: 'I knew a young man who came to Shanghai with a fine constitution and with excellent prospects; he used to boast that he drank 18 bottles of soda water daily, during the summer, and that he could *eat all kinds of fruit*. This, however, could not last, and after a short illness he died near the close of his second year.'

Exercise was only to be contemplated during the winter and spring months, 'to stimulate all bodily functions'. Walking was best though 'tiring and monotonous and . . . often impossible here on account of bad roads . . . riding on horse back is also very good' and it was 'much to be regretted that there is no cricket ground in Shanghai' (though it is recorded elsewhere that cricket was first played in Hongkew on 22 April 1858).

Henderson was convinced that 'more diarrhoea, dysentery and ague are induced by insufficient clothing during the Autumn than by any other cause … a blanket ought also to be kept on the bowels, even during the hottest weather. The extremities and chest may be exposed but *it is never safe to sleep without having the bowels well-covered*.' His advice was taken, one Hankow resident writing to his father in April 1863, 'Tell my mother that I wear a flannel band in summer, I thought I told her that Bella made me two in Alexandria.'[28]

In his remarks on clothing, Henderson recommended cotton as being cooler than linen. He went on, 'The great object of tropical prophylactics being TO MODERATE WITHOUT CHECKING THE CUTICULAR DISCHARGE [Henderson's mysterious capitals]; I would here enter a caution against too frequent changing of body linen, a habit confined to newly arrived Europeans principally.' Perhaps it was fortunate that Henderson disagreed with the experts who railed against bathing.

As a medical missionary, Henderson was as concerned for the welfare of the soul as for the body and recommended the mastery of 'Passions' through gospel study. Though some claimed that 'there is something peculiar about the tropics which excites certain passions in a higher degree than in temperate regions', he himself had '*never seen a man suffer from keeping himself pure*'. He recommended developing 'a taste for refined and elegant literature', particularly for the one book that will offer 'full information regarding his duty and his relationships towards his maker and his fellow-men'.

The Bible might serve as a corrective for some but many found it insufficiently powerful. Quite a number of early consular officers kept Chinese mistresses, including Robert Hart, who began his diary of consular service soon after his arrival in Hong Kong in August 1854. The entry for 27 August would have delighted Henderson: 'In order to live righteously and Godly, I must obey the commands of the Deity; and to do this I must know what they are: Therefore I must make the Bible my constant study ... I must take care that I sin not by encouraging evil desires or sinful imaginations.' But soon after his arrival in Ningpo that autumn he noticed that 'A couple of China women have been peeping in through my windows. I hope I may be able to control myself properly here. Many temptations surround me.' By 1865, he had had three children by his Chinese mistress, Ayou.[29]

Henderson concluded his tract with 'general remarks' which included a discussion of the complexities of the climate. The summer humidity encountered in all the treaty ports could be measured by its effects: 'boots and shoes become mouldy, glue and paste soon lose their tenacious qualities, furniture falls to pieces, and wall paper is soon destroyed'. Inhabitants were advised to seek elevated sites in order to rise 'above all malarious influence ... yellow fever and plague, marsh remittent and intermittent [fevers] never ascend beyond a certain altitude'.

In his few years in the city, Henderson observed a terrible mortality in Shanghai and made a plea for higher ceilings and faster construction of drains and sewers, despite the difficulty of their excavation in the city's boggy soil. Similarly, the preoccupation of later guidebooks with good drains and hygienic dairies makes it all too clear that sanitary conditions in the early days left much to be desired. The horrid state of the local water, filled with rubbish, excrement and 'putrescent bodies', meant that even laundry could make one ill. 'Clean' clothes smelled of filthy water, and 'washerman's itch' or eczema was so common that many people preferred to send their dirty washing to Japan on a two-week round trip.[30]

Despite these problems, it was not until 1870 that local residents in Shanghai began to clamour for a waterworks, and only after a disastrous fire in the French Concession in 1879, exacerbated by a lack of water to control the damage, did the municipal council call for plans and estimates. In 1882, pipes and mains were finally laid. Foreign residents paid for their water but most of the Chinese residents in this early phase continued to buy water drawn from the Whangpoo by the bucketful from members of the Guild of Water-carriers (who opposed any suggestion that purified water might be supplied free).

Like Henderson, many of the early missionaries in Shanghai were medical men who divided their time between prayer and cure and, because of their desire to reach the Chinese and convert them, offered their medical expertise to the local population. Henderson worked at the London Mission Hospital which had been opened for the benefit of Chinese patients near the south gate of the Chinese city in 1843 and which moved to Shantung Road in 1861. Though medical help was available, it was not until 1862 that the first hospital for foreigners, the French Hospital, staffed by the Sisters of St Vincent de Paul, was opened on the corner of the Rue Colbert and the French Bund. With the advent of faster steamships, most sick foreigners with any means rushed home for treatment and the French Hospital found itself in financial difficulties treating the 'destitute sick'. Though municipal funds were forthcoming, 'to extricate the institution from its encumbrances', even including the proposal that the municipal council should in future allocate 'a certain annual sum to supplement the deficiencies that seemed likely to recur', there was some automatic Protestant resistance. Anonymous letters were sent to the local press alleging that the Catholic sisters tortured patients by persistent efforts to convert them on their deathbeds. Eventually, the French Hospital became the Shanghai General and moved from its original site to the north bank of Soochow Creek.[31]

Despite medical efforts, decades of inadequate sanitation and dietary excesses meant an ever-increasing need for cemeteries. In the first Shanghai cemetery, established on Shantung Road after a residents' meeting in 1844, 20 per cent of the graves were of the 'sarcophagus type'. They included that of T.C. Beale of Dent, Beale & Co., the great rival of Jardine's. Beale, who also acted as Shanghai's Prussian consul, was one of the rare company heads who died and was buried in Shanghai (most, at this early stage, retired to the bracing climate and high ceilings of Scotland). The tomb of the French customs inspector, formerly librarian at the Sorbonne, Monsieur Arthur Smith, also lay in the Shantung Road cemetery, but by 1863 the cemetery was becoming dangerously full.[32] Subsequently, eleven different cemetery sites were acquired in Shanghai, several of which served distinct sections of the community. There was a Parsee cemetery, a Jewish cemetery and a separate cemetery for sailors.

If Shanghai's residents did not always live as long as might have been hoped, nonetheless the treaty port flourished. By 1860, with its population increasing in both size and variety, and its services, municipal or otherwise, expanding, Shanghai made a relatively comfortable posting for a consular officer or a tea-man. By contrast, some of the other treaty ports were struggling and their inhabitants were forced to contend with far greater difficulties.

3

The Smaller Ports

The coastal port of Ningpo, on the southern side of the Yangtze delta, had for centuries been a significant port of transshipment northwards up the coast and inland along the Yangtze, and the East India Company had, early on, earmarked it as a suitable place for settlement.[1] Such promise was not to be fulfilled, for though opened to foreign residence following the Treaty of Nanking, Ningpo's prosperity declined as Shanghai developed.

In the autumn of 1843 Robert Fortune, plant-hunting for the Royal Horticultural Society, described the town as standing at the 'junction of two fine streams who by their union form a noble river' about twelve miles inland from the sea. Over the river

> the Chinese have constructed a bridge of boats ... a most simple and ingenious contrivance, consisting of a number of large boats moored at equal distances across the river, forming the basis on which the upper woodwork rests, and enabling the whole to rise and fall to a certain extent with the tide. By this means there is sufficient space under the bridge to allow fishing and passage boats to pass under at all times of the tide, providing it is not running too strongly.[2]

Arriving some months before the first British consul, Fortune was at a loss to know where to go or to whom to apply for quarters.

> Leaving my boat and servant on the river, I strolled away into the city to reconnoitre, thinking that something might turn up which I could use for my advantage. I was soon surrounded by crowds of natives, and amongst them some blackguard boys who had been corrupted to a great

34

extent by the troops during the war but who luckily understood a little
of the English language . . . they informed me there was one *Hong mou
jin* 'red-haired man' – a term which they apply to all Western nations –
already in the city and immediately led the way straight to his quarters.

This was Dr Daniel Jerome MacGowan, an American medical missionary who 'was dressed *à la Chinoise*, tail and all complete, but truth
compels me to state that his dress was a rather ludicrous one . . . The
large flowing gown he wore was almost too fine for a mandarin, while
the hat was one commonly worn by servants and coolies . . . imagine a
London judge clothed in his fine black flowing gown and wearing the
hat of a dustman.'[3] MacGowan was still living in China in 1907 when
his photograph was reproduced in a compendium volume on the treaty
ports. Disappointingly, he appears bare-headed and wearing dark
clerical dress.[4]

In freezing weather, the wind whistling through the poorly papered
windows of MacGowan's house, Fortune spent his time in Ningpo
admiring wild azaleas on the hillsides and the cunning preparation of
dwarf junipers, peach and plum in the gardens of the rich. He was
cheated of a mythical yellow camellia, bargaining over two plants, in
bud but not in flower, which turned out to be white and perfectly
ordinary when they finally flowered in Hong Kong.

In January of that same cold winter, Ningpo was officially opened as
a treaty port by Robert Thom who had been a merchant in Venezuela,
Mexico and France since the age of 14. He had ended up in Hong Kong
where he had acquired a Chinese mistress and 'a creditable acquaintance with the written and spoken language'.[5] He had patriotically
'joined up' as an interpreter on the staff of the British Superintendent
of Trade Sir Henry Pottinger during the war and, on this basis, was
now appointed consul at Ningpo. He arrived with a medical officer, two
clerks, an assistant interpreter and an extra 16-year-old, M.C. Morrison,
who had come to study Chinese with Thom and to try to cure the
dysentery that he had endured for the previous eight months. Unlike
so many others, Morrison did recover and went on to several consular
appointments.

In Ningpo, Thom found it hard to rent suitable accommodation,
having to settle for a Chinese house outside the city reached by narrow
paths through rice-fields, and the city did not seem to attract foreign

settlement. In 1845 there were only three British residents apart from the consular party, a merchant who soon abandoned hope and moved to Shanghai and two unmarried lady missionaries. Though the numbers were unsatisfactory, the balance of the sexes might have seemed exciting to those Shanghai Freemasons who outnumbered their dancing partners by ten to one.

Despite his small constituency, Thom issued regulations for their conduct, requiring them to obtain his permission if they wished to go more than three miles outside the city or enter other cities and villages, or if they wished to shoot anywhere, and enjoining them to respect temples, tombs and local people. After Thom's departure, Consul Adkins, his successor, found his few fellow-countrymen 'not at all polished'; most of the ladies addressed him as Mr 'Hadkins'.[6]

In 1854, when the 19-year-old Ulsterman Robert Hart arrived to serve under J.A.T. Meadows in the Ningpo consulate, there were twenty-two foreign residents. As he sailed into the harbour, 'a dense forest of masts all but completely hid the City from view. A large Pagoda in the centre of Ningpo towered above all other heights.' Disembarking from the sampan that had brought him to the shore

> I observed a gentleman in white trousers and a snuff coloured coat; I at once made up my mind that this was Mr Meadows and such he proved to be. However with that perversity so peculiar to the British, I rather tried to avoid him. Altho' I did not know my way to the consulate, I chose rather to lose myself than ask directions from a Gentleman to whom I had never been introduced ... I walked on; but Mr Meadows overtook me; he bowed and said 'Mr Hart?' – I bowed and 'presumed he was Mr Meadows' – we shook hands and got to the consulate. Mr M. is tall ... his eyes are very light blue, and have a terribly wild expression – quite like those of a maniac in fact; his beard is cut in the French style (Henri IV, I think) ... on entering the consulate, we met Mr Fortune, the Celebrated Traveller.[7]

The very next morning, Consul Meadows took Hart to pay calls upon the foreign community. Like Fortune, he was introduced to Dr MacGowan who, apart from his work as a medical missionary, published the bi-weekly *Chinese and Foreign Gazette* and had written an explanatory sheet (in Chinese) describing the solar eclipse of 11 December 1852 and a *Treatise on Cyclones* (1853). He greeted his visitors with a book in his hand and wearing a morning-gown (which Meadows considered an 'affectation' although it was perhaps less so than his oddly assorted Chinese dress) and Hart elaborated upon the doctor's facial arrangements: 'He is a little fat man, a supporter of the Moustache movement but an enemy to bearded chins although he wears an Imperial.'

They then called upon Mrs Cobbold, wife of the Reverend Robert Henry Cobbold of the Church of England Missionary Society. The latter was as prolific a writer as Dr MacGowan. As well as many tracts, he had published a version of *The Pilgrim's Progress* in the Ningpo dialect 'printed in the Roman character' and *Directions for the Misguided* (on the evils of opium, the staple of foreign trade at Ningpo). Mrs Hobson 'of Shanghae' (the wife of John Hobson, also of the Church of England Missionary Society) was staying with the Cobbolds. 'She looks as if she could frown terribly: her upper lip is expressive to a most wonderful extent – pressed tightly against her teeth and drawn down in the centre.' Next they visited the 'unaffiliated' missionary Miss Aldersey, 'a very nice old lady' from whose house there was a fine view of Ningpo and where Hart (not for the last time) made a fool of himself with a Miss Dyer, daughter of the pioneer printer of the Scriptures in Chinese, Samuel Dyer. By the end of the day, Hart, ever susceptible to a neat ankle, declared that 'the sight of Miss Dyer has reconciled me to Ningpo'.

They then called upon the Roman Catholic bishop, who had a fine church under construction, and discovered that 'all the priests have adopted the Chinese dress'. Mr Russell (yet another Church of England missionary and the author of yet more works printed in the romanized Ningpo dialect) was out and Mrs Russell (who also published religious works in the romanized Ningpo dialect) was not receiving, which 'called forth a growl from Mr M. in which I could make out that he considered women great bores – had to fix their hair or put on a clean cap &c'. They proceeded next to the Knowltons where Miles Justus Knowlton of the American Baptist Missionary Union said 'he considers Chinese very easy! Ahem! It is said that those who form this opinion of Chinese are the persons least likely to succeed in making much progress in the study of it.' Mrs Knowlton was fresh-faced and red-haired and, though married, promised good conversation.

Crossing the river away from the walled Chinese city, they went to call on another American missionary, Richard Quartermain Way, who also ran a boys' boarding school for the mission. He was out but Mrs Way was 'a nice, agreeable lady'. Then there was Mr Nevius, another American Presbyterian missionary, and a prolific writer of religious works in Chinese (whose wife translated *Peep of Day* into the Ningpo dialect). The Nevius' (both in their early twenties) struck the 19-year-old Hart as 'young' and 'juvenile'. Nevius 'kept rocking in his rocking chair while we remained. His attire was very *negligée*.'

After the missionaries came the other consuls. First they called upon the American consul Mr MacCartee but only his wife, 'beautiful white teeth and red lips', was in. At the Portuguese consulate, Senhor Marquez

> gave us a polka on his harmonium. It was quite amusing to see the courtesy with which he treated Mr Meadows – and to know at the same time that they were on very bad terms. From his house we went to that of Mr Davison the most respectable of the Merchants of this place ... He seems to be a nice hearty fellow ... With him we finished the Foreign Community. A very tiresome job it was: going to so many houses with the same intention and making the same remarks to each one. I am surprised to find the ladies such students and such proficients in the colloquial of the District. They talk greatly about what they call the 'Romanized Colloquial'. I wonder is this an attempt to convert the Chinese into a tongue of classical renown. 'Fever-and-Ague' seems to be a favourite topic here.[8]

Two days after the round of respectable foreigners, Hart and Meadows went to pay a courtesy call on the Chinese authorities in the form of the Ningpo Taotai (Daotai or Circuit Intendant, the senior Chinese official). Riding in sedan chairs, they were preceded by two men with English flags stuck in their hats and followed by a man carrying their calling cards as they proceeded through the courtyards of the yamen (the official residence).

> At the last gateway but one ... We were saluted by the explosions of powder – not, I think, from guns but from Monstrous Crackers – and by the sound of a Gong, and the music of an instrument which in appearance resembled a clarinet, but in sound was like a Highland Pipe minus the Drone. Near the door of his Reception room, the Tao-tai, attended by two inferior mandarins, met us ... Tea was introduced; then

... cakes, fruits, preserves and various sorts of delicacies ... Before each
of us were Chop-sticks and one small silver-pronged fork.

Hart's plate was piled high by his host, according to the Chinese
custom.

Small cups were then brought in, each holding about half a wine glass;
these were filled with a sort of Whiskey. Each of the party raised his cup
in his hand – stretched it out to each of his companions – said *Ts'ing* and
then either quaffed it or tasted it ... Immediately the attendants poured
out what was left in our cups and refilled them ... As often as we drank,
we 'presented cups' and *chin-chinned*. I was greatly struck with the very
graceful manner in which the Tao-tai and the Mandarins waved their
cups.

Filled with 'Whiskey' and cakes, Hart and Meadows then proceeded
to meet the district magistrate where 'The same ceremonies were again
gone through: he feasted us with *meats* – a good substantial breakfast in
fact ... I could not use the Chopsticks so sometimes I took my fingers
– sometimes my fork.'⁹ Such was the ceremonial round in Ningpo.

Just down the coast from Ningpo was another treaty port, Amoy, which
was also coastal, with a harbour protected by islands. Amoy itself was a
large island, close to the mainland; opposite Amoy lay the small wooded
island of Kulangsu (Gulangsu), with sandy beaches beneath great round
rocks. Though the original foreign settlements were on Amoy, residents
gradually moved their homes to Kulangsu. The Reverend Pitcher's
guidebook *In and around Amoy* makes plain the reasons behind the
move. 'The streets are narrow and crooked, with the sewer underneath
and plainly in sight thro the chinks of the uneven flagstones ... there
are streets in Amoy so narrow that you cannot carry an open umbrella
... Several well-defined and distinct stenches greet the sense of smell at
every step.' One early missionary was described as leaving Amoy 'for
sanitary reasons'.¹⁰

Robert Fortune concurred in the view that Amoy itself was insani-
tary, 'one of the filthiest towns which I have ever seen ... worse even
than Shanghai, and that is bad enough. When I was there in the hot
autumnal months, the streets, which are only a few feet wide, were
thatched over with mats to protect the inhabitants from the sun.' He

was not entirely convinced that Kulangsu was any better. He saw it in a state of ruin, houses and ponds destroyed by troops. It was still occupied by British soldiers: those encamped to the south and west of the small island were 'all perfectly healthy' but fever and cholera prevailed on the north-eastern and eastern sides where 'the little English burial place was already nearly full and the earth was red and fresh with recent interments, scarcely a day passing without two or three being added to the number of the dead'.[11] Fortune found most of the shrubs in Kulangsu gardens 'common' and 'well-known'; presumably the enormous tree-size poinsettias that now tower over the garden walls were later introductions.

Once Amoy had been opened as a treaty port, English, German and American wholesale merchants began to arrive, handling sugar, tea, cotton, woollens and 'a variety of other goods' and also acting as agents for banks, steamship lines and insurance companies. Opium, too, continued to be a staple in trade. Early businesses included Bellamy & Co., J. Foster & Co., Giles & Co., H.D. Brown & Co., Fearon Low & Co., Lapraik Cass & Co., F.C. Brown & Co. and Dakin Bros, as well as the better-known American Russell & Co.[12] and major China traders like Dent, Jardine Matheson and Butterfield & Swire. Though their headquarters were in Shanghai, the latter two worked through agencies in Amoy until the late nineteenth century.

Hard on the heels of the merchants came Protestant missionaries. The Reverend David Abeel of the Reformed Church of America, whose 'mind was seriously arrested by religious truth' at the age of 17, arrived on Kulangsu in 1842 after working as a chaplain to foreign seamen in Canton and subsequently serving in Siam, Batavia, Malacca, Singapore and Macao. He was soon followed by members of the London Missionary Society, the Reverend John Stronach and Mrs Stronach, who arrived in 1844. Born in Edinburgh, John Stronach was the younger brother of Alexander Stronach who worked in the missionary printing enterprise which pioneered the use of movable type for publishing Bibles and tracts in Chinese. John Stronach opened a chapel in Amoy itself on 1 December and worked 'in harmonious co-operation with the American brethren'. His wife's health failed and she left for home with their four children in 1845 but died at sea, a story all too common in the early days of the treaty ports.[13]

In 1850, James Young of the English Presbyterian Mission arrived in Amoy and participated in 'the first union between the London Missionary Society and the English Presbyterian Mission' when he married Miss Harvitt who was 'engaged in educational work among the native girls'. Miss Harvitt died two years after her marriage and was buried in the missionary cemetery on Kulangsu Island in 1853; James Young's 'faculties were so far impaired' that he left for home in 1854 and died soon after.

The first mission school was opened in 1845, near the Russell hong and the Temple of the Sea in Amoy, by the Reverend Peet who left for Foochow after a year, when the establishment was taken over by Elihu Doty and his wife. Doty was 'an ordained minister of the Dutch Reformed Church in the United States'[14] and, though his wife died almost as soon as she had started her girls' classes, he remarried and continued the work until his second wife also died, in 1858. Doctors, too, began to arrive in Amoy to tend the moribund missionaries: Dr Cummings in 1842 who worked from Abeel's house until 1846, Dr Hepburn (1843–5), Dr James Young (1850–4), Dr Hirschberg (1853–8) and Dr John Carnegie (1859–62). The brevity of their tenure suggests that they regarded long sojourns as imprudent, a view borne out by the mortality of their cohabitants.

The first consular officials, who arrived in November 1843, reinforced the general view that Amoy was unhealthy no matter where one settled. Consul Gribble arrived in some style: 'a tall, fine-looking man', he landed from a warship with his pregnant wife and their four little girls, a European woman servant, a Chinese manservant, and a West Indian servant. His medical officer, C.A. Winchester, surveyed the city's 'narrow streets full of decaying vegetable matter, without sewerage or drainage and with a most abominable and universal stench' (which Fortune had ascribed to the local cuisine) and proposed residence on Kulangsu for reasons of health and hygiene. They may have chosen the wrong aspect on Kulangsu for within four months they were all ill and Vice-Consul Sullivan had been 'at death's door for weeks'.[15] The difficulty of their circumstances was compounded by the incompatibility of Mrs Sullivan and Mrs Gribble which, in turn, affected their husbands' working relationship.

Gribble was soon succeeded by George Tradescant Lay, who on

arrival sent for his pregnant wife and four children. It was not long before he too succumbed to illness, whether or not because a fleet of nightsoil boats (which collected human excrement for use as fertilizer) operated outside his office in the hot sunlight, it is hard to say. What is certain is that his illness proved fatal, confirming the view of Amoy as unhealthy.

Lay had come to Amoy from Foochow, another new treaty port which lay up the Min River some twenty miles from the coast. Large ships were unable to reach the city and had to stop at the Pagoda Island anchorage downstream. Fortune described the approach to Foochow in 1845.

> On the banks of the river are numerous temples ... built in the most romantic and beautiful situations. A Fig tree (*Ficus nitida*), a kind of Banyan, is a great favourite with the priests, and is always found growing beside the temples, where its dark green leaves and wide-spreading branches afford an agreeable shade from the fierce rays of the sun. About nine miles below Foo-chow-fu, a pretty little pagoda stands on an island on the left bank of the river: near this is the anchorage for large vessels which it would not be prudent to take up to the town.

Though he went on to describe the flat granite bridge that stood low, almost on the surface of the river, and the Chinese city on the north bank, after a couple of years travelling from treaty port to treaty port, he had clearly rather lost interest in such descriptions: 'The streets in all Chinese cities have much the same appearance: some are a little wider than others and have better and more attractive shops: but by far the greater part of them are narrow and dirty and Foo-chow-fu certainly forms no exception to the general rule.' Even so, he recorded that the local women all wore flowers in their hair: 'The rustic cottage beauty employs the more large and gaudy such as the red Hibiscus; while the refined damsels prefer the jasmine, tuberose and others of that description.'[16]

In Foochow, the first consuls were allocated houses of varying suitability within the city walls. Unlike the other early treaty ports, Foochow never had a foreign 'concession' and it was some years before a foreign settlement was established on the south side of the river, on sloping ground previously occupied by graves. The difference was technical: a concession was an area leased by a foreign power from the Chinese government for a nominal rent whilst a 'settlement' was an area which the Chinese government set aside for foreign residence and within which foreign nationals leased plots from Chinese landlords.[17] The difference was also economic: the foreign powers were themselves responsible for expensive building and maintenance works in the concessions, but this was not one of the responsibilities of the first consul in Foochow, George Tradescant Lay, in his decrepit consulate in the suburbs.

This was Lay's third consular posting in as many years. Married to Nelson's niece, George Tradescant was the first of a long line of Lays who lived and worked in China in either the Consular or Customs Service. He had arrived in Macao in 1836 as an agent for the British and Foreign Bible Society and was appointed consul on the basis of his knowledge of Chinese and service as interpreter to Pottinger during the First Opium War, but only after a warning that mission work was incompatible with his new duties.

Lay had first opened the Canton consulate in July 1843 and was ordered to move on to Foochow in July 1844. His was not a stately Gribble-style arrival for he was turned off his ship at Pagoda Island and forced to proceed in a native boat. The local authorities allocated him a house in a 'low-class suburb' built of boards, standing on piles over the river which flooded twice a day at high tide. He was later moved to another which 'kept out neither sun nor rain'. By the time Fortune arrived in 1845, Lay had already transferred to Amoy with fatal effect and had been succeeded by C.A. Sinclair.

The consulate was by then situated in a temple in the town, on one of the small pagoda-capped hills that still stand in Foochow. Fortune had some trouble reaching the consular eminence for 'nearly all of the streets in the suburbs were under water at the time, some to the depth of four feet'. Feeling that, under the circumstances, it was impossible to walk the distance, Fortune took a sedan chair and was soon surrounded by hundreds of noisy local people.

> Quang-yanga, quang-yanga – their term for foreigners – was rung in our ears, and frequently other appellations of a much worse signification. Our Chinese servants, who walked by our side, were attacked and reviled for having any connection with us. In one of the streets the water was so deep that I was obliged to stand up on the seat of the chair and

even then it reached my feet. Here the crowd became very abusive and commenced throwing water over us. At first our servants bore this treatment pretty well; but their patience was at last exhausted, and they turned upon the assailants. The scene was now both amusing and disagreeable. Luckily I happened to be a little in the advance, and was therefore pretty well out of the mêlée; but Captain Freeman came in for his full share of it, and was completely soaked through.[18]

If visitors were forced to endure such treatment, it is easy to imagine the difficulties experienced by permanent consular staff and their families.

The situation in Canton was somewhat different since it had seen foreign habitation of a sort for decades. Nevertheless, in defiance of treaty stipulations, the local Taotai continued to refuse foreigners access to the Chinese city so, with very bad grace, residents remained in their cramped factories. It was not until after the Second Opium War of 1856–60 that foreigners established themselves on the 'reclaimed sandbank' of Shameen (Shamian), still outside the city but much closer to it. The British consulate was then built on Shameen, but in order to reinforce the principle that foreigners had the right to enter the city, the consular residence was established in a former yamen of a Manchu general well inside the walls of Canton. It had a five-acre park, 'lofty trees, a herd of deer and the graves of [Consul] Robertson's cats and dogs', but it was cut off every night when the city's gates were closed.[19]

Relations between local and foreign residents of Canton had hardly improved since the days when William Hickey and his friends had made their illegal sallies into the walled city. Robert Fortune wandered around the environs of the city, visiting the Fa-Tee nursery on the far side of the river to view the azaleas, camellias, tree peonies and roses for which it was famous. He also walked out into the hills 'for the purpose of examining their botanical attractions' and was attacked, stoned and robbed of his money, hat and umbrella (he congratulated himself on having left his watch at home). Other visitors suffered worse fates, being stripped of all their clothes, and such incidents were by no means uncommon in the area.

Fortune was not alone in comparing the treaty ports according to their degree of squalor: Canton, which probably saw more visitors than any other treaty port at this period, got the worst press of all. 'P.G.L.'

prefaced his *Reminiscence of Canton 1863* with his experiences during the Crimean War. Nothing he had witnessed in that war equalled what he saw in Canton. 'It is impossible to conceive my emotions, the horror with which I actually witnessed evidences of inhuman barbarities of which I had so often read . . . My blood froze within me; each particular hair stood on end; never in my travels have I witnessed a more awful, loathsome, disgusting scene than that which I witnessed at Canton city.' Passing through the narrow streets in sedan chairs ('the streets of Canton are for the most part just sufficiently wide for two people to pass'), over the granite paving stones 'which are invariably loose and give way beneath one' and 'sloppy, not merely from rain but from the large quantities of water which are continually being carried through them in open buckets, suspended to bamboos on the shoulders of indefatigable coolies', he noted that the 'houses are small with only one storey, and all exactly resembling one another. Each has a long signboard suspended outside, treating of the honesty of the proprietor and of his wares, and as whole streets are generally devoted to one specific trade, there is a miserable sameness about the place.' Though he goes on to describe other horrors, P.G.L. was particularly revolted by the food market.

> I examined more minutely the sucking pigs. Alas! They were but dogs. It is indeed too true. Upon such diet do the poorer classes in China live. The tails had been most artistically twisted round . . . It is extraordinary what they will eat. It is only a few days since I buried a favourite horse. In the night they dug up his remains and stripped every particle of flesh from his bones. Next morning I found nothing but the head, tail and bones lying outside the grave . . . I need not say that for the next few days I was very careful of beefsteaks.

The removal of his horse from a shallow grave was surely carried out by such dogs as had escaped the sucking-pig treatment but the remark is characteristic of his portrait of the Chinese as unclean scavengers. He proceeded to 'one of the most filthy, loathsome and heart-rending sights I have ever been exposed to', Beggars' Square, where unfortunates died under the shade of a mat-tent with cups of water at their side. He then described criminals chained to stones or wearing the cangue, a great wooden collar placed around the neck of a prisoner who then became dependent upon relatives to feed him. Finally, there were the public executions. A morbid preoccupation with these horrors was characteristic of Western visitors to China: sets of postcards were produced in the early twentieth century so that the fascination could be carried home, and J.-J. Matignon wrote a whole book on the subject, illustrated and grandly entitled *Superstition, Crime and Misery in China.*[20]

P.G.L. seems to have had some doubts about his highly coloured reminiscences for in a later foreword dated 1866, he wrote, 'The following narrative, written during my earliest years in China, contains amidst a multitude of truths, a few inaccuracies and false impressions, which now perhaps from longer experience I might correct. I prefer however to leave it in its original state, because to attempt to modify or remodel it would I fear in a great measure be to destroy it.'

Even before Canton was opened as a treaty port, the first medical missionary had arrived there to deal with some of the horrors. The American Peter Parker opened an ophthalmic hospital in 1835 and also treated a variety of diseases, commissioning local artists to record some of the goitrous growths and carbuncles on his patients before treatment. He also introduced anaesthesia to China. One of his successes was to have fitted the Opium Commissioner Lin Tse-hsu with a truss for his hernia just before the First Opium War broke out. This was a delicate matter, for the Opium Commissioner clearly did not wish to expose himself to a foreigner; in his place another hernia-afflicted member of Lin's staff was sent for treatment to check the efficacy of the truss and its fitting; this was followed by a fitting for Lin Tse-hsu's brother who was considered to be the same size as the Imperial Commissioner. Parker was somewhat less successful in his later appointments as American chargé d'affaires in Canton and Minister Plenipotentiary.

In the city and its suburbs, other medical missionaries also treated the poor. Most of the victims of the annual summer cholera epidemic died but some apparently responded to the use of 'calomel and opium and hot rubefacient frictions'. In the city itself lived Dr Kerr (of the Medical Missionary Society) who, like Parker, specialized in ophthalmology and whose annual expenses in 1863 included more money spent on whisky and lard than on Chinese medicines.[21] Such dispensaries were supported by all the local notables – Smith, Archer & Co., N. Mody & Co., Arthur Sassoon, and Olyphant & Co., and by the

Chinese compradors of Sassoon's, Mody's, Gilman & Co., Lindsay's, Lapraik, and Russell & Co.

It is perhaps ironic that so many of these major firms, who had lobbied so hard for China to be opened up to trade, left Canton once it had become a treaty port and set up their headquarters on the nearby island of Hong Kong. Though technically not a treaty port, for it had been ceded in perpetuity to the Crown, Hong Kong's freedom from tariffs, and its relative security for foreigners brought about by the permanent presence of British armed forces, made it an attractive base.

The security of Hong Kong was relative. Like all of the South China coast, including Amoy and Canton, it was subject to periodic typhoons. Even when the weather was calm, southern China was uncomfortably hot and humid, and the weather and local insect life wreaked havoc upon foreign possessions. Soon after his arrival in Hong Kong as a young consular officer, Robert Hart checked the contents of his boxes and 'found them filled with cockroaches and mosquitoes: cloth clothes slightly damaged; and my best kid gloves destroyed'. At his first posting in Ningpo, conditions were no better. 'The weather is very damp, the floors of my bedrooms are quite wet and my clothes have a disagreeable musty smell.' At the end of April 1855, 'The weather was so fine that I had my clothes aired today: much need of it as they were becoming quite blue-moulded and musty.' His shirts occasionally provided comfort for undesired visitors: 'Yesterday evening when going to bed about 10 o'c. I found a great snake on a table in my bedroom among my shirts. I killed him with my stick: he measured 5 *feet*. Thickest part about 1 and a half inches in diameter. It is very disagreeable to find such things in one's bedroom.'

4

Consuls and Merchants

If snakes in shirts were disagreeable and the weather unreliable and prone to wreak havoc on possessions, the consuls found the foreign population of the new treaty ports equally unstable and occasionally just as disagreeable. The Foreign Office had to find and appoint dozens of consular officials, in considerable haste, to staff the newly opened consulates. Since knowledge of the Chinese language was desirable, some had been sought from amongst missionary ranks, others from among the Hong Kong merchants.

When Hong Kong was ceded to Britain after the First Opium War in 1843, the Governor-General, the senior British officer in the area, was given charge of all the consulates in China. From 1861, when, as we shall see, the first British diplomats were allowed residence in Peking, responsibility for the consulates was transferred from Hong Kong to Peking. The credentials of the senior British diplomats in China throughout this time varied according to their responsibilities. There were Envoys, Special Envoys, Ministers and Plenipotentiaries (empowered to sign treaties). Lord Macartney's credentials in 1792 had described him as a special Ambassador charged with the task, then unfulfilled, of arranging a trade agreement and residence for a British diplomat in Peking. When this object was finally achieved, in 1861, the senior diplomat in Peking, at this early period, was usually described as 'Minister' rather than Ambassador, Ministers being lower-ranking than Ambassadors.

For Her Majesty's consuls themselves, after they had opened their consulates as best they could, the work began of protecting British traders and promoting British trade. Neither task was made any easier by the lack of suitable accommodation and the difficulty of finding sufficient staff to deal with drunken and aggressive sailors and slippery traders as well as with the protocol duties of calling on Chinese officials. Obliged to meet such expenses from their own salaries, even the consuls found ends hard to meet. Junior members of staff, the trainee 'student interpreters', complained of the utter impossibility of survival on their pay.[1]

Most consuls had only one or two assistants to help with their daily duties and to deal with unexpected emergencies such as court cases involving British property and British subjects as plaintiffs or defendants. Though Her Britannic Majesty's Supreme Court for China – first based in Hong Kong and then from 1865 transferred to Shanghai – was supposed to try the more serious cases involving British subjects, the impracticality of transferring prisoners and witnesses meant that many murder trials had to be conducted in the consular courts of the treaty ports.

In exercising their judicial powers, consuls were also confronted with a diplomatic difficulty. Foreigners considered Chinese justice extremely harsh, although sentences were in fact more lenient than in British courts. Though murder was punished by execution, manslaughter was settled through compensation in a system that was far less severe than that of the Victorian courts in Britain.[2] Conversely, the Chinese viewed consular sentencing as biased and there were frequent Chinese protests, sometimes amounting to riots, at the lenient treatment of British defendants in British courts.[3]

Even when British subjects were found guilty as charged, the problem then arose of what to do with them. The post of constable was poorly paid and dangerous, and in consequence recruits were frequently inadequate and addicted to drink. The single outstanding exception was a splendid constable at the Amoy consulate in the 1860s, a Corsican called Pereira, capable of controlling three drunken seamen armed with knives who were on their way to prison. The cells of many consulates were makeshift and insecure, and filled with prisoners 'shouting, screaming and trying to break out at all hours of the night'. The Canton consular prison, designed for about a dozen prisoners, sometimes housed over thirty and was damp and dirty. At one point, most of its inmates had to be released because of the prevalence of dysentery and fever. The stench in the small consular prison in Ningpo was so awful in hot weather that prisoners were released on payment of a fine in lieu of a custodial sentence.[4]

Despite these horrible conditions, the Foreign Office usually refused all demands for better prison accommodation on the grounds of expense. Though Chinese prisons were sometimes willing to take consular prisoners, conditions there varied from extreme leniency (on payment of bribes) to disease-infested squalor, frequently worse than that encountered in the consular cells.[5]

Even if consuls did manage to contain their prisoners (one kidnapper, handcuffed and in irons, was rescued from jail by friends who tunnelled under the floorboards), their powers were limited: the maximum penalty they could impose was of twelve months' imprisonment (hardly a practical sentence given the condition of their prisons) plus deportation. As to securing convictions, juries in Hong Kong were said to consist of nothing but 'Portuguese and Parsees who understood English imperfectly and grog-shop keepers'.[6] To complicate matters further, the Chinese, traditionally unwilling to participate in legal procedures – and all the more unwilling to submit to a British justice that they perceived as biased – were often reluctant to come forward as witnesses.

Many consuls were aware of the severity with which Chinese were treated in the British courts and the relative leniency of sentences passed on British defendants, citing in their correspondence cases in Hong Kong where British murderers of Chinese had been acquitted. From afar, Lord Palmerston, the Foreign Secretary, attempted to enforce proper sentencing, criticizing the procedural slip-up that allowed Mr Compton (who had provoked a riot in Canton by objecting to the noise made by street hawkers) to escape punishment, and berating F.C. McGregor, serving in the Canton consulate, for his 'doctrine that the offence of getting drunk was a palliation of any offence which the drunken person might happen to commit'.[7]

Opium, still the mainstay of British and American trade, presented a further problem for the newly appointed consuls. Since most of them took their official duties and responsibilities very seriously, this illegal traffic was an embarrassment. Opium clippers brought their mail and they were sometimes compelled to travel on board them if no legal means of transport was to hand, though they generally made every effort to confine these ships to distant anchorages. The official attitude to opium was that 'no support would be given to British subjects detected by the Chinese in smuggling opium but that it was up to the Chinese to detect the smugglers and to bring them before the consular courts'.[8]

Consular embarrassment was not the only consequence of the opium trade. Much more serious were the violence and piracy that ensued. As a consular officer in Ningpo, Hart was visited by a Portuguese with a head wound and a broken collarbone who informed him that he was the sole survivor of a pirate seizure of one of Dent's opium ships.[9] Such violence often involved innocent foreigners. One naval surgeon, attempting to make an official visit to the consulate in Foochow, was held at gunpoint by fifteen Chinese looking for opium.[10] He got off lightly. When pirates boarded the boat in which he was returning to Ningpo from Shanghai, an American missionary, the Reverend William Lowrie, was thrown overboard and drowned.[11]

Another unsavoury trade, which consuls did feel they could roundly condemn, was that in 'coolies'. California, Australia, Chile, Peru and Cuba were amongst the destinations of these unfortunate indentured labourers, usually poor and illiterate peasants press-ganged by unscrupulous foreign merchants or ships' captains and their Chinese 'coolie-brokers'. Even if they survived the atrocious conditions on the long sea journey, they found themselves virtual slaves, bound to years of hard labour in sugar-cane fields or on railways far from home. British ships' captains were also involved in shipping small children from Shanghai to Siam in the 1850s. All the consuls protested: Rutherford Alcock in Canton called for international action and Winchester in Amoy applauded the accidental drowning and deliberate execution of various coolie-brokers in Canton.

In condemning the coolie trade, the consuls must also have been conscious of the danger of public (and anti-foreign) unrest that it provoked. In Amoy, in 1852, a British coolie-broker called Syme took it upon himself to rescue one of his Chinese employees from the yamen where he had been placed under arrest. His action provoked a riot in which two British subjects were injured, and a British naval party, summoned to protect British interests, in turn shot several Chinese. The local vice-consul, J. Backhouse, arrested Syme and fined him but failed to punish Syme's partner Connolly who managed to escape from the inadequate consular jail. This was not the first time that Syme had caused distress to his consul: in 1848, T.H. Layton considered his co-habitation (at the age of 28) with a much older maidservant, Mary Jones, to be open fornication and an insult to public morals, though the consul was informed that there was nothing he could do as this was an ecclesiastical matter and there was no ecclesiastical jurisdiction in China. Syme and Connolly moved their coolie business to the nearby port of Swatow (Shantou) where they were no longer subject to British consular jurisdiction since Swatow was not yet a treaty port.[12]

Trouble from coolie-brokers was perhaps to be expected, but even the most innocent of the consul's subjects could cause him endless worry. Though he might call on missionaries and their families, and enjoy an evening of 'music both vocal and instrumental ... the cakes superb; the jam delicious',[13] some missionaries were abrasive and obstreperous, and some became embroiled in religious squabbles requiring consular mediation between Protestants and Catholics (the latter officially outside the jurisdiction of the British consuls).

Many were also intent on preaching in the interior of China, beyond the officially sanctioned limits of the treaty ports. Such sorties were condemned by the Foreign Office: Consul Balfour in Shanghai was informed that should Medhurst's trips in disguise beyond the limits of Shanghai get him into trouble, the 'maximum permitted consular penalties' were to be imposed. Parkes in Canton had to accept delivery of the Reverend William Burns from the Chinese authorities after he was arrested on an illegal journey into the interior. Parkes exchanged letters with the Chinese authorities and gave an official warning to Burns, 'a most zealous but by no means prudent person'.[14]

The case of the coolie-broker Syme and his Mary illustrated the Victorian consul's difficulty in maintaining public decency at a time when there were very few foreign women within the treaty ports (in Canton in 1851 among the foreign community, men outnumbered women by a ratio of 7:1). Many men took Chinese mistresses, a very small number married them. Consuls themselves were not above succumbing to temptation. Robert Hart kept secret his liaison with his Chinese mistress Ayou in Ningpo. Other consuls were similarly secretive about their mistresses though Robert Thom (who served in Amoy, Canton and Ningpo) was quite open, as was Meadows, Hart's superior at Ningpo in the 1850s.

Much more troublesome were the male inhabitants of the treaty ports and not just because they were more numerous. Sailors came into port to get drunk with almost inevitable consequences. Hart in Ningpo

> watched a couple of drunken sailors this evening: crowds of Chinese were out gazing and laughing at them. Certainly very bad specimens of Western Civilization are to be met with here now and then. The natives are very much afraid of a drunken sailor – perhaps more so of one who is only on the 'wrong side of being jolly'. Jack comes staggering along, shouting and laughing; he throws his arms around some Chinaman – and shouting 'Come along my heartie!' makes the fellow screech as if he were about to be murdered.[15]

Worse were those involved in the dangerous and illegal opium or coolie trade who could be very rough indeed. In his everyday dealings at the consulate in Ningpo, Robert Hart came across a variety of bad hats, among them Captain Burton of the *Inglewood* and his crew. Two of Burton's sailors applied for a discharge on 3 January 1855, for they said he was 'a very nice, quiet, soft-spoken man on shore; but that he is the very opposite on board', an opinion borne out by his steward who complained of the captain 'and reached what Mr Ballard called "the summit of the climax" by telling me that the Capt. *cursed* every morning as soon as he arose. This from a sailor!'

It was not long before Hart heard more of the *Inglewood*.

> Yesterday morning a man named Wm. Kilburne, representing himself to be an American, came to this consulate to lodge a complaint against Norwood, one of the crew of the *Inglewood*. It appears that Kilburne was staying at Cymoon's lodging house and that Norwood had also been passing a day there: when Kilburne was going to bed on the evening of New Year's day, Norwood gave him a severe drubbing, blackening both his eyes to a severe extent. Now in what way the consul is to act here I don't know; I think it not impossible that *this case* is designed by the Portuguese to try how Mr Meadows will act towards an Englishman who had beaten an American, after a Portuguese had been flogged for striking a Chinese consular servant.

Though Hart did not record the outcome of this complaint (or its potential ramifications), worse was to follow in March of the same year: 'Another dispatch [from Hong Kong] asks Mr Meadows if the

Inglewood took away a cargo of children who had been purchased at Ningpo. Very fortunately Mr Meadows yesterday wrote a long dispatch about this.'

Six days after the *Inglewood*'s sailors had requested their discharge, Joseph Perry, 'the *Spec*'s gunner, came up to the consulate ... to let us know he had shot a Chinaman'. On 17 January 1855, Perry's case came before the consular court. 'He was accused of killing a Chinaman. He acknowledged having done so. Seven witnesses were examined against him, and three in his favour. The Chinese prevaricated – evaded – & contradicted in a most peculiar manner. The result was Perry's acquittal on the plea of self-defence.'

Far less straightforward a case than that of Perry was the matter of two mercenaries who had joined rebel forces fighting the imperial government and whom Meadows and Hart found chained up in the Ningpo yamen after their capture by the Chinese authorities. One told Hart that 'he was an American and that his name was Johnson' (although he was also known as Roberts and Jefferson); the identity of the other was even more complicated. He said his name was 'Akin' but Hart noted in parenthesis, 'He is Aldridge, sentenced to twenty-one years transportation for Homicide at Hong Kong – he broke out of prison – got to Shanghae – joined the Rebels – helped Jefferson to break out of the Shanghae jail & is quite a gallows bird.' Later that same day, Akin/Aldridge admitted he was an Englishman, 'a deserter from the *Salamander*', but Hart and Meadows left both in Chinese hands for transportation to Shanghai and punishment as rebels by the Chinese courts.[16]

With such subjects to defend, it was sometimes difficult for a consul to turn his mind to the promotion of British trade. Despite wars and treaties the enduring complaint of the merchants (law-abiding or otherwise) was that the British government did not offer enough support: they wanted pressure put on the Chinese government to open the entire country to British trade, to legalize the opium trade and to remove tariff and customs barriers, and they wanted the British government to provide them with greater protection in China through the dispatch of gunboats as required.

Relations between merchants and the Foreign Office's consuls in

China were frequently fraught with difficulties. The behaviour of some merchants and ships' crews, and their involvement in the opium trade, caused consular headaches and it was the consuls' unenviable responsibility to explain to them the caution of the home government. The merchants were prepared to lobby strongly at home: as early as 1837, Disraeli satirized the 'free-trading' merchants in his novel *Sybil*, depicting one election candidate as 'a Scotchman, richer than Croesus, one McDruggy, fresh from Canton, with a million of opium in each pocket, denouncing corruption and bellowing for free trade'.[17] Self-interest characterized the merchant lobby but the British government at the highest level was similarly concerned with its own interests and not particularly sensitive to Chinese feelings.

In 1850, as Prince Albert led the Royal Commission in planning his Great Exhibition of the arts and manufactures of the world, a letter was dispatched to the Tao-kuang emperor of China requesting official participation from China in the exhibition. Coming only eight years after the First Opium War and at a time when the British Foreign Office was pressing for further access to Canton city in an acrimonious exchange of letters, it is hardly surprising that the emperor did not greet the suggestion with enthusiasm, his reply of 22 June 1850 conceding only that he would not make it a criminal offence for Chinese subjects to participate.

The Royal Commission did not abandon hope. Edgar Bowring reported from Whitehall on 16 January 1851 that he was confident of 'ensuring a tolerable representation of Chinese industry at the exhibition by collecting from various private individuals . . . and I have reason to hope that we shall get many curious things'. Just over a month later he recorded that although attempts to procure any general action had been unsuccessful, nevertheless 'fifty packages are on their way hither, having been collected by private individuals'. Attached to his report is a Chinese banknote.

The Royal Commissioners also attempted to enlist the support of private companies for the exhibition though they had only one positive response when the P&O shipping line agreed in June 1850 to a request for assistance with the transport of exhibits from India and China. Obtaining the exhibits in the first place proved more difficult. Having failed with the Chinese government, the Royal Commissioners turned to the senior British government representative in China, Samuel George Bonham, Governor of Hong Kong and Her Britannic Majesty's Plenipotentiary and Chief Superintendent of Trade.

Bonham wrote from Hong Kong that Lindsay & Co. had 'collected some specimens of Chinese manufacture contained in 31 packages ... which it is their wish should be allowed admission into the exhibition'. However, though the response from Lindsay's was pleasing, it soon became clear that consular efforts to engage the interest of the merchants as a whole had failed: a committee of some sort had been set up in Canton and then abandoned. Furthermore, not all the potential exhibits that *had* been obtained were acceptable. Bonham had been informed 'by Vice-Consul Elmslie at Canton that Howqua, the China merchant, had collected a few specimens of crockery ware and other trifling objects which he desired should be forwarded to the Great Exhibition' but the Governor, in tones characteristic of the times, disparaged this Chinese offering: 'I was unable to forward Howqua's contributions to London which seem moreover of little value in themselves.'

In Shanghai, Consul Alcock had also been pressed into service but encountered a similar indifference amongst the merchants and reported to Bonham in December 1850:

> I have the honour to state that the British and French residents of Shanghai appear to have felt that the impossibility of gaining access to the great seats of Manufacture or to the producing districts for raw materials, placed them in too disadvantageous a position to do justice either to themselves or to the resources of this Empire which could only be very inadequately represented and in a way more calculated to mislead than to instruct by such objects only to be obtained at Shanghai.

The refusal to co-operate with the consul in Prince Albert's grand scheme represented an attempt to demonstrate, once again, to the British government that the merchants needed access to the interior of China in order to be able to operate properly and profitably.

Alcock was, nevertheless, able to forward seven cases and two extra packages which included specimens of porcelain from the great ceramic centre of Ching-te-chen (Jingdezhen), pieces of 'richly figured silk' from the Shanghai Taotai and such 'works of art and raw and manufactured produce as might be obtained ... [from] individual members of the community undeterred by the fear of giving [an] erroneous impression of the actual state of advancement in China'. Alcock himself collected a pair of scissors, a razor and some sewing needles which, in the light of his refusal to accept Howqua's 'trifling objects', Bonham might have been expected to reject. Despite the lack of interest shown by the British merchants in his jurisdiction, Alcock explained that he had chosen these implements with a view to the promotion of British trade.

> The three implements I have selected as of universal usage and of little variety in quality may be deserving of attention, were it only for the contrast they represent to the unequalled excellence and perfection of many other industrial works of a people presenting irreconcilable contradictions and anomalies whenever they are brought in contact with the habits and ideas of civilization of the Western World. But they may possibly attract with advantage the notice of our manufacturers from the fact that however rude or imperfect they seem, neither the iron of Sweden nor the hardware of Sheffield have hitherto been able to compete or find a market in China ... Whether the preference to their own productions is to be attributed to superior cheapness, greater aptitude and fitness for the work or to national prejudice or patriotism, to any or all of these, is a problem for the solution of those directly interested in the extension of the markets for one of our staple manufactures in which we are supposed to have distanced all rivals.[18]

In the end, it appears that Bonham and Alcock's efforts in the face of merchant indifference were to no avail and the Great Exhibition's Chinese exhibits were acquired in Britain by a Mr William Hewett: 'The committee in Canton for the purposes of the Great Exhibition having expressed their inability to persuade the Chinese to forward any contributions, I was applied to, at a very late period ... I finally succeeded in occupying the whole space allotted to China ... I borrowed a thousand pounds for the purpose of purchasing in London and Liverpool all that was rare, curious and beautiful ... I engaged a Chinese attendant at a cost of £50.' The Chinese attendant may have been a member of the rather curiously composed 'Living Chinese Family' which appeared in the Great Exhibition with the Chinese collection. The 'family' included Soo-Chune, aged 32, a 'Professor of

Music', and his two children, Miss Amoy aged 7 and Master Mun-Chung aged 5; C. Ashowe, 'an interpreter'; and Miss Pwan Ye-Kou, aged 17, 'a young lady with feet two and a half inches long', with her maidservant, Miss Lum-Akum.[19]

The merchants' refusal to participate in the Great Exhibition on the grounds that they were excluded from the tea- and silk-producing regions stemmed from their assumption that the potential of the China market was limitless. This view, held from the very beginning of the China trade, and prevalent even now, was based primarily on the sheer size of China's population and the belief that if one could sell a product to every inhabitant of the Celestial Empire, the financial results would be stupendous.

Such a view was not shared by Foreign Office officials. In 1852, Mr Mitchell, an assistant magistrate in Hong Kong, prepared a report on the potential of the China trade for the Governor of Hong Kong, Sir George Bonham (created a baronet in November 1850), though his report does not appear to have been widely circulated until 1858 when Lord Elgin (who had arrived in China to prosecute the Second Opium War) forwarded it to the Foreign Office. Mitchell revealed 'that the export of manufacturing stuffs to China was less by nearly three-quarters of a million sterling at the close of 1850 than at the close of 1844'. He did not consider that the failure to expand trade (or indeed, its contraction) was due to confinement to the treaty ports or excessive tariffs. The fact that the 'swarming millions' of Chinese consumed only 'one half so much of our manufactures as Holland' was due to the self-sufficient nature of the Chinese economy (a point that Alcock had struggled towards when proposing his scissors, razor and needles to Bonham for the Great Exhibition). 'When we opened the seaboard provinces of this country to British trade ten years ago,' wrote Mitchell,

> the most preposterous notions were formed as to the demand that was to spring up for our manufactures. Our friends in Manchester and even their counterparts on the spot out here ... seem to have all gone mad together upon the idea of an open trade with 'three or four hundred millions of human beings'. They straightaway began to bargain and barter, in imagination, with 'a third of the human race', and would not be convinced that it was not possible to throw more into the newly opened markets. Sir Henry Pottinger [Chief Superintendent of Trade, and first

Governor of Hong Kong] told them that he had opened up a whole new world to their trade, so vast, 'that all the mills in Lancashire could not make stocking-stuff sufficient for one of its provinces', and they pinned implicit faith in a statement to which their own fondness stood sponsor. Now as we could not possibly find a better one, I take Sir Henry Pottinger's own hyperbole and try to exhibit how utterly unfounded from first to last was this splendid fabric of His Excellency's imagination.

Mitchell conceded that hong book-keepers and shopkeepers might wear the 'neater, but less durable and far more expensive, British long-cloth' but he was convinced of the impossibility of persuading China's peasants to abandon their traditional products, markets and methods.[20]

Mitchell's arguments made little impression on the merchants, who were soon to bring further pressure to bear in their attempt to open up China to trade. In the meantime, they were beginning to have more influence within the existing treaty ports. The balance of power between the consuls and their subjects now changed with the establishment of local government in some of the larger concessions, in the form of municipal councils. Though these were often convened by the senior consul (usually British), they were otherwise independent, promulgating by-laws and regulations of extreme complexity without any particular reference to either the Chinese or home governments. Together with the law courts in the major treaty ports, which maintained the principle of 'extraterritoriality', these institutions ordered life within the concessions.

The first municipal council was set up in Shanghai in 1854 when the British, French and American consuls met together to revise the local land regulations to enable foreign land renters to elect a council annually to run the settlement. The consuls convened the meeting at which the election by ratepayers took place and the elected councillors undertook to maintain the roads, light the streets with oil lamps (at a cost of $12 per month) and spend an equivalent amount on sanitation. Most of the first year's budget went on hiring a superintendent of police (an ex-inspector from Hong Kong) and building a police barracks.[21]

In 1862, the French, 'fearing lest their interest might be overlooked', set up a separate concession, whose municipal council, though elected on a wider basis than in the neighbouring settlement, was only an advisory body, unable to act without the consent of the consul who was in sole charge of the police.[22] A year later, the British and American settlements merged to form the International Settlement. There, though the consuls called the ratepayers' meeting each spring, the municipal council, comprising nine 'unsalaried businessmen'[23] who met weekly to set the rates and to make or amend by-laws, ran everything else, including the police force. The police officers were all foreign, the constables either Chinese or foreign, the latter mainly ex-servicemen from India amongst whom Sikhs predominated. In 1865 the establishment comprised 1 officer, 61 'foreign' constables and 42 Chinese constables.

Local institutions grew apace. The Shanghai Fire Service was instituted in 1866. The Shanghai Volunteer Force, established in 1853 in the face of the Small Sword rebellion and reorganized in 1860 when yet another rebellion threatened the city, was virtually disbanded in 1862, leaving only a Rifle Club. However, the massacre of missionaries and the French consul in Tientsin in 1870 frightened Shanghai's inhabitants into convening a special meeting of the municipal council which resolved, 'That the Shanghai Volunteer Corps shall consist of Artillery, Mounted Rangers and three companies of Infantry' and 'that the management of the Corps shall be vested in the Municipal Council'.[24]

The Shanghai Municipal Council was the first, the largest and the most 'international' of all the councils in the treaty ports: in a later treaty port, Hankow, there were, eventually, British, Russian, French and Japanese municipal councils; and in Tientsin there was to be a similar separation (but including a German municipal council). In some places, like Chefoo (Yantai), opened as a treaty port in 1860, the same sort of international co-operation was seen with inhabitants from all countries contributing to the maintenance of a General Purposes Committee. Smaller treaty ports pottered on under consular supervision: Amoy's foreign inhabitants only organized themselves into 'an international settlement under the governance of a municipal council' in 1903.[25]

5

Small Swords and Imperial Chinese Customs

Those early foreign residents of China who were not personally involved in the illegal trade in opium and coolies and its concomitant violence were nevertheless justifiably concerned for their own safety and security within the treaty ports. By the middle of the nineteenth century, the Ch'ing dynasty had begun to lose control of large parts of China as a series of rebellions challenged its authority. Established by Manchus from the north-east of China in 1644, the dynasty was much resented for not being Chinese and, as it weakened, presented a specific focus for discontent. Shanghai and Amoy, in particular, were affected by these uprisings.

The first revolt to threaten treaty port security was that of the Small Sword Society (Xiao dao hui), a branch of the Triad (San he hui), or Heaven, Earth and Man Society, whose main aim was the extinction of the Ch'ing dynasty and the reassertion of Chinese rule. Its activities were widespread. The Triad was one of many secret societies that have existed throughout Chinese history. Some had religious affinities; others, like the mid-nineteenth century Triads, were more closely associated with specific social groups and areas. The Triad flourished along the coastal trade routes amongst boatmen and sailors, its members linked in brotherhood by secret rituals and passwords.

Since 1849 the Small Swords had been active in the Amoy area, causing considerable worry to the treaty port's tiny foreign population. In 1851, a Chinese named Ch'en Ch'ing-chen was arrested in Amoy at the order of the senior local government official, the Taotai, on suspicion of being the local leader of the Small Swords. Ch'en Ch'ing-chen had lived in Singapore, where he had acquired the status of a British subject.[1] He had also worked for Jardine Matheson, either as a clerk or in the trusted position of comprador. He was said to have been timid and quiet, his main hobby being the building up of his library of improving English books, and it seems likely that it was in fact his brother, 'a man of very different character', who was involved in Small Sword activity.

Since Ch'en was a British subject, G.G. Sullivan, now British consul, made efforts to free him, first sending his vice-consul to negotiate, only to be told that Ch'en was a Chinese, not a British subject. Sullivan himself then called upon the Taotai and after a four-hour discussion was informed that Ch'en would be returned. Unfortunately he was returned dead, though fully clothed and propped up in a sedan chair. Unconvinced by this macabre display, a British doctor examined the body and it soon became clear that Ch'en had died from a terrible beating.[2]

The judicial murder of Ch'en Ch'ing-chen was a shock to the small community and hinted at the seriousness of the Small Sword rebellion and the likelihood of bloodshed if the imperial government moved against it. In May 1853, the community's fears were realized as Small Sword rebels marched on Amoy.

When the treaty ports had first opened, the British government had sent not only consular officials but also naval forces to each port. However, the two services were entirely independent of each other, the consul receiving his instructions from the Foreign Office and the senior naval officer his orders from the Admiralty.[3] In practice, since instructions from the appropriate authority took months to arrive, both had to make their own decisions when faced with a sudden local disturbance; and, while their interests might be thought to have been identical, in practice the two men did not always agree on a single course of action.

When Vice-Consul Backhouse was informed that 3,000 armed rebels were advancing upon Amoy and were only perhaps a day's march away, the British gunboat HMS *Rattler*, stationed in Amoy to protect the foreign community, was at sea on a pirate hunt. So, on his own initiative, Backhouse requested that the opium 'receiving' ships of Tait, Jardine and Dent, tactfully anchored outside the harbour, should now enter. At the same time he moved his consular archives and cash to Dent's ship, the *Lord Amherst*.

Amoy was taken by the rebels on 18 May when the imperial government forces were driven out, and the opium ships retreated to their distant anchorage after HMS *Rattler* had returned from her pirate hunt. Though the safety of the government's consular property seemed to have been sensibly assured, and though Backhouse could hardly have waited for Foreign Office permission, he was nevertheless reprimanded by his senior officer, the Governor of Hong Kong Sir George Bonham, because he had been careless enough to offer the Chinese a pretext for saying that the British consular authorities abetted and encouraged the opium trade. Evidently, Backhouse should have found a way of suggesting that the opium ships had arrived of their own accord.

Official neutrality was preserved when imperial forces tried to retake Amoy by sea at the end of August. The Amoy Taotai requested help for the imperial troops but all the official British vessels moved to the east side of Kulangsu Island 'to leave room for the battle', with only HMS *Rattler* stationed in front of the foreign hongs, charged solely with the defence of foreign property. Less concerned with official neutrality, foreign residents were quick to profit from the situation, stockpiling gunpowder and weapons for sale to both sides. At the same time it was reported that Dent's ship *Lord Amherst*, doubtless taking advantage of the confusion, had fired on an imperial war junk. When this was confirmed, the British consulate issued an official reprimand.

At the end of the hostilities, whilst hundreds of local people were brutally executed by the victorious imperial forces, the foreign community on Kulangsu emerged unscathed. Not only had foreign merchants conducted a brisk trade in arms, they had also escaped customs duties since the imperial Customs House was out of action for eight months.[4]

The same self-interest and readiness to profit from the Chinese authorities' impotence characterized the reaction of the foreign community to the Small Sword uprising in Shanghai. Since 1848, the countryside around Shanghai had been filling with the characteristic recruits for rebel bands: disaffected men, landless peasants and some 13,000 junkmen discharged from the government junks that carried grain to the capital.[5] In those early days, foreigners who ventured outside the city did have something to fear. In March 1848, three missionaries, Drs Medhurst and Lockhart and the Reverend William Muirhead, had, against local consular orders issued in part for their own protection, travelled out of Shanghai and met an unruly crowd. Whilst distributing tracts, an argument arose and they only just escaped with their lives from junkmen armed with poles and bars. Little attempt was made by the imperial government to impose order on the surrounding country-side and when the Small Sword rebels, wearing red turbans, burst into the Chinese city on 7 September 1853, the birthday of Confucius, they met with no prepared resistance.

As British consul, Rutherford Alcock's first thought was for British trade. Faced with the disruption of the Chinese customs service, he agonized over his duties:

> If I let the ships depart without ... verifying ... duties and obtaining security for their final payment, British interests would be protected at the expense of the Chinese contrary to the express provisions of the treaty. If on the other side I detained the vessels until a Custom House should be re-established ... I run the risk of totally sacrificing British property and trade for the benefit of a government no longer in position to fulfil the conditions of that treaty.[6]

Two days later, on 9 September, a joint British-American notice was issued stating that in the event of the Chinese customs becoming inoperative, the consuls would collect promissory notes for the full amount of all duties owed to the Chinese customs, the only difference being that the British consul had to defer to the Foreign Office whilst the American consul could make his own decisions. Thus would treaty obligations be carried out, for 'the capture of an isolated sea-port [Amoy] on the coast of a great Empire can in no sense abrogate a solemn treaty entered into between the two Sovereigns of Great Britain and China. The obligations continue on both sides.' The American Minister Humphrey Marshall put it more succinctly: 'The treaty is not dead.'

Foreign merchants did not share the consuls' enthusiasm for fulfilling treaty obligations. One of the first activities of the Small Sword rebels had been to ransack and burn the Chinese Customs House.

Looking forward to not paying customs duties, Shanghai's merchants banded together to urge that the city be declared a free port, like Trieste. To some, it already was. On 8 September, the day after the uprising, T.C. Beale (donor of land for the cathedral and owner of the finest garden in Shanghai that boasted a *Magnolia grandiflora* and a *Cryptomeria japonica*) of the opium firm Dent, Beale & Co., who also served as Portuguese consul, Dutch vice-consul and acting Prussian vice-consul, had, in the latter capacity, allowed the *Preussischer Alder* to leave Shanghai without paying any duties on receipt of a promissory note absolving him from all claims.

Among the leaders of the Small Sword Society was Liu Li-ch'uan, a native of the same county as the Taotai, Wu Chien-chang, the senior Chinese government official in Shanghai. Liu had known Wu well, and may even have acted as his accountant at one stage in a varied career which included service as an interpreter to various Western merchant houses, a spell as a sugar-broker in Canton, probable opium smuggling and (most improbably) a period as a physician to the poor of Shanghai whom he treated for free.[7] Another acknowledged leader of the rebels was Chin A-ling, from Fukien, who had worked as a mafoo, or groom, for Mr Skinner of Dent, Livingstone & Co. Liu Li-ch'uan, described by one anti-rebel source as 'an emaciated opium smoker', 'informed the American Minister, who happened to be in Shanghai at the time, that the rising was against the Manchus, and that foreigners had nothing to fear'.[8]

Initially, the foreign inhabitants of Shanghai, aware that they themselves were not threatened, regarded their local rebels favourably and enjoyed a profitable relationship with them, supplying food and arms. Perhaps, too, their reluctance to condemn the rebellion stemmed in part from a shared dislike of the Chinese government, which was seen by many foreigners as a major impediment to their own ends. The ease with which foreigners could move amongst the rebels was illustrated by their rescue of the Taotai, Wu Chien-chang, who had been trapped within the Chinese walled city when the rebels attacked. Leaving his office to be plundered by the rebels, he hid himself and appealed to Beale and others for help. Disguised, wearing glasses and clutching an old umbrella, he was lowered from the walls of the Chinese city in a basket (some say a strong cotton sling) by Dr Hall and Mr Caldecott, and taken to Russell & Co.'s hong where Colonel Marshall, the American Minister, was also staying.

His fellow-countryman Liu Li-ch'uan, leader of the Small Sword rebels, appears to have suggested to Marshall that Wu should be reinstated as Small Sword Taotai but Wu was evidently reluctant to accede, fearing eventual imperial punishment. For his failure to protect the Chinese city and for his association with Russell & Co., which was condemned by the imperial government for selling arms to the rebels, he was later sentenced to banishment, although this was commuted owing to his generous contributions to the imperial coffers. He re-emerged in Shanghai in 1858, in a slightly lower official position.[9]

Though the Chinese government sent imperial forces to try to put down the rebellion, its duration was much extended by the supplies provided by opportunistic foreigners. In November 1853, acting upon information that guns were being delivered to the rebels by a foreign firm, imperial troops raided the foreign settlement. When they seized the guns, they claimed they were attacked by 'rebels in foreign disguise'.[10] These were in fact sailors from HMS *Spartan*, who, in defence of the gun-runners, killed three imperial soldiers and wounded fourteen others.

In the months during which the Small Sword rebels held the Chinese city, immediately adjacent to the French settlement and close to the British, there were frequent skirmishes between the rebels and imperial forces which were noted by Dr Yates whose house was close to the city walls. The victims of both sides were taken to Dr Lockhart's London Missionary Society hospital which was situated near the scene of the fighting (next to the Chinese Egg-hatching Establishment). There were also sporadic attacks on foreigners throughout 1853: Dr Medhurst and his missionary companions were threatened, Mr Henry Reeve was fired at near his back door, and Mr Arthur Smith (of Birley, Worthington & Co.) was set upon when out walking with a lady near the New Park. She managed to escape but he was so severely wounded by sword cuts that 'for some time his life was despaired of'.

Before the seizure of the Chinese city, the foreign residents of Shanghai, alarmed by stories of the rebellion, had banded together to establish the Shanghai Volunteer Corps for their own defence. British, American and French consuls and naval officers presided over a meeting on 12 April 1853 at which Captain Tronson of the 2nd Bengal Fusiliers assumed charge of the corps in order to maintain 'an armed neutrality'.[11] After much enthusiastic drilling, the corps prepared for its first major encounter. This was not with the rebels, as might have been expected, but with the imperial troops who had surrounded the walled city to besiege the rebels. Chinese soldiers were not, by tradition, disciplined forces and their foraging was seen as a threat by the foreign residents of Shanghai. Thus it was imperial forces, on the outskirts of the city, who were attacked by 400 British and American volunteers and sailors on 4 April 1854. The Battle of Muddy Flat lasted for two hours and left two sailors (one British and one American) dead, two volunteers fatally injured and thirteen others less seriously hurt. The Chinese camps to the north of the British settlement were set on fire and some thirty imperial soldiers were killed. (In his account of the battle, a local resident Mr Wetmore maintained that the ground was not muddy but dry and dusty, though in crossing the small creeks that traversed the area, the troops doubtless got muddy feet. Some think that the battle was originally called the Battle of Muddy Feet and that the change in name was the result of a rather serious misprint.)[12]

The Battle of Muddy Flat or Feet saw foreign settlers and the sailors who were there for their protection pitted against the Chinese imperial army. It may or may not have involved the rebels (depending upon whether or not some wounds were thought to have been inflicted by their gingal guns), but in its wake the foreign community and its plenipotentiaries (who offered their support some time later) gradually came to the conclusion that the rebellion was, in the long run, bad for trade, not least because it encouraged a general lawlessness. The rebellion was subsequently crushed within a month, in mid-February 1855, by walling off the Chinese city and cutting off supplies.

The most important result of the Small Sword rebellion in Shanghai was the formation of the Imperial Maritime Customs Service in 1854. There had been a Chinese Maritime Customs House in Shanghai since 1658 on the Bund, next to the 'large umbrageous compound of Messrs Dent & Company', in 'a Chinese temple, the fantastic roofs and curved gables of which constitute the only break in a line of European architecture'.[13] However, the payment of customs duties was all too often a matter of bargaining. The resultant inequality of treatment, unjust exactions and exposure to the rapacity of underlings had long been a subject of complaint amongst foreign merchants.[14]

After the disruption of the Small Sword uprising and the interim arrangement by which local consuls collected customs duties, the same consuls proposed the introduction of foreign methods and discipline, which, in the view of the time, could only be brought about by the employment of foreigners in the Chinese service.

On 29 June 1854, in the foreign settlement outside the Chinese walled city, and in the presence of their consuls, the first three foreign customs inspectors, Thomas Francis Wade (later Minister in Peking and the first Professor of Chinese at the University of Cambridge), Lewis Carr (an American) and the surprisingly named Frenchman Arthur Smith, swore 'truly and honestly to discharge all the duties of . . . office as Inspector of Maritime Customs'. The Shanghai Taotai, Wu Chien-chang, temporarily restored to office after his narrow escape during the uprising, was present as Superintendent of Customs, representing the Chinese government in whom responsibility for the service was 'ultimately vested'. And so, according to a later resident of Shanghai, Samuel Couling, 'Honest and efficient administration was established. Trade was freed from underhand arrangement. Accurate statistics were provided. Honest merchants were protected. The Chinese government received a valuable revenue which vastly improved its financial position.'[15]

6

The Taiping Rebellion

The Small Sword uprising was partly ended through the withdrawal of foreign guns and supplies. A rebellion of far greater extent and duration, that of the Taipings, was harder to suppress. Though for ten years from the beginning of the rebellion in 1850, foreign consuls maintained a neutral stance in the defence of business interests, they were not above negotiating with the Taiping rebels in order to obtain permission for their subjects to trade freely.

The decline of the Ch'ing dynasty had seen the concurrent uprising of many different opportunistic rebel bands in various parts of the country. But the Taiping rebellion could also be said to have resulted, at least indirectly, from foreign influence in China, for its leader, Hung Hsiu-ch'uan, was deeply affected by Christian missionaries whom he encountered in Canton. In 1836 he was given tracts written by Liang Afa, the first Chinese Protestant convert, who had been baptized by Robert Morrison in 1814 in Macao.[1] Hung Hsiu-ch'uan seems not to have read the pamphlets until 1843 when he decided that an old man who had appeared to him in delirious visions was God and that he himself was Jesus' younger brother, called to destroy pagan idols and establish the worship of the true God.

In 1847, Hung studied with the Reverend Issachar Jacox Roberts from Tennessee, a member of Karl Gutzlaff's Christian Union in Canton. Though Roberts considered baptism 'in the rolling surf off the shores of Hong Kong or in the flowing rivers of China' to lie at the heart of Christian conversion he appears to have refused to baptize Hung Hsiu-ch'uan who made off into the wilds of Kwangsi (Guangxi) province to continue his own preaching work.[2]

In his stronghold at Thistle Mountain in Kwangsi, Hung gathered together a band of disaffected peasants, uprooted from their land by the terrible famines that occurred in southern China in 1847–9. To these followers he preached the establishment of a Heavenly Kingdom of supreme (*tai*) peace (*ping*) incorporating the sharing of possessions, agrarian reform and rebellion against the enfeebled Ch'ing dynasty. By the time the Taipings took Nanking in March 1853, they had established their own government, including a ministry charged with responsibility for foreign affairs (something which did not fully exist in the Ch'ing government at the time). A new calendar was promulgated that included a Western-style Sunday for rest and worship (not a concept incorporated in the traditional Chinese calendar); land was reallocated, and, though the sexes were segregated, women were permitted relative equality and allowed to serve in the army.

Though the Taiping advance was resisted by Ch'ing government forces, for a time they carried all before them. In the winter of 1852–3 the rebels took the cities of Hanyang, Hankow and Wuchang, just up the Yangtze from Shanghai. In March 1853 they established themselves in Nanking which they held until 1865, and later that year they seized Tientsin, frighteningly close to Peking. In June 1860, Soochow (Suzhou), close to Shanghai, also fell.

As the tide of war ebbed and flowed (Hankow was retaken by the Taipings for the fourth time in 1855), so too did the attitudes of observers in the treaty ports. Throughout the 1850s the rebels harried Canton, and in 1855 they approached Ningpo. Robert Hart, then a young consular officer, recorded in his diary for 27 February 1855 (after mention of Mr Nevius' erysipelas), 'Some of the Shanghai rebels have come to Ningpo; but as they are few in numbers it is not likely that any disturbance will ensue.' On 21 May, he saw frogs brought out by a thunderstorm and a snake 'sneaking along very stealthily . . . I never saw anything like the personification of cunning and stealth as this gentleman.' He was pestered by beetles and mosquitoes, tried Chinese tobacco as he had almost run out of cigars, and reported that the rebels had taken a town about 400 miles away.[3]

Hart was far removed from the worst of the fighting, so his insouciance is perhaps not surprising, but in fact the Taipings, like the Small

Swords, were not anti-foreign. In April 1853, Sir George Bonham, Governor of Hong Kong and and Chief Superintendent of Trade, went to Nanking to negotiate with the Taiping rebels and obtained permission for British subjects to travel and trade freely in Taiping territory. However, his mission also had a second purpose which reflected the ambivalence of the foreign attitude towards the Taipings. Determined to maintain neutrality, Bonham had already made it clear to the Ch'ing government that they could expect no assistance from the British, for earlier in the same month he had informed Wu Chien-chang, the Shanghai Taotai, that Britain would not send troops against the rebels but would act only to defend British life and property. (In a similar vein, in December 1854, the new Governor of Hong Kong Sir John Bowring refused a request for aid against rebels attacking Canton, and in December 1859 the Earl of Elgin and Kincardine insisted that Britain would not assist the Ch'ing against the Taipings.) Nevertheless, on his visit to Nanking in 1853, Bonham was also keen to establish the long-term prospects of the rebels, in case it should prove politic to ally with the winning side.[4]

Bonham was not the only foreign representative who was anxious to see the Taipings at first hand. The French Minister, Alphonse de Bourboulon, accompanied by his English Protestant wife, went to Nanking to enquire about the treatment of Catholics. He was impressed by the savage punishment of opium smokers (whose severed heads were hung on the city walls), the free distribution of warm winter clothing, the continuous printing of the Gospels and the cannon shots that announced that the Heavenly King Hung Hsiu-ch'uan was at prayer. Discomfited, like Bonham, by the 'imperial' position assumed by the Taiping leaders who sat on a raised dais above him and set a tone of superiority in their treaty proposals, de Bourboulon nevertheless concluded that the Taiping rebellion was 'one of formidable character and proportions' with a strength and a 'moral force which gives them great superiority over their adversaries'.[5]

The American Minister, Humphrey Marshall, was irritated to have been beaten to Nanking by the British and the French, his own efforts to get there being scuppered when his boat, the *Susquehanna*, ran aground. Unable to find a replacement with a shallower draught, he made the attempt once more in late May 1854 and reached Nanking on the 27th, only to find, like the French and the British, that he was caught in the convolutions of treaty responsibilities.

Visiting Nanking in an unofficial capacity, the journalist Frank Blakiston described his meeting with Hung Jen-kan, one of the Taiping leaders. A fellow-countryman of Hung Hsiu-ch'uan, Hung Jen-kan had spent four years in Hong Kong studying with missionaries and had, on the strength of his Hong Kong experience, been made Foreign Minister of the Taiping Kingdom. He greeted visitors with a handshake and a 'How do you do' in English. His studio, facing a garden full of flowers, was filled with European effects:

> There is a telescope on a moving pedestal (broken), a gun box (gun gone), three Colt's revolvers (all useless from rust), a box of gun caps, ditto of Vestas, two solar lamps that can't be made to light, and a cake of brown Windsor soap; the Woolwich Manual of Fortification … five or six clocks, an alarum, broken barometer … three English Port Wine bottles, and one ditto of Coward's mixed pickles … an engraving of the Holy Well in Flintshire …[6]

This touching collection of European possessions, together with the unorthodox Christianity that the Taipings professed and their serious military challenge to the Ch'ing court, presented foreign residents in China with a dilemma. Missionaries were torn. Some felt that the unorthodox Christianity of the Taipings was almost worse than straightforward idolatry; for others, unorthodox Christianity was infinitely preferable to idolatry and required gentle support to steer the Taipings on to the correct path. Among those of the latter view was Issachar Jacox Roberts who had previously refused to baptize Hung Hsiu-ch'uan. He had been trying to make his way to Nanking for seven years ever since receiving an invitation from his former pupil to preach there. Hampered at first by the treaty restrictions that forbade foreigners from travelling into the interior, he eventually made the trip in October 1860 after British and French attacks on Peking compelled the emperor to rescind his prohibition on travel outside the treaty ports (see Chapter 7). Both he and the British missionary Joseph Edkins tried hard to disabuse Hung of his belief that he was a son of God, Edkins writing theological letters in very large characters for the increasingly short-sighted Taiping leader. Their efforts were unsuccessful, for Hung insisted upon annotating Edkins' letters in scarlet ink, crossing out references to Jesus as God's 'only' son.[7]

Divided views amongst the missionaries and the failure of men such as Roberts and Edkins to correct Taiping unorthodoxies meant that the Taipings were increasingly viewed askance. When Roberts left Nanking in January 1862, he described Hung as 'a crazy man, entirely unfit to rule ... without any organized government'. The official consular (and Foreign Office) view, after an early mild flirtation with the rebels when they were at the height of their power, was that they were bound by the treaty not to interfere on either side.

However, it was to be the views of a third group, the foreign merchants, that were to prove decisive. Like others, the merchants were at first divided: gun-running to the rebels proved lucrative and the relatively pro-foreign views of such Taiping leaders as Hung Jen-kan allowed the hope that the Taipings might succeed in overthrowing the Ch'ing dynasty and establishing a regime more favourable to their commercial interests. Others were less sanguine. John Gavin, a Scottish engineer turned architect, then residing in Hankow, wrote to his family in Edinburgh:

> I believe before long you will see a different policy pursued in China. I was reading in some home papers that you are now beginning to find out that little is known of the state of affairs here, they thought the Rebels were nobody, but now they find that they have it in their power to dictate to the Emperor and Britain, peace or war. My policy from the first was to leave them alone and you will see that will be right, [though] there's no doubt cause for the present govt. to be found fault with.[8]

Eventually, fear of greater unrest prompted both the foreign merchants and the Chinese bankers of Shanghai to take unofficial action. In 1862 they raised money to support an army to suppress the rebellion, known by the Chinese as the Ever Victorious Army and by foreigners, at least at first, as the Disciplined Force. Ultimate control of the army was complex. Theoretically it was independent and 'co-operated' with the Chinese imperial forces. In practice, the provincial governor, Li Hung-chang, increasingly assumed command. The first leader of the Ever Victorious Army was an American adventurer called Frederick Townsend Ward.[9] A somewhat garbled account of Ward, which reflected Shanghai gossip of the time, was given by John Gavin in a letter to a colleague in 1863 in which he referred to his Shanghai experiences of the previous year:

> You may have heard of General Ward's name who has been taking an active part here to put down the Rebellion. He was a low Yankee of neither character nor position. He commenced business near Shanghai by training a few Manillamen and took a small village from the Rebels, the plunder of which amply paid him and brought him to the notice of the mandarins who gave him money to purchase arms and train Chinamen to the use of them. For doing so he was taken prisoner on board a British man of war. He said he was now a Chinese subject and on that ground had to be set free and all at once our Admiral made a friend of this Filibuster and used to go out with him and send men to assist in attacking the Rebels in the neighbourhood of Shanghai.

To some extent, the Taipings brought the Disciplined Force upon themselves. After many years in which Taiping troops had approached Shanghai but had always withdrawn, in 1862 the Taiping general Li Hsiu-ch'ing led thousands of troops towards the city, demanding that the British and French withdraw from Shanghai, although he promised not to allow the plunder or destruction of foreign property. This substantial Taiping army was stopped in its tracks just outside Shanghai by an unexpected snowfall and a month of abnormally cold weather. The threat of the Taipings and the harsh weather caused the peasants in that area terrible hardship, and they fled towards the safety of the city. Despite severe measures such as the closure of the Chinese city gates, the raising of drawbridges on the canals, the imposition of a curfew, and the issue of passes to 'legitimate' Chinese only, the British consul reported in the summer of 1862, 'We are once more overrun with refugees . . . camping out on the Bund in front of the house, and on the roads near the stone bridge. It is frightful to see the numbers of women, aged and children, lying and living out in the open air, and not over-abundantly supplied with food.'

During the cold weather of early 1862, a local newspaper, the *Daily Shipping and Commercial News*, contained increasing numbers of notices of missing dogs, among them 'Teazer', 'Smut', a pregnant Pekinese called 'Chin-chin', and the liver-and-white pointer belonging to General Staveley who was in charge of the British forces in China.

Presumably they had been eaten by the starving poor sleeping rough in Shanghai's streets. As many foreign merchants began to support resistance to the Taiping army, the *Daily Shipping and Commercial News* also began to fill with reports of charges against men like 'P. Lodie, aged 31, Scotland, resident Shanghai, selling arms to rebels and W. Hardie ... having charge of a cargo boat with arms and rebel passes'. Even General Staveley was involved in supplying the rebels, selling off the weapons of the 22nd Punjab Native Infantry and the 5th Bengal Naval Infantry when they were posted home.[10]

Despite the Taiping threat, the inhabitants of Shanghai attempted to live life as usual. It was not always easy. John Gavin, though admitting that he must 'stop writing about the rebels for my Mother is always in a state of great fright about them', nevertheless recorded that he

> did not get much work done as the Rebels made their appearance in the neighbourhood of Shanghai. As the slip [dockyard] was on the opposite side of the river from the city, they on one or two occasions came within the slip grounds. As the very naming of the word 'rebel' would make a Chinaman take to his heels, it was impossible to get to work. I did what I could for some time. I had to go there every day with a Revolver in my pocket and row boats ready for the workmen to cross as soon as they heard they were coming. They did not come down at that time in large bodies, perhaps from fifteen to twenty would come rushing down on horseback and the first you would know of them would be seeing the villains within a couple of hundred yards of you. At last, thinking there was no use erecting works to run the risk of getting them burned down, I suspended work altogether and wrote home to the owner that I had done so.

As the Taipings encircled Shanghai, the treaty port's inhabitants organized themselves with bravado. John Gavin was among their number:

> we got up a Volunteer Corps, to defend the settlement should there be any disturbance. We got plenty of Drill Sergeants and were at drill morning and night and in six weeks we were tolerably efficient, at least able to shoot a Chinaman ... We were never called into active service, but always had to be in readiness, as every day we had the pleasure of seeing a few rebels within gunshot of us, and we did not know when they

would pay us a visit. The work we had was quite action enough. We had two lines of defences within the British Settlement, all the streets were barricaded and for two months the Volunteers had to stand sentry at night ... However, time passed away and with all the threatening dispatches the Rebels sent us from time to time, they seemed afraid to show fight ... They used to send us word the day and hour that they were coming to make an attack which is a Chinese custom. They don't try to take the enemy by surprise. It is a custom that may do very well amongst themselves as they never fight, they are better up to running away. We got some soldiers up from Hong Kong and then we commenced to show the offensive and, I think little to the credit of Great Britain, our Admiral used to send our men along with the Imperialist soldiers, which gave them more courage, although our men generally got all the fighting to do.[11]

Evidently unconscious of the irony, Gavin always referred to the Chinese government forces as 'the Imperialists' and was scornful of their achievements.

By the summer of 1862, the Taiping army under Li Hsiu-ch'ing had given up any thought of taking Shanghai, and the Taipings were forced on to the defensive on many fronts, not least around their capital of Nanking. In September 1862, Frederick Ward was fatally wounded near Ningpo. Though the British consul in Shanghai, Walter Henry Medhurst (son of the missionary of the same name), proposed that an officer of the British Army should succeed him, Ward was temporarily replaced by an American, who had been his deputy, Henry Andrea Burgevine. However, Burgevine's drunkenness, his failure to keep accounts for his Chinese superior and his method of obtaining money by physically attacking bankers, led to his dismissal in January 1863.[12]

Meanwhile, General Staveley, commander of the British forces in China, had been keeping the Taipings back behind a thirty-mile limit established around Shanghai and, in May 1862, had enlisted his brother-in-law, Charles Gordon of the Royal Engineers, to assist in capturing walled cities held by the rebels in the Shanghai area. According to Staveley, Gordon was 'of the greatest possible use to me, especially in reconnoitring the enemy's defences, and in arranging for ladder-parties crossing the moats, and escalading'.[13] He also constructed defences around Shanghai in swampy land filled with 'the croaking of frogs, the stinging of mosquitoes, the noise of bats ... big beetles flying about, and the stench of dead Chinamen'.

Staveley had tried to get Gordon appointed as Ward's successor at the head of the Ever Victorious Army but it was not until after Burgevine's assault on the Shanghai banker Yang Fang that his name went forward, and he was confirmed in his appointment in March 1863. His appointment had been opposed by Frederick Bruce – now, as British Minister in Peking, the senior diplomat in China – who had written to the Foreign Office in defence of British neutrality which, he said, would be compromised by Gordon's service; however, the steamer carrying the dispatch was wrecked off Ceylon and the British government issued an Order in Council allowing British Army officers to take up temporary service with the Chinese. Bruce's letter was rescued and dried out and did eventually reach London, but too late to affect Gordon's command of the Ever Victorious Army.[14]

With his staff surgeon, Andrew Moffitt (who would later marry his sister), and four other British officers, about 4,000 Chinese troops and a few American, British and German mercenaries, Gordon soon proved his worth by taking the rebel-held city of Fushan, sixty miles north-west of Shanghai, in two days. He also set about reforming the Ever Victorious Army. Looting and alcohol were forbidden, a medical service was set up, and Gordon established a working relationship with Li Hung-chang. In the first days of May 1863, he went to the rescue of Li's brother who had been wounded in the posterior when attempting to recapture the walled town of Taitsang (Taicang), now on the north-west edge of metropolitan Shanghai. Whilst the Chinese imperial forces had rushed at the town, pushed through a gate and found themselves surrounded by murderous Taipings, Gordon made a proper reconnaissance, conducted a lengthy bombardment and then ordered a calculated assault. The battle was fiercer than any he had seen in the Crimea, though he led it 'from the front, unarmed, smoking a cheroot and carrying his cane'.[15]

One of the complications of such a widespread rebellion was the difficulty of manning so many fronts. Gordon's concern was to retake the towns on the Yangtze delta, but further inland, up the Yangtze at Hankow, the foreign residents of what had become a new treaty port (see Chapter 7) were also vulnerable, although they faced the Taiping threat with customary phlegm. The local Taotai showed less fortitude, as John Gavin, by now living in Hankow, reported in April 1863:

> A few of them paid us a visit a fortnight ago, the inhabitants flying in every direction, there was a terrible hubbub for a couple of nights. I hope if they come the Taotai will be the first to lose his head. Govt. sent us about a month ago some rifles for the Volunteers here and the Blackguard would not pass them from the Customs House, he said he did not wish foreigners to have firearms in their possession and an old wife of a consul would not interfere. However, when the panic arose about the Rebels, he sent word to the consul asking the assistance of a gunboat and saying that the rifles were lying in such a place and would be delivered as soon as sent for – he tried to pacify the people asking them not to run, that there was no danger, at the same time he was shipping off his wives, goods and chattels and would be the first to run himself.[16]

Gordon was a difficult man, neither sociable – he did not eat with his fellow-officers but might consume ten or twenty raw eggs alone in the mess late at night after the others had dined – nor one of nature's subordinates. 'I act for myself and judge for myself. This I have found the best way of getting on,' he wrote to his mother; his superiors had to find this out for themselves. As leader of the Ever Victorious Army and in charge of the campaign against the Taipings he found himself, nevertheless, under the overall command of the Chinese government and he was soon to experience all the difficulties that that delicate position implied. Later on, the foreign employees of the Imperial Maritime Customs were to find themselves similarly placed as foreigners linked to the treaty ports but officially appointed to promote Chinese interests.

For Gordon, the most tragic result of his ultimate subordinacy to the Chinese was the execution of the Taiping Wangs (kings) at Soochow. Aware that the Taiping rebellion was failing and that his own terrifying reputation was a persuasive factor in bringing the insurgents to heel, in December 1863 he negotiated the surrender of Soochow, guaranteeing a safe conduct for the rebels and assuring the inhabitants that there would be no looting. The Taiping Wangs surrendered without a fight. However, disregarding Gordon's promises, Li Hung-chang, Gordon's Chinese superior, then proceeded to have all the Taiping commanders brutally executed. Gordon, who had given his word as a British officer and gentleman, was appalled. Li Hung-chang, for his part, could not understand 'how Major Gordon should take the matter so much to heart. What was he to the Wangs, or the Wangs to him?' The remark was made to Sir Samuel Halliday Macartney, an army medical officer who had also temporarily transferred to work directly with Li Hung-chang against the Taipings (although he later married a relative of one of the Wangs). Macartney, who seems to have failed to urge Gordon's practical view that clemency and restraint at Soochow could have produced an early and peaceful Taiping surrender, was 'about to read Li a lecture on foreign ideas of honour when I was brought to a standstill by his advancing the undeniable fact that China was China and the foreign country the foreign country'.[17]

In an effort to reconcile Li Hung-chang and his loose foreign cannon, Macartney visited Gordon whom he found

> sitting on his bedstead ... sobbing .... and before a word was exchanged, Gordon stooped down, and taking something from under the bedstead, held it up in the air, exclaiming: 'Do you see that? Do you see that?' The light through the small Chinese windows was so faint that Macartney had at first some difficulty in discovering what it was, when Gordon exclaimed: 'It is the head of the Lar Wang, foully murdered!' and with that burst into hysterical tears.[18]

Five days after the massacre he was still described by a colleague as 'in a truly sorrowful state: he could not speak for emotion, his eyes were full of tears',[19] although Hankow gossip had him in a more fiery mood. John Gavin wrote on 19 December 1863 to his father:

> Captain Gordon who is now in charge of the disciplined Chinese has taken Soochow from the Rebels. They surrendered on his promising that their lives should be spared. The first thing the Mandarins did was behead several of the Chiefs altho' they promised to the contrary. And when he [Gordon] interfered they gave orders to the soldiers to take him into custody; he took out his revolver and shot six of them. He retired from Soochow at once which has since been retaken by the Rebels. I expect this will lead to the breaking up of the disciplined Chinese force, at least to the English giving them any moral support. We have not yet heard full particulars but I do hope that the Rebels got hold of the Mandarins when they retook Soochow.

Alas, the rebels failed to retake Soochow and so were in no position to exact their revenge.

Gordon's despair at the failure of Li Hung-chang to understand that, even in war, an Englishman's word was his bond almost unhinged him. Nor can his peace of mind have been restored when he found himself blamed for Li's duplicity. The Bishop of Victoria (Hong Kong), Dr George Smith, protesting to the Foreign Office about atrocities against Taiping prisoners, roundly condemned Gordon; and even after his death in the Sudan in 1885, when he was nationally acclaimed as a hero, a pro-Taiping China missionary who had known him said, 'I can only look upon him as a murderer of native Christians and a wild mercenary soldier.'[20]

Though Gordon found it hard to recover from his experience and the Ch'ing government was seriously shaken by the length and extent of the Taiping uprising, the foreign community in Shanghai lost no time in taking action to stabilize its position once the rebellion had been suppressed. For it was then that many of the institutions required in an established foreign community were founded. As has been noted, the Mixed Court, a police court which dealt with matters involving foreign interests, was first held in 1863. Ostensibly presided over by a Chinese magistrate in the presence of a consular assessor, in practice, the latter could overrule the magistrate's decisions. In the same year, the American and British concessions were formally 'united under one rule', creating the International Settlement (the French Concession remaining separate) and the Shanghai Club was founded, a gentleman's establishment where senior partners gathered at lunch-time. In 1865, Her Britannic Majesty's Supreme Court for China and Japan was moved from Hong Kong to Shanghai. In this the Taiping rebellion was said to have been instrumental, for the city had 'attracted large numbers of low adventurers to China, whose outrages and lawless acts had often gone unpunished', though civil cases were also becoming more complicated with the growth of trade.

In Shanghai, the legal duties of the British consul were transferred to the Supreme Court, though cases involving other nationalities were still tried by their consuls and the only other 'supreme court', the United States Court for China, was not set up until 1907. In all other treaty ports, the consul retained judicial authority, although a Supreme Court judge would be sent to try very serious cases involving British citizens wherever they occurred in China.

7

The Second Opium War

Whilst Small Swords and Taipings were an intermittent distraction for treaty port residents (at times watching battles was almost a spectator sport), of much greater concern to many was the need to open China still further to foreign trade. Though the Sino-British Treaty of Nanking (1843) had been followed by further treaties with the Americans and the French which expanded the provisions of the British treaty, the merchants remained unsatisfied. The opening of the coastal treaty ports had not led to the vast expansion in trade that they had hoped for: indeed in 1850 the Manchester Chamber of Commerce complained that the government of China 'endeavours in secret and indirect ways to oppose itself to the introduction of foreign manufactures by encouraging native jealousies and screening native aggressions . . . The strictly enforced limitation to five places on the seaboard prevents the growth of better personal feeling between the races and keeps concealed the causes of our stunted trade with China.' There was 'disappointment universally felt in respect of the results expected from the Treaty of Nanking' and 'the mistake made in limiting the right of ingress to five coastal ports'.[1]

Though not everyone was convinced that expansion of the treaty port system would increase Britain's export possibilities, in 1854 the British decided to press, with the French and the Americans, for the renegotiation of the treaty. The American treaty of 1844 had stipulated renegotiation after twelve years, though the British treaty had not. However, the British treaty had also contained a 'most favoured nation' clause by which additional privileges subsequently obtained by one country were also to be extended to Britain. In applying this clause to the issue of renegotiation, and reckoning the twelve-year period to date from the Treaty of Nanking's signature in 1842, rather than its ratification in 1843, the British acted with consummate sophistry. Perhaps mindful of the fact, and certainly aware of the Ch'ing government's predicament in the face of the Taiping rebellion, Lord Palmerston as Foreign Secretary wrote to Sir John Bowring, Governor of Hong Kong and Chief Superintendent of Trade, 'The Chinese Authorities may perhaps, and with some degree of plausibility, object that the circumstances of the time are unsuitable for the commencement of such a work.'[2]

Any scruples Palmerston may have entertained were soon overcome. In February 1854, he further proposed to Bowring that he prepare to demand revisions in the Nanking treaty to allow the British access to all of China (or, at least, the Chekiang coast and the lower Yangtze), legalization of the opium trade (the only profitable British import to China), abolition of internal duties or levies on foreign goods in transit, and residence of a British ambassador in Peking. He also wanted to insist (in the light of problems in Canton, especially) that the English-language version of the treaty be considered superior in any disputes.

Accordingly, in mid-October 1854 Sir John Bowring, accompanied by French and American envoys, arrived in Taku, a fortified coastal town on the river approach to Tientsin (and thence, further inland, to the emperor's capital, Peking) to propose the revision of the Nanking and subsequent treaties. Their proposal was dismissed out of hand and, after almost a month in Taku, they returned south, concluding that only a display of military force would move the emperor.

In December of the same year, the governor of the province of Canton, Yeh Ming-ch'en, who had himself earlier refused to contemplate revision of the treaty, thus prompting Bowring's journey north to Taku, wrote to the Governor in Hong Kong, asking for British naval assistance in the suppression of the Red Turban revolt in Canton province; unsurprisingly Bowring refused. Yeh Ming-ch'en was well known to Bowring and his predecessor, Bonham, not only for his continued refusal to allow any attempts at treaty revision but also for his persistence in debarring foreigners from entry into the walled city of Canton which, in British eyes, was contrary to the original provisions of the Treaty of Nanking. Throughout 1855, Bowring, the French envoy and the American Commissioner in China, Peter Parker, who had earlier served as a medical missionary in Canton, continued to press for permission to go north to Peking to pursue renegotiation of the treaty.

Diplomatic approaches having failed, a new excuse for a military campaign was found when a lorcha (a small vessel with a Western-style hull but Chinese-style masts and sails)[3] called the *Arrow*, Chinese-owned but flying a British flag, was boarded in Canton on 8 October 1856 and all its (Chinese) crew seized on suspicion of piracy. On the same day, Harry Parkes, British consul at Canton, protested to Yeh Ming-ch'en who, though he released all the crew on 22 October, refused to apologize. As Bowring had discovered in the interim that the *Arrow's* British (Hong Kong) registration had, in fact, expired on 27 September, Yeh's actions might have been considered sufficient amends, but against the background of the continued closure of Canton and the stalemate over treaty revision, the Royal Navy was dispatched to uphold British principles. On 25 October Admiral Sir Michael Seymour seized the Hai-chu fort which lay before the city of Canton. On the 27th, Canton was shelled, and on the 29th, Seymour entered Yeh Ming-ch'en's yamen. A week earlier American warships under Commodore Armstrong had taken the Barrier forts down-river from Canton.[4]

In response, on 30 October, Yeh Ming-ch'en placed a bounty on every English head – a condition which further restricted the activities of the foreign merchants in the factories on the shore, who were already inconvenienced by the British warships shelling over their heads. He also continued to refuse to see Bowring, who travelled up from Hong Kong for the purpose in mid-November; however, he denied any involvement in the great fire of 15 December which destroyed the foreign factories. On 29 December the postal steamer *Thistle, en route* for Hong Kong, was seized by mutineers who killed all eleven foreign passengers on board. Some said that the mutineers were wearing the insignia of Yeh's militia.[5] On 12 January, British troops burnt thousands of houses in Canton.

In Hong Kong, the effects of the crisis in Canton were soon felt. Mysterious fires broke out on the island, servants suddenly abandoned their masters and assaults on Europeans became common. The Bishop of Victoria, Hong Kong, said in retrospect that he and his fellow European inhabitants felt 'exposed, not merely to the ordinary danger of a foreign residence, but to the cup of the poisoner, the knife of the assassin and the torch of the midnight incendiary'.[6] The 'cup of the poisoner' was no mere rhetoric for on 15 January almost the entire foreign community was violently ill after breakfast. The baker had filled their bread with arsenic. Fortunately he had put in so much that most were sick immediately and suffered no long-term ill-effects. Lady Bowring, however, had 'been a bad case, as it is thought some arsenic got into her lungs'. Her health remained poor and when she died in September 1858, her death certificate ascribed the event to 'Ulceration of the stomach – long-standing atrophy'.[7]

In January 1857, the Foreign Office in London authorized the Governor-General of India to send an artillery regiment to China, and in February it ordered Admiral Seymour to proceed to the Yangtze and blockade the Grand Canal to try and starve Peking into submission by interrupting the imperial rice barges. The government also ordered Bowring to continue to press his demands for ambassadorial residence in Peking, more treaty ports and access to the interior. These actions provoked a series of parliamentary debates in which the government was defeated by the combined forces of Gladstone, Disraeli and Cobden. The government resigned but on 13 March 1857, a 'special plenipotentiary', Lord Elgin, was appointed to deal with affairs in China. Elgin had served as Governor of Jamaica and Governor-General of Canada. His brief was to take over the demands for treaty revision that had been unsuccessfully prosecuted by the British, American and French representatives in China. It made no mention of Canton or of Yeh Ming-ch'en.

Elgin travelled to China via Paris in order to concert policy with the French. Anchored off Ceylon on 26 May, he wrote in his diary, 'Bad news from India'. On reaching Singapore, he was forced to make the difficult decision to turn back the transports of troops intended for China to deal with the Indian Mutiny.[8] Elgin himself left Singapore for Calcutta where communications with London were better, and it was not until September that he recommenced his voyage to Hong Kong where he was to meet the French envoy, Baron Gros, and his troops.

Elgin had to spend some months in Hong Kong awaiting reinforcements. He dined with Admiral Seymour: 'An opium ship had just arrived [bringing letters and dispatches as well as opium] so we had a plentiful crop of topics for conversation. The news from India is rather better.'[9] Not until December did he finally embark on HMS *Furious*, bound for Canton. The ship was a paddle-steamer, her captain 'Sherard Osborn of Arctic regions notoriety'. Canton was taken in early January 1858 and Yeh Ming-ch'en was captured and sent to Calcutta where he died in 1859.

Elgin and Gros then made a leisurely progress up the Chinese coast, calling in at treaty and other ports. Swatow, though not yet open to foreign residence, demonstrated the worst of foreign influence, Elgin writing that it

> consists mainly of the agents of the two great opium-houses, Dent and Jardine ... This, with a considerable business in the coolie-trade – which consists in kidnapping wretched coolies, putting them on board ships where all the horrors of the slave-trade are reproduced, and sending them on specious promises to such places as Cuba – is the chief business of the 'foreign' merchants at Swatow ... I went to the house of one of the 'shroffs' connected with Jardine's house, and I found the gentleman indulging in his opium pipe. He gave us some delicious tea.

Elgin also met Mr Burns, 'a missionary, whose case is narrated in the series of "insults by the Chinese authorities" submitted to Parliament'. Burns, whose presence inland was illegal according to the Treaty of Nanking, 'wears the Chinese attire ... He does not boast of much success in converting.'

Like Robert Fortune fifteen years before, Elgin found the approach to Foochow very attractive. He was amused by 'the landscape, consisting mainly of hillocks dotted with horseshoe graves, and monuments to the honour of virtuous maidens and faithful widows, surrounded by patches of wheat and vegetables. Kensal Green or Père Lachaise, cultivated as kitchen gardens, would not inaptly represent the general character of the rural districts of China which I have visited.'[10]

Near Ningpo, he visited a temple where 'a very dirty lad without a tail, proved to be the priest', for, like all Buddhist monks, his head was completely shaved whereas laymen shaved only the front of their heads and wore the long remainder in a pigtail. (The pigtail or queue was a hairstyle imposed upon Chinese men by the Manchus when they conquered China in 1644. All men had to shave the front of their head, grow the rest of their hair long and wear it in a plait.) Next Elgin called at the Chusan archipelago and remarked of the main island, 'This is a most charming island. How any people, in their senses, could have preferred Hong Kong to it, seems incredible.' He tried unsuccessfully to buy 'perfumed sticks of Mosquito Tobacco' and was taken by a French priest to see the beautiful view of the walled city of Tinghae (Dinghai) 'surrounded by rice fields; beyond the sea studded with islands of the Chusan group'. (It is still a wonderful area but it would hardly look the same now if it *had* been preferred to Hong Kong.)

In Shanghai on 29 March 1858 he reported, 'Here I am in the consul's house, a very spacious mansion. The climate, character of the rooms &c., all make me feel in Europe again.' He also addressed the British merchants, himself convinced that Mitchell's 1852 report on trade which he had rediscovered in Hong Kong contained important truths, unpalatable to the merchants. He felt that they must acknowledge China as a 'laboriously manufacturing' society of considerable self-sufficiency, and that British trade would be increased not by the removal of trade barriers but by 'proving that physical knowledge and mechanical skill, applied to the arts of production, are more than a match for the most persevering efforts of unscientific industry'.[11] He was also critical of the missionaries who travelled illegally into the interior, to little effect and considerable danger to themselves and such converts as they made.

After these civic addresses, the still small flotilla finally reached the mouth of the Pei River, the approach to Tientsin and Peking, in April and began the serious business of the mission. By the end of May, Elgin had established himself in a temple in Tientsin: 'It consists of a number of detached rooms, scattered about a garden. I have installed myself in the joss-house, my bedroom being on one side, and my sitting-room on the other, of the idol's altar.' On 29 June, despite pressure from the Americans, French and Russians to abandon the demand for ambassadorial residence in Peking and permission to trade in the interior (points that they felt would be refused and which might jeopardize their separate negotiation), the Sino-British Treaty of Tientsin was signed. It included the right to appoint an ambassador to reside in Peking, protection by the Chinese authorities of Protestant and Roman Catholic missionaries, unhindered travel for British subjects on consular passports, the right of British ships to trade on the Yangtze, the opening of more ports, an indemnity to be paid by the Chinese to compensate for 'losses at Canton, and ... the expenses of the war' and a fixed single charge on the transit of goods.[12] The treaty was rapidly followed by American, French, German, Dutch and Spanish negotiations establishing the same concessions.

Elgin had accomplished what he set out to do. He went on to visit Japan (and signed a treaty there) and returned to Shanghai in September for further tariff negotiations, including the setting of a very high duty on opium, effectively legalizing the trade. He then proceeded to Nanking to see the Taiping rebels. When he finally left China in March 1859, he met his brother Frederick Bruce in Ceylon. Bruce had been newly appointed the first British Minister to China and it was he who was to ratify the new treaty in Peking.

It soon became apparent that though the Chinese might have signed the treaty, they were very far from accepting it. When Bruce arrived at the mouth of the Pei River, on his way to Peking in June 1859, he found the river barred. Fired upon from the Taku forts, he was forced to retire home. To deal with persistent Chinese intransigence a large force was ordered from Britain and India, the French were also involved and Lord Elgin was summoned once again to return to China 'on an errand of which the issue is almost more than doubtful'.[13] Though shipwrecked off Ceylon, he managed to save a considerable portion of his effects, 'some a good deal damaged', and met his brother at Shanghai. There he worried 'how best to prevent my mission from impairing in any degree Frederick's authority and prestige ... but it is so much in accordance with their notions that an elder brother should take the part which I am now doing, that I do not think the risk is great'.[14]

When the British and French forces arrived at the Taku forts for the second time in August 1860, they took them, though not without considerable difficulty and loss of life. As the French and British troops marched on Peking, the Hsien-feng emperor left for his summer retreat-cum-hunting park at Jehol, about 100 miles north-east of the capital. The combined army arranged to gather at the old Imperial Summer Palace, the Yuan-ming-yuan or 'Garden of Perfect Brightness', an eighteenth-century mixture of traditional Chinese buildings and elaborate baroque palaces built by Jesuits for the Ch'ien-lung emperor some miles north-west of Peking.

By the time they had departed twelve days later, the Imperial Summer Palace had been laid to waste. There is still considerable dis-agreement as to how the looting started (the French say the British did it, the British say it was the French) but after the event, General Sir Hope Grant and his French counterpart, General de Montaubon, called in all the treasures that had been taken, 'Chinese curios and handsome clocks, bronzes … silks … jade ornaments and porcelain',[15] and auctioned them amongst their officers, raising the sum of £8,000. The proceeds were divided amongst the ordinary soldiers, each man receiving £4. The remains of the palace were set alight at Lord Elgin's suggestion (and in this the French did not participate).

In the face of such destruction, the Chinese government had little choice but to co-operate. On 24 October 1860, in the magnificent Hall of Audience in the imperial palace in Peking, Prince Kung, sixth son of the Tao-kuang emperor and brother of the Hsien-feng emperor, met Lord Elgin and signed the Convention of Peking, thereby ratifying the Treaty of Tientsin.

Elgin stayed on in Peking, choosing a house for his brother Frederick, who was to live in a grand *fu* or princely residence as the first British Minister. From an 'elevated place' in the Forbidden City, Elgin made the first of many similar descriptions of Peking. The city's single-storey grey-roofed houses were arranged around courtyards invariably planted with a tree for summer shade.

> Peking is so full of trees and the houses are so low, that it hardly had the effect of looking down on a great city. Here and there temples or high gateways rose above the trees but the general impression was rather that of a rich plain densely peopled. In the distance the view was bounded by a lofty chain of mountains, snow-capped. From the park-like emin-ence we looked down on the Imperial Palace – a large enclosure dotted with yellow-roofed buildings … the yellow roofs, interspersed here and there with very deep blue ones, had … a very brilliant effect in the sun-shine.

Having formally introduced Frederick to Prince Kung, Elgin left Peking and made a leisurely return home, noting the French destruction of the suburbs of Shanghai and the rebuilt factories in Canton and reading Trollope and '*Aurora Leigh*, which I admire greatly' and Darwin's *Origin of Species* 'which is audacious'.[16]

The Treaty of Tientsin, as ratified in the Convention of Peking, was to have enormous consequences for China, long isolated from the West. Foreign missionaries and merchants could now travel freely throughout the country and both were officially to receive the protection of the local authorities wherever they went. Churches and houses could be built in the hinterland. The Yangtze, which flowed through the western province of Szechwan (Sichuan) and the tea- and silk-producing central provinces, was opened to trade, and new treaty ports were established at the Yangtze towns of Chinkiang, Hankow and Kiukiang.

Nanking, also on the Yangtze, was opened through a treaty with the French, but was not formally occupied by a British consul until 1899. Tientsin itself was opened, as were others in the north: Newchwang or 'Cow village' (now Yingkou) in the far north on the Liaotung (Liaodong) peninsula, an eventual source of beans, millet, bean-oil, bean-cake and Fushun coal; and Chefoo on the Shantung (Shandong) coast, another source of bean-cake, also vermicelli, very good peanuts (still), pongee and other silks, hairnets, lace and fruits, and the eventual site of a number of missionary seaside sanatoria and the famous Chefoo schools which were attended by almost all missionary children until the Japanese invasion. In the south, Swatow on the Canton coast was opened, source of yet more bean-cake (apparently used there as manure), sugar, oranges and unfortunate coolies;[17] and Hoihow (Haikou) on the tropical island of Hainan (sugar, pigs, sesame seeds and dried fruits). There were also to be treaty ports on Pagoda Island (Luoxing) and on Formosa (Taiwan).

PART II

Widening Horizons
1860–1900

8

More Treaty Ports

In opening the Yangtze to the British, the Treaty of Tientsin fulfilled a long-held ambition, for it was felt that better access to the vast river that ran from west to east across the centre of China would throw open once and for all the previously forbidden interior. British residence was assured with the establishment of concessions in Hankow, Kiukiang and Chinkiang. Hankow, which was to develop into the most important of the treaty ports in central China, was one of three cities (now merged as Wuhan) that stood at the confluence of the Han and Yangtze rivers. On the south bank of the Yangtze lay Wuchang and on the west side of the Han lay Hanyang which was to see much Chinese industrial growth in the late nineteenth century with the development of the Hanyang arsenal, iron and steel works, and chemical and engineering establishments. Situated at a point on the Yangtze which could still be reached by ocean-going steamers, and in close proximity to Wuchang and Hanyang, Hankow had long been an important entrepôt for river-borne trade.

The treaty port of Hankow was opened in 1861 and work on the British concession began immediately. The first requirement was to make the riverside safe and accessible to shipping. As the Yangtze rose and fell dramatically between seasons, it was necessary to construct a stone embankment or bund – 'a noble and lofty river wall and fine flights of stairs, ascending 40 feet from low water'.[1]

Above the bund, the promenade of the British concession was soon lined with trees, though below on the river the view was somewhat spoiled by the presence of six hulks or wharves around which water-borne traffic flowed.[2] Despite the fine promenade and palatial houses, very similar to those of Shanghai and Singapore, surrounded by large gardens and shaded by exotic trees, and the Sikh policemen who 'make a goodly show', the traveller Isabella Bird found the flatness of the broad river dull.[3]

Though the British concession was eventually joined by a German concession (1895), a Russian concession (1896), a French concession (1896) and a Japanese concession (1898), Hankow remained above all a commercial city, a centre of transshipment and of industries that included Russian tea-brick factories, a match factory, six albumen factories, the British-American Tobacco Company, cotton spinning and weaving, iron and steel works, and electricity companies. It did not offer the same entertainments as Shanghai, although there was a club, a racecourse and a golf course. The main pastime for foreign residents, 'the natives apparently caring little for it', was shooting pigeon, geese, duck, pheasant, snipe, white herons, hares, deer, wild dogs and other game to be found in the neighbourhood.[4]

Despite its growth as an industrial centre, Hankow remained quite a dangerous place of foreign residence for several decades. Though Consul Challoner Alabaster, temporarily in charge in 1875, reported that ladies could walk freely in the concession (though not in the neighbouring cities of Hanyang and Wuchang), attacks on missionaries in the street and on tennis parties, during which stones were thrown, continued. The culprits were described as either coolies and out-of-work boatmen or nationalistic students, and from the beginning consuls urged the constant provision of a naval gunboat, for whenever a gunboat was not present, there were disturbances.[5]

Kiukiang, further down-river, on the southern bank of the Yangtze, was opened in 1861 but such had been the destruction there during the Taiping rebellion that, as late as the 1880s, three-quarters of the city was still in ruins. The depleted population managed, nevertheless, to stone the British consul and naval gunboat captain as they tried to mark out the boundaries of the new concession. In the following months, the British doctor was attacked, as was the consulate, and all the foreign houses were broken into. The 1880s were recollected by the then consul as 'pleasant' with some fifty foreign residents, half of them British, living in the concession. But almost from the beginning trade at Kiukiang was slow, perhaps partly due to the city's relative proximity to Shanghai. In

1895, Isabella Bird found it had a sleepy air though there was 'a pretty shady bund, and pleasant foreign houses in shady gardens'.[6] By the end of the century, Kiukiang's main significance was as a stopping point *en route* for the hill-station of Kuling, established by the Reverend E.S. Little (subsequently of the chemical company Brunner Mond) who was described by the vice-consul as a 'terrible man!'[7]

Chinkiang, 160 miles east of Shanghai, on the south bank of the Yangtze where the Grand Canal crosses the river, was only slightly more successful as a treaty port. The foreign concession stood on the river-bank, under Jinshan Hill with its temple and fine pagoda. Isabella Bird (whose vocabulary on the subject of the treaty ports, like Fortune's, is disappointingly repetitive) found it

> an attractive place. It has a fine bund and prosperous-looking foreign houses, with a British consulate on a hill above; trees abound. The concession roads are broad and well-kept. A row of fine hulks connected by bridges with the shore offers great facilities for the landing of goods and passengers. Sikh police are much in evidence, the hum of business greets one's ears, traffic throngs the bund, the Grand Canal is choked with junks.[8]

Appearances apart, little of this bustle represented trade in foreign hands. In 1877, Chinkiang had thirty-one residents (not including missionaries) and six British businesses, and it was not a happy place. The small community's penchant for personal feuding and inability to run the concession properly made Chinkiang an uncomfortable post for its consul.[9] The municipal council was described as a farcical scandal. When in 1879 the consul asked (as was his right) to examine the council's books, Mr Bean, a British merchant, concurrently chairman and treasurer of the municipal council, 'a coarse cantankerous man of low tastes and malignant disposition', beat him up. Mr Bean's relations with his fellow British merchants were no better: in 1888, he was again elected chairman of the council at a meeting which another British merchant, Mr Duff, refused to attend. Mr Duff was in turn elected to the same office at a meeting that Bean would not attend, leaving the consul to deal with a double administration.[10]

Relations with the Chinese were scarcely any better: in 1889, after a Sikh policeman was accused of striking a Chinese man, there was a riot in which both the British and the American consulates were burned down and the foreign community had to retreat to a steamer on the river for safety. The required gunboat did not arrive, much to the fury of Consul Mansfield whose family lost everything but the clothes they were wearing and whose wife never recovered from the ordeal.[11]

Four ports in southern China were also opened in 1861: at Pagoda Island (the anchorage downstream from Foochow), at Swatow on the coast between Amoy and Hong Kong, on Formosa, the island to the east of the mainland where the East India Company had briefly dwelt in the last years of the eighteenth century, and at Hoihow on the tropical island of Hainan. Swatow, which already had a Customs post and which had long been visited illegally by opium clippers and coolie traders to avoid consular interference, was, like Foochow, a treaty port with no concession area. Though most of the foreign businesses congregated in the eastern side of the town and most foreigners lived in the quiet suburb of Kia-lat, 'free from the bustle and noise of the native town', these areas were not exclusive.[12]

In its early days, Swatow was extremely dangerous, although not so threatening to British life and limb as Chaochow (Chaozhou), inland up the river. Chaochow had in fact originally been designated as the area's treaty port, but it had proved impossible to establish foreign residence there owing to the hostility of the local population. Instead, Swatow was selected as it already had a British community of about forty-five, and regular steamer traffic. The violence of Swatow's pirates and kidnappers was witnessed by Consul W.M. Cooper in 1867 when the door to his house was blown open with gunpowder and twenty armed men burst in. Cooper managed to drive them off but the shock was too much for his wife (who had just given birth to their second child) and she returned to England.[13]

Cooper and his successors, hardly surprisingly, made frequent calls on British naval gunboats whose arrival often led to further trouble. However, the depredations of pirates and the violence with which the local clans did battle also worried the Chinese provincial authorities who sent General Fang Yao to pacify the area. Though his methods were brutal (he boasted of having struck off several thousand heads), by 1872 it was said that the Swatow area was as safe as Shanghai.

Consular life in Swatow had, nevertheless, its contradictory aspects. Life itself was relatively pleasant. Double Island at the mouth of the port was used as a weekend retreat, there were games of cricket, and, in the brief cool season, the obligatory shooting parties bagged geese and duck. The consul's residence was a fine house with a large garden, and the foreign community appears to have caused few problems, in marked contrast to the coolie-traders and opium-dealers of pre-treaty port days. But the traffic in human beings was still a major business, and ships continued to leave the port carrying 'voluntary' emigrants, driven, particularly from the province of Fukien, by the pressure of population to seek work abroad. Humane consuls tried to ensure that British ships carrying this human cargo took safety precautions and did not pack their cargo, as one consul put it, 'like herrings'.[14]

The treaty port on Formosa was opened in 1861 by Robert Swinhoe. He is still best-known not for his consular work but for his interest in Chinese wildlife (a number of Latin species names are taken from his), being 'the first to give a proper attention to the study of Chinese birds'.[15] His arrival was inauspicious: during the voyage his baggage had been ruined by sea-water and he had lost ten shirts and six nightshirts whilst his assistant, Braune, lost twenty shirts and six pairs of white (tropical) trousers. It had been intended that the treaty port should be established at what is now called Tainan but Swinhoe, assessing potential for trade there as negligible, asked permission to transfer to Tamsui (Danshui) on the north of the island (though its trade was no more promising). Formosa was a difficult station, not because of local opposition but because of the tropical climate – 'rain, fog, damp and monotony' – and the sense of isolation. Indeed, Swinhoe recommended the east coast of the island as suitable for a British convict settlement because it possessed a 'rocky shore in front and ... savages in the mountains behind'.[16]

Swinhoe flitted back and forth to Amoy for medical treatment and then to England on sick-leave, and the British consulate moved with similar speed from Tamsui to Takow (Dagou), near Tainan, and then split itself between all three, further adding a branch consulate at the coaling station of Keelung (Qilong). The foreign community on Formosa was tiny at the outset, consisting only of one or two consular officials and a similarly sparse scattering of officers of the Imperial

Maritime Customs. Adkins, whose first consular posting was at Ningpo, served in Takow for a few months in 1864 and 'messed' with the local Customs commissioner. They had fruit, tea or coffee for break-fast and fish, meat, eggs and fruit for lunch and dinner, drank very little wine, avoided beer completely 'in such a warm climate' and played cards or went sailing (both of which Adkins disliked).[17]

The arrival of a missionary doctor in 1866, welcomed by Mrs Swinhoe who was about to give birth, signalled the beginning of mis-sionary work on Formosa and a new series of consular problems in con-sequence, for the determination of the missionaries to venture to other cities and travel in the interior provoked local opposition, stonings and wild accusations. The relative isolation of the post also led to rash actions on the part of its consuls; at Takow in 1868, Gibson called for a gunboat when a Chinese Christian was murdered, several British mer-chants were attacked and 'British trade in camphor was obstructed'. As he also acted as consul for France, Germany and Denmark, his protest was pan-European, which did not stop the local Chinese intendant from hitting him twice with his fan. A British naval party then stormed a nearby town and killed several Chinese, to the anger of the Foreign Office. Though Swinhoe (based in Tainan) defended the action, he himself was soon in trouble with the Foreign Office for supporting the use of torture in the case of a Chinese accused of anti-foreign violence.

The sense of isolation in Formosa became increasingly real: in 1884 the island was blockaded by the French and by 1895, apart from those in the consulate, the only other British residents in Takow were a doctor, a Customs officer and their families. In that year, after China's defeat in the Sino-Japanese War, the island was ceded to Japan and the treaty port there ceased to exist.

A treaty port on the island of Hainan was officially prescribed in the Treaty of Tientsin but no action was taken to establish it until 1872. Kiungchow, the administrative capital of the island, had originally been selected as its site but in the event the nearby port of Hoihow was chosen. This was hardly a practical improvement for the port was inaccessible to any vessels other than flat-bottomed sampans, and then for only twelve hours a day, and the major items of trade (sugar and pigs) did not attract British firms. In the mid-1880s, there were twenty-two foreign residents, of whom ten were British, and the four 'British' firms were actually Chinese-owned and dealing in opium. The consulate was grandly established in a former rope warehouse whose courtyard was used as a piggery and latrine by a substantial number of neighbouring families and whose structure was constantly threatened by white ants and dry rot.[18]

The northern treaty ports, opened in 1861, were generally more successful. Chefoo in Shantung was to become renowned as a summer resort, Newchwang was the first port opened in Manchuria, and Tientsin was to become one of the most prosperous of the treaty ports, second only to Shanghai.

Chefoo, opened by M.C. Morrison, was later described as 'the Brighton of China' for its seaside sanatoria and prep schools. It was originally to have had a proper concession area but Morrison spent so long arguing with the French that nothing ever happened and in the end there was only a foreign quarter, controlled and managed by a General Purposes Committee, which derived its revenue from voluntary contributions. It also tried to levy a poll-tax on all male residents, but without the necessary staff this proved impossible to enforce, and in consequence the Committee often found itself short of funds.[19] (It is ironic that after Morrison's endless quarrels with the French, his successor, Challoner Alabaster, found himself concurrently acting as French consul.)

Chefoo was never much of a trading port, with only four foreign trading firms (three of them British) active in 1891, shipping beancake, vermicelli, peanuts, silks, hairnets, lace and fruits. It had been (and remains) a seaside fishing village and much of the excitement there in the early years resulted from consular inefficiency. In 1874, the consul W.H. Lay (who was terminally ill) and his interpreter Cooper ('an alcoholic') made a mess of the trial of an Englishman named Fawcett who had shot a Chinese during a dispute over the construction of a lighthouse. A decade later, Consul McClatchie died at his post before anyone could fully investigate the fact that he kept no accounts and made no distinction between private and public expenditure.[20]

The treaty port of Newchwang in Manchuria was established in the wrong place. It had been intended to site the port at Newchwang itself, forty miles up the Liao River, but when it was discovered that foreign shipping could not navigate the river, Yingkow (Yingkou), on the mudflats at the mouth of the river, was chosen instead (though confusingly it was always called Newchwang).

Unprepossessingly sited, and described in 1867 as 'dreary in the extreme', it was, nevertheless, quite liked by many of its consular inhabitants, for its freezing but sunny winters afforded bracing riding weather, and the summers were relatively cool and dry. When T.T. Meadows arrived to open the consulate, he found only a mud village and so proceeded to occupy a temple with characteristic open courtyards. As the dining-room, sitting-room and bedrooms were ranged around the courtyards, these had to be crossed in all weathers. Meadows was compelled to live like a Chinese, wrapping himself in furs in the winter because his stoves did not adequately heat the room; and despite the port's famed lack of humidity, a successor complained of the 'luxuriant growth of herbage on the dining-room floor and walls in the hot weather'.

There was a concession at Newchwang but it was something of a failure for few of the lots were leased and the river kept washing bits of it away.[21] Though the port was ice-bound for four months in the winter, there was usually an armed naval guard stationed there to protect its inhabitants from endemic banditry. The foreign community, swelled by over-wintering pilots, was predominantly masculine, and fights over Chinese concubines and drunken brawls were common. Meadows sourly recorded in his dispatches the story of a British pilot, bitten on the nose either by a German or by the German's dog, who then bit off part of a German tide-waiter's nose, and the behaviour of Mr MacPherson, the American consul, who got drunk with another resident and fell into the mud 'where they both rolled about for some time, plastering each other's faces with mud and laughing idiotically'.[22]

In the last years of the century, Newchwang's position in Manchuria became less isolated as railways linked it with Tientsin and with the Russian port of Port Arthur (Lushun). However, increasing Russian and Japanese rivalry over the northern territories of China found British consuls fighting a protracted but losing battle to prevent British interests being squeezed out of Manchuria.[23]

Of all the treaty ports opened after the Treaty of Tientsin, the eponymous city was the most successful, though it was perhaps not the most attractive. As many residents would testify, 'the country is flat and uninteresting . . . the many waterways with which it is surrounded are, for the most part, of a dirty yellow appearance, and certainly do not add to the attractiveness of the district . . . the climate is one of extremes'.[24] The British, French and German concessions were laid out to the south of the Chinese city (joined by a Japanese concession in 1895 and Russian, Belgian, Italian and Austro-Hungarian concessions in 1901).

The British concession area was established without some of the dangers attendant elsewhere, for British troops were still stationed in the city after the Second Opium War. At the beginning, a vice-consul was also posted at Taku, at the mouth of the Pei River, site of the Chinese forts and of battles past and future. His business was to attend to sailing ships which could not proceed further up the muddy shallows, but with the increasing use of steamships his function declined and the post at Taku was abandoned in 1877.

In June 1870, one of the most serious massacres of missionaries in China took place in Tientsin. Resulting in the deaths of sixteen French missionaries, some thirty Chinese converts and a hundred Chinese orphans, as well as the French consul and a number of foreign merchants, it was nonetheless viewed somewhat unsympathetically by the Protestant British, who considered the actions of the Roman Catholic missions unnecessarily provocative (see Chapter 11).

Despite the shock of these events, the economic development of Tientsin and the building of solid banks, offices and fine residences within the concessions continued steadily. Each concession maintained its own municipal administration and each displayed its own national character in its buildings. Scottish baronial and rusticated stonework distinguished the British concession. In the French concession there arose buildings with grey-tiled fairy-story towers like so many small châteaux. The German concession filled with heavy brick residences reminiscent of the suburbs of Hamburg.

In the second half of the nineteenth century, further negotiations with the Chinese government continued the process of opening more and more Chinese cities to foreign trade and residence. In 1874, Augustus Raymond Margary, then serving as consular interpreter in Shanghai, was appointed interpreter to a mission from Burma led by Colonel Browne. Margary was to meet the mission on the Sino-Burmese border in Yunnan province but was killed there in February 1875. Official British protest and demands for reparation gave rise to the Chefoo Agreement of 1876 which pushed British influence further up the Yangtze, opening Ichang and Wuhu and, in an additional article signed in 1890, Chungking (Chongqing). The terms of the Chefoo Agreement were not restricted to Szechwan province: Wenchow (Wenzhou), on the coast of Chekiang south of Ningpo, was added to the coastal ports, and Pakhoi on the southern Kwangsi coast, not far from the Vietnamese border, took British residence close to French-dominated Indo-China.

The Chefoo Agreement also marked a change in British policy towards concessions and settlements. Hitherto within most treaty ports a concession, 'rented' by the British government which then 'sub-let' plots to its nationals, had been laid out wherever local conditions permitted. Now, with so many new cities being added to the list, the expense of building works within such concessions, especially where river embankments and wharves needed to be constructed and maintained, was questioned. In future, though new foreign settlements continued to be established, the land on which new buildings arose would now be rented directly from its Chinese owners and not from a lease-holding British government. And though such a change was undoubtedly prompted by economic considerations, it was also, in the face of rising Chinese nationalism, politically prudent.

Like the other small Yangtze ports of Chinkiang and Kiukiang, Wuhu remained a sleepy post although it had plenty of passing steamer trade. Living amongst the thatched, mushroom-shaped local houses and by a pretty lake, most of its foreign residents were missionaries although Wuhu, perhaps because of its sleepiness, also attracted a disproportionate number of opium traders, said to be mainly 'Jews' who claimed British nationality owing to birth in India. One surprising local resident was the son of the great modernizing Chinese official and diplomat, Li Hung-chang, who promoted the building of railways and telegraph systems and the use of steamships. His son spoke excellent English and lived in the small river port 'in a finely furnished European-style house with electric lighting and comfortable armchairs and sofas'.[25]

Apart from opium-dealing British subjects, missionaries caused the greatest consular headaches in Wuhu. The China Inland Mission, as its name suggested, was far keener than the Foreign Office on penetrating

China's interior, and its servants regularly set off from the Yangtze ports to brave its dangers. In Wuhu itself, missionary activities gave rise to anti-Catholic rumours and accusations of the kidnap and murder of babies which prompted a mob to storm and burn down the Jesuit mission in 1891. The mission was, unfortunately, next to the British consulate whose inhabitants had to flee, dressed in Chinese clothes, to the relative safety of a hulk moored on the shore.

Ichang, the second treaty port to be opened on the higher reaches of the Yangtze, lies at the end of the river's famous gorges, spectacular and dangerous narrows filled with huge boulders, and treacherously covered by rushing water, which were, until 1898, impassable to modern craft. The city of Chungking and the great interior province of Szechwan lies beyond the gorges and so Ichang was an important port of transshipment for local goods.

The first consul, W.E. King, who opened the treaty port in 1877, had had to wait several months for the river to rise sufficiently to allow HMS *Kestrel* to get him to Ichang, and even then the ship grounded seventeen times. His post was to prove no easier. King was instructed to secure land for a concession (although the Foreign Office was still debating the cost), but after three attempts in which he was attacked by an angry mob, he was forced to establish his consulate on three junks moored on the river. Even there, the small staff were jeered at and stoned and after King left (to retire on medical grounds) the Foreign Office finally decided not to bother with a concession after all. The consulate was established in four sheds, built to store cotton, and a small toolshed served as the consular lavatory (until the roof fell in). Only a decade later was a proper consulate built.

Steamers began to make their way up as far as Ichang with some regularity in the 1880s, though only in spring when the water was high enough, and in 1896 Isabella Bird found it transformed and

> very attractive. At low water it stands high on the river bank, on a conglomerate cliff above a great level sandbank, but in summer it loses whatever dignity it gains by height, and is nearly on the river level ... On the river bank are the buildings and godowns of the Imperial Customs, including the Commissioner's house and large garden, dainty dwellings for the staff of twelve Europeans, and a tennis ground, with a fine bund and broad flight of stone stairs in front. Near these are the large houses

of the Scotch Church Mission, and beyond a new plain building put up by the China Inland Mission ... There are a few foreign hongs and godowns, and a Customs pontoon moored in the stream. Behind the British consulate, a substantial new building with a tennis lawn used for weekly hospitalities, breezy hills, much covered with grave mounds, roll up towards a mountainous region, and below, the Yangtze, with its perpetual rush and current, swirls in a superb flood half a mile wide.

At the time of my first visit, a British gunboat, a wholesome and not unneeded influence, lay at anchor opposite the town.[26]

There were about forty-five foreign inhabitants, almost half of them missionaries, who spent their spare time playing tennis, shooting, enjoying boating parties and dodging missiles. Inside the hall of the Commissioner of Customs' house were several 'cairns of stones which were nearly as big as a human head ... which had been collected in the dining and drawing rooms after their windows had been smashed in an anti-foreign riot a few days before'.[27]

Ichang was a port of significance: the southern ports opened by the Chefoo Agreement never fulfilled their promise. Pakhoi's trade remained firmly in Chinese hands. In 1879 there was a nil return on foreign trade. In 1900 the consul, still stationed there to report on British interests, recorded foreign trade as 'virtually nil'. Not only was there nothing to do at Pakhoi but it was also a desperately uncomfortable and isolated tropical posting for it was in effect no more than a fishing village and was constantly threatened by pirates. It had been opened in 1877 by A.S. Harvey who, only a few months later, went mad in Hong Kong, descending to the hotel dining-room for breakfast with nothing on. His successor, W.G. Stronach, also appears to have become paranoid.

Wenchow, twenty miles inland from the Chekiang coast, seems to have had a more soothing effect on consular nerves. It did not attract traders, the foreign community consisting entirely of officials (consular and Customs) and missionaries. There was no foreign settlement, though the disposition of the foreign community was divided, with the Customs north of the town walls and the consulates and residences on an island in the river, opposite the city. The local inhabitants were described as 'lethargic and unenterprising but they have frequently indulged in riots'.[28]

An additional article to the Chefoo Agreement, signed in 1890, opened

Chungking, far up the Yangtze River, above the dangerous gorges. According to the Chefoo Agreement, a 'consular agent' could be stationed there but full opening to trade was to wait. In the interim period, consular officials, charged with finding out as much as possible about western China and ensuring the proper provision of transit passes, spent more time struggling to get to Chungking than actually residing there. In 1881, one of them, W.D. Spence, took fifty-eight days to travel the 400 miles of river upstream from Ichang to Chungking. Floods delayed him for weeks on end, two men were killed in a junk collision, the steersman was washed overboard to his death, and the junk finally sank. C.T. Gardner and E.C.C. Wilton (in 1883 and 1900 respectively) lost all their possessions in steamer accidents on the same stretch of river.[29]

In 1898 the businessman Archibald Little, who was convinced that steam navigation would greatly expand trade possibilities, managed to navigate the gorges and ascend the river in his steamer, the *Leechuen*, but until then all the river junks had to be hauled through the narrow gorges against the current by 'trackers'. Their shoulders deeply callused by the bamboo ropes they pulled, they struggled barefoot up steep flights of steps or along trackers' paths

> a foot or so wide, some only fifteen or twenty feet above the river, others at a giddy height on which the trackers looked no bigger than flies ... On all of these ... the life of the tracker is in continual peril from losing his foothold owing to the slipperiness of the rock after rain and from being dragged over and drowned by the backward tendencies of the heavy junk tugging at the end of 1,200 feet of a heavy bamboo hawser as thick as an arm.

Mrs Bird saw two bad accidents. In one

> a big junk dragged by 300 men ... in two hours made hardly perceptible progress, slipping back constantly, though the drums were frantically beaten and the gangers rushed madly along the lines of struggling trackers, bringing their bamboo whips down on them ... Suddenly the junk shivered, both tow-ropes snapped, the lines of trackers went down on their faces, and in a moment the big craft was spinning down the rapid; and before she could be recovered by the bow-sweeps she flew up into the air as if she had exploded, a mass of spars and planks with heads bobbing about in the breakers.[30]

One missionary, whose family travelled up through the gorges after the Boxer rebellion, demonstrated piety beyond the call of duty in his description of his infant daughter's death on the river. 'A hurricane swept down the mountainside, caught our sail and capsized the boat.' He, his wife and his two elder children were pulled from the rushing waters but the Chinese nurse had 'dropped the baby, and we could not find the wee corpse'. The nurse was terribly upset but 'we assured her that there was no blame attached to any one and thanked God for saving so many of us'.[31]

When they managed to reach Chungking, a city almost permanently covered by cloud, perched above the confluence of two rushing rivers, its steep, stepped streets slippery in the mist and humidity, consular agents and subsequent consuls found little to please them. The consulate was first situated in a dilapidated house in a filthy area and the dangers of shipment through the gorges meant that the foreign goods (tinned foods, beer and wine) essential to consular happiness were difficult to obtain and inordinately expensive when they could be found. Before the arrival of the first British merchant in 1897, Chungking consuls prospected widely for British trade, travelling throughout Szechwan, Yunnan and Kweichow (Guizhou) provinces and into the Himalayan foothills. As steamer transport increased, Chungking gradually became less isolated but the steamship captains, having struggled up the gorges with their 'two Chinese pilots ... their two quartermasters, their baggage and their "makee-learn" [apprentice]', felt no more enthusiasm for Chungking than did most of the consuls.

In his little book, *Excelsior: being an inadequate description of the Upper Yangtze* (1934) which he dedicated 'to those who served with him on the Upper River 1926–8 and 1932–4', 'Charon' made no attempt to describe Chungking for two reasons: 'The first is economy in matter and the second is that Chungking beggars description ... Only those who have visited Chungking in the Summer can appreciate the beauties of its wonderful Climate. And what a happy hunting ground it is for anyone interested in the smaller varieties of Insect Life.'[32]

Whilst the British were busy extending their influence inland along the Yangtze, a terrible blow was struck at Chinese pride when China was defeated in the Sino-Japanese War of 1894–5 (which had started over their rivalry in the neighbouring country of Korea). That such a tiny nation as Japan, traditionally both politically and culturally subservient, could inflict military and naval defeat was a deep humiliation. Japan seized control of Formosa, and Britain and the other foreign powers made the most of the provisions of the treaty that concluded the war. Soochow and Hangchow (Hangzhou), both in the Yangtze delta area, and Shasi were added to the list of treaty ports.

Shasi was on the Yangtze, eighty miles below Ichang. The first consul arrived in 1897 at the end of an epidemic which he estimated had killed 17,000 people, and the following year there was an anti-foreign riot. However, the consulate was closed down in 1901 as was that at Soochow. Yochow (Yuezhou), at the confluence of the Hsiang and Yangtze rivers in Hunan, was opened in 1899 but also closed in 1901, and Samshui (Sanshui) in Canton province, which had been opened in 1897, proved equally short-lived. Of all the newly acquired treaty ports, only Hangchow survived as a full consulate but was never to be of any significance.

A number of the new treaty ports, like Pakhoi and those in Szechwan (viewed as bases for exploration westwards), were in the far west and south-west of China, close to the border with Indo-China. They were chosen to provide not so much a base for British trade as a means by which information on French interests and activities might be gathered. By the beginning of the 1880s the French were established in Indo-China and were still expanding their empire there (Laos was absorbed in 1893). Just as the British regarded the Yangtze as a British 'sphere of influence', the French looked on south-western China in a similarly proprietorial manner. Both powers were moving beyond the idea of confinement to the treaty ports and looked forward to dividing China (for the purposes of trade and industrial development) into sections within which British or French companies would build railways or extract minerals and other raw materials. The Chinese government was time and again compelled to give ground on the basis of an incident (like the Tientsin massacre or other anti-missionary attacks) for which it had no responsibility and over which it had little control. Whereas the eighteenth-century emperors had been able to play European embassies off against each other, now Europe played out its own commercial rivalries on Chinese soil.

Another 'listening post' set up to superintend the French was the British consulate in Ssumao/Szemao (Simao) in south-western Yunnan which had been opened as a treaty port as a result of a Sino-French convention in 1895. It was formally 'opened' in 1897 when the consul, J.W. Jamieson (a 'deep-drinker' and skilled linguist), was greeted by a crowd shouting 'Kill! Kill!' Jamieson concluded that consular activities should be transferred to the provincial capital at Kunming, and although he was succeeded by another consul, Ssumao, like so many other short-lived small consulates, was effectively closed in 1901. The title of Ssumao consul was not, however, allowed to lapse. In 1902, W.H. Wilkinson established himself in Kunming, which was not a treaty port and there-fore not open to consular residence, as 'Consul-General at Ssumao', a fiction maintained for several years until the Chinese accepted the *fait accompli* and addressed Wilkinson as Consul-General for Yunnan.

Tengyueh (Dengyue) on the Yunnan–Burma border was officially opened by a Sino-British convention relating to Burma in 1894, although the first consul did not arrive there until 1899. Its management was complicated by its location and by British interests in Burma. The consulate's expenses were supported in part by the Government of India and the first consul, Jamieson (who had just transferred from Ssumao), engaged in bitter arguments with the commissioner from Burma. Subsequent incumbents of the post were less combatively involved in Burmese affairs, travelling widely through the neighbouring tribal areas along the undelimited border and participating in annual Sino-Burmese meetings to settle issues arising from tribal raids.

The isolated border posting was enlivened by shooting. Consul C.A.W. Rose kept a pointer and a red setter to help retrieve game, and organized a dark-room in the consulate to pass his time. He also left instructions for his successors on how to dress (formally for the cross-border meetings, with a dinner jacket for evenings) and recommended a vast medicine chest stocked with quinine, Epsom salts, castor oil, iodine and embrocations for distribution to the local tribespeople.

Whilst the British and the French watched each other carefully in the west, Germany staked out its own 'sphere of interest' on the other side of China, in Shantung province on the eastern seaboard. Just like the French after the Tientsin massacre and the British after Margary's murder in Yunnan in 1875, the death of two German missionaries in

Shantung in November 1896 became the German pretext for the seizure of Kiaochow (Jiaozhou) Bay. Germany's sphere of interest was secured by the end of 1897. At the same time, anxious to have her share, Russia sent warships to Port Arthur on the Chinese side of the Sino-Russian border 'as protection for Chinese interests against a German invasion' and the Russian government offered China a loan on condition that Russia be allowed to 'keep' Port Arthur.[33]

No sooner had Germany seized Kiaochow Bay and Russia Port Arthur than Britain re-entered the competition, demanding territory in Shantung from the Chinese to counterbalance the presence of the Russians. In 1898, at the same time as a ninety-nine-year lease was arranged on Hong Kong's 'New Territories', the small territory of Weihaiwei on the northern coast of Shantung was leased to the British 'for as long a time as Port Arthur shall remain in the occupation of Russia'.[34]

Though plans were made to develop Weihaiwei as a naval base and fortress harbour, the expense involved and the costs of the Boer War put an end to such plans. In 1902 it was announced that 'It is not the present intention of His Majesty's Government to refortify the station, but to retain it as a flying naval base, and as a depot and drill-ground and sanatorium for the China Squadron in North China'.[35]

Double the size of the Isle of Wight, Weihaiwei never developed much trade beyond the export of local peanuts to Hong Kong and Canton and some salt and rice which was spasmodically re-exported to Vladivostok. It did however provide a pleasant summer holiday resort for British residents in China who stayed in 'neat little bungalows, sparsely furnished', or in greater luxury in the King's Hotel, 'under the management of Mr J.W. Loureiro', and who enjoyed the medicinal sulphur baths at Narcissus Bay. There were two golf-courses and, in late August, duck, geese, snipe, curlew and quail to shoot. Pheasant and partridge had been practically exterminated but in 1902 it was hoped that a 'closed season' would allow stocks to recover. Family holidays were well catered for, but Weihaiwei does not seem to have offered much amusement for sailors: 'a certain type of naval man may feel inclined to grumble in moments of depression at the absence of facilities for indulging in the festivities he enjoys at many other ports in the East, but even he generally admits that from the point of view of healthfulness, Weihaiwei in the summer is not to be equalled.'[36]

This double Isle of Wight with its happy families and discontented sailors was, from 1902, governed by a commissioner, the Hon. J.H. Stewart Lockhart (who came up from Hong Kong where he had been in charge of the New Territories), a secretary (who also served as magistrate in the Port Edward district), a medical officer, a resident chaplain, and a district officer and magistrate (for the interior district), R.F. Johnston, who was later to be seconded to serve as tutor to the ex-emperor, Puyi.

The second half of the nineteenth century saw a huge growth in the number of treaty ports and it became almost inevitable that the system should begin to break down, with some ports closing within a few years, for the enclaves themselves had served their purpose. The treaty ports were the vanguard of foreign penetration: now the whole country was being forcibly opened up and carved up. Yet against this background of political pressure, the changes that were being forced upon China made the country more attractive to foreign residence.

9

Private Life and the Social Round

By the second half of the nineteenth century, despite the upsets of the Taiping rebellion and the Second Opium War, life in the older treaty ports was well-established, municipally directed and relatively secure and comfortable for foreign residents. With the opening of further treaty ports and Customs posts, however, many new foreign communities were developing across China, experiencing much the same difficulties as had early treaty port residents. There were also a considerable number of new arrivals, appointed to staff the new consular posts or attracted by the greater openness and freedom to trade achieved through the Treaty of Tientsin. These new arrivals, isolated from family and friends, had to get on with superiors, business acquaintances and Chinese servants and subordinates, often in tiny, not necessarily congenial, communities.

John Gavin, a Scottish civil engineer, first encountered in Shanghai when he had stopped work on the 'slip' or dock he was building because of a threat from Taiping rebels, moved up-river to Hankow in early 1863. Unusually well-documented, his experiences there must have rivalled those of many new arrivals in the smaller treaty ports. Hankow, opened by Consul W.R. Gingell in December 1860, was important to foreign merchants, particularly for its proximity to the tea-growing areas. Once there Gavin turned his hand to the construction work required in the new port, designing and building houses and godowns for new settlers and newly arrived banks and businesses, and shoring up (or 'bunding') the river front.

Though later to be described as the 'mateyest' of the treaty ports,

Hankow was very thinly populated in the mid-1860s so it was not surprising that Gavin's main thoughts were for home and its distant comforts and friendships. Supplies from Scotland were welcome: he wrote to his sister on 27 February 1863, 'My bun, shortbread and etc., have made their appearance at last. They are very nice and have kept beautifully, they were the same as if they were newly baked. A gentleman was telling me to write home how much they were admired so that you might be sure to send out some more.' Other items were not so welcome, for he instructed his mother on 3 June 1863, 'Dinna send me a Gordon cheese, they don't go down in this climate. I would rather have a supply of jams and jellies, 6 shillings a pot is cheap here. If you send any it ought to be put in a supply of small-necked jars and the jars not too large, for a big one does not last any longer than a small one.'

Apart from food, he obtained great pleasure from photographs of family and friends sent out by mail steamer.

> I have just been busy for two hours examining my albums. My mother is not so good as the one that was sent out to me some time ago. The one [of himself] I sent home first she said she would not have known had it not been for the hair. If it was not for her hair, I would have taken it for Aunt Marion . . . My Father is the best by far of any that he has got taken yet. Sarah is an awful fright. Why didn't she dress her hair before she went to get her likeness taken? . . . Mary and Janey are capital but Uncle Peter and Uncle Bob . . . is that the best they can afford? . . . What duffer-looking chap is that Mary Walker has got beside her? I could not make out for a long time who Dr Finlay was, now that I see it is him, I think it a good likeness. I have been trying all afternoon to make out who the young lady and gentleman was and took it out to see if there was anything written on it and I find that it is the Prince and Princess of Wales; every person here has been getting her likeness . . . Miss Brown and Kathy Murray are awful yellow-looking chickens.

A sense of Hankow's distance from civilization is underlined by John Gavin's letter to his mother in March 1863 in which he lists the articles he needs:

> 2 pair long boots glazed leather to wear outside of pants; to be no longer than to the knees
> 2 pair of thick lacing boots
> 2 pair of thin boots elastic-sided

1. An early Western view of the implacable and inscrutable, *c.* 1830. An earnest merchant offers cherry brandy in an attempt to interest Chinese officials in free trade on Western terms. The body language is unpromising

2. The foreign factories at Canton in the late eighteenth century, by a Chinese artist.
Bravely flying their flags, these substantial buildings with cool verandas and shutters
against the oppressive heat were office, godown and home to foreign merchants.
Their only permitted area of recreation was the strip of foreshore between the
factories and the river. Nevertheless, an optimist has imported a horse

3. An unusual view of Shanghai, painted by a Chinese artist in about 1850.
On the horizon are the Whangpoo and its shipping where, within fifty years, massive
office buildings along the Bund were to give the city its characteristic skyline.
In the foreground, grand buildings, incorporating office, godown and residential
quarters, as in Canton, also reflect the imported 'compradoric' architectural style
with verandas running around both lower and upper floors

4. Pagoda Island anchorage, down-river from Foochow, painted by a Chinese artist in the early nineteenth century. Opened as a treaty port in 1867, the anchorage was used by large ships that were unable to travel further up-river. The small port was manned by an equally small number of consular and customs staff who were subject to depression and frequently quarrelled

5. Kulangsu Island, opposite Amoy, c. 1890. Foreigners preferred to live on Kulangsu which had a summit of huge round boulders and much greenery. Their houses, even at this late stage, still reflect the early style

6. A tea-taster's life and work in China, from the *Illustrated London News*,
13 October 1888. Combining the scientific and the satirical, the tea-taster
enjoys a busman's breakfast before facing mounds of paperwork in the office
and more tea to taste

7. Chinese labourers with their employers, *c.* 1875. Victorian gentlemen in three-piece suits and ties, together with a well-dressed Chinese foreman or comprador, survey an unhappy group of rattan workers, presumably engaged in some badly paid form of basket-work

8. Laying the foundation stone of the new Hongkong and Shanghai Bank in Hankow, 1917. A model of the elegant, colonnaded building complete with flag is surrounded by an interesting architectural ensemble. The life-size flags include the double triangle of the Bank

22. Consul F.E. Wilkinson and Vice-Consul W.W. Myers on parade at Pagoda Island near Foochow, during the First World War: two of the rare consular officials who did not go mad or become depressed during their posting at this isolated treaty port

7. Chinese labourers with their employers, *c.* 1875. Victorian gentlemen in three-piece suits and ties, together with a well-dressed Chinese foreman or comprador, survey an unhappy group of rattan workers, presumably engaged in some badly paid form of basket-work

8. Laying the foundation stone of the new Hongkong and Shanghai Bank in Hankow, 1917. A model of the elegant, colonnaded building complete with flag is surrounded by an interesting architectural ensemble. The life-size flags include the double triangle of the Bank

9. Edward Little, missionary-turned-businessman and land speculator, at home in Shanghai, 1912. Little established the summer resort or hill-station of Kuling in the late nineteenth century but is seen here making useful political contacts

10. Studio portrait of Sung Pah-zung, the comprador at the Shanghai office of the Mercantile Bank of India, 1930–1

11. Sir Robert Hart, Inspector-General of the Imperial Chinese Customs Service from 1863 until his death in 1911. Hart transformed the service into a massive and modern bureaucracy and set up the Chinese Post Office and the Customs College. His diligence on behalf of the Chinese government did not protect him during the Boxer uprising when he had to flee to the Legation Quarter and his home was destroyed

12. Sir James Stewart Lockhart in the garden of a Chinese official. Lockhart served in the British Consular Service, first in Hong Kong where he administered the New Territories and then, from 1902 to 1920, in the Weihaiwei leasehold which was returned to China in 1930 owing to rising costs

13. Participants in a 'tennis tea', a major event in the social round in Chengtu, *c.* 1908. All the players are heavily dressed, one man (seated at front with a child on his lap) evidently playing in an ankle-length Chinese gown

14. The grandstand at the racecourse outside Peking in the summer of 1899. In all the larger treaty ports, the races were the most important social event of the year. At the centre of the photograph is Prince Heinrich of Prussia

15. Two daughters of Consul F.E. Wilkinson balance on a Chinese wheelbarrow in Shanghai, 1907. Smaller consular or missionary children were often transported in baskets suspended from carrying poles. Chinese wheelbarrows are better designed than their British counterparts with the wheel at the centre and the weight, whether animate or inanimate, placed either side so that the wheelbarrowman must balance the conveyance but expends less energy pushing

16. A meeting of the Anglo-American Chinese Society for Harmony and Friendship in Shanghai, February 1913, held to welcome James Stewart Lockhart, Commissioner of Weihaiwei, and his wife. Mrs Lockhart sits in the centre, in a stole made from the skins of many small animals, surrounded by women and girls in a variety of Shanghai dress styles

17. 'Victims of the Taiyuan Massacre'. Dr and Mrs Lovitt with their son and Mrs Lovitt's father all wear Chinese clothes, a rather unsuccessful disguise or sartorial gesture assumed by many missionaries which neither concealed nor protected them. Forty-four, including children, were killed in the government office in Taiyuan in 1900 in one of the first and most serious anti-foreign attacks of the Boxer uprising

18. Missionaries setting out from Shanghai, c. 1890. They demonstrate adaptability in their choice of transportation but they are not of the group that assumed Chinese dress or Chinese ways

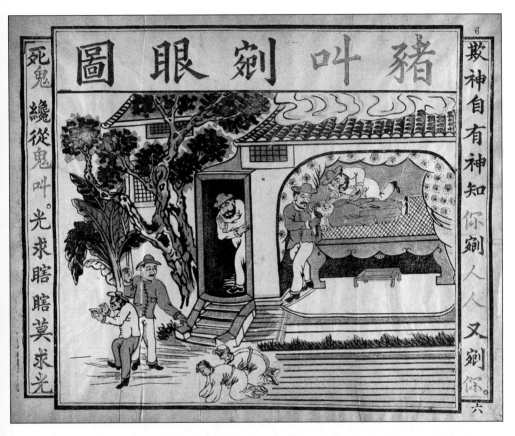

19. A Chinese attack on missionaries, 'The Cause of the Riots in the Yangtze Valley', 1891, shows missionary doctors extracting the eyes of unfortunate Chinese. Perhaps because of the high mortality rate in missionary hospitals, as a result of prevailing medical conditions and despite the best intentions of doctors, rumours circulated that missionary doctors wanted Chinese body parts. It was said that eyes were essential in the manufacture of silvered mirrors and that European eyes did not serve the purpose

20. Western visitors pose beside a criminal condemned to a slow death by strangulation in a cage. Suspended by his neck, the prisoner could not quite reach the ground. Though Western courts were frequently more savage in their sentencing than their Chinese equivalents, foreign residents and visitors to China were fascinated by Chinese punishments. Many brought back photographs or sets of postcards of Chinese executions, of decapitated heads displayed on city walls and of prisoners in the cangue, a version of the medieval stocks

21. Not a postcard but an official photograph of foreign retribution against the Boxers, 1900. Japanese troops, from the international relief force that rescued the diplomatic community from the siege of Peking, and Chinese imperial troops stand over the bodies of decapitated Boxers

22. Consul F.E. Wilkinson and Vice-Consul W.W. Myers on parade at Pagoda Island near Foochow, during the First World War: two of the rare consular officials who did not go mad or become depressed during their posting at this isolated treaty port

23. A consular review of the Boy Scouts of Shanghai, 1930s. Acting Consul-General Davidson takes the salute, followed by Acting Consul Ogden. The Boy Scout movement mushroomed in treaty port China but national and social distinctions were maintained. By the beginning of the Second World War there were nearly thirty different troops in Shanghai alone

24. Even within the Shanghai Volunteer Corps, first founded in 1853 to defend Western interests against the Small Sword Society uprising, there were divisions. ICI (China) had its own group members, here photographed in 1937 with the managing director in the centre of the front row

25. Western business methods were taken up enthusiastically in Shanghai. Western typography gradually replaced the traditional method of wood-block printing and Shanghai became a publishing centre, known for its progressive press. The Chinese writing system was a barrier to Western methods but many Chinese in the treaty ports took up Western ways, even learning to type

26. International businesses were tremendously interested in the China market, as the East India Company had been in previous centuries. Brunner Mond (later to become ICI) built a large business in China. Outside their godown or warehouse in Shanghai, local porters arrive to transport sacks of chemicals

3 pair of thin French shoes 11/3 is my size

1 suit tweed ordinary thickness

1 suit thin tweed or flannel same colour as tweed

1 pair pants tweed or flannel same colour as tweed

1 black alpaca sack coat trimmed with braid, and pockets as in an
ordinary coat but no lining in any part of it. The coats not to be
made too large or the sleeves too long

3 or 4 tooth brushes and boxes of tooth powder

3 or 4 silk umbrellas

6 pair large sheets

6 small pillow cases

6 towels

4 quires of overlaid notepaper with envelopes: a kind my writing can
be read from

2 quires common notepaper with envelopes

half a quire large ruled paper 12 × 8

3 doz. large envelopes

half a doz. plain ruled books three-eighths of an inch thick

2 doz. drawing pencils marked HB

4 bundles of quills

1 doz. Copybooks ... notepaper size

1 book of carbonne paper

In addition to personal effects, he was obliged to have recourse to them
for many much larger items required in the course of business:

1 veranda railing for 9 windows

8 imitation marble chimney-pieces, similar to those made in York
Junction Road, don't send any black, they must be well-packed,
divisions put in the box for each piece and packed with something
soft and not too many in one box. I have seen the marble ones sent
out and not one piece but was broken through carelessness in the
packing

railing for 2 or 3 staircases as tracing

4 dining room grates

12 bedroom ditto (fire brick backs). Not the most expensive kind, just
what you would call very good grates, they must be well and carefully
packed, a great many get broken

6 fenders and 6 sets of fire irons

1 100 ft. good tape lines

1 50 ft. ditto
4 dining room locks
4 drawing room locks
2 doz. Bedroom locks
1 doz. dining room door mortice locks, all with handles, screws and
    complete.

To keep up his spirits, he requested further volumes of *Home Truths* (he
had seven already), as well as 'Spurgeon's *Sermons* (I have *The Saint and
His Saviour*) and the 3rd vol. of *Lives of Engineers*'.

Clearly many of his purchases, both personal and professional, were
unobtainable in China, although his order of silk umbrellas seems a
luxury in the land of the red paper or yellow oiled-cloth parasol.
(Presumably anything other than black silk would have been considered effeminate.) And although the treaty ports were to become famed
for their overnight tailors, Hankow was then still a new town whose
tailors were unused to serving foreigners.

But if Gavin's Chinese tailors were unable to comprehend his
requirements, his family in Edinburgh were no more understanding of
conditions abroad.

> I have not got all the suits etc. turned out yet but they seem to be all
> right except the tweed, twice too thick. If I was to wear that now [8 July]
> I would be laid up with fever. I am going to have coats made out of what
> you sent for shirts, it is just the thickness. The least difference in the
> thickness makes an awful difference to the feel in this weather. Do you
> remember my sleeping pyjamas that you made out of 2 different kinds
> of cotton that you thought (my mother I mean) there was no difference
> in? I can tell as well as anything which it is when I put them on. During
> this weather you cannot catch cold. Just now (9 pm) the thermometer
> stands at 93 degrees in the house. Yesterday morning I put it out in the
> sun exposed to the wind and it rose to 120 degrees . . . The silk shirts you
> have sent me were undershirts, that is not what I meant. I don't know
> any other name for them, the one kind are shirts, the other underhose.
> However it does not matter. I am not much caring for them now. I took
> a fancy to them when I first saw them.

To continue his work of constructing his commissioned buildings in
the European style, he requisitioned his father for a further '3 sets of
stair railings, 2 marble mantle pieces, 6 imitation marble mantle pieces,

100 pairs of room door BRASS hinges with screw, double elephant drawing paper' and rolls of tracing paper and tracing cloth and, in return for all this ironmongery, sent home '6 boxes of tea, 2 for Mother, 1 for Aunt Sarah, 1 for Aunt Morton, 1 for Aunt Merricks and Annie and 1 between Dr Finlay and Mr South', and reported on the shipping of bronze gongs for a Mr Hay. He also appears to have succumbed to a little opium trading, getting into a tangle of mutual suspicion over 103 'bags of medicine' in which his partner was a Mr Dudley and which never showed a profit.

The working year was interrupted by festivals, particularly the Chinese lunar New Year. On 2 March 1863, he wrote to his sister, 'It is now a fortnight since the New Year (Chinese) commenced and business has scarcely begun yet. The 8th day of this year was the first lucky day in the almanac so there was no work done till then. Their almanac which is published every year by the emperor, has got its lucky and unlucky days and the stupid beggars would die of starvation rather than go out and look for work on a bad day.' As he was writing, he could hear the festivities continuing, 'last night and tonight is the Feast of Lanterns. There are strings of lanterns hung up at every door and as usual the beating of gongs from night till morning.'

He lived, or 'messed', with two other Scottish gentlemen, and their social life revolved around thrice-weekly prayer meetings and collecting money for the widow and orphans of the Reverend Robert Wilson, one of the three foreigners to die in Hankow in August 1863. Though social contacts with the Chinese were almost non-existent, there were some exceptions. He wrote to his mother on 1 December 1863,

Yesterday I was at a Chinese marriage. The Bride was dressed in scarlet silk, a scarlet veil on her face which is taken off after the ceremony. The lady who gives her away stands at her side supporting her on her little feet and telling her what to do. The husband has a lot of gymnastics to go through: one minute he is down on his knees, the next he has his head between his feet. The dinner was their treat. As in everything else, Chinamen begin at the wrong end so we got dessert first, all sorts of fruit, sugar candy and stinking stuff which we had to take with chopsticks, then came the substantial dishes which we also had to eat with chopsticks.

The meat is cut into small pieces and set in the middle of the table.

We all sit round the table and dab our chopsticks into the centre dish every mouthful. If you want to be polite and help your neighbour, you draw the chopsticks through your mouth to clean them before using them. In the afternoon, the Bride sits in a very disconsolate mood on the front of the bed receiving visitors.

I called on her in the afternoon dressed in my uniform as I was coming from drill. I have no doubt that she considered herself highly honoured as red is their favourite colour. Everything in the room was red: the bed, tables, chairs and all the furniture.

After his description of chopstick cleaning and meals back to front, it is hardly surprising that the Chinese in Hankow responded in kind. Invited to breakfast at the consul's house, the local mandarins

had everything on the table upside down. As soon as they began to breakfast, each of their servants came in with their pipes. An old beggar next to me sat with fork in one hand and pipe in the other, smoking all the time, his servant standing at his back with a light and a bagful of tobacco ... they went onto everything that was put on the table. They thought knives and forks a grand institution but they did not make much use of them, their fingers were more serviceable. They had to taste everything. One customer upset nearly the whole of the cayenne pepper bottle onto his plate. He thought it was all up with himself after the first mouthful. They walked into the bread. They were asking what it was made from, where the flour came from and what was the price of it. They took a piece of bread and a pinch of salt time about. I expected to see them tight before they were finished. They had wine, beer, tea and finished off with Gin.

Gavin's account of a trip into the countryside with a 'gentleman resident' from Kiukiang illustrates the precautions taken by the Victorian resident on tour in China.

Travelling ... is very inconvenient as the resources of the country can give no support and the means of travelling is very slow. The object of our journey was to get to the top of the mountains lying between Kiukiang and the Poyang lake and as they could not be ascended from the Kiukiang side, we had to cross to the other first. With our escort we made a pretty large party; 11 in all. We had two chairs with three coolies to each, two coolies carrying kit and provisions and one man to superintend. The chairs were most comical-looking articles made entirely of bamboo and tied together with string, with a covering of brown paper to shelter you from sun or rain. About 10 minutes after we started, I came to grief. The chair broke down and landed me on the ground. From the look of the chair I expected every 10 minutes to be landed on the ground. However we got it tied together again and it was all right for the rest of the journey.

Starting from Kiukiang at two o'clock in the afternoon, they reached the village of Sha-li-pu some two hours later, where they stopped to allow the coolies to get a cup of tea and a smoke. By five o'clock they were under way again and had reached the village of Yung-chan-nan at the foot of the Wuchang pass where they were to cross the mountains.

All the roads in China are merely footpaths winding through patches of ground which are cultivated by the country people ... For the first three or four miles from Kiukiang there is not much to be seen but as we got nearer the mountains, the scenery was much finer and the Country well-cultivated. The only thing grown is rice, which is the main staple of support used by the Chinese. The rising ground on the hills is all ter-raced and cut into flats not more than 50 feet wide, and as the rice plant must always have 3 or 4 inches of water, the streams from the hills run down those terraces, from one to the other, irrigating them all ... When we got to the foot of the pass, we got out of our chairs as it was a very steep climb and more agreeable walking, rather a degrading thing to do in the eyes of a Chinaman as he would never think of moving from his chair to save his own life or that of his coolies. From the top of the pass we did not get a good view as it was very thick. Descending on the other side the scenery was beautiful, the country was interspersed with patches of trees which was quite a treat of itself as I had not seen trees for many a long day. China is far worse than Scotland in that respect.

By half past six they had come to the village of Ssi-shi-chan where they planned to put up for the night.

It was anything but an attractive place. We went into every house and it would have been difficult to say which was the filthiest ... We at last fixed where we would put up: a wooden box about 14 or 15 ft square with mud floor, one side had half a dozen doors which at the same time served as windows; the top half was a sort of sparred work which in the cold weather is covered over with paper ... The herdsman's hut on the top of the Pentland hills to shelter them from the weather is a mansion compared to our Chinese house ... During the time we were looking for lodgings we were followed by nearly all the men, women and bairns in the village and when we got to our quarters, as many of them as could get in came in too and stood and looked at us, no doubt as great curiosities from one of the outside barbarous countries. The first thing to be done was to get dinner, which we had brought with us, and all the time we were at it we were suffocated by a crowd looking at us.

When we turned out knives, forks, spoons, glasses etc, they seemed very much amused. They could not think what they were for, and when the Chinaman with us told them, they did not seem inclined to believe him.

They were much amused at our style of taking food, when we did anything that appeared to them strange, they burst out in a scream of laughter.

When dinner was over, we thought we would finish with a cup of tea. After a great deal of talking they brought us a kettle that would have made tea for a Soirée. We could not get milk so we asked for an Egg or as they call it a Ki-dan (Hen's bullet). Switching up a couple of eggs rather took their fancy. When they saw the Operation completed they thought it rather a strange way to drink Tea. They always take it alone and at any break.

We got a couple of tables for a bed and turned them all out or they would have stood till next morning. They stood outside looking through the grating of the doors until we put the lights out . . it was the hardest bed I ever slept in.[1]

In the same year that John Gavin was exploring the cloud-covered hills of the Yangtze, a young Customs officer made his way across the bare northern plains to his first posting in Tientsin. Edward Bowra, the son of an inventor (of inflatable muffs to save ladies who fell into water, and rubber railway sleepers), had already seen adventure, volunteering to fight for Garibaldi in Sicily in 1860, and endured the constitution-threatening regime of the P&O liner on his way to China. 'Eating is the principal occupation on board,' he wrote, and went on to list the daily round of breakfast (9–10), luncheon with beers and wines (1–2), dinner (4–6), tea (7–8) and supper and grog (9–10).[2]

Bowra was unusual in being sensitive to the beauty of the north China plain which most people dismissed as merely flat, like Noël Coward's Norfolk. The French poet Paul Claudel, who served as French consul in Tientsin in 1906, described the countryside as 'horrible and ugly' though he admitted that the sky was 'admirably pure'.[3] Bowra joined the Customs mess, hiring six personal servants: a teacher of Chinese, a boy 'who performs all the multifarious duties of valet, house-maid and boots', two coolies to sweep the yard, fill and empty his bath, and carry him in his chair, a mafoo and a horse (apparently granted the rank of personal servant). Cooks were joint property in the mess and he found he could live very cheaply on 'two or three kinds of wine, joints, poultry, game, fish, vegetables and fruit such as Covent Garden could scarcely rival'. The daily round of meals was hardly less filling than that on the P&O liner. Breakfast was at 9.30, office work from 10 till 2, fol-lowed by tiffin, 'a chop and a glass of Bass's bright pale ale', and a return to the office to write letters and talk to the clerks. At 4 p.m. he would 'wash, dress and saunter round to the reading and billiard room, gossip for an hour or so and then ride out, returning in time for dinner at eight. Afterwards a cigar and a chat, a walk on the roof and turn in about ten or half past.'[4]

He found the Tientsin missionaries 'uneducated, characterless nonentities' but enjoyed the company of Dent's agent, Mr Hanna, and that of the 'rather addlepated' Hector Maclean of Jardine's, Mr Waller (Chairman of the Municipal Council, Superintendent of Works in the Settlement, Chief of the Municipal Police, Steward of the Race Course, Secretary of the Fives Court, Captain of the Cricket Club, and 'Best shot, best horseman and best billiard player') and Mr Meadows whose dinners were 'much the best here'. Bowra worked for Robert Hart in the Customs, much as in his previous career as consular officer Hart had served under J.A.T. Meadows in Ningpo. Meadows, however, after marrying a Chinese wife, had had to resign from the Consular Service and turn merchant.

Lacking enough work, Bowra studied Chinese, rode his pony, 'The Biter' (which he later hoped to sell in Shanghai where nobody would know why it had acquired its name), and 'shot the teeming wildfowl'.[5]

He also enjoyed riding out into the countryside, describing the beauty of the distant mountains encircling the plain in rather over-blown prose: 'As the sun lowers his crest, it seems as if the hills that bound the horizon, their summits crested all with cloudy crowns, are fairy palaces, castles of ivory, pagodas of gold.' Most other foreign residents ignored the hills and only ventured into the countryside to rid it of wildlife. Oliver Ready, a Hankow resident, entitled his memoirs *Life and Sport in China* and devoted three of his ten chapters to 'shooting', 'riding' and 'sailing', the last being mainly a way of getting close enough to waterfowl to shoot and eat them. The great thing about China for the shooting enthusiast was the lack of control. Back in England, 'to trespass a few yards on the grounds of another man will probably result in legal proceedings ... keepers flourish and wax fat on contributions levied on the friends of mine host ... hand-raised game is driven into the jaws of death, and ... the sportsman's friend, his dog, is practically banished'. By contrast, 'one can look on the whole empire of China and say, "Here is my ground, here I can take my gun and dogs and ... shoot what I will, stay as long as I like without asking anyone's leave, and where keepers and game licences are unknown." '[6]

The freedom to trample over anybody's fields, denied to all but the rich in England, raises an interesting aspect of foreign residence in China. Oliver Ready may have paid to hunt hand-raised game back home (he dedicated his book to his cousin, Alfred, Viscount Milner) but most foreign residents in China were not of the upper classes and did not enjoy the same privilege. The Professor of English Literature at Tsing-hua University in Peking, Wang Wen-hsien, a specialist in seventeenth-century drama, became interested in guns through his father who had served as a senior police officer in Hong Kong, Shanghai and Tientsin in the late nineteenth century and whose 'acquisitive resistance' in the matter of firearms was 'absolutely nil': 'the average Britisher when he moves into the outposts of empire usually saddles himself with a private arsenal in the hope of something to shoot at. A very respectable collection of sporting weapons is thus accumulated in the colony and must be got rid of when members of the community return to their homeland.'[7] In the late nineteenth century, this was not for fear of gun laws but because the social class and means of the gun-owner often meant that his passion, and his weapons, had to be surrendered when he returned home.

Oliver Ready's favourite hunting-ground was the Yangtze area, although the shooting was not so good as it had been because the foreign community in Shanghai had grown and there had developed a hunting industry with 'native gunners who, as a means of livelihood, scour the country with foreign breech-loaders ... The first essential for shooting trips on the Yangtze is a good house-boat or light draft yacht ... your floating shooting box.' The boy got everything ready,

> guns, dogs, provisions, and a good fire in the saloon ... you make your-self comfortable, have afternoon tea, read, smoke, dine, chat with your friend over the fire, and after spending the evening as comfortably as if in your own house, retire to rest, awakening next morning to find your-self on the scene of action and very possibly to hear the pheasants crow while still in bed.

Ready shot over fields abandoned after the Taiping rebellion and in the hills (deer and pheasant), in riverside swamps (snipe, woodcock, racoons, wild cats, swans, geese, mallard, goosanders, teal and duck), among graves (hares, 'wretched little animals, all bones and felt') and on the plains (quail and bustard). On one occasion he even shot fish through the ice of a frozen stream.

Tigers could be found near Amoy, although Ready never bagged one, but Robert Hart as a young consular officer went for smaller, prettier prey:

> Today I shot a bird which sings like a Black bird. Were it not for some white feathers on the wings, I shld. pronounce it a 'Chinese "English Blackbird"'. Perhaps it is a sort of Mina ... shot a dove this evening. The Ningbo people call it *pau cheu*: its back is of a slate colour; round its neck is a ring of black spotted feathers. It is a very beautiful bird.[8]

Practically the only drawback for hunters in the Ichang region was spear grass. Shooting without leather leggings, Ready collected grass 'the size of a bee-hive' in his socks, and his dog grew to the size of a sheep.

> When at length the boy proceeded to take my stockings off it was found they were practically sewn to my skin by the spear-grass, the tiny barbed points of which had passed in hundreds through the wool and worked like fish-hooks into my calves ... for days I was lame and sore, while my dog lived in misery for weeks. I did not even see a Reeves pheasant.

Dogs, too, were sacrificed to sport. European dogs seldom lived for more than three or four years in China, and often less, so it was nec-essary 'always to have puppies coming on if you do not want your shooting to be spoiled for it is useless to try and get pheasants out of thick cover without them'. The dogs succumbed to dysentery and

> worms in the heart ... thin, white worms resembling vermicelli [which] cluster around the heart, living on the blood, until they become so numerous as to eventually choke an artery, when death is instantaneous. In the case of a favourite dog, on which a doctor kindly performed a *post-mortem* examination, these worms were in such numbers that I positively could not see the heart at all.

The sacrifice was necessary for, in the eyes of the nineteenth-century foreign resident, practically everything that was locally available was inferior, dogs included: 'Native dogs are useless for sport, as they seem to be devoid of that friendly intelligence so noticeable in our own breeds, while their powers of scent are much inferior.'

Not all those who imported dogs for shooting found them satisfactory. The journalist and writer J.O.P. Bland, who was to collaborate with the unreliable Edmund Backhouse on a series of books on Chinese history, acquired a setter named Hector from Australia who appeared to have been exclusively trained in the pursuit of kangaroos: 'Hector had a mournful way of mooning about the country, indifferent to any birds in his vicinity, which said, as plainly as a dog can speak, that he was looking for the familiar things of his youth; and as the chances of flushing a kangaroo grew daily less, his interest in our proceedings waned visibly and finally expired.' Hector was disposed of by public auction.[9]

Oliver Ready spent Christmas 1889 shooting near Chinkiang, bagging three geese, fourteen pheasant, two deer, three woodcock, seven duck and one pigeon before settling down to his Christmas feast:

> Pigeon soup
> Woodcock
> Boiled pheasant
> Cold roast beef
> Plum cake ('a Christmas present from a Norwegian
> lady') ablaze with Whisky
> Cheese
> Pumelo [a giant grapefruit grown up-river in Szechwan]
> Whisky and water
> Tea

There was no holly or mistletoe to remind one of Merrie Englande, but I drank to 'the Old Folks at Home' with the sadness peculiar to wanderers on such occasions, and then gave myself up to nicotine and reflection.

In Shanghai, lacking foxes, foreign residents continued to combine the delights of riding and the chase in paper-chases in the suburbs.[10] Oliver Ready, when not walking out with a short-lived dog to shoot, was interested in riding and racing and was, like everyone else, contemptuous of the quality of the local ponies, though he looked at more than the common 'China' pony (from Mongolia) and had viewed 'a small, well-shaped pony from Turkestan, a large stringy horse from I-li and a weedy, cowhocked pony from Szechwan'. The China pony had a 'large, ugly head carried low on a wedge-shaped neck, so that when mounted you have practically nothing in front of the saddle'.

With riding, as with shooting, China provided opportunities that foreign merchants and residents would probably not have had back home, their youth notwithstanding.

The majority of men taking up appointments in China are barely out of, if not still in, their teens, and whether they come straight from school, from business in the city or from the universities, it is seldom they have had any large experience of horses. In very many cases, they do not even know how to mount, but finding ponies so cheap, or better still, getting a racer as a cumshaw [gift or bribe], they take to riding as naturally as if to the manner born, so that there are few residents of either sex who cannot ride ... From hacking to racing is but a step. The man who has learnt to ride (or thinks he has), being already a member of the race club, takes his steed for a quiet canter round the course. The old racer no sooner finds himself on the familiar track than he is off with the speed of flames, and our young friend, being powerless to check him, with his feet out of the stirrups and hanging on to the back of the saddle for dear life, is carried a mile or so before a sudden swerve at the exit rail deposits him on the turf. No bones are broken but the damage is done. Unless the dismounted cavalier be devoid of all enthusiasm the spirit of racing has assuredly entered his veins!

Despite decades of experience, in Shanghai at least, judging the qualities of a China pony remained a dangerous affair for the 'idea of feeling his legs, drawing out his tongue, examining his hoofs or peering into his eyes quickly evaporates [when with] a vicious eye ... the brute, snorting with anger and alarm ... attempts to rush one'. Even when broken in, they were skilled at cowkicking and their tempers remained untrustworthy.

Not everyone could afford to buy or own ponies: Paul King, a long-serving Customs officer whose promotions were few and far between, used to ride with his wife on 'Bund ponies' in Tientsin, 'discarded racers kept by the Chinese for chance hire to the bluejackets of the British Navy ... A friend once remonstrated with me, "What an extravagant fellow you are! I see you and your wife constantly out on different ponies." '[11]

Despite the savagery of the ponies, race meetings in Hankow in the second half of the nineteenth century resembled a huge picnic. Early in the morning, the prospective runners (ridden by their owners) trotted and galloped on the course, watched from the rails by 'the sporting members of the community, stop-watch in hand' whilst others 'follow proceedings from the grandstand while breakfasting on hot rolls and coffee'.

In autumn, as the level of the Yangtze fell, Hankow riders, released from the confines of the racecourse and the river bank, could gallop for miles along the dry riverbed, until spring when the river levels began to rise again. Further up the river during the autumn, at Ichang, golf was played on the dry riverbed forty feet below the level of the bund. There Paul King, now moved from Tientsin, and the harbour-master Mr E. Molloy, 'reckoned as one of the longest drivers in the Far East ... teed ... for a down-river trip. It was the old original Scottish game, straight ahead for seven miles, with the bones of sunken junks and high stone boulders as "hazards".'[12]

In summer, when the river was full and high, residents of Kiukiang 120 miles downstream from Hankow could find no satisfactory area to exercise their horses until

> the brilliant idea was conceived of using the city wall, which stands about twenty feet in height and is four miles in circumference.
>
> Entering by the western gate and turning sharply to the right we rode up the stone steps, much worn by time and human feet, to the top of the wall which is some twelve feet in width ... We usually made the circuit twice before descending. Where the steps adjoin the wall two

large right angles are formed, into which Chinese houses have been built in such a manner that their roofs are coterminous with, and slope at the same angle as, the steps.

All went well until one pony had had enough.

As a friend of mine was passing this point for the second time, his pony tried to bolt down the steps with the intention of returning to stable. A violent pull at the near rein brought the brute's head round, but without stopping him, so that he passed sideways from the steps on to the roof of one of the houses, and together with his rider instantly disappeared through it, amidst a cloud of dust, a crashing of timbers and the rattle of falling tiles.

Emerging from the debris, and smothered with dust, my friend led his pony through the front door into the street, where a crowd had already collected, neither apparently any the worse for their remarkable feat. An old woman who was in the building at the time had a narrow escape from being crushed by the falling animal, but she soon recovered from the shock, and a liberal sum in dollars with which to repair the roof probably caused her to regret that similar accidents did not more frequently occur.[13]

Kiukiang's foreign community consisted of a few married couples and perhaps half a dozen bachelors who were noted for their exuberance. For the luckless local inhabitants, it must have been like living with a rugby team in a permanent state of celebration. Oliver Ready regarded the jamborees that he enjoyed in Kiukiang as comparable to the almost entirely alcoholic bump suppers of boat crews at Cambridge. A jamboree was 'a bachelor entertainment consisting of an enormous dinner with plenty of wine, tales, songs and general hilarity, occasionally verging on riotousness with breakage of household furniture and other effects'. On one occasion at Kiukiang, a dinner at his mess was held for an Italian, a 'tall American of stern and unbending nature', two Russians and 'two Scotchmen, all we could muster'. 'After a jovial repast, we sallied forth on to the bund, and being a bright moonlight night, romance entered into our souls and we started to serenade the various ladies of the port.' They sang 'God Save the Queen' on the consulate lawn at 2 a.m. and were halfway through 'My Bonnie lives over the Ocean' in another garden when a thunderstorm broke. The lady of the house appeared 'in a commanding attitude on the upper veranda in her dressing gown, almost speechless with emotion, but gesticulating frantically'. They made their way to the Russian's house where the American unbent sufficiently to climb through the serving hatch between pantry and dining-room when 'a terrific crash of crockery told its own tale: the Russian's best dinner service was no more'. Then they went upstairs and grabbed 'the struggling form of our host's Chinese housekeeper, clad in nothing but her night garments. She was laid tenderly on the dining table and comforted with some *Veuve Clicquot* champagne.' The American, withdrawing with the declaration that they were all (himself excepted) 'inebriated and unfit for the society of respectable citizens', went to bed but was soon woken. 'The mêlée lasted probably five minutes, during which brief period his furniture was hurled in chaotic profusion all around the room, my black mess jacket was divided up the back from the tail to the collar, his pyjamas carried away, and the skin was detached from his bare feet by my boots. So ended a glorious evening.'[14]

Alcohol-fuelled high spirits were to be found in Hankow, too. Ready described a reception and banquet arranged at the Club for a visiting Russian Grand Duke. Despite the midsummer heat (Hankow is one of the 'five furnaces' or hottest cities in China), black dress was to be worn and two hundred people were crammed into a room filled with 'hot dishes and a great many lamps'.

> To still further increase the torture, a crowd of Chinese which had collected in the streets below commenced to throw stones through the open windows. One passed between my right-hand neighbour and myself, shivering my wine-glasses to atoms. The windows and shutters were hastily closed and very shortly the temperature must have still further increased by several degrees.

Champagne flowed and there was a sulphurous firework display. His eyes streaming from the fumes, Ready decided to set off home but found it hard going and ended up prostrate on the pavement where he was joined by a friend and could 'distinctly remember our sitting side by side in the gutter and swearing eternal friendship'. Though he found his bed eventually, his friend, it was said, 'attempted to go to bed in his bath, where he was discovered in full evening dress, scooping the water over himself and complaining he could not keep the sheets up'.

Such drunken mess dinners were partly the result of a continuing lack of respectable white women in most of the treaty ports. Slightly more decorous and well-organized men-only 'messes' were set up for young Customs officers. Paul King, serving in Swatow in the 1870s, described his bachelor life:

> Breakfast, tea or coffee and an egg – each man on the veranda or in his bedroom.
>
> Tiffin at noon in the mess-room, preceded by the inevitable and noxious cold drink in cocktail shape. Tiffin was quite a substantial meal, the feature being spatchcock chicken. We had no ice. Any meat had to be quickly cooked and eaten, and could only be got from the good-natured skippers of visiting steamers.
>
> Office hours in the Customs were ten to four. A cup of tea also served on the veranda to the consumer lying in a long cane chair helped tone up the system for the evening exercises. Sometimes when credit was more plentiful than reason ... a small bottle of champagne, from the cool depths of the Club well, was substituted for the tea ... The chit system was in full swing and the 'end of the month' troubled only a few.
>
> Dinner was late – eight to half-past as a rule. White linen mess-jackets and duck trousers – the dandies with red sashes – were mostly worn. Sherry, claret, and bottled beer were generally drunk at table with whisky and soda afterwards – sometimes, when card-playing was in vogue – deep into the night. Dinner was necessarily largely 'metallic'.
>
> Tinned soup, tinned fish, tinned meat, tinned vegetables and Christmas tinned plum pudding ... Tinned sausages were the great stand-by in those days, served with green peas (also from a tin). No wonder the white man's digestion not seldom failed him after years of exclusive feeding on chicken and tins.

Prejudice in Swatow against local produce (with the exception of chicken) was only cast aside on summer visits to a Customs Retreat Club on the bathing beach where rock cod was served by a Chinese cook.

In other messes a reliance on imported food was less marked. Charles Dyce was in charge of the provisions of his Shanghai mess in the 1870s and, noting the expense of pepper, salt, oil, vinegar and sauces, all imported from England, chose to use local raw materials which were cheap although subject to the cook's little extras: 'though every single article he bought from rice to woodcock was subject to the squeeze, he did not take an undue toll as things went'.[15]

The Mess and the Club were a male preserve, as was most social life unless sudden opportunities were seized. Robert Hart, whose susceptibility to a neatly turned ankle in Ningpo has already been noted, was still, ten years later, looking for a respectable wife. At the Shanghai races, he quite lost his heart to three or four young ladies: 'The fourth is so far, the favourite', but she 'turned out to be a married woman who dropped her aitches'.[16] Eventually he found himself a wife while on home leave.

The arrival of white women was an occasion to celebrate. Ready recalled

a small port where for a long time there had only been one lady, who was naturally regarded as the belle of the place. Presently a rival appeared and with her two pretty unmarried sisters: whereon my messmates and I forthwith gave an impromptu dance.

We cleared out the dining-room for the occasion, but found the carpet to be so old and so tightly nailed down that it would not bear removing, and we decided to dance on it.

No sooner, however, had we commenced to the strain of an accordion, not having a piano, than the floor, which was laid on round joists over the entrance hall, began to vibrate so violently that glasses on the sideboard were smashed and ornaments fell from the walls, while dust from the carpet, which evidently had not been beaten for years, rose in such clouds that, coupled with the heat of a stifling night, we were literally choked off and obliged to take refuge in the garden. Fortunately it was a beautiful night and full moon so we diverted our dance to a game of hide and seek, and a merrier evening I have seldom spent.[17]

Ready was lucky that only the floor bounced: in Wuhu, the Customs commissioner's house, though new, proved almost fatal. The house possessed a huge entrance hall. One night, the newly arrived commissioner, Paul King, was disturbed by a loud crack like a pistol shot, apparently coming from the roof. 'The sound was repeated, and next day I went up the roof ladder ... I am not an expert but I knew enough to wish for expert opinion on the extraordinary jumble of badly placed timbers which constituted the roof.' He consulted the engineer-in-chief who reported that the trouble was in the too flat arch in the hall ... There was supposed to be an iron girder in the flat arch but 'soundings' failed to locate it. I unearthed a wizened little man, who had worked as a carpenter under the contractor who built the house. The contractor himself was nowhere to be found ... The house was practically without foundations and the bricks and mortar, especially the latter, of the poorest quality. The little carpenter was doubtful about the iron girder but 'opined' ... that there was some iron somewhere ... At last the carpenter found it. It was a thin rod of iron about half an inch in diameter! The engineer-in-chief tore his hair and said the roof must come off at once to save the house from instant collapse ... It was a relief when the last of the old roof was safely on the lawn ... When it came to hoisting the heavy tie-beams into position, the four walls simply crumbled away and huge fissures in them were apparent ... We made a strong solution of liquid Portland cement and poured it into the cracks from above ... and a light new roof of corrugated iron.[18]

During the period of rooflessness, Paul King's superior, the Inspector-General of Customs, Sir Robert Hart, was characteristically unsympathetic. Having lived for years in tottering consulates in the south (though now comfortably ensconced in a Peking mansion), he said that many houses condemned by commissioners had lasted for years and sarcastically threatened to send the King family to the distant and inaccessible Customs post at Ssumao on the Burmese border where the commissioner's house was a bungalow.

Some of the earliest European buildings in Shanghai had been put together in Hong Kong and shipped for assembly on site but soon architects arrived and set up shop. Their designs then had to be interpreted and constructed by Chinese builders. Enterprising contractors from Canton and Hong Kong, used to building 'foreign' houses and offices and able to communicate with foreigners, made their way northwards to Shanghai and along the Yangtze to profit from the building boom of the mid-nineteenth century. Commissioned to draw up plans for the bunding of Kiukiang, John Gavin informed William Tyers of the Kiukiang Municipal Council in April 1863, 'In accordance with your request I have obtained the services of a Canton carpenter to superintend your Bunding operation.' He was to use another Cantonese, named Afoon, in the bunding of the concession at Hankow.

Bunds, like bungalows, derived from the Indian experience: the term was glossed as 'Hindustani *band,* an artificial causeway or embankment'.[19] The opening of ports all along the Yangtze necessitated an awful lot of bunding. However, such embankment work could only be done in the autumn and winter when the water was low. John Gavin wrote nervously on 11 February 1863 about the Kiukiang embankments: 'I forwarded you on 16th Ult. Plan for the Bunding of your Concession which I hope duly reached you and that you are by this time proceeding with the work. The season for that work is fast slipping past, during the last few days we have had a rise in the Water of 4 feet. I hope that it will rise no more for some time as we still have a great deal of work to do.'

Part of the Hankow bund collapsed a year after it was built:

on account of the dilatory way in which the Contractor went on with the erection of it, the water rose which prevented him erecting the lower part of it in such an efficient way as it ought to have been done. As my urging him from day to day to push on with the work before the water rose was of no account, at my request 900 taels of the Contract money was kept in hand to repair and make good any of the lower part when the water fell which may have been damaged. But before the water had fallen to its lowest, most of the said Bund work gave way, first the centre part of the work, then the remaining portion opposite Mr Ballance's Premises ... The cause of the accident I consider was the water from the land draining through the bank, this season to a much greater extent than usual on account of the river having fallen so rapidly. The water draining through the Bank which is of a sandy soil undermined the stonework of the Bund which gave way. My opinion is that even altho' the work had been efficiently finished by the Contractor, that the said Bund would sooner or later have given way under the pressure of water from within.

Gavin was happier using Europeans to supervise building works, although qualified European building contractors were about as common as pretty, unmarried European women in China. 'I don't know how to advise you with regard to the Superintendence of your house. You would no doubt be much better off with a European than with a Chinaman. I doubt whether Whitfield and Kingsmill would condescend to superintend another person's plans, especially mine as I am a particular friend of theirs having done them right in the eye.' In the event of a Chinese contractor working on the house and godown, 'You should get the contract written out in Chinese, same as the one in English and get both Contracts together with the Plans stamped at the Consulate. It is necessary to have the contract written in Chinese in the event of a dispute, as he will make the plea that he did not understand it if only written in English.'

Despite his preference for European supervisors, Gavin's advice on contracts seems relatively objective when compared with the laboured and repetitive jokes about Chinese servants and their corrupt and un-hygienic ways that appear in even the earliest accounts of foreign life in China. As Oliver Ready reported, from the moment of

> first arrival at an out-port ... as you are crossing the pontoon ... from the steamer to the bund, a most beaming celestial meets you and pre-sents an open letter, which reads something like this: – 'I hereby certify that the bearer, Lao San, was my boy for eight months and I found him honest and willing. Tom Jones' ... Reaching your quarters, you find two or three more beaming natives, also armed with letters of recommenda-tion, probably borrowed for the occasion, and who severally inform you, 'My b'long welly good boy.'[20]

Thus two of the standard clichés are introduced immediately – the dis-honesty apparent in the bare-faced borrowing of letters of reference and the use of 'pidgin' which was not a Chinese invention but imposed (like baby-talk on babies quite capable of normal speech) by foreigners to the point where it became an essential 'second language' skill in a Chinese servant.

The third, endlessly repeated, foible of Chinese servants was said to be their inventive borrowing of essentials from the houses of various foreigners so that dinner guests in someone else's house always claimed that they ate from their own plates 'borrowed' to make up an insufficiency. An embroidery upon this theme was offered by Oliver Ready.

> A Scotchman who had recently married brought from London a goodly supply of fine glassware for their new home. At one of the dinner parties given in honour of himself and his new bride, after replying to the toast

of the evening he proposed the health of his host and requested the company to drink it with Highland honours by placing one foot on the table and one on the chair. Bumpers having been tossed off he added that it would not be fitting for glasses consecrated by such distinguished service to thereafter descend to ordinary usage, and suiting the action to the word, flung the tumbler over his shoulder, so that it was shivered to atoms against the wall, the other guests numbering upwards of a dozen, following suit.

His boy's placid comment on the proceeding was, 'Truly master b'long too muchee foolo, he no savez b'long he new glass.'

They were indeed his own beautiful tumblers, borrowed for the occasion without his knowledge.[21]

The most common complaint about Chinese servants was of their dishonesty in 'squeezing' extra money out of their masters by controlling the shopping and either claiming to have bought excessive quantities of food or inaccurately representing market prices. The position of cook 'is also a lucrative post, for besides wages and a heavy squeeze on every article brought into the kitchen, the remains of each meal, whether half a chicken, half a leg of mutton, or both, are carried off for sale to native restaurants'. Oliver Ready became preoccupied with watered milk. 'At Hankow the supply was so adulterated that a friend of mine actually found a small live fish in his morning cupful. With a view to exposing fraud I purchased a lactometer and found the usual proportions of milk and water to be half and half.' He summoned the dairyman to milk the cow in front of him. But 'after shivering in my dressing-gown during the milking ... on testing it there was still a large percentage of water'. Milking the cow himself he pronounced the source pure and when he 'seized the dairyman with a hazy idea of making an end of him ... there slipped from his capacious sleeve a piece of thick bamboo containing about two pints of water'.[22]

Nevertheless, many servants were satisfactory. Though Robert Hart complained that 'My servant is a very stupid fellow – he brought me *fish* after I had partaken of all the other dishes', he was nonetheless grateful for the manner in which he was served tea. 'My boy comes in with the little Chinese tray on which is a pygmy Tea Pot – sugar bowl – Cream Ewer – Tea cup and two biscuits.'[23] And even the critical recognized some qualities, such as the ability to rustle up (and rustling is perhaps the word to use) instant meals at a moment's notice (by borrowing, according to Ready, from the cook next door). Chinese barbers were so gentle that they could shave a client in his bed without waking him and Chinese tailors were fast and effective. Despite this last acknowledgement of efficiency, Ready could not resist a joke about someone who asked a tailor to copy an old suit only to discover that the tailor had 'let a couple of patches into the seat of the new trousers in order to make them correspond exactly with the pattern'.[24]

Young female relatives of foreign residents who came out to visit were the focus of much attention, and not only from bachelors. Dyce considered that they had a hard time because 'the natives think that the natural freedom of our women is licence' and even Ch'i-ying, a Manchu official who had signed the ratification of the Treaty of Nanking in 1843 and who was brought out of retirement to negotiate the Treaty of Tientsin, reported that he had been quite horrified to be 'saluted' by a foreign woman in Hong Kong. Chinese women of a decent class were kept inside the home, not only because their bound feet made movement difficult but because it was considered improper for women to associate with men not of their immediate family, and even then there were proprieties to be observed. Walking in the streets, talking directly to men, and dancing were unthinkable activities for demure Chinese ladies and such behaviour from foreign women not unnaturally attracted critical attention.

Missionary wives were no exception. Members of the Wesleyan Missionary Society arrived in Chinkiang in March 1865.

> We made for the British concession, and on our way passed amongst very rude huts, the occupants of which came out in astonishment to stare at us, or I should say, to stare at Mrs Smith, for *she* is the great object of interest to them, and they seem anxious to find out whether she has small (that is compressed) feet ... The English inhabitants here number 28 and they cannot boast a lady, hence the surprise of the natives on seeing Mrs Smith.[25]

Missionary wives came out to China to help their husbands, braving the long and dangerous sea voyage and setting up home in the Chinese countryside where they were faced with frequently violent and hostile neighbours, floods or drought and unrecognizable diseases. Despite the difficulties of their surroundings, they took on the additional work of teaching Chinese women and girls, nursing and dispensing, and supervising Sunday School. The wives of consular staff, merchants and Customs officers had nothing to do but run the family home. They were once described as spending most of their time in a nightdress, not necessarily out of indolence but because a thick cotton Victorian nightdress with high collar and long sleeves was less likely to offend the servants than any other form of dress.

The childless Mrs Archibald Little arrived in China in 1887 to join her entrepreneur husband (who was to take the first steamship up the Yangtze in 1898) and was scathing about the indolence of foreign wives in China. She did, however, acknowledge that they were doubly hindered. They were not allowed to join their husbands' clubs or, in these early days, take part in any of the health-giving sports that the men practised. The failure of all but the missionary wives to take any interest in Chinese women was addressed by Mrs Little. She travelled widely (and bravely) both with and without her husband, made contact with Chinese women whenever she could, and was particularly impressed by missionary efforts to discourage foot-binding. In 1895, she founded the Natural Foot Society in Shanghai with ten other women, wives of consular officials and merchants. Apart from natural feet, one of her aims was to 'offer a splendid opportunity for genuinely benevolent work to European ladies in China who not infrequently must have felt the need of something to usefully occupy themselves beyond domestic chores'.[26]

Mrs Little married late and had no children: most wives had to brave the dangers of child-bearing and the difficulties of raising children in a strange land. The resultant domestic chores probably took up most of their time and all of their physical and emotional energy. Childbirth was particularly fraught. In January 1855, Robert Hart reported, 'Mrs Gough was confined: the child had to be cut to pieces in her womb as it was *overgrown* – Mrs G. is going on well' (and so she continued for some time, for she died in London in 1861).[27] Many women were not so fortunate, and even if mother and child did survive the birth, infant mortality was common in missionary families. The McConnells lost their first child at 11 months and the Coopers lost a daughter at about 18 months in Chefoo.[28] Robert Morrison's first wife and child died at the birth and Gutzlaff's first wife and daughter soon after birth. Samuel

Gayley's youngest child died at 20 months in 1862,[29] Mrs Hall saw two children and a husband die of cholera and her remaining infant die on the voyage home in 1862, and Mrs Henderson's baby died soon after her husband in 1864.

Another missionary wife, Lucy Soothill, survived the birth of her second child on the boat that was taking her to hospital in Shanghai in 1887. On her return to Wenchow, she sought, like other wives, to run her household as it might have been run at home but with the added complication of local ingredients. Her major preoccupation was proper English bread. Yeast was unavailable but 'Cook and I knew the ingredients to perfection. "A pinch of hops, a slice or two of potato, and a teaspoonful of sugar"; these innocent items had to be boiled together, put in a bottle with a little of "the old leaven" and left to ferment till next day, when the mixture should, properly speaking, have been ready to use. All we produced by our combined efforts was bread too sour and bad to eat!'

Undeterred, she continued to tend her yeast like a baby. 'In the cold weather it was encased in flannel and kept by the stove for fear of a chill', but her husband described the resultant bread as 'So hard that not a chopper could cut it! Whereupon it served as a footstool. After that we threw it on the fire; but it refused to burn. A brick it went in; a brick it came out.' She was only rescued by the arrival of Ah Djang who had been dismissed for 'delinquencies' by his previous foreign master but who could make yeast and bread 'fit for a king', and butter from water-buffalo milk.

When her daughter was tiny, Mrs Soothill hired an amah to look after her but this relationship broke down when she discovered that the baby's skin was 'irritable and red and, when I kissed her, she had a salty, sharp taste'. The amah had been using 'extra strong American baking-powder' instead of talcum powder. Every aspect of daily life in the hot, humid south of China posed a problem: furniture had to be of hard teakwood 'into which the white ants could not sink their teeth whereas they gobbled up our ordinary local wood while we slept'. The springs and webbing of couches mouldered in the damp and gave way; the webbing was replaced with 'native leather because this would not rot', but then the couch squeaked whenever it was sat on. Carpets had to live 'in a moth-tight tin-lined box six months of the year'.[30] Textiles suffered other depredations. David Hill, a Wesleyan missionary in Hankow, reported in 1865 that 'the long-tailed rats of China had discovered that [dirty] English pocket handkerchiefs form for them a hearty midnight meal'.

In Chungking, food was the foreigners' main concern. There were, as yet, no wives to solve the problems of bread-making, so provisions had to be brought up-river. W.D. Spence, the consul at Ichang, was sent up as a temporary consul for a short visit in 1882 and took with him jam, marmalade (into Szechwan, a province filled with oranges, though not Seville oranges), butter, coffee beans, baking and curry powder, two casks of Apollinaris water and nine dozen bottles of wine and spirits, all these considered a perfectly reasonable quantity of provisions by his superiors.[31] Less well-supplied than the consuls, missionaries in Fukien province grew to enjoy a breakfast, not of coffee, porridge and cream but of tea and 'a great plateful of plain boiled rice, with buffalo milk and sugar . . . It is not a quarter as heating as porridge and it tastes much nicer.'[32] For some, there was no substitute for coffee; in order to round off meals in European style, Mr Soothill bought 'a large, second-hand coffee grinder at a sale in Shanghai . . . and with much ado succeeded in grinding the beans'. Unfortunately the coffee tasted vile because the grinder 'had previously been used by a chemist in Shanghai to grind his castor-oil seeds'.[33]

When not wrestling with tainted coffee-grinders, the gentleman of the house faced different problems from those of his wife. She might be isolated, perhaps the only white female for hundreds of miles. He, however, had to get on with other foreign residents, both at work and socially. It was not always easy. Arguments between the members of the often tiny foreign communities were common and sometimes involved the consular staff: at Chefoo, the consul C.T. Gardner engaged in a heated argument with his Russian neighbour over the smell from the Russian's cowshed. At Newchwang, the isolated and somewhat eccentric consul T.T. Meadows (younger brother of J.A.T. Meadows who had shown Robert Hart around Ningpo twenty years earlier and then left the service) had not noticed anything unusual about his consular assistant, J.J.M. Beatty. Beatty's social conduct was, however, obvious to others in the tiny foreign community and became so outrageous that in 1867 the leading British trader in the town, Mr Platt, protested to

Meadows. Apparently Beatty smoked opium with his servants 'and liked describing in company the ... details of his homosexual relations with them'. Meadows was compelled to act and became perhaps the only Victorian servant of the Foreign Office to have included four-letter words in an official dispatch.[34]

Though getting on with a restricted and not necessarily congenial group may have been difficult, isolation seems to have been the hardest aspect of much foreign life in China beyond the crowded cities of Shanghai and Tientsin. Protestants and Catholics, often the only foreign inhabitants of distant mission stations, were doctrinally opposed and unsympathetic to each other, and a couple of consular posts appear to have been particularly bad for the mental health of those who served there. The rapid descent into lunacy of A.S. Harvey after a posting at Pakhoi has already been noted. Pagoda Island, though down-river from Foochow and quite a busy place, was equally unsettling. One vice-consul, P.F. Hausser, became paranoid there in 1891, convinced that there was a plot to murder him and, in 1900, E.T.C. Werner was (not for the last time) involved in a 'phenomenally foolish quarrel' with the local doctor.[35]

Werner was, of course, quite lucky to have a doctor to argue with. In some treaty ports, medical help was frighteningly distant. Consul Meadows suffered a complicated accident near Newchwang in 1861 when dismounting from his pony. As he got down, the pony shook itself, setting off a loaded revolver in a saddle holster. Meadows was shot in the thigh, the bone shattered. A doctor, summoned from Tientsin, took eleven days to reach him.[36]

It was not only in consular outposts that medical help remained difficult to find (and sometimes hard to bear once it was found). The medical missionary James Cantlie of Hong Kong was consulted at a distance by William Tyler, an officer on one of the revenue cruisers of the Chinese Maritime Customs that tended light stations, surveyed the approaches to Shanghai, hunted pirates and pursued opium smugglers. When his captain fell ill near Hong Kong, Tyler sent Payne-Gallway, a junior officer, ashore in a pinnace with a letter for Dr Cantlie describing the symptoms. Payne-Gallway returned with a parcel and proceeded to 'cup' the captain. Blistering the ship's paintwork with ignited spirit, he applied a 'white-hot tumbler' to the captain's back, 'twisted it and bored right through the skin'. Captain Ross 'bore it like a Briton . . . his mouth full of feathers which he had bitten from his pillow'. Dr Cantlie approved the damage the next day and explained that the treatment 'was the equivalent of the cautery counter-irritant only given up by the profession on account of its painfulness'.[37]

Those who served in the Imperial Maritime Customs, like William Tyler, were amongst the loneliest foreigners in China, serving at sea or stationed in tiny ports, away from their compatriots. Where there were more than a handful of Customs officers, their habitual isolation often made them difficult companions. In Swatow, the harbour pilot, Mr Frewen, was a 'Free-thinker, total abstainer and a vegetarian', though he would mutter darkly that *in extremis* he would eat anything. None of these characteristics were shared with his fellow Customs officials. In the 1890s, for no known reason, he took against his colleagues, the Swatow pilots stationed at Double Island, and would walk for miles along the coast to intercept incoming vessels before they could reach the official pilots. It may have been because one of the pilots, a 'haggard, wild-looking man', was rumoured to survive only on gin. Another colleague, however, considered that even when terribly drunk he could still safely ride every local current and shoal.[38]

Attitudes to life and drink may have separated the coastal community in Swatow; in other places, politics divided them. Hosea Ballou Morse, Customs commissioner in Lungchow (Longzhou) near the border with French Indo-China, found that the other foreigners in town, with whom he might have dined and conversed, were French and unwelcoming. The French consul, in particular, kept well away from him, out of suspicion of what he considered to be the pro-English stance of the Ulsterman Robert Hart, the Inspector-General of Customs. Hart was, himself, a difficult man to get on with. In his dealings with Paul King over the collapse of his house, Hart showed himself to be unsympathetic to the discomfort of his subordinates. According to King, he even took pleasure in perversely posting them where they did not want to go; not necessarily the recipe for a happy life in an isolated Customs post.

IO

Conflicting Loyalties: The Imperial Maritime Customs Service

The Customs officers, employed by the Imperial Maritime Customs Service, were among the first arrivals in the new treaty ports. The service, established in 1854 on the initiative of the foreign consuls in Shanghai, in the aftermath of the Small Swords rebellion, was administered by the Chinese government but run by foreign, mainly British officials. Within a decade it was employing about 400 foreigners and some 1,000 Chinese. By 1916, of 38 Customs commissioners, 23 were British, 4 French, 2 American, 2 Russian, 2 Japanese, 2 Danish, 1 Dutch, 1 Norwegian and 1 Portuguese. There were also 13 British deputy commissioners, 4 French, 2 German, 1 American, 1 Norwegian and 1 Dutch.

Divided into 'outdoor' staff (tide-surveyors, harbour-masters, boat officers, tide-waiters and so on) and 'indoor' staff (commissioners, assistants and clerks), the Customs Service operated mainly in the treaty ports but it also expanded beyond them, sending foreign servants out to many more distant outposts. In 1864, there were Customs houses at 14 ports; by 1916 there were 41 Customs 'ports' with 35 'sub-offices' under them. They ranged from Harbin (Haerbin) and Newchwang in the frozen north to ports like Ichang and Chungking on the upper reaches of the Yangtze and small ports such as Ssumao on the Burmese border and Hoihow on Hainan Island.

One year after the Imperial Maritime Customs Service had been established, the first Inspector of Customs, Thomas Francis Wade, resigned to return to the Consular Service (he eventually became the first Professor of Chinese at Cambridge). He was succeeded by Horatio

Nelson Lay, the son of George Tradescant Lay who had served as consul at Canton, Foochow and Amoy. After their father's early death, Horatio Nelson (named for his mother's uncle) and his brother William Hyde Lay, at the age of 15 and 13 respectively, had been sent off to Hong Kong to learn Chinese with the Pomeranian ex-missionary turned Hong Kong colonial administrator, Karl Friedrich August Gutzlaff. Both had then entered the Consular Service. William Hyde Lay was to die in 1876 while consul in Chefoo.[1] Horatio Nelson served in the Shanghai consulate before transferring to the Customs Service and had strengthened his Chinese connections by marrying a daughter of Dr James Legge, a missionary and translator of the Chinese classics who was to become the first Professor of Chinese at Oxford.

Robert Hart, who was in turn to succeed Lay as Inspector of Customs, had first met him in Shanghai in 1854 when Hart was on his way to his first consular posting in Ningpo. He wrote of Horatio Nelson and his brother William Hyde, 'Indeed I like him and his brother very much.' He was to revise his opinion of William Hyde Lay when he made a trip to Ningpo:

> This morning in company with Mr Meadows we visited several parts of the city – all the temples and public buildings. Mr Meadows hinted to Lay that he should not push the Chinese about ... Mr L. makes quite a child of himself – throwing stones at the dogs – and makes enemies by ill-treatment. However he is a very nice Chap – but what a precocious youth he is! So fond of the other sex &c. His constitution I fear is getting damaged to some extent.[2]

Horatio Nelson Lay, who was also described by many (though not by Hart) as intemperate, was the first long-term British Inspector of Customs and the first to experience the conflicting demands of the position. Sir John Bowring, Governor of Hong Kong and Superintendent of Trade, though he had had reservations about Lay's appointment, came to see him as useful: 'There is no foreigner in China who has equal opportunities for ascertaining the feelings of the High Mandarins, and probably none who has so much of their confidence.' Lay in fact worked for the provincial authorities rather than the 'High Mandarins' but he was important to the Chinese, 'used as a source of information about the attitudes, information and objectives of the foreigners while also being used to control their commercial and trading operations'.[3] Indeed in carrying out his duties for his Chinese masters, he incurred the enmity of many British traders and was frequently attacked in the columns of the *North China Daily Herald.*

In this early period, no one was quite sure of the exact status of the Inspector of Customs, and Lay did nothing to clarify the matter. In 1856, at the height of the Taiping rebellion, which threatened the Chinese government above all but which also caused serious disruption to trade, he proposed the establishment of a flotilla of ships which would (like him) serve a variety of masters in a variety of ways. Run by the Chinese Customs, the ships would protect trade and Chinese government revenue by pursuing pirates and preventing smuggling, and could operate as gunboats against the insurgents. However, Lay also saw the flotilla as serving British interests in securing the Yangtze, for by then the British were beginning to press for the opening of the river to foreign, especially British, trade. In addition, the flotilla would relieve British taxpayers of the burden of supporting the Navy in China which hitherto had carried out most of the anti-smuggling and anti-piracy work.

Plans for the flotilla were shelved with the outbreak of the Second Opium War in 1857 when Lay impulsively abandoned his Chinese masters to accompany Lord Elgin to the north of China to press the Chinese for a second treaty. After some hesitation, Lord Elgin had invited Lay to join him as official interpreter, despite the fact that he was an employee of the Chinese government, a nicety that did not bother the British and which, under the circumstances, Lay's employers were in no position to resist. He appears to have spent much of his time drafting the commercial sections of the Tientsin treaty that legalized the traffic in opium (so that imperial revenue could be collected upon it) and that opened many more inland ports to foreign trade with the concomitant Customs establishments. When he did participate in negotiations, he was described by a later recruit to the Customs Service as hectoring and truculent.[4]

Lay's own description of his role in the Customs illustrates his ambivalent attitude towards his employers: 'My position was that of a foreigner engaged by the Chinese government to perform certain work *for* them but not *under* them. I need scarcely observe in passing that the notion of a gentleman acting *under* an Asiatic barbarian is pre-posterous.'[5] His Chinese employers were well aware of their employee's divided loyalties: 'Lay is the most crafty of the barbarians ... the said barbarian was afraid of being disliked by the ... various barbarians, so he accompanied them to Tientsin and made a great display of violence and ingratiated himself with the barbarian chief [Lord Elgin] in order to show his public spirit. When he returned to Shanghai, he was as compliant as ever in our employ.'[6]

Back in Shanghai in 1859, Lay had to expand his Customs Service considerably to staff the new treaty ports but he also devoted much effort to his proposed flotilla. Travelling to London, he commissioned a fleet of eight ships which sailed for China in 1863. The project foundered expensively and almost immediately over the question of command: the Chinese government wanted Chinese officers in command, Lay insisted on a British commander-in-chief. It was not even possible to recoup costs by selling off the ships in China since they might fall into the hands of Taiping insurgents, so the fleet was returned to India and England for dispersal and Lay was dismissed in November 1863.

On 27 November 1863, Hart recorded, 'Lay's note of 16th says the Chinese have dispensed with his services and appointed me to succeed him. Very pleasant to be at the top, but I have difficult times before me.' Two days later, he received his first dispatch from the Tsung-li yamen (Zongli yamen; the Chinese foreign ministry) but, before opening it, 'I ate my breakfast in my usual way, and then, as usual, read my morning chapter and prayed.' When he finally did turn his attention to the dis-patch, he found it contained letters from Sir Frederick Bruce, British Minister in Peking, and J. McLeavy Brown, assistant Chinese secretary at the British legation (and a fellow Ulsterman), congratulating him on his appointment, official notification from the Tsung-li yamen of his appointment, 'a dispatch from the Yamun relative to Tls. 375,000 to be borrowed by Lay, which I don't quite understand', and his first piece of business, 'a dispatch directing 2/10th Tonnage dues to be forwarded as heretofore by a Chinese Weiyuen'.[7]

Though Lay had described himself as a 'middleman between China and foreign Powers', using his influence 'honestly ... in the interest of all', the efficient imposition of Customs duties and the suppression of smuggling were not welcomed by the foreign merchants who were perhaps happier smuggling their opium and gambling (or bribing) their way through the traditional system. The same was true of many Chinese traders. A Hankow resident reported in 1863 on the method adopted by local boatmen to avoid the taxes and bribes demanded by provincial mandarins.

> To strike at the roots of rebellion they must shoot all the Mandarins, as long as that system of squeezing is carried on the people will always be discontented. Europeans are here very much against the wish of the Mandarins altho' the people do not dislike us so much. The reason is that we hurt the trade of the Mandarins a great deal, especially on the river here. The mandarins of each district have a fleet of Gun boats, 12 or 15 oars to each boat and every junk that passes they stop and demand £50, £100 or £200 as they think best. If they refuse, they take cargo and Junk too, but now since the river has been opened up, most of the trade is carried on by steamers and they are afraid to stop them. Chinamen trading with junks on the river will pay £100 or £200 to be towed so as to escape the Gun boats, which rather annoys the Mandarins.
>
> On one occasion in coming up the river we took a few junks in tow at Etching [Ichang] and just as we were getting under way, when they thought that all hands were otherwise occupied, one of those Gun boats pulled alongside the junks and 5 or 6 fellows from the Gun boat with rusty swords over their shoulder jumped on board. I saw them and having an idea what they were after, i.e. Squeezing money from the owner, I ran into the Cabin and brought out a Rifle which I pretended to be loading in a great hurry. If you had seen how they bolted, the owner of the Junk was most delighted.[8]

It was just such lawlessness that Robert Hart sought to bring under control when he took over the Imperial Maritime Customs Service as Inspector-General, but he was also conscious of the modernizing potential of the service. Thus in addition to their normal Customs work, Hart instructed his commissioners to collect statistics, to produce medical reports and materials for international exhibitions, to work on river conservancy and harbour improvements, and eventually to run the Chinese Post Office.

Conscious too of the ultimate Chineseness of the Customs Service, Hart also set out to train young Manchus and Chinese in foreign languages and foreign science, to prepare them for service in the Customs and the world outside. To this end he established the T'ung-wen-kuan (or Shared Culture College) in Peking in 1863, and a smaller version in Canton. He appointed its staff himself, sometimes detaching men from the Customs for the purpose.[9] However, not all the teachers or subjects were appreciated by the students. Emile Leverrier, formerly in charge of the Imperial Observatory in Paris and a somewhat truculent character (described in the local satirical press as a 'boule-dogue'), was appointed by Hart in 1866 to teach not, to his disappointment, astronomy, but French. He was supposed to have twenty-five students but frequently found no more than three present in class. In an attempt to get them to write their homework neatly (rather than scribbling on thin Chinese paper), he bought them pens and European paper but they made no use of them. In 1869, French lessons were terminated.[10] The college, however, survived. In 1933, John King Fairbank, author of *China's Response to the West, 1839–1923* and editor of Hart's papers, taught courses on the history of the Customs at the college, although he found that the

> Chinese direction of the college in Peking made it a training ground for bureaucrats. Foreigners in the service told me they favoured holding open examinations, which would pick up Chinese trained abroad and bring in men of calibre to be commissioners. But instead the college kept on producing clerks for the lower echelons ... I found little intellectual vitality among my students and spent little time with them.[11]

Despite this subsequent decline, Hart's concept was a grand one, going far beyond the original conception of a Customs administration. The Inspector-General ruled his personal empire for over forty years, finally retiring in 1909. Paul King, who himself served in the Customs for forty-seven years, was first introduced to Hart by his father at the Berkeley Hotel in St James's Street in London in 1866: 'I remember how he came forward from a dark corner of the room and shook hands with us in a curious shy manner.' He offered the young man an appointment as Fourth Assistant at the silver equivalent of £400 a year if he could pass an ordinary Civil Service examination.[12] However, it soon became apparent that Hart, 'the great IG', was also a man with a long memory and distinct prejudices. King's uncle, Colonel Man Stuart, had served in the Customs as private secretary to Horatio

Nelson Lay before his replacement by Hart. Man Stuart continued in the service as Hart's secretary but did not share 'the common deceit in the service' that Hart was a benevolent despot. 'Despot he certainly was, but his victims were rarely the objects of his benevolence.' Conscious that his uncle's views on Lay and Hart were not likely to assist his prospects, on his second meeting with Hart, Paul King mentioned that he was a very good swimmer, unaware that Hart hated all men of athletic tendencies and accomplishments. King, who devoted much of his memoirs to his sporting activities in China, felt that his chances of early promotion had been dashed. Indeed his advancement was very slow and on one occasion when he requested a promotion, Hart ignored the request and merely wrote to say, 'Dear King, you are transferred to Kowloon [in Hong Kong]. And let me tell you, you won't find it a bed of roses. Hart.'

On a later occasion, suffering from sprue and armed with a medical certificate in the hope of getting a posting by the sea, preferably at Shanghai, King called on Hart who had himself 'adopted the air of an invalid and sat with a blanket around his knees'. Hart's response was 'You can go to Ichang or you can have home sick leave. I have no other port for you.' Ichang was 1,000 miles up the Yangtze, sick leave meant enforced resignation, and there *was* another port available, as King observed:

> It was known that the man designated for Soochow, a place in close proximity to Shanghai, was anxious to return to Ichang, so a solution agreeable to two of his older employees only awaited a stroke of his pen! But no doubt, once again 'something within him' psycho-analysis perhaps could explain, kept him back from an obviously graceful act.

At the mercy of the IG, the King family were sent in 1898 to Hangchow. Though it is considered one of the most beautiful cities in China, with its great West Lake traversed by elegant dykes built by poet-governors of the past, King viewed his newly built Customs commissioner's house with justifiable foreboding. The veranda looked out over dreary swamps and they were informed by the local doctor that 'every time you open a window, you suck in malaria'. King's wife soon contracted the disease and King, though himself suffering from carbuncular boils, spent much time nursing her.

Whilst at Hangchow, King was ordered to perform a service for the Customs that underlined his position as a Chinese government servant rather than a British citizen. Prince Heinrich of Prussia, brother of Kaiser Wilhelm II, arrived in China in 1898 to lead a detachment of German troops in the taking of Kiaochow Bay in Shantung for the purpose of establishing a German 'area of interest' and to inaugurate the new German railway in the same province. He also visited Hangchow with his wife and there King was deputed to entertain him. King found him pleasant and, despite his mission, apparently rather depressed, fearing that Germany's actions in China would lead Britain and France to follow suit and carve up China between themselves. Anglo-German rivalries in China notwithstanding, King helped the Princess to buy dolls and toys for her children and took the Prince riding: 'he was inclined to ride rather recklessly, and did not know that in a Chinese street one must ride in the middle . . . else one might get a glancing blow on the head from the overhanging shop signs'.[13]

King's fellow Customs officer, Hosea Ballou Morse, was likewise involved in the reception of the Prince when he visited Hankow. It was fortunate that Morse did not have to entertain the Prince at home for he had just arrived and had discovered that in his residence 'there is not one plate – soup, meat, cheese or dessert'.[14] Instead Morse acted as adviser to the newly arrived governor, Chang Chih-tung. The governor was in a slight panic over the use of a yellow sedan-chair provided by the German consul for the Prince's procession through the streets, for it was thought that if a chair of the colour normally associated with the Chinese emperor was used by a foreigner it might provoke a riot and embarrassment to all sides. Morse advised that he offer the Prince variously coloured conveyances rather than forbid the use of yellow, for a prohibition might be seen as an insult by the German consul.

Not all Customs work was confined to China. In March 1866, Edward Bowra was sent by Hart to accompany Pin Chun, the Chinese Secretary of the Imperial Maritime Customs, on an overseas tour. They travelled to London, Paris, The Hague, Copenhagen, Stockholm, St Petersburg and Berlin before returning via Washington, San Francisco and Japan. Hart himself was with them for some of the time but was preoccupied with finding a bride, so he kept disappearing to Ireland where he found and married a Miss Bredon in August 1866. Bowra, too, though unable to leave the mission as easily as Hart, also managed to marry in London in August 1866 and took his bride with him on the return voyage. Though satisfactory in personal respects, the trip was not otherwise a success. The Chinese Secretary was elderly, homesick and not up to the endless improving visits to button factories, shipyards, mines, silk-weaving factories and museums, although he did seem to recover from his indisposition when offered lighter entertainments. At the Théâtre de l'Ambigu in Paris, so Pin recorded in his diary, he saw, 'Fifty or sixty females, actresses ... of whom one half were noticeable for good looks, the great majority being nude to the extent of half their persons'. In London, he turned down all official engagements on 18 May but 'managed ... to stagger ... as far as the Haymarket Theatre'. Two days later, 'he was too weak to visit St Paul's Cathedral or watch, at University College Hospital, a surgical operation by Sir James Fergusson, but by the evening he had recovered his strength sufficiently to face a performance at the Primrose Theatre'.

Bowra's next European venture under Hart's direction was to organize Chinese participation in the Vienna Exhibition of 1873. Though the Chinese emperor and British merchants in China had failed to rally to Prince Albert's call for Chinese exhibits for his Great Exhibition in 1851, Robert Hart was able to direct Customs staff to prepare exhibits for later 'universal' exhibitions. Edward Bowra was responsible for the transport and display of such raw materials and manufactures as peppermint oil, fireworks, joss-sticks, thirteen varieties of tea, five varieties of fan, medicinal centipedes and his own collection of Chinese wood-carvings.[15]

Apart from directing his Customs officers in foreign affairs, Hart also lent them out to Chinese enterprises as required. Hosea Ballou Morse, who served in the Customs in Shanghai, Hankow, Tientsin, Pakhoi and Kiungchow, was seconded by Hart in 1885 to advise the China Merchants' Shipping Company. The company had been set up in 1872, using steamships rather than sailing junks to compete with foreign steamships in China's coastal carrying trade. It had run into trouble with a market collapse in 1883 followed by the Sino-French War the next year, during which the ships had been nominally 'sold' to the old opium-trading enterprise Russell & Co. to avoid possible seizure by France. Morse was to organize the return of the ships and to prepare an audit of the company which had been heavily subsidized by the Chinese government. The company also owned much river-front land in many of the treaty ports and Morse tried to organize this more logically and to promote refrigeration to preserve perishable products in transit and in storage in the company's godowns. His efforts proved fruitless: 'When I say that a certain step may show loss in the present ... but will be greatly to the company's advantage in the future, I find no one will assume responsibility for anything except the immediate present; drifting is the sole policy and the future may care for itself.'[16]

Both Paul King and Morse also served under the German Gustav Detring, Customs commissioner at Tientsin. Detring remained in the same post for twenty-five years because he was liked and trusted by Li Hung-chang, by then governor of Chihli (Zhili) province (which included the capital, Peking) and the figure most associated with efforts to industrialize and modernize China. Hart had originally been convinced that Detring's lisp meant he would never speak Chinese properly and that therefore he would not be of much use. Indeed when recruiting Americans through the Customs commissioner Edward Bangs Drew, a Harvard graduate, Hart specified that he wanted young men 'with no lameness, stammering, deafness or bad sight ... who could write a fairly good clerkly hand and ... cipher quickly and correctly'. However, with an eye to Chinese political developments, Hart reversed his verdict, writing in 1881 that Detring

> is a first-class man – has done excellent work – has German proclivities of course, but is first of all for China, and he is more loyal to me than are most others; he naturally has more influence than anybody else with Li and Li is for the moment more go-ahead than any other man in China ... Li is the man for the moment, and D. is his right hand.

Under Detring, Morse supervised Customs dispatches and looked forward to winter when he 'closed the year's trade returns in the middle of December, and after they were off there was nothing to do except tend to the mails (tri-weekly), ride over the plains and work up private theatricals'. In the latter, Morse was very successful. Wearing a dress lent by Mrs William Forbes and playing the part of Miss D. Gruffin 'in love with Villikins' in *Villikins and his Dinah*, he 'was much in request as a dancing partner in the dance after the play, supplementing the other six ladies'. Not all his activities in Tientsin were as light-hearted. In the summer before his theatrical success, Morse had had to participate in a painful service on behalf of the Chinese government. In 1877–8 north China was stricken by famine, brought on by three years of drought and exacerbated by grain hoarding and corruption. As 90,000 refugees crowded into Tientsin, dying in their dozens daily, relief funds were collected and Detring dispatched Morse and a colleague to the countryside to distribute them. Morse recorded in his diary that in one village the many dogs

> had all been eaten … Sheng Taotai informed me that human flesh had certainly been eaten in Shansi, but not in Chihli. Children had of course been sold – especially girls – to be taken south … The appearance of the children is most horrible – mere bones, with the skin dried on them, pot bellies (their food is weeds and the bark of trees), faces pale, haggard, eyes staring.

An official report to Detring elaborated on the effects of the famine:

> A family presented themselves before us when we called, the father aged 60 and three sons aged from 25 to 40, four gaunt figures; the questions were asked, the register compared, the amount fixed and the father told to rise to receive his tickets. He could not do it; in that one minute, the old man, overcome by the excitement acting on his weakened frame, had died before us of starvation.[17]

A decade later, Paul King arrived in Tientsin to serve under Detring, to whom he reported every day 'all that was happening in the office. He never listened, as his mind was always full of schemes in which Customs business had little part, but he never criticized.' King was advised by his doctor not to go out and administer help to the refugees from another natural disaster, this time the flooding of the Tientsin plain, for smallpox was prevalent. Unfortunately, though taking the doctor's advice, he was one of the only two foreigners in Tientsin itself to catch smallpox. Once recovered, he and his wife enjoyed skating, dancing, ice-boating and 'pai-tzu' (ice-sledge) picnics. He also, as usual, indulged his passion for sport by setting up a gym in the Club where he and William McLeish, 'an old Dulwich master … boxed and whacked one another about with basket-handled single sticks to our hearts' content'. Gymnastics played a part in Christmas pantomimes. One resident,

J. Boyce-Kup, 'gave a most thrilling performance on the flying rings'. King, who was playing Harlequin, wisely checked the trap-door through which he was to make a flying leap and discovered that the two sailors deputed to catch him had disappeared, and Columbine 'was so tightly laced in by the stage-manager, Alfred Smith, that her internal economy gave way and she had such a pain inside as to necessitate the application of various "liquids" before she could go on at all'.[18] On a more serious occasion, a debate was organized during which Archdeacon Moule upheld 'the credibility of miracles' against Dr Jamieson ('pleading for the examination of all phenomena'). The debate so excited a young man sitting next to King that he developed violent religious mania and had to be placed under restraint. He was eventually shipped off home.

Tientsin and Shanghai offered a sizeable community, schools, churches, entertainments and access to doctors, hospitals and shops selling imported goods. However, many Customs commissioners were less fortunate in their postings. Hosea Ballou Morse, though promoted to the rank of commissioner, had to move to Pakhoi on the Kwangsi coast. Since the treaty port was inaccessible to steamers, which had to anchor beyond the harbour's sand-banks, and since most shipping from Haiphong in Indo-China went straight to Hainan Island and back, bypassing Pakhoi, there was almost nothing for a Customs officer to do. Instead Morse spent much of his time working up an address on 'Currency and Measures' for the North China Branch of the Royal Asiatic Society.

Mrs Morse organized her household as best she could. To Chinese servants, many foreign obsessions were incomprehensible and, indeed, foreigners might have found life easier had they adopted more Chinese ways. Chinese medicine holds that cold drinks are unhealthy and so the Chinese always drank boiled water, with or without tea-leaves. In a foreigner's household, where cool drinks were welcome in hot weather, water had to be boiled and filtered, or perhaps filtered, boiled and filtered a second time. Then it was essential to make sure that servants, who probably did not understand what all these processes were for, did not through negligence allow flies or dust to make their way into the boiled and filtered water. As a missionary's wife remarked, 'To tell a Boy once to do a thing is never enough. The perpetual daily alertness of the mistress, the repetition of instructions over many months is what finally produces care in the hygienic preparation of our food and cleaning of our rooms.' The preparation of locally available foods in the foreign style might also be a problem, particularly in such a tiny outpost as Pakhoi. Beef in the far south of China was 'aged water-buffalo' and mutton 'scrawny goats', and whilst Shanghainese cooks had had decades of experience in cooking for foreigners, this was not the case in Pakhoi. Despite all the filtering and boiling, it seems likely that Morse suffered intermittently from water-borne schistosomiasis.

The Morses left after a year and their next posting was to Tamsui on Formosa where Morse organized the building of bridges, pontoons and sheds, and the repair of roads damaged by typhoons. Much of his work there, fifty years after the First Opium War, was reminiscent of the very early days. A chestful of opium was stolen from the warehouse where 'official' opium was stored, so he set up a permanent guard on the godown. Like consuls in Fukien province in the 1860s, he also attempted to curb the kidnapping and export of women, advised local officials on the trade in the famous Oolong (Wulong) tea produced on the island, and tried, unsuccessfully, to promote and improve the local production of camphor in the face of competition from Japan.

Life in Tamsui was uncomfortable. The climate was hot and humid, even in winter when clothing mouldered. Mrs Morse collected and sketched local plants, and some specimens were sent to Kew, but she noted in her sketchbook that fevers had prevented her from carrying on throughout the summer and second winter. Morse with difficulty persuaded the IG that facilities were required for recreation and he built up a library of 200 volumes and had a tennis court laid out. The foreign community was small: Christmas Eve 1892 was spent at the home of the British consul W.S. Ayrton, the Morses were 'at home' on Christmas Day and New Year's Eve, and the harbour-master, Mr Trannock, gave a dinner on New Year's Day.

In 1897 Morse was sent to another godforsaken outpost at Lungchow, close to the border with Indo-China. Home life was no easier there than it had been in Tamsui. The Morses' luggage arrived three months after they did and they had to live on a small boat until a residence and Customs house were built. The town's foreign community consisted of the French consul, French missionaries and a few French businessmen;

there was no doctor and no hospital. The only other woman was the French consul's wife. To add to the impossibility of maintaining a genteel household in the humidity, Mrs Morse was being slowly poisoned by her head boy. The cook betrayed the head boy's activities to his employers, explaining that the boy 'had wanted to get better control of the household accounts', and the head boy was dismissed immediately. The only long-term effect on Mrs Morse was a not unnatural hatred of all things Chinese.[19]

Hardly had the poisoner been dispatched than the Morses were sent back to Pakhoi, a move which did nothing for Hosea Ballou's health. In less than a year they were moved on, to be replaced, to his horror, by a French Customs official. One wonders whether, with the French expanding their interests in neighbouring Indo-China, the new arrival would have remembered that his first allegiance was to China, not France.

One Customs servant who was conscious of where his loyalty should lie was the ex-naval officer, William Tyler, who spent much of his working life on the Customs ships but who was occasionally posted ashore on special secondment. He was in Shanghai in 1898 when the condition of the river approaches became the subject of serious discussion. 'Mr Hewett, the P. and O. Agent, a man prolific of ideas drew up a scheme ... and tried to get me to support it. But it was teeming with defects; it took away from China the sovereignty of the river; it required China to pay half the cost, and the only representation given to her on a board of nine was the Customs commissioner – a foreigner.' Some years later Tyler was happy to see a better scheme carried out although he still had to overcome the suspicion of the German consul-general in Shanghai that he was promoting British, rather than Chinese interests.[20]

By the end of the nineteenth century, the Imperial Customs was a far-reaching and fully professionalized organization. Men like Tyler commanded a fleet of ships patrolling the coast, guided by charts produced by the Customs and by buoys and light-houses set up and managed by the Customs. The Customs produced annual volumes on China's internal and external trade and a variety of special papers on aspects of production, taxation, medical conditions and transportation. It also ran the postal system (set up in 1896) and its officers continued to man dozens of ports, both inland and coastal.

With the advent of a modern Post Office and a wider network of tele-graph lines, communications began to improve. The first telegraph lines, set up in Shanghai in 1865, had been torn down, and the line from Shanghai to Hong Kong set up in 1871 by the Great Northern Telegraph Company had to be brought ashore in great secrecy. In 1881, the Chinese government allowed land lines to be erected and the network grew fast, although it was restricted to the major treaty ports. The last decades of the nineteenth century saw a concurrent growth in railway construction, whilst the passage of steamers up the Yangtze also increased the speed and efficiency of transportation.

The spread of Customs officers and the development of communica-tions across the country, beyond the normal confines of the treaty ports, was only paralleled by the growth of Christian missions in the interior of China. Though most of the treaty port hospitals were mission-run and churches and worship were important features of treaty port life, most missionaries were drawn to the goal of converting the millions of Chinese rather than serving their fellow-countrymen. Customs officers might feel that their lives were often lonely and uncomfortable but missionaries had it far worse.

II

A Mission to Convert

Most of the modern medical care available in China was provided by medical missionaries who arrived in increasing numbers after 1843, following the Treaty of Nanking. Though establishing hospitals in the major treaty ports, many missionaries voluntarily set out to man isolated stations in the interior of China where they hoped for closer access to the Chinese people as potential converts.

The Church had long been interested in China and when the Ming dynasty was overthrown by the Manchu Ch'ing dynasty in 1644, Jesuit missionaries began to establish themselves there. Like the Mongols before them, the Manchus in China were alien rulers, but they were less antagonistic towards foreigners, perhaps partly because they had to rely on non-Manchus to assist in government. The Jesuits found some favour at court through their astronomical skills. They translated the Chinese classics into Latin and astronomical works into Chinese and Manchu, and Father Giuseppe Castiglione served as a Western-style court painter and helped other Fathers to design palaces in Jesuit baroque style in the Yuan-ming-yuan (Garden of Perfect Brightness), one of the imperial summer retreats just outside Peking. Though they established churches in Peking, in Shensi (Shaanxi) province, in Fukien and, with the help of a local convert Hsu Kuang-ch'i, at Siccawei near Shanghai in the late seventeenth century, their success, their proximity to the court and their enthusiasm for Confucianism led to jealousy in Europe amongst the other Catholic missions and in 1773 the Pope suppressed the Order. By then, however, the Yung-cheng emperor had already issued a decree forbidding Christianity. Thus, whilst missionaries did not quite disappear from China, their influence at court was gone for ever and they were driven into hiding.

As the Yung-cheng edict was not revoked until the mid-nineteenth century, missionary activity in China during the eighteenth and early nineteenth century was difficult, dangerous and often achieved only through compromise. To some extent, the reopening of China to such activity by way of the treaty ports caused further difficulties, particularly to former Chinese converts to Catholicism. In the decades following the Yung-cheng edict, Chinese Catholics had continued to meet and worship, and their church had developed its own characteristics. In particular, women were awarded a position of some importance. From 1800 to 1850, the Nanking 'Catholic' Church was led by a widow, Ho Ta-kuan, who maintained the chapel, taught children, led prayers at Mass and supported visiting clergy.[1] The return of orthodox, celibate and male missionaries naturally meant the end of female church leadership and the re-establishment of foreign domination of the Chinese Church.

Protestants had no base to recapture nor any base from which to work. Some regarded the Roman Catholics with admiration, especially for their determination to penetrate the interior of China despite prohibitions in the period before the full 'opening' of China in 1860. 'Entering by stealth, living in concealment ... ever and anon meeting with imprisonment and torture, and death itself, they have presented a remarkable example of fidelity to their calling,' wrote the Protestant missionary Hudson Taylor.[2] The United Reform Church in Swatow took a sterner anti-Catholic line: 'Alas, China knows far more of Popery than of true Christianity, and if we ourselves dread the political influence of a religion which has an earthly head in an alien country, we can sympathize with the Chinese in their fear to some extent.'[3] From the earliest days, Catholic missionaries in China had adopted Chinese dress, even to the extent of attaching a false pigtail to their black silk skull-caps. Protestant missionaries, however, were divided on the matter.

A young Australian missionary, Nellie Saunders, had her own views:

> The opinions of missionaries in China appear to be divided on the question of the desirability or otherwise of adopting the native dress. At the ports where Europeans are constantly seen there may not be, perhaps, any necessity for doing this, and there may even be very strong reasons why it should not be done. But in the interior, where the sight of a

foreigner is a rarity, exciting intense curiosity and even, in some cases, terror, the rule would appear to be different.

Her reasoning was perhaps based on her experiences whilst on a trip into the interior from Foochow.

> One thing one has to remember is this, that in China you must not have a waist. They think an Englishwoman's figure nothing more or less than shocking. It is much the same to them as if we were to see a lady parading the streets in tights ... Now, though Mrs Stewart and I knew this, we forgot all about it, and both of us having on tight-fitting bodies were much commented on. Topsy, having on her out-door jacket, was all right, and Frances wears Chinese dress.[4]

Eventually, she herself adopted Chinese dress, writing to her mother on 4 January 1894, 'Chinese dress is so comfortable. I don't know how I shall ever care to go back to the old style; it is so light and loose; one can pile on any amount of clothes, and then there are no gloves or hats to bother about ... except in the summer-time when they all wear pith helmets – girls and all.' Poor Nellie never had to face a corset again for she was murdered the following year.

Before the Treaty of Tientsin, when foreigners were officially confined to the treaty ports, consuls despaired of controlling missionaries who were determined to break out and convert the Chinese masses in the hinterland, and even after 1860 Christianity and missionaries remained the cause of much consular concern. Anti-foreign views among the Chinese, already firmly entrenched, were exacerbated by the practices of some religious orders. Roman Catholic orphanages in particular were regarded with suspicion. Despite the care provided by the missions for many sick or abandoned children, and the useful skills such as embroidery that were taught there, many Chinese were sceptical of the Christian practice of baptism, believing that the bodies of dead or dying children, often taken in by the missionaries as a last act of charity, were being used for sinister practices. In one case Consul Robertson in Canton had to intercede with the local governor on behalf of a female Chinese Catholic convert who had been condemned to death on an accusation that she extracted babies' brains and eyes during baptism. It was not really Robertson's business but as the French consul was 'on the verge of insanity', the French bishop had turned to him for help, with some success.[5]

Throughout the second half of the nineteenth century, there were a succession of attacks on foreigners. The residents of Hankow and Canton in particular were regularly subjected to stonings, often the result of protests by the Chinese against the coolie trade, but it was the missionaries in the interior who suffered most. Far from the treaty ports with their police forces and volunteer armies, they and their Chinese converts were at the mercy of unsympathetic local provincial governors. In March and April 1860, Catholic orphanages, churches and converts' houses were attacked in Nanchang. In 1863, the Catholic church in Chungking was destroyed and the following year the French Catholic missionary François Mabileau was killed in Szechwan. In August 1868, 10,000 people attacked the Protestant China Inland Mission residences in Yangchow (Yangzhou): in reprisal Consul Medhurst in Shanghai ordered four gunboats to proceed up the Yangtze to Nanking to capture China's new steam warship. In January 1869, Mabileau's successor, Jean-François Rigaud, was burnt to death and a hundred Chinese Christians were murdered in Szechwan. Six months later more Chinese Christians and Catholic churches were attacked in Kweichow.

Rumours of evil practices in the matter of the baptism of children reached a pitch in Tientsin in June 1870, when a mob gathered not at the church of Notre Dame des Victoires nor at the hospital run by the French Sisters of Charity, but outside the French consulate. When he emerged to make a protest, Consul Fontanier was murdered. The consulate, church and hospital were all set on fire, the nuns and perhaps a hundred orphans being burnt to death. A French attaché from Peking and his wife also perished, as well as several Russian and French merchants who were killed by the mob when they tried to intervene. (The Protestant view, however, expressed in a dispatch from the British legation in Peking, was that the massacre 'was entirely the fault of the RC missionaries who endanger the British and American citizens' lives'.[6])

The sad catalogue of martyrdom did not end there. In May 1873, an American church was damaged in Jui-ch'ang (Ruichang) and, in the summer of the same year, Catholic missionaries and converts died in Ch'ien-ching (Qianjing); in 1883, more died in Yunnan province and in 1890 there were anti-Catholic riots in Ta-tz'u (Dazu). In 1891, the establishment of a Catholic orphanage provoked attacks on Catholics and Protestants in Wuhu on the Yangtze and there were similar attacks in Ichang and Wuhsi (Wuxi). In 1893, two Swedish missionaries were killed in Ma-ch'eng (Macheng) and two years later there were anti-Christian riots in Chengtu (Chengdu).

It was in that same year, 1895, that poor Nellie Saunders was killed at Ku-ch'eng (Gucheng) during a massacre of Christians by members of a sect who misleadingly called themselves the Vegetarians. A missionary child who survived the massacre later described what had happened in one of the houses attacked.

> Mildred and I were just outside the house ... picking ferns and flowers because it was Herbert's birthday and we were going to decorate the breakfast table. We saw men coming along ... Milly saw their spears and told me to run, but I was so frightened I lay in the grass, thinking perhaps they would not see me. The men did see me, and took hold of me and pulled me by my hair along towards the house. Just as we arrived there, I fell down. They then began beating me. I got away from them and ran to the back door. I tried to shut it, but could not at first, as the men put their sticks in; but afterwards succeeded and bolted it. Then I went into our bedroom and got under my bed. Mildred lay on her bed. Soon the men broke open the door, pulled off all the bed-clothes, opened the drawers, and took what they wanted; smashed windows and things; then began beating Mildred, and cut her with swords; afterwards they left the room. One man saw me under the bed as they were going out, and gave me a knock on the head with a stick. We next saw Topsy Saunders with her face very much cut, being walked backwards and forwards by the men who were asking her questions; and if they were not answered quickly they dug a spear into her ... We saw Nellie Saunders lying by the door moaning. From the window we saw four men outside the back door beating and killing the Kuniongs [Chinese women converts]. One Kuniong's head I saw quite smashed up in a corner ... Very soon ... I found the house on fire. I went back to tell Mildred, and we went into the nursery, where we found Herbert covered with blood, Lena lying on the ground (I think she was dead – she was covered with blood), with the baby beside her, and Evan sitting crying.[7]

In 1899, in Fan-ch'eng (Fancheng), up the Yangtze from Hankow, a Lutheran missionary, Halvar Ronning, was more fortunate. Ronning was pursued through the streets by an anti-foreign mob. As the gate-keeper barred the mission gates against the crowd, Ronning scrambled on to the wall. His skull-cap, to which his 'false queue' was firmly attached, was snatched off his head. Fortunately for him, the shock of this sudden hair-loss and the revelation that he wore a false queue caused the mood of the crowd to turn from brutality to hilarity and nothing further happened.[8]

Such assaults, though terrifying and often fatal, were nonetheless localized and for the most part unorchestrated affairs. Far worse was to follow. In 1899 and 1900 a series of concerted attacks on both missionaries and railways, each an obvious manifestation of foreign intrusion, marked the beginning of what came to be known as the Boxer rebellion. Whilst the Taiping rebellion of the mid-nineteenth century had been viewed almost as a spectator sport by many foreign residents in the areas affected, the Boxer rebellion terrified all foreigners in China, caused the death of several hundred missionaries (and many thousand Chinese Christians) and culminated in a siege in Peking where the entire legation quarter, filled with foreign ambassadors, ministers, hotels, post offices and shops, was terrorized and cut off from 20 June to 14 August 1900.[9]

Though the origins of Boxer beliefs and their ambitions remain unclear, it was evident from the beginning that anti-foreignism was a major component. Contemporary Chinese who opposed the movement referred to its adherents as *quanfei* or 'boxing bandits'. More formally, they were known as the *Yihetuan* or 'Militia united in righteousness'.[10] Foreigners simply called them 'Boxers'. The 'boxing' aspect arose from their practice of a form of martial art which was supposed to ensure spiritual protection: 'When you've reached the field of battle, as soon as the gods have entered your bodies you'll go up to heaven, and the devils [foreigners] will have no way to attack you,' bellowed one commander at his followers.[11]

Though the prevailing drought in north and north-east China, which caused enormous suffering as peasants were forced to abandon their desiccated fields, was probably one stimulus to the uprising, Boxer attacks focused not on local landlords and officials but on foreigners and foreign importations. On 10 June 1900, the Peking–Tientsin telegraph was cut. At the same time, Boxers destroyed the railway machine shops at Fengtai (on the outskirts of Peking) and local railway stations, and dug up as much of the Peking–Tientsin railway line as they could. The railways were obviously new and alien (and foreign-owned), but they were also thought to interfere with the *fengshui* or geomantic harmony of an area. Such was the fear of railways bringing topographical bad luck that the enormously powerful K'ung family (direct descendants of the sage Confucius) had managed to get the railway diverted in a great loop away from their home town of Ch'u-fu (Qufu) (which is still an inconveniently long way from the nearest station). Their reasoning was that the railway would 'shake the tomb of the Sage' and prevent the spirit of K'ung ancestors from resting in peace.[12] In an outbreak of anti-foreign hysteria, many Chinese also alleged that foreigners buried a dead (Chinese) body under each railway sleeper (a belief perhaps extrapolated from their suspicions over orphanages).

As well as aiming at the railway system, Boxers also attacked missions and missionaries and seem to have found powerful allies in their assault among some local provincial governors. The considerable number of books commemorating the massacre of Protestant missionary families in Taiyuan in 1900 (with angry titles like *Fire and Sword in Shansi* or the more defiant *A Thousand Miles of Miracles in China*)[13] all concur in their condemnation of the provincial governor, Yu-hsien. Governor of Shantung province when Boxers killed two German missionaries there in 1899, and removed from office as a result of German pressure, he was nonetheless appointed governor of Shansi (Shanxi) province in March 1900 despite missionary and ambassadorial protest. Not long after his arrival, Boxers appeared in Shansi (his enemies assumed he had brought them with him) and the rumour spread that foreigners and Christian converts were poisoning wells. Whilst Peking was under siege, 2,000 Chinese Christians and over 60 foreign missionaries were murdered in Shansi, 44 of them, including children, executed under the governor's personal supervision in his yamen in the grim, grey provincial capital of Taiyuan. Yu-hsien's open support for the Boxer rebellion was soon reflected at the highest level and on 21 June, perhaps believing that the means of ridding China of the foreign powers was at last at hand, the court renamed the Boxers 'righteous people' and absorbed them into the local militia: it also declared war on foreigners.[14]

Surviving missionaries from all parts of Shansi made their way across hostile country in two provinces to Hankow and safety, although the

journey itself killed a number of children and one woman survived only
to die in childbirth a few days after her arrival. The Boxer threat to
foreigners was confined to the provinces of Shantung, Shansi and
Chihli. Those in treaty ports in Szechwan, Fukien and the south were
unaffected personally, though disturbed at the menacing press reports:
the Siege of the Legations in Peking, as it became known, was front-
page news throughout much of the world. Such news was neither reas-
suring nor accurate. On 5 July 1900, the *New York Times* informed its
readers, 'All foreigners in Peking dead'; on 16 July it offered 'Details of
the Peking Tragedy – Foreigners all slain after a last heroic stand – shot
their women first'. In fact almost all survived.[15]

The nearby treaty port of Tientsin was also seriously affected by
the Boxer uprising and endured its own siege. On 17 June (before the
official declaration of war), Chinese troops began shelling the foreign
settlement, and within a few days many foreign residents had retreated
into Gordon Hall, the British town hall constructed in 1889 in the
Scottish baronial style with its battlemented skyline and, providentially,
'bombproof catacombs underneath'.[16] The Hall was named after
General Gordon, not to commemorate his efforts in curbing the
Taipings but because as a Royal Engineer he had fixed the boundaries
of the new concession after the Treaty of Tientsin.

The Tientsin volunteers, aided by a small force of Russian and
Japanese soldiers, held a perimeter ring against the Boxers, but the
streets of the foreign settlements were unsafe. Those who ventured out
faced a barrage of shots with bravado, 'anything less than the puncture
of one's hat or bicycle tyre by a bullet was considered of no especial
moment'. The foreign houses and buildings were solid: not proof
against bombs but largely impervious to bullets. Chinese houses in the
foreign settlements were the usual northern Chinese single-storeyed
mud and brick constructions with wood and paper windows. Flimsy
and little more than temporary dwellings, they were particularly vulnerable and were destroyed in their thousands. As in Peking, where the
highest casualties were suffered by Chinese Christians, so in Tientsin far
more Chinese – some Christian, some employees of foreign firms – died
than did foreign residents. Fired on by Chinese soldiers, their houses
within the foreign concessions were set on fire by the foreigners themselves who feared that they might harbour Boxers. One Chinese

resident described how, 'Day after day, my family members all lie on the floor on mats, the window lattices sealed off by wooden furniture to keep shells from entering.' Another saw the house next door shattered by a shell.

Boxers patrolled the streets outside the foreign concession, and there took their revenge on anyone or anything that seemed foreign. Local Chinese inhabitants were randomly identified as Christians and subjected to ordeals that were not so different from the methods used in medieval Europe to try witches. The accused had to burn pieces of paper and if the ashes rose upwards, they were deemed innocent. Those found guilty were killed, as were women with normal as opposed to bound feet since that suggested they had been in contact with foreigners. The pursuit of 'foreignness' meant that businesses had rapidly to change their names, eschewing the character *yang* (foreign) which had frequently been used for its connotations of newness, modernity and glamour. Churches and business premises selling foreign goods were burned. 'Foreign' kerosene lamps were banned and kerosene was poured away in the streets. The Boxers also issued a series of arbitrary regulations. Women, regarded as unclean, were ordered to stay indoors after dark and not to defile their courtyards by throwing out dirty water. Local Chinese were also ordered to cover their chimneys with red paper as protection against foreign shells and at the end of the fifth lunar month in 1900, the besieging Boxers effectively announced the abolition of June and July because the eighth month, which falls in August/September in the traditional Chinese calendar, was regarded as lucky, and the Boxers could not wait for it to arrive in the normal way.[17]

A combined foreign force of British, Japanese, Russian, American and French troops, assembled from divisions stationed in China, reached Tientsin on 14 June, and the city was taken. Relief among the foreign residents was not shared by many of the Chinese inhabitants of the treaty port, for Russian and German soldiers in particular embarked on a campaign of rape and terror. Hearing that valuables were sometimes hidden in coffins along with dead family members awaiting an auspicious date for burial, they broke open any coffins they could find and even dug through the cemetery, flinging bodies away to be eaten by stray dogs (according to Chinese beliefs, such a dispersal of body parts means eternal restlessness for the soul of the deceased). James Ricalton, an American photographer, recorded scenes of death in the city, foreign gentlemen posing beside dead Boxers on the city wall, and dead Boxers floating in the river in the French concession. Lines of decapitated Boxers were also the subject of a 'stereograph' by B.W. Kilburn.[18]

The siege of Peking was relieved on 14 August 1900 by an international force dispatched from Tientsin. The chancellor of the Japanese legation, Sugiyama Akira, had been killed on 11 June 1900, the German Minister Baron Freiherr Klemens von Ketteler on 20 June. At least 66 other foreigners had also been killed, 150 or more had been wounded, and Chinese Christians had died in uncounted hundreds.

One man, who as a loyal servant of the Chinese government might have presumed himself safe, had been compelled to leave his luxurious Peking house with its large garden where his own band played at garden parties. Sir Robert Hart, Inspector-General of the Imperial Maritime Customs and close adviser to the imperial household since 1863, lost everything: his house was destroyed, his belongings disappeared and he had to take refuge in the Legation Quarter. In August 1900, just after the relief of the siege, he wrote an essay about the events that had taken place, beginning, 'We cannot say we had no warning ...' He spoke of missionary arrogance, 'the arrangement by which missionaries were to ride in green chairs and be recognized as the equals of Governors and Viceroys', the refusal of Chinese Christians to take part in or share the expenses of village festivals and the interference of Roman Catholics in litigation. He wrote of the military seizure by the Germans of the port of Tsingtao (Qingdao) in 1897–8 and the increasing determination of the Chinese court to resist such foreign incursions. He also made it clear that though, at the beginning, the besieged had 'only the Boxers armed with sword and spear to fear', after 20 June 'rifles began to be used, and soldiers fired them' – imperial soldiers joining forces with the rebels once the Chinese government had officially espoused the Boxer cause.

Convinced that foreigners had only themselves to blame, Hart nonetheless took some pride in the way in which they had conducted themselves during the siege. 'Crowded numbers, limited accommodation, and the absence of everything in the shape of privacy, comfort, and ordinary convenience, were naturally disagreeable factors for a Peking summer, but the thought that all were in the same boat and must make the best of it ... inspired each and all with courage, resignation and sympathy.'[19]

Not everyone was full of sympathy. A young American, Mary Hooker, who was holidaying with her cousin (wife of the first secretary at the American legation in Peking), found herself trapped in the Siege of the Legations and also under fire from the wife of the American Minister, Mrs Conger, who was rather shocked to find her improperly dressed during an attack. 'Do you wish to be found undressed when the end comes?' Mrs Conger demanded. Mary Hooker thought that it made 'very little difference whether I was massacred in a pink silk dressing gown ... or whether I was in a golf skirt and shirt waist that I was in the habit of wearing in the day hours of this charming picnic'. Mary Hooker found it helped her morale to make light of things, and she shocked Mrs Conger by telling her, 'I was going to stay in bed unless something terrible happened when I should don my dressing gown and, with a pink bow of ribbon at my throat, await my massacre.'

Mary Hooker was relentlessly frivolous during the first weeks of the siege, listing the menu when Sir Robert Hart came to dine on tinned peas and two potatoes and 'broiled chicken procured at risk of cook's life'. She was unsentimental about horseflesh: 'Horse is the principal article of diet ... The May races having come off before the siege, most of the diplomats had not disposed of their horses and polo ponies and now the all-important question is not if "Cochon" will win more cups in future but whether his steak will be tender.'

But as the weather grew hotter and steamy with summer rain, her dancing partners began to die at the defences. 'Last night young Warren of the Customs was carried through the compound on the way to the hospital, his face almost entirely shot off. I knew him quite well – had danced with him often; he was a charming fellow. He died at daybreak this morning.' Nearly two months into the siege, 'Another European baby died yesterday, simply from lack of food. It lay in its little coffin looking so white and tired.'[20]

Retribution for the siege was severe. The court fled Peking, the Imperial Palace was occupied and sacked (as was the Summer Palace), Yu-hsien and many others were executed, others involved were ordered to commit suicide, the Taku forts were razed and the Chinese government was forced to repair damaged foreign property and pay an indemnity of 450 million taels ('the tael to be reckoned at three shillings'), a sum which was nearly twice the Ch'ing government's annual income.[21]

The suppression of the Boxer rebellion had far-reaching effects on traditional China. The splendid isolation of the Ch'ing court was broken for ever when the empress dowager (who had been forced to flee the capital in 1900) began in 1902 to hold receptions for the wives of foreign diplomats. The traditional examination system, by which officials were recruited through writing essays on Confucian subjects, began to break down as the result of a foreign stipulation in the Boxer protocol that no examinations should be held for five years in cities where anti-foreign atrocities had taken place. In 1905, the traditional examination system was abolished and the Chinese sought to establish a modern, national school system based on models seen abroad. The nationalism of the Boxers, expressed as anti-foreignism, was to some extent discarded as young Chinese looked critically at their traditional institutions and developed new theories of nationalism and modernization. Despite the empress dowager's international tea-parties, however, the same spirit of enquiry was not seen at court.

PART III

Advance and Retreat
1900–1943

12

From Boxers to Warlords

After the Boxer rebellion, the Chinese government, under the Manchu Ch'ing dynasty, was hopelessly enfeebled. It was also both out of touch and out of step with the rest of the world. It had been established in 1644, nearly two hundred years before the Treaty of Nanking and the opening of the first foreign treaty ports, and for the past fifty years had been unable to resist the increasing parcelling up of its territories into spheres of foreign 'interest' as well as effective foreign occupation. Though it is a simplistic view, it is difficult to look at China in 1900 and not be struck by the antiquated nature of its institutions, faced with the encroachments of the West and the growing ambitions of Japan. The disparity was evident even in the most superficial respects. In Japan, the emperor sometimes wore full Western dress; in China, the inappropriately titled 'Motherly and Auspicious' empress dowager and her court wore long embroidered robes, tottering on white platform-soled shoes in processions with richly dressed eunuchs. Such Westernization as there was – the full permitted extent of modernization – was firmly restricted to the treaty ports with their bank and office buildings, racecourses and railway stations.

There were Chinese who wanted to change China: K'ang Yu-wei, who as an official had been an adviser to the Kuang-hsu emperor, had advocated the establishment of a constitutional monarchy and sought to revive China by a reinterpretation of the Confucian classics and the presentation of Confucius as a political reformer; Chang Chih-tung, a senior official and provincial governor, promoted the building of railways and advocated educational reform and the adoption of Western military systems and machines; Li Hung-chang, another senior official who had led the imperial forces against the Taiping rebels, fostered the adoption of Western technology such as steamships, modern armaments, railways and telegraphs; and the empress dowager's own nephew, the Kuang-hsu emperor, who may well have been killed at her order in 1908, supported the ill-fated Hundred Days Reform movement in 1898 which advocated educational change, abolition of old-fashioned essay-writing in the civil service exam system, Western military training, the establishment of a Western-style university in Peking, budgetary and administrative reform, and the abolition of sinecure offices.[1] Conservative officials, however, resisted all such changes with vigour.

At the same time, external pressure on China continued. In 1897 Germany occupied Kiaochow Bay in Shantung as its own 'sphere of influence', whilst Russia and Japan, too, began to move in as they saw other nations developing their hold on a weakened China. For strategic and material reasons both were interested in the very north of China, the Liaotung peninsula where Russia had already occupied Port Arthur and the adjacent great plains of Manchuria, with their rich mineral deposits below fertile soil. In 1904, Russia and Japan went to war over this potential sphere of interest and in the following year Russia was defeated. The Japanese now took over the Russian lease on the Liaotung peninsula and control of the northern end of the Chinese Eastern Railway.

Inevitably, Sino-Japanese treaties and agreements had consequences for British interests. Changsha in Hunan province was opened as a treaty port in 1903 as a result of a Sino-Japanese treaty; the first British consul arrived there in 1905. Following on the German presence in Shantung, a British consulate was opened in the provincial capital in 1906, and in 1919, after the First World War when Japan took over Germany's Chinese territories, a British consulate was established in the coastal port of Tsingtao.

Russian, and later Japanese, intentions in Manchuria also needed monitoring, so British consulates were established at Mukden (Shenyang), the provincial capital, in 1906, at Antung (Andong) on the Korean border in 1908, and in the far north at Harbin in 1910. Antung was closed down eighteen months after opening and Harbin was frozen in for half the year.[2] The banquets and drinking imposed by the numerous Russians there made it a more than usually ruinous posting for British consuls who declared it the most expensive place in the Far East.

Mukden was a political post whose object was intelligence gathering; similar political posts aimed at monitoring other nations' interests were opened elsewhere in China in the early twentieth century. British interests in Szechwan, close to French Indo-China, were strengthened by the addition of a consulate in Chengtu, the provincial capital, in 1902. There, the consul dealt directly with the Chinese viceroy, attempted to counter French designs on the province and watched developments in Tibet, an area of great interest to British India. To monitor Tibetan developments more closely, a distant consular outpost in the far west of Szechwan, close to Tibet and inhabited by many Tibetans, was opened at Tachienlu (Dajianlu) in 1913. The first consul was L.M. King, son of Paul King who had served for many decades in the Chinese Customs. Tachienlu was one of the remotest of consulates, cold, desolate and mountainous, and accessible only by slow-moving yak caravans. Though King was occasionally joined by a British representative of the Government of India, the main social contact there was 'a semi-insane frontier commissioner', so it is not very surprising that King should have announced to the consul in Chengtu that he planned to marry a Tibetan and requested the consul to conduct the marriage service. The consul rudely refused, insulting letters were exchanged and an appalling row ensued. Though King was finally married (by a consular junior), he had to leave the service.[3]

Another short-lived consulate was established at Kongmoon (Jiangmen), up-river from Macao, in 1904. It closed the following year. A more successful establishment was that at Kashgar (Kashi), in the far west of China. Though technically on Chinese soil, it was staffed by the Indian Consular Service for it was considerably nearer India than Peking. It was, nevertheless, a vital link for travellers from China to India. Sir Aurel Stein, for example, who made three major trips to the Silk Road cities of China's westernmost province, shipped all the precious documents, artefacts and wall paintings he had acquired there back to London through the consul in Kashgar.[4]

Whilst the foreign powers competed for access to China, the suppression by the court of attempts at reform drove modernizers like K'ang Yu-wei and the young Western-trained doctor and revolutionary Sun

Yat-sen into voluntary or enforced exile abroad where their overseas Chinese compatriots, resident in Canada, America and Singapore, were more willing to support ideas for change in China. In China itself, the only modernization undertaken outside the treaty ports by the imperial government had been the development of more modern army regiments. Drilled in Western style, they were armed with weapons supplied by the descendants of the gun-runners of the early days, companies like Olof Wijke & Co. of 6 Kiangse Road, Shanghai, H.M. Schultz & Co. of Tientsin, Nanking and Tsingtao, and Messrs Telge & Schroeter of No. 16, The Bund, Shanghai (who furnished most of the Chinese torpedo flotilla), Von During, Wibel & Co. of Shanghai, Tientsin and Tsingtao, agents for the Erhardt gun works in Düsseldorf and the explosives produced by the Westfaelisch-Anhaltische Sprengstoff Act. Ges. in Berlin, and Hugo Reiss & Co. of 4 Canton Road, Shanghai, sole agents for the Birmingham small-arms manufacturer Webley & Scott.[5]

The 'modernized' army was led by General Yuan Shih-k'ai and was to form the base for his own ambitions. In 1908, the elderly empress dowager and her nephew, the Kuang-hsu emperor, died within two days of each other, and the 2-year-old Aisin-Gioro Puyi ascended the throne. With a minor as emperor, the Ch'ing government had little hope of restoring its fortunes, and a series of anti-dynastic movements culminated in an uprising in Wuhan (of which Hankow was part) in 1911, and the overthrow of the Ch'ing dynasty. In 1912 Sun Yat-sen, who had engineered many of these uprisings from abroad, was elected first President of the Republic of China and the young emperor was forced to abdicate. Sun, however, was soon outmanoeuvred by Yuan Shih-k'ai who set out to subvert the new republic and have himself proclaimed emperor. His ambitions proved short-lived, however, for he died in 1916. China now fell under the sway of warlords, some of them formerly leaders of Yuan's modern army and all of them enjoying virtual territorial autonomy with the allegiance of their own military forces.

The uncertainties of warlord rule were, for foreign residents, not very different from previous uncertainties. Though Eric Teichman (Chinese counsellor at the British legation in Peking) might write that, before the 1911 revolution, 'the foreigner could come and go through the length and breadth of the eighteen provinces of greater China proper in greater safety than in most countries of the world', the perception of those who had lived through anti-missionary riots and the Boxer uprising was probably rather different. Assessing the current situation Teichman continued: 'after the revolution, the collapse of local government and law and order over vast areas produced a situation in which in many districts it was impossible to venture on the roads without the risk of meeting bandits and being robbed or murdered or carried off and held for ransom'.[6]

For those outside China, warlord rule was even more difficult to grasp, involving as it did forgettable names and constantly shifting alliances. The American humorist S.J. Perelman complained,

> I just can't seem to tell those Chinese warlords apart. The trouble started a long time ago when Chiang, the Premier of China (have I made any mistakes so far?) went over to borrow a cup of opium from Chang and exchange gossip ... This Chang is 'Young' Chang and should not be confused with 'Old' Chang, his father, the one-time ruler of Manchuria ... Just when I had all this neatly pegged ... Chang decided to kidnap Chiang ... 'Young' Chang ('Old' Chang's son ...) offered to return the Generalissimo ... to Soong. At this point two more generals ... entered the scene. They might just as easily have been named Rosencrantz and Guildenstern but no; they had to be named Yang and Feng. Yang was a Chinese version of General Jubal A. Early, who hoped to hijack the whole enterprise; Feng, who is called the 'Christian Marshal' (as opposed to Feng, the Jewish marshal, I guess) had no real business there.[7]

Treaty port residents had slightly less trouble since they usually took notice only of the local warlord; many is the child who was given a 'warlord' medal by whoever happened to be in control in Peking or Tientsin.

The reaction of foreign residents to the 1911 revolution itself had been muted. It all appeared to be happening very far away. The greatest concern was expressed in the capital, although Cecil Bowra, a Customs officer stationed in Peking, noted that there was 'no anti-foreign element whatever in the insurrection and no cause for concern as to its repercussion on the Customs Service'.[8] The writer Hope Danby, resident in Peking, watched with horror as 'armies of coolies busily painted all the beautiful earth-red walls of the Forbidden City and imperial properties and temples with a violent Reckitt's Blue wash, and flags of blue and white were flown everywhere. It was strange what a difference the new colour scheme gave to the city, but fortunately nothing could be done about the golden roofs of the palaces.'[9] There was some effort to protect foreign interests: a detachment of 2,000 British, French, German, Japanese and American troops was sent to Peking in March 1912, on stand-by, but elsewhere matters went on much as usual. British troops took Yadong and Gyantse in Tibet in May, the Russians took I-li (Yili) in Sinkiang (Xinjiang) province in June and, with a nineteenth-century flourish, the British Minister issued a formal protest against Sun Yat-sen's ban on opium.

As a precaution, missionaries in far-flung outposts were called into the cities by their consuls. Grace Service, wife of an American missionary, together with the entire 'Anglo-Saxon' community in the Chengtu area, moved into the unfinished building of the Canadian mission hospital in September 1911. There they stayed until the end of November, with their sewing machines, entertainments and a concert. Though the Services' gardener came every day with armfuls of flowers – 'our chrysanthemums were never more prolific than that year' – a faint sense of urgency was conveyed by a strange communal effort to sew together an immense cloth chute from strips of rice sacking. 'The idea was to facilitate getting the women and children down from the city wall should we have to leave the city suddenly.' Mrs Service thought it a ridiculous idea and refused to participate (though such a system was to be used in an escape from Nanking in 1927). In her diary she recorded:

> *September 11th.* Fighting is reported from various places. Some say 1,000 or so were killed on the Tzechow Road, only about 50 *li* [a Chinese mile, one-third of an English mile] away from Chengtu.
> *October 4th.* Lucy Bell's birthday. Cook made a dandy coconut cake and we ... had tea together in the Assembly Room ... In the evening I knit. Bob played chess. We heard 130 bags of mail have arrived. Situation no better.[10]

In mid-November, they were all informed they could go home. Nothing had happened to them: some friendships were made in the cramped conditions and others, apparently, broken. In Shanghai, the

British consul Everard Fraser declared the International Settlement to be neutral and, apart from fighting around the arsenal outside the city, it was only the appearance of the new Nationalist flags that signified the change within the city. Charles Lepissier, French vice-consul (and member of a volunteer fire brigade called The Torrent), took photographs of revolutionary soldiers on the outskirts of Shanghai, carrying rifles and wearing Western uniforms of jacket and trousers and peaked cap but with their long pigtails still evident, some hanging down their backs, others tucked into their caps.[11] As soon as the 1911 revolution occurred, radicals had cut off this symbol of oppression, imposed when the Manchus came to power in 1644. It was therefore ironic to see revolutionary soldiers still wearing their hair long, but these were early days.

The outbreak of the First World War was to be a far greater preoccupation for foreign residents than any continuing turmoil in the China that lay beyond their concessions. Neutrality was not the order of the day. The British embassy in Peking received an anonymous letter accusing the Belgian lady who ran the Tientsin hat shop of being a German spy. From the German concession of Tsingtao, a noted local resident, Dr Gilbert Reid, wrote pro-German letters to the Tientsin press and when his birthday celebrations in 1917 were attended by 'the highest Chinese officials', the British Minister, Sir John Jordan, made a formal protest, for Reid (who was subsequently deported) was 'a person notoriously working in the interests of the enemy'.[12]

In Shanghai, the local German newspaper *Der Ostasiatische Lloyd* included reports on 'Operations at sea' and German invincibility: 'an engagement took place on the 29th February between the German auxiliary cruiser *Greif* and three British cruisers and one British destroyer. The *Greif* during the engagement torpedoed and sank one large British cruiser of about 15,000 tons. The *Greif* blew up herself' – a locution suggesting a somewhat careless invincibility.[13] Another journal, not obviously German but unquestionably pugnacious, *The War* (produced, however, from 33d Nanking Road, right on top of the *Ostasiatische Lloyd* which was at 33c), published a poem on a similarly nautical theme by Alexander Fuehr which ended with a challenge to Britain:

Where are your ships of yesterday?
Your ships of yesterday are where
Drake hurled the argosies of Spain
When to your pirates' noisome lair
He skulked with rapt, ill-gotten gain ...

On page 4 was an article entitled 'England on her knees'.

In our last number we drew attention to Putnam Weale's clever appeal
to the Chinese government for a division or two of picked Chinese soldiers to help England. Now it is whispered about in Shanghai that His
Britannic Majesty's consul has assembled the compradors of English
firms and urged them to subscribe to the English war-loan ... We
believed from the moment she declared war on Germany that England
would come to her present predicament of mendicant ... the obviously
conscious falseness of the present boasting is absolute proof that they
have lost the last vestige of self-respect and are ready for anything. Do
you remember the great ado with which the great English war-loan was
advertised a few weeks ago?

Another correspondent, Bernard B. Ridder, refuted the British claim
of 'Starving Germany' in an article which described bumper German
harvests. The paper's pages were also enlivened by advertisements. A
picture of a dog chasing a cat encouraged all to 'Read Wau-wau satiric
weekly' (likewise published from 33d Nanking Road), and Arnold
Karberg & Co. had in stock amperes, volt meters, Naumann sewing-
machines, dynamos, Koppel's light-rails and cars, and Glaeser's paints
and cranes, lathes and drills.[14]

In Tientsin, H.G.W. Woodhead, editor of the *Peking and Tientsin
Times,* fought back. He had already found himself in a difficult editor-
ial situation in Peking where he had worked for the *Peking Gazette*
which was financed by Alfred J. Eggeling (of the Deutsche Asiatische
Bank). In 1913 Eggeling maintained that 'there is no German interest
of capital in the paper ... So long as you follow the general policy of
supporting Yuan Shih-k'ai and the policy of centralization of the
government, I am perfectly indifferent whether you adopt a pro- or
anti-German policy, though I must in my own interests request you not
to attack the German Bank by name as long as I am associated with it.'
After the outbreak of war, however, Eggeling launched into a tirade
against Reuters for its pack of lies, and when Woodhead set a leader of

27. Advertising transformed the streets of Shanghai and Tientsin.
A local painter, in baggy trousers but with a fedora, paints an advertisement
for cosmetics on a Shanghai wall, *c.* 1930

28. Once drains, dairies, horse-racing and golf courses had been established in
the treaty ports, many other Western innovations were enthusiastically adopted
by local and foreign residents alike

29. Many Chinese grew rich in the treaty ports and led lives that reflected the mixed composition of the cities. Lo Hun-chun and his family lived in a grand brick house in Shanghai whose interior boasted separate Western and Chinese rooms and furnishings

30. The separation of Shanghai into International and French concessions,
each with its own police force, allowed some to dodge the various authorities and become
rich through opium, gambling or prostitution. The trappings of gangsterism were readily
available. This, however, is the car of the leader of the Pan-Asian Assembly photographed
in 1931 with driver, bodyguard and a news photographer

31. Riding was a favourite pastime of foreign residents in China from the earliest days. The staff of the Hongkong and Shanghai Bank's agency (with the agent's wife) were photographed outside the Bank house in Chefoo in 1935 on their China ponies

32. Because of the lack of foxes, many foreign residents took to paper-chasing in lieu of hunting. The Shanghai Paper-Hunt Club's exploits were recorded by the cartoonist Edmund Toeg. Ditches and other obstacles had to be negotiated and local residents were not always enthusiastic about the paper hunt's passage over their land and crops

33. A race meeting at the Tsingtao racecourse in the early 1930s demonstrates not only the fashionable interest in racing but also the increasing power of the Land of the Rising Sun. Japan had been granted all of Germany's former concessions in China (centred on Tsingtao and Shantung province) at the end of the First World War

34. China was a home-from-home and Caledonian balls were held in all the major treaty ports. One of the dancers shown here in Hong Kong in the 1930s remembered Caledonian balls in Hankow where her stepfather worked. He had been 'Chieftain' for a while in Hankow and when her mother was home in England, she acted as his 'Chieftainess'

35. The Chinese traditionally abstained from milk, disliking the taste and regarding it as a rather revolting by-product of the beast. When foreign families began to settle in China they established dairies wherever they could

36. For small Western children a Chinese amah was the centre of life. Here Jieh-jieh holds Pat Power, brought up with his brother Brian in Tientsin

37. Though some sent their small children home to boarding school, many children grew up in China and went to school there, enjoying (or not) the usual round of exams, festivals and plays. The American School in Peking, which had both Chinese and foreign pupils, organized an annual play

Ways of Travelling

Written and Illustrated by Mervyn L. Peake, of North China, aged 10½ years.

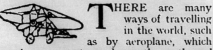

THERE are many ways of travelling in the world, such as by aeroplane, which travels at a great speed over the earth, and by submarine under the water. These were much used in the Great War.

In Africa the bullock wagon is used by the natives. It has a cover something like a Peking cart.

The camel is a very good journey maker, because it can carry very heavy loads, and also can go without food or drink for many days. One day when I was in a motorcar in Peking, when I was seven years old, I counted about one hundred camels.

I am now going to describe some ways by which I have travelled myself.

The first travelling I ever did was in a mountain-chair, from Kuling, when I was only five months old. I was carried shoulder high by four very sure-footed Chinese, while one false step on uneven ground would carry all five of us hundreds of feet below. From the chair I went on to a Yangtsze river steamer. The steamer was very nice and comfortable. I know, because I have been on some since. They are much smaller than any ordinary sea steamer.

From Changsha I went into a "native house-boat" or junk for several hundreds of miles to Hengchow.

The Chinese junk can travel in four different ways. Firstly, the boatmen can pull up the sails so that the wind catches them and then the boat goes very fast. secondly, the boatmen go on to the shore and pull the junk along by ropes. That is called tracking. They also can take long poles and walk up and down the deck pushing them into the mud, shouting "Hey-ho."

This is called poling. The fourth way is to paddle or row with long oars to get along when the water is very deep. When the wind is blowing hard against, then they have to tie up to the shore until the wind is over. Once the boat that I was on was stuck in the Tung-Ting lake and for ten days we could not get away because of the wind.

The rickshas are about the commonest ways of travelling in the ports of China. They are like a chair with wheels, drawn by a man between two shafts. They are very convenient to go to any place, not very far away, for a few coppers.

I used to go to school on a donkey, and it was great fun, because he used to gallop like anything, but now I go to school on a bicycle. It is very useful for getting about on nice smooth roads, but one must look out for punctures.

I once rode in a Peking cart in Tsang-Chow. There is a mule between two shafts pulling a covered over cart. The cart has no springs, so that it bumps terribly, so that it makes your bones very sore.

The driver sits on the shafts very near the mule's tail. The people inside are usually very cramped.

I have been on many train journeys, but my longest was from China across Siberia to England. It took us just twelve days from Tientsin to London. We passed through Russia and we had Russian tea. Many of the Russian women sold us eatables like bread, milk and eggs.

My longest sea trip was from England to China in a Japanese steamer around the Cape. The whole journey took two months, and it was pretty risky because at that time the war was on and the German submarines were out.

Motor-cars are not at all rare in the streets of China now.

But the usual mode of travelling is on your feet, and it is generally the most convenient and the best.

---

38. The artist and writer Mervyn Peake, whose father was a missionary, spent his early childhood in Tientsin, with summer sorties to the mountain resort of Kuling. The travelling life of a foreign child in China is reflected in an early article, written and skilfully illustrated at the age of 10

39. Apart from the mountain resorts, there was also the seaside resort of Peitaiho where many of the residents of north China, in particular, repaired during the hot and humid summers. The Talati family's beach-hut is a sort of Chinese pavilion with a boss at the apex and upturned eaves

40. Summer holiday resorts were very important, especially for missionary families who were often separated for much of the year between inaccessible mission station and boarding school at Chefoo. The resorts offered tennis, swimming and many organized activities for children and parents. A group photograph in summer holiday clothes taken at Mokanshan, 1930s

KULING, Ki., 1934

AMERICAN CHURCH MISS.—
See Missions Section

貝 克 爾
Baker, Henry E.
Civil Engineer
West Valley

道 正 甘
Kan-chen-tao
Berkin, John
*Surveyor, Engineer, and Real
Estate Agent*
Lot 37A TA Berkin
Berkin, John
Berkin, C. M.
Representative of—
Hongkong Fire Insurance
Co., Ld.

Canossian Institute
Lot 61B Central Avenue

中 華 抽 繡 公 司
*Chung-hua-chou-hsiu-
kung-sze*
China Embroidery Co.
*Manufacturers and Exporters
of Swatow Drawn Thread
Work, Mosaic Work, Cross-
stitch Work, Underwear,
etc. (Wholesale and Retail)*
Summer Branch: 36A Kuling
Head Office :
20 Broadway, Shanghai

CHINA EMBROIDERY—cont.
Factory :
11 Siang Yap-st., Swatow
Ong Pek Liang, gen. mgr.
Ong Heo Yu, mgr.

CHRISTIAN MISSIONS IN
MANY LANDS.—See Mis-
sions Section

翰 約 都
Duff & Co., J. L.
*Provision Manufacturers and
Merchants :   Forwarding
and Commission Agents*
Duff, J. L.
Duff, J. F.

僊 客 岩 寓
Sien-ngai-keh-yu
Fairy Glen
Private Hotel
J. L. Duff & Co., agents and
managers

Kuling American School
Allgood, Roy, M.A., B.SC.,
headmaster
Allgood, Mrs. Roy, R.N.,
home mgr.
Day, Dr. Clarence B., PH.D.,
M.A., B.D., chaplain
Day, Mrs C. B., B.A.,
grades, music

KULING AMERICAN
SCHOOL—cont.
Ingram, Miss Kathryn,
B.A., lower grades
Ekvall, Miss Grace, B.A.,
lower grades
Hann, Miss Anne, nurse
Lauridsen, Frank P., B.A.,
mathematics and Boy
Scouts   [and music
Rohde, Mrs. R., French
Tapley, Miss Alice M.,
dietitian
Tooker, Dr. F. J., res.
phys.
Townsend, S. R., Latin,
French
Townsend, Mrs. S. R.,
violin, general science
Turner, E. A., M.A., LL.B.,
asst. headmaster, athle-
tics, boys' house master
Turner, Mrs. E. A., PH.B.
Underwood, Rev. Richard
S., M.A., English

Kuling British School
*Boarding and Day School for
Girls and Boys*
Lot 37A
Berkin, C. M., sec.

**Kuling Community
Hospital**
*General Hospital for
Foreigners and Chinese*
Tooker, Fred, J., M.D., hon.
med. supt.
Lewis, S, C., M.D., res.
physician

Kuling Estate Council
Johnson, Rev. Wm. R.,
chrmn.
Tooker, Dr. F. J., vice-chrmn.
Craighill, Rev. L. R., hon.
treas.
Johannaber, Rev. C. F., hon.
Anderson, Rev. D. F. [sec.
Franklin, Rev. E. C.
Tyng, Rev. W.
Wahlquist, Rev. D. R.
Wu, Dr. T. P.
Allgood, R.
Berkin, John
Wong Kwong, Mrs.
General Secretary—
Arndt, B.

嶺 牯 華 中 普 仁 醫 院
Kuling Medical Mission
Hospitals for Chinese
Sun, T. W., M.D., res. physi-
cian   [med. supt.
Tooker, Dr. Mary F., hon.

**Kuling Private
Sanatorium**
Lot 65 TA Nizreb
Berzin, Dr. A., med. dir.
Hambleton, Mrs. R. L.,
R.N. (U.S.A)   [(U.S.A.),
Sutherland, Miss J., R.N.,

牯 嶺 備 辦 公 司
Kuling Store
General Provision Dealers
Lot 36
Duff, J. L., propr.
Hsin, C. F., mgr.
Hsia, C. K.
Sole Agents—
J. L. Duff & Co.'s "Kuling
Brand" Preserved Provi-
sions

普 通 公 司
Pu-tong-kung-sze
Kuling Universal Agency
House Agency, Insurance
36A Kuling TA Universal
Herbert, G., F.R.G.S., F.R.C.I.,
mgr.

麗 昌 照 相 號 牯 嶺 支 店
*Lai-chong-chau-seang-ho-
ku-ling-che-din*
Lai Chong Studio
*Photographers · Developing,
Printing and Enlarging*
Liang, K. C., mgr.

李 博 德
Li-po-teh
Lipporte, J. H.
*Kuling Real Estate General
Agent and Architect ; Fire
Insurance Agent*
89 Central-av.
Tel 19
TA Lipporte
Lipporte, J. H.
Lipporte, H. H.
Gittins, J. S.
Agent for—
Heywood, Wilkinson &
Clark
Dollar Steamship Lines

Redcroft School
Redcroft, Lot 20
Gilbertson, Miss Ruth, B.A.
Anderson, Miss Esther,
B.A.
Ekstrand, Miss Dorothy
Landahl, Miss Lillian, B.A.
Lindell, Mrs. Selma
Anderson, Palmer I., B.A.,
and Mrs.
Myers, Miss Margaret, B.A.
Shirley, Miss Alma

41. The mountain summer resort of Kuling was a real-estate project masterminded by the ex-missionary Edward Little. Though created primarily for missionaries and missionary organizations, Kuling was served by many other institutions, from the American School to photographic studios and general stores

42. Many foreign residents ignored the fact that they were living in China. But below their mansion flats in purpose-built tower blocks local residents also dwelt. William MacQuitty, working for Shell in China in the late 1930s, photographed refugees living near him, the children playing diabolo in the shadow of skyscrapers, with their cloth shoes scrubbed and drying on the fence, and bamboo poles thrust through the sleeves of their newly washed jackets

43. Natural disasters were not uncommon in China, often causing tremendous havoc and destruction. The Hongkong and Shanghai Bank in Hankow withstood the Yangtze floods of 1931 when the Bund became a waterway with the highest water levels seen since records began in the 1860s. Nearly 100 million Chinese suffered from the effects of the floods

44. Some of the foreign buildings in China's treaty ports are more eccentric than anything that might be seen at home. This fairy-tale castle was built by Eric Moller, a Swedish inhabitant of Shanghai

45. Other treaty port residents built themselves the sort of palatial home they might have inhabited had they lived in Godalming. Stockbroker Tudor was much favoured in Shanghai's outskirts. H.E. Morriss, owner of the *North China Daily News,* built himself this estate on the Avenue Père Robert in the French Concession

46. Here dressed as a Buddhist monk, the con-man and adventurer Trebitsch Lincoln was one of those who found China's distance and lack of coherent policing something of a relief when they had to leave Europe or America fast. Trebitsch Lincoln, briefly MP for Darlington until financial scandal forced him to resign his seat, was involved in further financial and political scandals in America and in most countries in Europe and ended up in China where he became a Buddhist monk. Rare in his enthusiastic support for the Japanese invaders, he died in Shanghai in 1943, safe from internment as an Austrian citizen

47. Sir Edmund Trelawney Backhouse, photographed as a sage, arrived in China to escape vast debts incurred at Oxford. He confused the Bodleian Library by offering generous benefactions of important Chinese palace editions but eventually sent material of little value; he also defrauded arms dealers and wrote two extraordinary pornographic 'memoirs'. Marked as a 'suspicious person' by the British embassy, he died in Peking in 1944

48. Among visitors to China in the 1930s were Harold Acton, Osbert Sitwell and Robert Byron. Acton lived and worked in Peking, teaching English literature at Peking University. Here he is photographed (*back row, second from the left*) in front of a typical Peking courtyard house surrounded by fellow teachers and other foreign researchers

49. George Bernard Shaw, invited to China by a progressive group, spent a day in Shanghai where he met the venerable ex-Chancellor of Peking University (*right*) and the writer Lu Hsun. Lu Hsun's elegant essays and memoirs remain popular in China today but when he met Shaw (not a tall man), he was self-conscious about his height

50. Sir Reginald Fleming Johnston (1874–1938), *c.* 1920. Johnston served in the Hong Kong colonial service before being sent in 1904 to Weihaiwei as second-in-command to Sir James Stewart Lockhart. From there he was dispatched to act as tutor to the last emperor of China, Puyi, from 1918 to 1925

51. Shanghai rioters set fire to a British diplomat's car in 1905. This riot was provoked by a British judge overruling a Chinese colleague in the Mixed Court but it was part of a long series of boycotts and attacks on foreign businesses provoked by American Exclusion Acts which discriminated against Chinese immigrants and spurred the growth of Chinese nationalism in the twentieth century

52. An attack on the British concession in Hankow, 1925. All the Yangtze treaty ports suffered such attacks in 1925–6, complicated by Chiang Kai-shek's march northwards during which Hankow was taken from the local warlord in 1926. In 1927, the concessions in Hankow and Kiukiang were returned to the Chinese

53. Japanese bombs fall on Shanghai in 1932. The Japanese had invaded Manchuria in 1931 but this particular attack on Shanghai was brief as they concentrated on the invasion of north China, taking Peking in 1937 and most of eastern China in 1938 as part of their plan to establish the 'Greater East Asian Co-Prosperity Sphere'. It had very little 'co-prosperity' in it from the Chinese point of view

54. Eric Cumine's cartoon of 'How the Japs had us coming and going' from *Lunghua Cackles*. Foreign residents of China were interned from 1942 in a series of camps across China. They went off to internment dressed in their warmest clothes, carrying suitcases and packages, but four years later, released in the summer and considerably thinner, they wore home-made shorts and tops, their few surviving possessions stuffed into baskets and string bags. By the time they were released, the remaining foreign concessions had been returned to China

55. The official view of the arrival of foreigners in China, in a painting from a Canton museum, 1970s. Three foreign sailing ships, loaded with opium and recklessly firing cannon, are attacked by valiant peasants who fight with one hand raised in a clenched fist. Some foreigners who have attempted to land are driven back to the sea, fleeing in terror

56. In many of the old treaty ports, the only reminders of the century of foreign occupation are the solid Western-style houses which still stand today, although their occupants are very different. The former Shanghai home of Benjamin Ezra, a businessman whose family came from Baghdad and who co-founded the English-language Zionist newspaper *Israel's Messenger*, is now part of the People's Armed Police compound. The European pitched roofs with chimneys and the broad verandas surrounding the house recall the earliest treaty port style of architecture, developed in Macao in the late eighteenth century

his own entitled 'The Truth about Germany' against a scurrilous pamphlet of German origin entitled 'The Truth about Great Britain', he received a 'hysterical screed from Mr Eggeling informing me that he was not going to have Germany attacked when she was down on her back'.[15]

Woodhead enjoyed some aspects of the war. In 1915, he greeted the new German Minister, Admiral von Hintze, with posters all over Peking and Tientsin which read 'Hintze's 57 Varieties', and he marked the Armistice with posters printed in red ink reading simply, 'Der Tag!' ('The Day!'). He also helped to organize food parcels for British prisoners-of-war in Europe and was pleased to note that though the German community had started such a scheme earlier, their parcels were routed through Russia where the Russians insisted that there must be a parallel address in the Cyrillic script. It transpired that the '*soi-disant* German Pole' who wrote the Russian addresses 'had been addressing all parcels to friends in Russia'.[16]

In Shanghai, Henri, brother of the vice-consul Charles Lepissier, was one of the twenty-six '*Français de Changaï morts pour la Patrie*' whose names were carved on the war memorial.[17] Though China was neutral, that did not prevent the combatants from fighting on her territory. Japan declared war on Germany on 23 August 1914 and moved on 'German' Shantung province. In October, Japanese troops occupied the Bavarian-style railway station at Tsinan (Jinan) and in November they took Tsingtao, capturing the 2,300-strong German garrison.[18] Japan's intentions were clear. At Versailles during the peace conference that followed the end of the war, Japan demanded all Germany's Chinese territory. Despite strong protest from the Chinese government, her demands were granted by the Allies on 30 April 1919. This action enraged and united China's students and intellectuals, drawing them into a cultural reform movement, called the May Fourth movement after the day of its first mass demonstration in Peking.

They were not the only group to protest. From the beginning of the twentieth century, workers and Chinese residents in the treaty ports had led a series of strikes and boycotts directed against the foreign powers. In 1905, there was a boycott of American firms, in protest over increasingly stringent laws and rough treatment of Chinese immigrants in America. Later in the same year, the Mixed Court Riots broke out in

Shanghai. The Mixed Court which dealt with cases in which foreigners were either directly or indirectly involved was presided over by a Chinese magistrate with a foreign consular assessor in attendance. In 1905 a British consular assessor overruled the Chinese magistrate over the imprisonment of fifteen Chinese girls, thought to have been procured as prostitutes. On 22 December, the *North China Daily Herald* reported that in the Nanking Road

> Rickshaws were overturned. A foreign lady was hustled and her cloak torn off. A motor car belonging to G.D. Pitzipios, the British vice-consul, came along, the crowd seized it, maltreated the occupants, turned the car over and set it on fire ... Several foreigners on bicycles were stopped and their machines thrown onto the bonfire ... Then the mob turned their attention to the Town Hall, which they stoned, smashing the windows. A body of police ... arrived and were greeted with a volley of stones. They fired two rounds of blank cartridge without producing any effect on the mob and then fired a round of ball cartridge killing three men.[19]

There were further strikes and protests by Chinese businessmen and workers in Shanghai in June 1919, after student protest against Japan's takeover of the German concession there. In Foochow in November, many Chinese students supporting a boycott of Japanese goods were injured and one killed when Japanese residents turned on them. Strikes and boycotts were not only political: in 1921, 10,000 workers in the British-American Tobacco Company in Shanghai went on strike over wages and conditions.

Against this background of increasing student and worker unrest, and in the absence of a strong central government, banditry flourished. In 1923 the Blue Express, the Chinese *train de luxe* plying between Shanghai and the capital, was derailed by bandits in the mountains of Shantung. British, American, French, Italian, German and Danish tourists and members of the Shanghai community were held for a month at Lin-ch'eng (Lincheng) before frantic negotiations secured their release. Two years later, the Tientsin newspaper editor H.G.W. Woodhead was captured at sea by pirates when *en route* to Weihaiwei. The captain of the *Tungchow* was shot and Chinese and foreign passengers' possessions looted before the ship was abandoned by the pirates near Hong Kong.[20]

Worker unrest in the 1920s came to a head on 30 May 1925. For some months, Chinese workers in Japanese-owned textile mills in Shanghai had been demonstrating for higher wages and improved conditions. Though the conditions in which they worked were often better than those in local mills, there was the added irritant of foreign ownership. On 15 May, a Chinese striker was killed by his Japanese foreman. A major protest march was organized on 30 May and during it police from the International Settlement killed nine demonstrators and wounded fifty or so more. In reaction to what had happened in Shanghai, strikes and demonstrations spread throughout China, especially in the treaty ports (martial law was declared in Shanghai and twenty-six gunboats arrived full of Marines from the concessionary powers).

In Amoy, from the upstairs windows of Butterfield & Swire's offices, the British consul Meyrick Hewlett watched the demonstration of 'scholars, boys and girls, down to tiny mites of very young age' yelling, 'Annihilate the Imperialists, Abolish Consuls, Give us back the Concessions, Britons have slain our compatriots in Shanghai'.[21] Hewlett decided that the arrival of a British gunboat would be inflammatory but all foreign women and children were assembled to take flight in a ship 'kindly detained by the Netherlands consul in case of need'. Hewlett negotiated with the principal agitator, a student aged 27 named Lim Tiong-hock who was organizing a strike and a boycott of all British goods: 'I ... pleaded with him to believe that the British government had really no wish to retain many of the concessions, and could he not believe they were really better held in trust by us, seeing the perfect manner in which they had been developed and administered.'

On 27 July, at 3 a.m., Hewlett awoke to find a man in his bedroom and assumed the worst; six hours later, a Chinese, secretary of the municipal council, was shot, and Lim Tiong-hock was murdered in Amoy city on the 28th. Although in the event the threatened strike in Amoy never took place, at the neighbouring port of Swatow all the servants at the consulate abandoned their posts. In the interests of comfort, Hewlett took action: 'I was able with the help of a Dutch skipper to smuggle in to my colleague there a boy, cook and coolie.'[22] Not only servants were smuggled in to Swatow: for many months, all provisions had to be imported from Hong Kong as local shops and markets refused to serve foreigners.

If the worst was avoided at Amoy, there was more serious trouble elsewhere. In Ningpo, the shop which stocked provisions for the foreign community was destroyed, as was the junior Customs mess (where two young assistants hid in huge water jars). In Chungking, women and children were evacuated and after the consulate was damaged, Consul H.A.F.B. Archer worked from a small gunboat. Anti-foreignism was also rife in Chengtu. A Canadian missionary woman was beheaded there and an American woman set upon in her rickshaw. On the Yangtze, the British consulate at Chinkiang was besieged for four hours and women and children were evacuated by ship to Shanghai; at Kiukiang, there was an attempt to wreck the consulate and set it on fire; and at Hankow, the British navy was involved in a skirmish in which several demonstrators were killed.

In Canton, a demonstration on 23 June appeared to have passed off peacefully until firing broke out. The British consul J.W. Jamieson said it came from the French concession where 'the French had lost their heads'.[23] Several dozen foreigners were killed or wounded, and over two hundred Chinese died. Jamieson, like Hewlett in Amoy, advised against a naval blockade (shades of a century or more earlier) but he was censured by the newly arrived legation counsellor, Owen O'Malley, who accused him of being unnecessarily afraid of assassination and drunk from lunch-time onwards.

In the wake of the events of 23 June, most foreign women and children living in Canton were sent away. Those who stayed on – 'consular officials, bank employees, heads of great oil companies' – had to fend for themselves, for all the Chinese servants had fled.[24] They lived from moment to moment: 'every foreigner must have a small bag ready and packed with toilet necessities and a change of clothing, and be prepared at any hour of the day or night, to board one or the other of the foreign gunboats anchored just off Shameen jetty'. A young American journalist, Hallett Abend, who arrived in Canton in the summer of 1926, a year after the first demonstration in the city, was advised to wear long trousers in the sticky heat because 'Most Chinese associate shorts exclusively with Englishmen, and the English are highly unpopular here just now. Wear long trousers please; to do so may save you from insult and even from violence.'[25]

Abend found Shameen, the foreign concession area, virtually cut off.

'On the island side were blockhouses, barbed wire, sandbags, machine guns and British and French sentries with rifles and hand grenades. Night and day since June of the year before, Shameen had lived under fear of new attacks.'[26] On the Canton city side of the bridge 'were more sandbags, more armed guards, Chinese this time. They searched every person coming from the island. Persons going to the island were not permitted to take anything with them – not a newspaper, not an orange, not a cigarette, not a letter or even a clean sheet of paper.' On the island, 'shaded by giant banyan trees, peppers, and palms' with 'great splashes of cerise [bougainvillaea] blossoms against the walls of massive granite and brick buildings', there were only a few men in residence.

Though the immediate threat felt by foreign residents throughout the treaty ports was from workers and students demonstrating against foreign occupation and exploitation, the political situation beyond the treaty ports was becoming increasingly unstable. And though the twists and turns of Chinese politics were probably of more interest to foreign newspaper editors than to most treaty port residents, the latter did not always escape the endemic warfare that ensued. The north of China was largely held by warlords who were frequently at odds with each other. In the south, the remnant of Sun Yat-sen's Kuomintang (National People's Party) government, effectively led from 1926 by the leader of the New Revolutionary Army, Chiang Kai-shek, was based in the Canton area. In 1926, Chiang Kai-shek led his Nationalists, as the Kuomintang were also called, on a Northern Expedition against warlords and the growing Communist Party (with which, under Russian encouragement, he was nominally allied). In October 1926, his troops took Hankow; in November, they captured Kiukiang and Nanchang; and in March 1927, they seized Shanghai and Nanking.

There was considerable tension on the Yangtze throughout 1926 and 1927. Two British river steamers were captured at Wanhsien (Wanxian), just above Ichang, in September 1926 and only released after the town was shelled, with considerable loss of life. In Chungking, a particularly unpleasant warlord seized the city and there were anti-Christian riots and tremendous shelling of foreign buildings. In Hankow, before the Nationalists took the city, tension gave way to violence when a mob attacked the British concession in January 1927. The withdrawal of a naval force was a matter of fierce argument: the British Minister in Peking, Miles Lampson, held that British control should have been maintained at all costs but Rear-Admiral Cameron felt that the risks of war were too great. Lampson had similarly instructed that the concession at Kiukiang should be defended to the death but the consul, A.G.N. Ogden, had evacuated women and children as soon as he heard of the attack at Hankow, and when the expected attack on Kiukiang came, the remaining men left safely.

In February 1927, the *Manchester Guardian* correspondent, Arthur Ransome, visited Kiukiang, where there was evidence of looting, and Hankow. In Hankow, he found that the only damage had been the destruction of 'the obnoxious barricades' marking the boundary of the British concession. Now, Chinese were allowed to sit on the benches on the British bund. Stories of massacre and danger had also been much exaggerated.

> For example, it is not true that the Hankow Club was sacked and its valuable library damaged. The library is intact and recalcitrants who refused to be immured in the Asiatic Petroleum Company's building were going to the club as usual during days when the outside world was informed that it was unsafe for any Britisher to show himself in the streets.[27]

Ransome was in Hankow to report on negotiations between the Chinese and the British over the return of the British concessions at Hankow and Kiukiang to China. He found that the news

> had been received quietly. It seems to be generally recognized by all but a few die-hards in Shanghai that the time has come when a change in the relations between British and Chinese is inevitable. It is, of course, hard not to sympathize with those Englishmen who have grown accustomed to the established ways and now look forward rather gloomily to life in a Chinese world very unlike the old. It is easy to understand the pained surprise of businessmen who have for years been able to count on Chinese labour at a stable wage, low in comparison with wages at home, at finding themselves face to face with trade unions which have yet to learn the difference between extravagant and economically justifiable demands. At the same time, one can but feel that they have had a long and profitable innings … They have been jerked in a few months from the Victorian era to the present day.[28]

Despite Ransome's tranquil account of post-riot Hankow, all along the Yangtze foreign residents had fled as the Nationalist Army arrived, fearing not so much the army itself but that they might be caught up in battles between local warlord forces and the Nationalist Army and attacked by mobs stirred to anti-foreignism by the Nationalists' growing success. In Nanking, Alice Tisdale Hobart, whose husband worked for Standard Oil and whose experiences as an oilman's wife in the frozen north of China and in Changsha provided the background for her romantic novels *Oil for the Lamps of China* and *The City of the Long Sands*, listened with increasing horror to the news of the Nationalist advance. She and her husband had just left Changsha, a city with a long history of anti-foreignism. The worst of the Changsha incidents had occurred in 1910, when the rising cost of rice transported on British steamers, and the British consul's insistence on using skilled builders from the neighbouring (and hated) province of Hupeh (Hubei) in the construction of his consulate, led to several days of rioting. All foreign buildings except the offending consulate and the Yale Missionary Hospital were completely destroyed.[29] For Mrs Hobart, Changsha had been wild and different, with 'its calamities, its chaos, its threats to life and property'. Now she was to live within a walled city that had not been provocatively divided by concessions. The Hobarts' home, the Standard Oil house, stood high on Socony Hill, looking down on the massive city wall that abutted the Yangtze: 'Nanking was different. There was no white man's settlement, no concession here. The foreign houses were scattered about over the city. There was plenty of room for everybody within this huge sprawling city.' Furthermore, there was order and government in Nanking, and she had confidence in the local warlord, General Sun.

Though General Sun appeared to be holding his own, in late October 1926, a month after she arrived, Mrs Hobart noticed 'an air of panic about the house. The coolie had left his dishes half-washed, the cook had prepared nothing for tiffin, his pots and pans stood unwashed, the boy's dusting cloth lay on the floor.' The Number One Boy announced that he was off, explaining, 'Missie my too much fear. Kuomintang just now catch Kiukiang.' She in turn insisted that he stay: 'Wang, no can go. No b'long proper custom ... S'pose you go, other man allo' wantchee go ... My think so Kuomintang no come.' As the streets of Nanking began to fill with fleeing inhabitants and the panic grew, Mrs Hobart fetched the long rope for descending the wall which had been kept for years in the attic for just such an event.

But the moment passed. By spring, she was intent upon the daffodils and tulips in her garden. 'Mrs Williams, wife of the university dean, sent me a basket of violet plants.' In February, General Sun's eastern front collapsed. The house on Socony Hill was used as a beacon, to signal to the British gunboats on the river below, and as Nationalist soldiers began to cross the river, Mrs Hobart packed 'a small dispatch case in which I placed toothbrushes and hairbrushes, the little things needed in case mobs or soldiers suddenly got out of control'.[30] Soldiers did get out of control. The dean of the university was shot dead as his house was looted and at the British consulate-general, the British doctor and harbour-master were killed and an Indian soldier and the British consul wounded.[31]

The American community gathered at the Hobarts' house and Mr Hobart negotiated with the first group of Nationalist soldiers that approached: they were Hunanese and his ability to speak the appropriate dialect defused tension for a while. However, as time passed, more and more soldiers threatened the house, shooting at random until, at a signal from the roof, the gunboats on the Yangtze below began to lob shells over the house. The refugee inhabitants, including Mrs Hobart, now had to do what they had never done before.

> When I got to the wall some were already over. 'Here,' someone called, 'we'll tie you into this rope.' Rope? – Sheets, blankets, curtains knotted together. 'Won't it cut me in two?' I asked. 'Can't say,' whoever it was tying me in, answered . . . I let them help me up to the top of the parapet. I swung my feet over, dropping, as it seemed to me, into space, for the bottom of the wall looked very far away. I feared the rope drawing tight and I feared it breaking, but I held on tight and watched the vines and the little trees growing out of the wall slip slowly past me and the marshy plain get nearer. I felt solid ground under my feet and I heard them above calling, 'Hurry up, down there,' and, with fumbling fingers I helped untie the knot.

Her husband broke his ankle – 'The sheets broke,' said a Mr Jordan.[32]

On a Jardine Matheson steamer on the Yangtze, below the city wall, Chester Ronning, a Canadian teacher, and his family, who had been ordered by the consul to leave Hankow when the foreign concessions were seized, witnessed the escape. To Ronning, it must all have seemed rather familiar – his father had vaulted over a wall twenty-five years before to escape an angry anti-foreign mob. In the end, fifty-two men, women and children escaped from Nanking to the safety of the gunboats *Emerald* and *Noa*.

Nationalist troops entered Shanghai in late March 1927, and as they did so 20,000 foreign soldiers were massed in the International Settlement and French Concession to protect foreign lives and property. Though Chiang Kai-shek's spokesman announced that it was the Nationalists' intention to recover the Settlement and Concession and abolish extraterritorial privileges, he stressed that this would be done peacefully and diplomatically. The Nationalists were far more concerned to eradicate Communists from Shanghai: this they did on 12 April, killing 20 and later executing 145. Foreign property and lives were spared and on the same day as the massacre, the municipal council magnanimously acknowledged the changing times by extending a welcome to Chinese visitors to Jessfield Park, Kongkew Park, and the Bund lawns and foreshore. Dogs, however, were still not allowed.[33]

Admitting well-dressed Chinese into Shanghai's public parks was a local gesture: at the same time, the official recognition of the impracticality of maintaining British concessions in some of the Yangtze ports that had led to the return of the Hankow and Kiukiang concessions to China in 1927 (followed by Amoy in 1929 and Chinkiang and Weihaiwei in 1930) did not imply a full-scale British retreat: in justification it was noted that national concessions as such were no longer necessary to the maintenance of British (or anybody else's) trade, indeed 'in each case, the British government were well rid of embarrassing responsibilities' for 'these small concessions, no larger than a London square and surrounded by Chinese urban areas, were of no practical value and a constant source of trouble, danger and anxiety'.[34]

In many of the treaty ports, foreigners lived outside concession areas altogether or at least outside their own country's concession. In Tientsin

The German concession ... was the most favoured residential area for foreigners of all nationalities ... The British concession and extension contained the most important foreign banks, offices and shops, and a considerable Chinese population ... The Italian concession ... was becoming the most popular centre for the palatial residences of retired Chinese militarists and politicians.[35]

Whilst abandonment of some of the smaller concessions may not have signalled the end of the British government's interest in China, the means of maintaining that interest were changing. 'Gunboat diplomacy, with or without gunboats, was swiftly yielding to the gentler arts of co-operation and understanding,' writes one commentator.[36] Co-operation and understanding were not always the hallmarks of consular views and activities, but the consuls were working under extremely trying conditions. China was divided. Though Chiang Kai-shek had taken the Yangtze towns and Shanghai, and moved his seat of government to Wuhan on 1 January 1927, only to move it again, to Nanking, on 18 April, some members of the Nationalist government stayed on in Wuhan and set up a short-lived rival establishment under Wang Ching-wei. Nor was it certain that Chiang would be able to take or hold north China. The Nationalists did manage to capture Peking and Tientsin in June 1928, and the Manchurian warlord Chang Hsueh-liang proclaimed his allegiance to Chiang Kai-shek on 29 December, more or less completing the unification of China, but the warlords kept making and breaking alliances. The Communists, too, though retreating to remote mountainous regions of China after the Nationalist assault of 1927, were regrouping and attracting wider support.

In the midst of such uncertainty, the British government in particular was also subjected to considerable pressure from British residents in China to safeguard their interests. As the return to China of the Hankow and Kiukiang concessions was being discussed (ironically, with the breakaway Nationalist regime in Wuhan, not Chiang Kai-shek), the British also issued proposals on treaty renegotiation to the Chinese Nationalist Party. Austen Chamberlain summarized them thus:

> The principal changes the Chinese desire in the old treaty are: (1) The extraterritorial position of foreigners who can only be tried by their own courts; (2) the tariff provisions preventing China from raising her duties on foreign goods; and (3) the quasi-independent status of foreign concessions. Britain is prepared to change all these points because the present system is antiquated and unsuited to modern conditions. It no longer provides the necessary security and protection for the peaceful avocations of our merchants.[37]

Arthur Ransome devoted many pages to a description of those in China who opposed these changes. They were the 'Old China Hands' whose 'attitude is distinctly bellicose', who 'think of "anti-foreignism" as China's original sin, to be exorcized by periodic penances', and who 'look round on their magnificent buildings and are surprised that China is not grateful to them for these gifts'. In a chapter on 'The Shanghai Mind', he went on, 'The Shanghailanders hold that loyalty belongs at home and that their primary allegiance is to Shanghai.' Their reaction to Chamberlain's proposals was firm:

> They proclaim that British property is in danger when they need British troops to defend them, but have shown during the last few months that acceptance of this assistance does not in any way prevent them from doing what they can to make impossible the realization of a British policy which they do not like ... English prestige is at stake when their interests are threatened, but unless English policy coincides with their own, they are prepared to be the Ulster of the East.[38]

Those foreign residents who were prepared to accept the end of concessions were nonetheless alarmed at the prospect of the abolition of extraterritoriality. When H.G.W. Woodhead arrived in China, his first job was to report on court proceedings in Shanghai. He was hardly complimentary about the extraterritorial foreign courts. 'Proceedings in the American Court beggared description. Lawyers strolled round the courtroom ... expectorating loudly and frequently. They bullied the witnesses and threatened the judge.' Despite bearing a name from a Marx Brothers film, Judge Lebbaeus R. Wilfley attempted to improve matters, insisting that lawyers sit an exam before appearing before him but the lawyers 'combined to impeach him in Washington'.[39]

But if proceedings within the foreign courts were unsatisfactory, they were a great deal better than the alternative. Woodhead went on to state that the idea of the rule of law was quite alien to the Chinese and that 'the administration of justice, unsatisfactory as it was under the militarist regime of 1926, became infinitely worse with the accession to power of the Kuomintang'. He cited the intolerance of political opposition, the corruption of local authorities (prepared to levy loans at gunpoint), and the difficulties presented to motorists which led the British consular authorities to advise 'their nationals not to motor on any roads under

Chinese police control unless their cars were driven by Chinese chauffeurs'. The principle was that 'the owner or driver of a motor car is held responsible for any accident that may occur, whether it was stationary or moving at the time it happened'. The unfortunate German vice-consul in Mukden was ruined financially and 'made such a nervous wreck that he had to leave the country' because his car was merely in the vicinity of a mule-cart which bolted.[40] Though Woodhead was no doubt right to worry in such unstable times, extraterritoriality was still being discussed by Britain and China when the negotiations were interrupted by the Japanese seizure of Manchuria in 1931 which put an end to the talks.

Japanese actions in China were to dominate the last decade of the treaty ports but British diplomacy, in front of or behind the scenes, continued to pursue British interests. Some British businessmen felt that the uncertainties of life there were becoming too great. Others were more optimistic. Swire's, one of the oldest British firms that had traded in China since before the First Opium War, felt that it could still adapt to the changing times, though the entrenched conservatism and lack of faith of the Shanghailanders drove one director to despair. Another Swire employee was shocked by the attitude of Sydney Mayers, director of the British & Chinese Railways Corporation,

> who turned to me very gloomily at the soup and in his most pompous and pontifical manner said . . . 'Get out of China, it is Ichabod. You will get no help from home and will go the way of the merchants in Smyrna. We came to China with the sword and gun in our hands . . . the Chinese never asked us to come, they never wanted us, they don't want us now.'[41]

Nor were the directors of Swire's very impressed by the British legation which was, nevertheless, continuing to try to exert influence. In 1926, it attempted to control the appointment of the new Inspector-General of the (no longer Imperial) Maritime Customs. This was none of its business, for it was a Chinese appointment, though the leading candidates were both British. Just before his dismissal in 1926, the current Inspector-General Francis Aglen acknowledged, 'My position does not depend so much now on the power and prestige of the British government. If it depended solely on that I am afraid it would be a very poor outlook because British prestige has never been at such a low ebb.' Nevertheless, the British legation pressed hard for its favoured candidate A.H.F. Edwardes, Aglen's de facto deputy. When it appeared that Edwardes was losing out to the Shanghai Customs commissioner, Frederick Maze (a nephew of Sir Robert Hart), the commercial counsellor to the British legation in Peking thundered to the Foreign Office:

> are we going to sit still and let a hardly-fledged Chinese government dismiss for purely personal reasons a British subject who has rendered his predecessors loyal service in a position of great responsibility and has worthily maintained that high tradition set up by the great Englishman who first gave the Chinese their Customs Service? ... It is not only Edwardes' battle that we are fighting but the claim of every Englishman and foreigner in China.[42]

When he was Commissioner of Customs in Canton in 1912, Frederick Maze had cultivated Sun Yat-sen, inviting him to a garden party and meeting to discuss harbour improvements. Later, when the Nationalist Army entered Shanghai, he overlooked a strike, remarking, 'I find it quite natural that Chinese members of the staff, especially Cantonese, desired to participate in the celebration of such an important occasion.' One member of the British legation staff, Sir John Pratt (Boris Karloff's brother), a dark-skinned Anglo-Indian, jovially known as 'Black Pratt' and 'Uncle Tom's Cabin', began to see that 'in supporting Mr Edwardes we have unfortunately backed the wrong horse ... The plain fact is that Mr Edwardes is *persona non grata* to the Chinese. He lacks the one thing that is essential for anyone in his position to have, namely, the knack of getting on with the Chinese. On the contrary, he always seems to rub them up the wrong way.' Edwardes, feeling himself outmanoeuvred, private British thundering notwithstanding, resigned in 1929.

Maze's appointment was not welcomed by the *North China Daily News* – 'It would be idle to pretend that Mr Maze's appointment as Inspector-General of Customs is pleasing either to foreigners or to the most responsible Chinese' – and Maze was asked to resign from the Shanghai Bowling Club. But he was not to be ostracized for long. His tenure of office was significant for his acceptance of the principle that the Customs should be staffed by Chinese (except where very specific qualifications were required), although the gradual process of sinifying the Customs was, like extraterritoriality and everything else, to be conclusively interrupted by the arrival of the Japanese.[43]

13

Four Hundred Million Customers

Despite riots, strikes and boycotts, the early years of the twentieth century saw a rapid increase in the number of foreign enterprises opening up in an increasingly open China. The new businesses were indeed new, for companies dealing in chemicals, tobacco, petroleum and modern necessities such as electric lighting, clean water and personal and business insurance, joined the old trading houses which, in their turn, were taking on agencies for modern products as well as continuing to buy raw silk, pigs' bristle, beancake and peanuts. Owen Lattimore, the son of a missionary, who had grown up in remote Paoting (Baoding) where no Chinese children were allowed to play with him, worked for a firm in Tientsin 'that dealt with everything. As agents we bought for buyers in Europe and the US everything that China exported and imported everything that China imported.'[1]

At business headquarters in the treaty ports, all modern conveniences were now to be had. Office buildings and grand houses were designed to demonstrate the permanence and importance of foreign firms and their proprietors. Grander municipal buildings were also constructed to house the business of running the foreign concessions, and the treaty ports in China began to take on an imposing Western appearance so solid in construction that it long outlasted the concessions themselves.

In Tientsin, there were now separate British, French and German concessions on the right bank of the Pei River and Japanese, Russian, Austro-Hungarian and Italian concessions on the left bank. Thus as Dr A.H. Hardy put it, 'All the Powers, except China, are now accommodated with commodious waterfronts.'[2] Tientsin's Gordon Hall housed the law court, the offices of the British Municipal Council, the police station and an assembly room for concerts and public meetings. It had two round towers and Gothic pointed windows and doors, and its exterior walls were battlemented like a castle. Its architect, a Scottish missionary, had described its style as Victorian Tientsin, 'but Mad Mac, the piano tuner, said it reminded him of a prison hospital on the outskirts of Edinburgh'.[3]

The Tientsin Club was designed by Messrs Algar & Beesley of Shanghai, its foundation stone laid in 1903. Above rose a bar, a five-table billiard room, card and board rooms (the latter also able to accommodate dances and concerts), a bowling alley and a library. Electric lighting was installed throughout, and hot and cold water with a steam-heating plant completed the arrangements. It stood opposite Gordon Hall, near the Astor House Hotel (built in 1894 with seventy bedrooms, an 'excellent' cuisine and a 'carefully selected' wine list), and overlooked Victoria Park. There a military band occupied the bandstand (with its Chinese pavilion roof) on Sundays and there, as in most treaty port parks, Chinese were only admitted if accompanied by small foreign children, and bicycling and ball games were forbidden.

The Club Concordia ('an international club in all respects, except that members of the committee must speak German'), built in 1907 in the neo-Romanesque style favoured by Kaiser Wilhelm I, had five tennis courts, a theatre seating 300 and 'modern extinguishing appliances' in case of fire. The Cercle d'Escrime Français included bachelor rooms and a large hall for fencing, boxing and gymnastics, and there was an open-air swimming area 'on the Extra-French Concession'.

Tientsin's banks included the Hongkong and Shanghai Bank building with three rows of arched verandas in the earliest treaty port style and the Yokohama Specie and Russo-Chinese banks, built at road junctions, both boasting domes, the Russo-Chinese Bank's dome being set behind a row of Dutch gables. Some of Tientsin's buildings were vaguely international in style. The Chinese Engineering & Mining Co.'s offices were Italianate; the residence of Wilhelm Kleeschult – importer of chimney cowls, washing machines and storm flares, exporter of straw braids, bristles, wool and skins – was timbered in stockbroker Tudor; and the Kailan Mining Co. headquarters were colonnaded like a Greek temple. More often, however, there was a distinct national character to the buildings so that it is still possible to walk through Tientsin and see when you are leaving, for example, the French for the German concession.

The arms dealers Von During, Wibel & Co. had their headquarters in a square residential-style building, exactly like a turn-of-the-century private house in the leafy Berlin suburbs, surrounded by its own garden. West Station, built in 1910, was said to correspond to the standard of German railway stations at the time though the façade was thought to be extremely overwrought; and the house at No. 29 Xuzhou Dao (formerly Mumm Street, off Wilhelmstrasse) exemplified the East Asian Jugendstil favoured by the architect Curt Rothkegel (elaborate stucco curlicues and circular moon-gate forms surrounding the rectangular doorways). Rothkegel's signature was the inclusion of carved wooden animal motifs, and in the centre of the door of 29 Xuzhou Dao is a larger-than-life cat's head with its tongue sticking out. The house built for J. Faust in 1904 was a similar mixture of East Asia and art nouveau. The two gables were rounded, borrowing the top half of the favoured circular form of Chinese moon gates, filled in with striking black-and-white chequered tiles and finished with elaborate art nouveau balcony railings. It also boasted a square tower, topped with a decorative Jugendstil grating and wedding-cake ironwork. Faust ran an import–export company (bristles, furs, skins and wool), held the agency for Western Assurance of Toronto and owned the *Tageblatt für NordChina*. He sold his house, which sadly no longer exists, at an enormous profit to Prince Tsai-lun, a minor member of the imperial family, in 1912 – Tientsin by then becoming a desirable place of residence for those who found Peking too stuffy.

Shanghai's buildings were less eccentric and their nationality less evident, but they were bigger and grander. Though the old arcaded style was beginning to go out of fashion, the offices of Carlowitz's agency for German industrial products (1899) and Becker & Baedecker's design for an office building at No. 138 Kiangsi Road (1908) still reflected the old form. In contrast Becker's Russo-Chinese Bank building (1899–1902) was in the classic Renaissance style, and Becker & Baedecker's Shanghai Club Concordia (knocked down in 1934 and replaced by the Bank of China building which still stands on the Bund) resembled a German Renaissance palace (though still surrounded by verandas in the old style).[4] Despite the boggy soil, the price of land in Shanghai was such that buildings started to grow upwards. By 1904 there were seven-storey structures erected on a foundation of timber piles (imported from Puget Island Sound).

One of those who made his fortune from building and property ownership was Henry Lester who had, like John Gavin, arrived as an architect and land surveyor in Shanghai in about 1863. He died in 1926, leaving a fortune 'entirely due to his investments in land in the early days'. In his will he left money to Holy Trinity Cathedral for the rebuilding of the cathedral school, deanery and church house, an endowment to the cathedral school, a large sum of money to the Shantung Road Hospital, 'thereafter to be called the Lester Chinese Hospital', a smaller sum to St Luke's Hospital which could keep its name, and yet more money to the Institution for the Chinese Blind, the Children's Refuge, the Little Sisters of the Poor, the Shanghai Missions to Rickshawmen and St Joseph's Asylum for the Poor. The Henry Lester Institute for Medical Education and Research was to be 'erected and equipped', as was the Lester School for Chinese and foreign scholars.[5]

The bulk of Henry Lester's wealth may have derived from shrewd investment in land but he was also one of Shanghai's characters. 'The owner of many fine apartments, he lived in the meanest . . . without any tendency toward either luxury or liberality.' He travelled by tram because it was even cheaper than a rickshaw, so his generosity to rickshawmen appears to have been mainly posthumous. He was said never to buy a collar or shirt, 'depending on a business associate to give him his slightly worn and discarded haberdashery'.[6]

When the Chinese arrived in increasing numbers in the International Settlement, living in 'lane houses', two- and three-storey terraced buildings packed close together on narrow lanes off the wider, shop-lined main roads, foreigners less parsimonious than Henry Lester moved further out of the city and built themselves grand houses surrounded by luxurious gardens.

Out on Avenue Joffre in the suburbs of the French Concession, Becker & Baedecker (still promoting the German neo-Renaissance) built red-roofed villas topped with tiny cupolas and decorated with huge carved stone gables. Further out still, on Siccawei Road, was

'Dennartt', the residence of Mr V.W. Drummond, born in Highgate in 1841, barrister-at-law, Chief Law Officer for Foreign Affairs, owner of the Perak Sugar Co. and the Kalumpong Rubber Co., decorated with the Imperial Order of the Sapphire Button (third rank) and the Red Button (second rank), and a 'strong supporter of Mr Joseph Chamberlain'. Dennartt was huge and was set in a shrubbery beyond which stretched infinite lawns. The centre bay owed something to Hardwicke Hall, the flanking bays were topped with Tudor gables over flimsy ironwork, and a long, low conservatory-like building adjoined the main house. Carl Seitz's residence on Kiaochow Road looked like a hotel on the Côte d'Azur with a huge veranda and pendant stuccowork; H.J. Craig's massive house on Bubbling Well Road was decked with a veranda of romanesque and doric columns; and even the stables at 'The Elms', where J. Johnston lived, had battlements like Gordon Hall. Though most buildings in the treaty ports were now constructed to the designs of local architects, foreign at first but increasingly Chinese, some commissions were still offered to distinguished architects from home such as Clough Williams-Ellis who built the Butterfield & Swire mansion.[7]

Business life in China was divided between those who worked in company headquarters in the comfortable treaty ports, and those who lived outside or travelled all over China for their companies. Owen Lattimore, who found business circles in Tientsin 'hopelessly philistine', moved to an insurance company and, 'as I wanted to get out of Tientsin as much as possible, not only on insurance business, I made myself into the firm's principal Chinese-speaking trouble-shooter', working with Chinese agents in the interior.[8] Such a move was perhaps wise, for within the treaty ports some of the Victorian excesses decried by Dr James Henderson fifty years before still persisted. When the journalist Carl Crow arrived in Shanghai in 1911, 'there were half a dozen business concerns which maintained private bars where business or personal friends could drop in for a drink at odd moments during the day … the *China Press* on which I was city editor, maintained a private bar for the staff though there was nothing free about it'. To be invited to 'enjoy' the bar at the Hongkong and Shanghai Bank 'was an honour reserved for exchange and bullion brokers and people with heavy overdrafts ... A more democratic bar was that of Lane, Crawford & Co., general storekeepers. Every morning at 10.30 the venerable Mr Crawford, who had been doing the same thing for more than twenty years, would empty a bottle of gin into a pitcher of ice, add other ingredients and serve a drink which was known as a "Crawford Special".'[9]

Drinks and virtually all other purchases were still made by the chit system. Elsie McCormick described the way it worked:

> A person may enter practically any restaurant or café and merely inscribe his name and address on a piece of paper at the end of the festivities. The boy who receives the chit has no means of checking up the statistics on it, nor does he ever attempt to do so. He simply files away the memor-andum and trusts to the various joss that the signer of it will not feel urged to board any of the numerous trains or boats leaving the city before the first of the month.[10]

The failure to check meant that after visits from the American fleet, many establishments found themselves left with chits signed by Donald Duck or George Washington.

Even without a Crawford Special so soon after breakfast, work in China seemed to many (at least in retrospect) to have been more fun than it would have been at home. The comfort of daily life with an unaccustomed number of servants and the great distance from head-quarters doubtless helped. Edward Ward described his management of the Reuters office in Tientsin in 1934 as 'a kind of comic opera', particu-larly when it came to the quarterly audit of the office accounts (a drawer full of chits and IOUs). He also amused himself by designing a multi-coloured uniform, reminiscent of the male chorus from a Strauss operetta, for the coolies who cycled about Tientsin delivering copies of British and American stock and commodity exchange quotations to local subscribers.[11] He did, however, stress that he managed to increase Reuters' Tientsin revenue considerably.

Whilst those in the larger treaty ports worked in their offices (with the usual round of snipe-shooting and paper-chasing at the weekends), those who travelled for their firms saw a different China outside the settlements, described by several as a medieval world. That medieval countryside was now traversed by a number of railways, a late nineteenth-century Western introduction that had, as has been seen, attracted Boxer animosity.

The first railway line to be constructed was the Shanghai–Woosung line, begun in 1876. However, owing to 'the fanatical prejudices of the populace acting in conjunction with the bigoted opposition of the official classes',[12] or, to be more precise, 'the death of a native hit by the locomotive',[13] the line proved short-lived, and in 1877 it was broken up and the rolling stock shipped to Taiwan and dumped on a beach. It was not until 1896 that the Chinese government, under pressure from modernizing officials such as Li Hung-chang (the man who had so disappointed General Gordon by executing the Taiping leaders), issued an edict promulgating an active railway policy. The edict was the signal for a great scramble for railway concessions on the part of various foreign interests.[14]

The pursuit of railway concessions reflected the (mainly) European division of China into spheres of interest which spread far beyond the confines of the treaty ports. France, with its interests in Indo-China, had its eyes on south-western China, particularly Yunnan province and areas bordering Indo-China. Germany, after its seizure of Kiaochow Bay, regarded Shantung province as its special preserve. British interests were less easy to define: the Yangtze was 'British' but so was almost everywhere else, at least in British eyes. British capital financed the Peking–Tientsin railway which was torn up by the Boxers as a symbol of foreign control. British capital was also involved in the Shanghai–Nanking railway (in the British sphere of influence) which involved 25 major and 277 minor bridges, 405 culverts and heavy charges incurred 'for coffer-dam, timbering, pumping and piling'.[15] Belgian capital provided the initial finance for the Peking–Hankow railway in 1899; this too was partly destroyed by Boxers. The Russians built railways and connecting lines in the far north, the French built a narrow-gauge line from Kunming in Yunnan to Hanoi, the Germans built railways in Shantung, and the Japanese (some decades before they invaded the region) set up the South Manchuria Railway (Managing Director, Baron S. Goto), with railway hotels like the Yamato at Port Arthur.

The arrival of the railways and railway hotels made commercial travel somewhat easier. Richard Dobson, a representative of a tobacco company, travelled through China in the 1930s visiting Chinese district managers. Tobacco was an extremely successful introduction to China, the opium of the twentieth century. Dobson told the story of how an American, Mr J.B. Duke,

> when they brought him a machine that would make as many cigarettes in a minute as a man had hitherto made in an hour, said, 'Bring me the atlas.' When they had brought it, he turned over the leaves, looking not at the maps but at the significant figures at the bottom, until he came to the legend, 'Pop. 430,000,000'. 'That', he said, 'is where we are going to sell cigarettes.' When they told him that the Chinese did not smoke cigarettes, he said he supposed they could learn. In the best season I can remember, our company alone sold six thousand five hundred million cigarettes in China in a month.[16]

Based initially in the province of Honan (Henan), at Chengchow (Zhengzhou), 'a tenth-rate Chinese Crewe ... a railway station with a few streets of shoddy houses scattered around it', Dobson travelled by train, sometimes in cattle-trucks, compelled to keep to the 'railway zone' because the country round about was infested with bandits. His task, like that of all the other travellers, was to deal with local Chinese agents: to check their books and supplies, and to make sure that they were sticking to the agency and not dealing with competitors. Dobson's work also included the ritual of a call on the local tax bureau to protest against the hand-rolling of cigarettes. It was illegal, he said, as the rollers were evading tax, though he knew that 'it would have taken an expeditionary force to eradicate the illicit trade in the country as long as the Japanese smugglers kindly provided the paper'.

Train travel was still quite slow and had its own peculiar problems. Even today, the train timetable in China is fantastically complicated and requires a certain knowledge of classical Chinese since some of the lines are designated by place-names current in the third century AD. In the 1930s trains were frequently full so one resourceful commercial traveller would 'get into a freight truck and sit on top of bags of beans, which was at least in the fresh air, but it could be damn cold in winter'. Overcrowding was not the only difficulty: 'there was no schedule ... You just went to the station and joined the general bivouac, which might be for one hour, half a day or a whole day ... Then there was a scramble for the best places on the roofs of the carriages because there was no room inside.' Some trains had no glass left in the windows, so it was no warmer within, and since the trains were invariably over-loaded, they travelled very slowly indeed.[17]

Many commercial travellers found that their destinations lay beyond the major towns served by railways and they had to resort to a variety of forms of transport beyond the railhead. There were, in the north, the infamous Peking carts, in which foreign travellers had suffered since 1793 when Lord Macartney's embassy arrived in them in Peking. 'A Peking cart was a two-wheeled unsprung cart with a canopy covering of blue cloth', its lack of springs on deeply rutted roads leading to bruis-ing bouncing. One traveller preferred to walk, not because of his dis-comfort but to relieve the mules which had sores on their backs.[18] Some travelled by chair, 'not the glorified telephone box in which the élite of the Regency did their afternoon calls, but a crude contraption of bamboo' of the type used by travellers in China from the 1860s.[19] Others employed the passenger wheelbarrow,

> rather like an Irish jaunting car but with seats suspended over one wheel. You could sit on either side. Your baggage would be on one side and you would sit on the other side ... And no wheelbarrow in China was any good unless it had a built-in squeak ... It was propelled by a man who held the two shafts in his hands with a strap attached to the shaft round his neck.[20]

Travel by car or lorry became increasingly common as the century advanced although roads were slow to develop (and still leave a lot to be desired). Richard Dobson acquired a company lorry to use on a newly built military road from Canton to Hankow. Leaving Canton before dawn, in pouring rain, 'I took a wrong turning; five minutes later we were arrested, and were escorted back to Canton in disgrace.' Recommencing the journey, he discovered that his driver 'had been employed by the bus company but he was not a driver. I had never driven a lorry myself, but was forced to it eventually by the driver's determination to decelerate when changing down.' It was not just the driver who was at fault; the road was also a problem. 'It was easy to see why there had never been a road there before. It was an impossible bit of country, and I doubt if the road ran straight for fifty yards anywhere.

The surface was of mud, which of course the heavy rains had not improved.' After dark, they crawled round interminable hairpin bends and frequently had to stop to make a reconnaissance of the next corner on foot. The following day they became completely stuck in mud and had to pay some road-menders to push them clear; the day after that they had to stop on a frozen mountain for fear of skidding off it. Fortunately, 'two carloads of Europeans came roaring up the hill, one car with chains clanking on its wheels', so they followed in the path made where the chains had cracked the ice.[21]

Travelling in the hinterland was as dangerous as it had ever been. Though such organized threats as that of the Boxers had receded, banditry increased as the country began to fragment under warlord rule. As one Butterfield & Swire traveller reported, between one warlord's sphere and the next 'there would be a no-man's-land which was bandit country and you could be kidnapped. My predecessor ... at Hankow was in fact kidnapped on one of his trips up the Han River.'[22] Bandit groups sported exotic names and were not above threatening Western enterprises. In April 1914, when Linan was sacked by the White Wolf bandits, the Asiatic Petroleum Co. reported considerable losses as a result of the destruction of buildings and stores.[23]

It was not only businessmen who ran the risk of kidnap. A Norwegian engineer, Sigurd Eliasson, was employed to plan what turned out to be an impracticable irrigation scheme on the Yellow River in Shansi province in 1933. Depressed by local opposition and corruption, he was kidnapped and held for several weeks by local bandits. He escaped, only to find that a ransom had already been paid.[24] The year before, the young daughter of a much-loved doctor in Newchwang was also kidnapped by one of many bandit groups operating in Manchuria. It was said that the flat country, covered with fields of kaoliang (a kind of millet) which grew taller than a man, offered special protection for bandits skulking invisibly amongst the stalks. 'Tinko' Pawley had gone riding on the Newchwang racecourse when she and her companion (and their three dogs) were seized and

> lashed up in a terribly uncomfortable fashion. A noose was passed round
> our necks, tied at the back with a slip-knot, crossed and looped twice
> round the upper arms, then taken again and knotted between our shoul-
> der blades with a lead rope to our captors. In this manner our elbows

were dragged back and any vigorous forward movement tightened the rope and threatened to strangle us.

Beaten with their own riding crops they were quickly driven into the fields because 'the bandits were terrified of being spotted before they could reach the high close-growing kaoliang where they would be in safe cover'.[25] She, too, was rescued by a combination of ransom and Japanese military activity after five weeks of constant movement from village to village through the millet.

The novelist Stella Benson, whose husband Seamus Carew O'Gorman Anderson was in the Customs Service, experienced a narrow escape in Manchuria. In freezing winter temperatures, with an unreliable cook – 'Missy, I am plenty drunk, dinner no can do' – her only foreign neighbours were German and Canadian missionaries and a hospitable Russian with an insufficiency of utensils who 'ate curds and nuts out of the lid of a saucepan and drank his vodka out of a jampot'. The short summer brought some compensations, for then Stella could grow tomatoes and cabbages, beans and peas, lettuces, radishes and carrots, and apricots, loganberries and sweetpeas.

In 1927, a new Customs levy on goods entering Manchuria enraged the local Japanese shopkeepers. A mob broke into the Customs warehouse so Stella Benson and her husband

> sent the dogs and horses away to a place of safety, committed my jade beads, synthetic pearls and priceless S. Benson manuscripts to the missionaries' care, hid the safe in a thicket in the compound, decided on the point where we could most easily climb over the compound wall should the mob come in at the gate, dressed ourselves in dark clothes (and any woman will realize how difficult it was for me to find a pair of low-visibility stockings in these days of insolent champagne-colour) and sat down to wait, reading *Northanger Abbey* with ears pricked.[26]

Fortunately nothing happened, though when Stella published an account of this 'Storm in a Manchurian Tea-cup' in the August edition of the *Nation and Athenaeum* it provoked a complaint from the Japanese authorities and a prohibition on further publication by the Inspector-General of Customs.

Business rivalries could also become dangerous. At Hsuchow

(Xuzhou), in Honan, Richard Dobson noted that foreign tobacco buyers had

> cut into the profits of the local merchants ... a few weeks before, our
> 'No. 1 Chinese', a first-rate man, had been shot dead outside our com-
> pound ... I was quick to catch the infection of nervousness from the
> little community. One night, I woke one of them up, and he was out
> of bed, menacing me with a revolver, in a couple of seconds ... A few
> weeks later the American manager was killed ... and our leaf-buyers
> were withdrawn.[27]

On the road between company compounds, mission houses or large towns, travellers had to use what accommodation they could find. On his lorry trip northwards Dobson was given the only free room in the Muilik inn, 'a cupboard under the stairs measuring no more than five and a half feet in any direction, and full of bugs'. Overnight accommodation in villages had not changed much for centuries and the inhabitants were as curious as those John Gavin had met on his moun-tain trip in 1863. In the north of China, one traveller recalled, windows, including those of inn rooms, were covered with paper rather than glass, and 'all the village children would come round and poke holes in the paper windows to have a look at the foreigner ... the broken paper windows would also let the draught in, and in the cold weather, I can remember staying in some of these places with sleep impossible it was so cold.' In one inn, maddened by the noses pressed against his paper windows, he went outside to invite them in in order to get it over with and keep his windows intact.

> There were about six people including, I gathered, the village school-
> master. And he said, 'We've never seen a foreigner before, do you mind
> if we do?' I said, 'Certainly not.' So the schoolmaster came in, looked at
> my socks and shoes and asked me what they were made of. I was able to
> tell him and we had other simple exchanges, until he ended up by saying,
> 'Thank you very much indeed; that's been the most interesting experi-
> ence for me.'[28]

North China inns were constructed around a courtyard, with low, single-storey buildings facing into the court, the façade windows made of decorative latticework plastered with the all too penetrable paper. Their rooms were occasionally provided with a bed but more commonly with a *kang* or hollow brick platform. Sanitary arrangements were limited. Water might be provided for washing and there was usually a frightful lavatory, 'horrible even to think about'. 'As far as possible, one used the fields.'[29]

In western China, inns were differently constructed, of timber rather than the solid brick and mud of the north, with a restaurant downstairs and bedrooms upstairs, but they lacked the relative privacy of a courtyard enclosure. The dusty arrival would have to wash downstairs, as Archibald Carey wrote, 'in full view of the other diners and of the passers-by in the street outside. The latter would usually collect in a vast throng when they saw a foreigner washing – especially if he happened to be shaving, too.' Carey, who travelled for Asiatic Petroleum, longed to be able to sit down in a bath rather than 'sponge down from a portable tub about the size of an ordinary hand-basin' and was of the opinion that inn-keepers used to let people in to watch the foreigners wash on payment of a small fee.[30]

In the bedrooms upstairs in a Szechwan inn, the rooms

would have one, two or three beds and varied in price accordingly. Illumination was provided by a small flat dish of vegetable oil over the end of which a lighted end of wick would be hanging. There would be a rickety table and one or two simple chairs or stools; and on the table a cracked China teapot which contained drinking water and a couple of tiny tea-bowls in case you wanted to entertain a friend or clean your teeth.

Bugs were the worst problem, as Carey explained: 'In winter, the creeping variety waited until one was asleep and then came out from the crevices in the floor and walls to share your warmth, and partake of your blood. The jumping variety were not so coy … We frequently referred to lice as seam-squirrels.'[31] A single eiderdown quilt was also provided 'which you could use in place of your own bedding if you were the adventurous type'. The experienced traveller carried a well-oiled piece of ground sheeting to put beneath his own bedding, DDT powder to sprinkle around the bed and a mosquito net.[32]

Those who travelled varied in their attitude to the local food: one man carried iodine, aspirin, whisky, bread (he did not like the soft, damp steamed bread of the north, preferring his own, even if it did get greener and harder as the trip proceeded), tinned pork, tinned beans, stewed lamb (also tinned) and Aquarius Water bottled by Watson's the Chemist of Tientsin.[33] Archibald Carey carried most of his own food although he would buy eggs and chickens along the way: 'Such staples as white bread and Irish potatoes were a luxury to be enjoyed only after returning.'[34] Bernard Llewellyn, a volunteer driver for the Friends' Ambulance Unit's China Convoy in south-western China, sent in response to the Japanese threat, relished the local food:

> piping hot, and tasting more delicious than any roadside meal you could find in any country of the world. Fried chicken, bean curd, liver and onions, scrambled eggs, bean sprouts, noodles in delicious soup and, if the restaurant was near a big river, a whole fish cooked in a sauce of surpassing excellence ... to add flavour to the bowls of steaming rice.

Whatever their attitude to Chinese food, all those who visited their local agents were compelled to attend a banquet offered by the agent, with dishes of native delicacies such as birds' nest soup, pigeons' eggs, sharks' fins, frogs' legs and sea slugs. Very often the banquet would comprise sixteen dishes washed down with warm rice or kaoliang wine.[35] One of Butterfield & Swire's representatives recalled a northern banquet that 'had seventeen courses all of water-originating food – water chestnuts, fish of various kinds, duck and so forth ... And I remember it was my first experience of eating not with ordinary chopsticks, but with ebony chopsticks with pointed silver tips and that did test my skill very considerably.'[36] If the banquets were exotic, they were as nothing compared to an occasion on which Stella Benson entertained the wives of Chinese Customs officials in Manchuria.

On that occasion, however, food was not the topic of conversation.

> Conscious of her splendour down below, Mrs Kao said (evidently), 'My dear, you haven't half enough on,' and lifting up the flap over Mrs Chia's tight satin ham disclosed red satin embroidered underclothes – and – the red satin flap being lifted, a layer of black satin. Mrs Chia was very proud to be thus examined but her face fell when Mrs Kao lifted her flap and showed *white fur* underclothes. Neither had anything that would wash.[37]

Commercial and other travellers quite often stayed in mission houses when far from home. Bernard Llewellyn regularly frequented the China

Inland Mission in Kuan-hsien (Guanxian) on the edge of the Chengtu plain.

> The mission station was in the main street ... built in the foreign style, and the first time I went into the living room there was a volume of Winston Churchill's speeches lying on the table. There was always this element of the unexpected and familiar which you were sure to encounter ... you were shaken by the sight of a book you had on your own shelves at home; by the music of a familiar record; by a table laid for English tea.

In the Methodist Mission at Kweichow he 'had been entranced to hear Gilbert and Sullivan melodies transposed, by the magic of the portable gramophone'. His favourite mission however, 'open to [foreign] travellers of any faith or no faith at all', was that of the Friedenshort Deaconess Sisters in Pichieh (Bijie) which offered room service beyond a commercial traveller's dreams.

> Sister Margarete, with her fat rosy cheeks ... would lead the way to our bedrooms, telling the servant girl to bring jugs of hot water, towels and soap. The tin baths would be brought in and while we were bathing, Sister Margarete would enquire about the missing buttons on our clean shirts ... After many protests, a naked arm holding a garment would appear round the corner of the door and Sister Margarete, making sure that none of the younger sisters was nearby to glimpse a masculine arm not even clothed in white samite, mystic, wonderful, would take the shirt with averted eyes and hasten to her workbox ...
> They gave us foreign food ... What puddings and cakes I have eaten in Pichieh – cakes cooked by smiling Sister Jo ... with long German names.

In the evening, Sister Jo 'would get out her flute and play it while someone pedalled away for dear life on the harmonium' and Sister Margarete would tell the unlikely jokes of isolation

> about some of her church people who had been given some cast-off underclothes from a parcel sent from Europe, and who in the fullness of their gratitude had attended the next Sunday services with the newly acquired undergarments (which included ... items so positively unmentionable that Sister Margarete could not even describe them to us ...) worn proudly on top of their ordinary clothes.[38]

*

Commercial travellers in early twentieth-century China included not only those responsible for supplying and checking up on agencies, but also specialists investigating the state of native industries in order to see where they could penetrate the market. Companies were finally beginning to learn the need to survey the market and learn about local conditions instead of, like their predecessors decades before, simply hoping that China would buy British shirtings if they became available.

The chemist Henry Glendinning arrived in Shanghai in 1899 representing the chemical company Brunner Mond (which in 1926 was to become part of ICI). He visited the silk softeners and dyers of Hangchow who used wood and straw ash with fatty pig-belly to soften the silk, although he encountered suspicion and the concealment of trade secrets and concluded that 'getting information out of China is an unhappy business'.[39] He also instructed up-country merchants on the manufacture of washing soda and soap. In Tientsin, he reported on dyes used in the cotton industry and noted the eternal problem: 'Some time ago the dyers started to use foreign indigo but gave it up because it was too expensive.' He did, however, conclude after extensive research in the market and amongst local agents that 'even here, at the headquarters of the soda trade, your products are quite capable of competing in price with the much inferior native stuff'. Emmens, the Tientsin manager of the American Trading Co., was equally optimistic: 'the spread of your products need not *necessarily* be slow if you would, after making the necessary arrangements with the foreign firms to act as bases, employ a man or men to go round and push it'.

By the end of his first year in China, Glendinning had appointed the man he felt could open up the alkali market in China, Edward Selby Little. Little was an Englishman who had originally intended to join the Consular Service. However, while studying at Cambridge he had fallen under the influence of American evangelists and had instead become a missionary for the American Methodist Episcopalian Church. He had served in Chinkiang since 1886 but was growing disillusioned with his prospects of advancement within the Church and had already embarked on an ambitious alternative career as a property speculator, developing the resort of Kuling on Lushan mountain as a summer retreat for foreigners residing in the hot and humid cities on the Yangtze.[40]

Little established Brunner Mond's headquarters in Shanghai where by 1906 an impressive residence with a huge lawn in front of it was erected for him at No. 30 Gordon Road. The house's arcaded verandas recalled the earliest treaty port architecture but they were dominated by massive chimneys and gables ornamented with Chinese Tudor timbering. Little set up a network of subordinates, comprising 24 European staff (many of whom were Littles or married to Littles), and 113 Chinese staff, distributed between eastern Siberia, Harbin and Dairen in the frozen north, Tientsin, Hankow, western China and the south as well as at headquarters in Shanghai. Below them were the agents for Brunner Mond chemicals: in the Shanghai area alone, there were 54 agents supplying 400 outlets in the provinces of Chekiang, Anhwei, Fukien and Kiangsi (Jiangxi). In the course of his business as a property speculator, Little also acquired land for Brunner Mond godowns and offices in – amongst other places – Harbin, Dairen, Tientsin, Chefoo, Kalgan (Zhangjiakou), Tsinan, Hankow, Chengchow, Changsha, Shanghai, Nanchang and Chungking.

Like Brunner Mond with its stress on travelling to the interior and examining the native industries that it intended to supplant, Standard Oil, keen to introduce its 'Brilliant' kerosene to millions, distributed below cost many thousands of small kerosene 'Mei-foo' lamps so that Chinese peasants would have something to put the kerosene in. It was perhaps the sight of an inn-keeper in Honan 'carefully pouring the oil into a drain' since 'he really had no use for the oil, but the tin would prove extremely useful' that provoked the project.

Other schemes to supply China's millions with things that they did not yet know they needed came to grief. 'Someone in London had calculated that as China was now open to Western ways, out of the 200 million women there [the calculation was made in the late 1800s], at least one in every 200 would surely wish to learn to play the piano. As a result of that logic, thousands of unwanted pianos rotted in the godowns of Hong Kong and Shanghai.'[41] Most of the few pianos that were wanted in China were acquired by missionaries and warlords and provided work for Mad Mac, the itinerant piano-tuner, who had so firmly expressed his view on Tientsin's Gordon Hall. He travelled far into the interior to keep them going and also tuned the piano kept on the warlord Feng Yu-hsiang's private train. Feng Yu-hsiang may have acquired his piano through missionary influence for he was known as 'the Christian General' and was supposed to baptize his troops whole-sale with a hose-pipe.[42]

Consuls, too, were often expected to cover considerable distances in the pursuit of duty, and the tasks they faced at the end of their journey were not always pleasant. When serving as consul at Kiukiang in 1906, E.T.C. Werner was informed of a massacre at Nanchang, about 100 miles south, which included among its victims British missionaries. As the nearest consul, he was instructed by the British Minister in Peking to proceed 'in a gun-vessel to investigate and settle the case'.

This was easier said than done for the case involved all sorts of Chinese complexities. The British missionaries, the Reverend H. and Mrs Kingham and their elder daughter Gracie, had been 'jumped on, with nailed boots, and crushed with heavy stones' and the only survivor of the family was 5-year-old Vera who had been saved by her amah. Her family had died at the hands of an anti-foreign mob, stirred up by a strange series of events.

The Catholic Mission and the local magistrate had been in dispute for an inordinate length of time over 'a trifling question of the wording on, or placing of, a small signboard next to a Chinese shop'. Père Lacruche invited the magistrate to dinner and pressed him to sign a document to settle the matter. The magistrate signed 'under protest' and then slipped away to cut his throat in another room in the French Mission. This was a traditional Chinese way of apportioning blame: if an aggrieved person committed suicide in another person's home, the home-owner was seen as guilty of murder and would be tried for the crime. To the magistrate and to the Chinese mob that killed not only the Kinghams but also seven French missionaries, the matter was appar-ently not as trifling as it appeared to Werner, who spent the next three weeks 'in investigation, examining the sites, taking evidence'.[43]

Werner merely sat in on the Chinese court to see the Kinghams' murderers found guilty. In Weihaiwei, the district officer and magis-trate, Reginald Johnston, had to preside in local courts himself. Without any other legal officers in the area, there was plenty of scope for drama when the plaintiff and defendant appeared in person, each to conduct his own case, with 'practically unlimited freedom to say what he likes about his opponent and about things in general'.[44] The difficulty of reconciling British judicial practice with freedom of expression was apparent to Meyrick Hewlett, secretary to the British Minister in Peking, who visited Weihaiwei and reported on one case tried there. The 'principal witness, a poor coolie, had lied and lied and lied'. After he had been imprisoned for contempt of court he explained that 'the truth is very valuable, you can use it only once'.[45]

When not administering justice or trying to see it done, many consuls had to open new consulates in conditions that did not differ very much from those that had obtained fifty years before.

On arriving in Weihaiwei in 1902 Stewart Lockhart found that Government House consisted of seven small rooms which 'hardly conjured up an image of the power and magnificence of the British Empire'. Such was the isolation and cold of the winter months there that his wife spent much of her time away.[46] Though the summer months were busy with Hong Kong visitors seeking a cooler summer resort and the arrival of the China Naval Squadron, Stewart Lockhart was extremely isolated, relying largely on correspondence with his junior officer, Reginald Johnston, stationed in the south of the territory, for entertainment. When not covering Weihaiwei's barren slopes with trees, establishing fruit orchards, collecting taxes and dispensing British justice, they exchanged letters filled with the doings of the imaginary figures of Mrs Walkinshaw and the Quork.

Meyrick Hewlett may have been the fourth consul to arrive in Changsha, where he was posted in 1908, but since his first two predecessors had suffered from TB (fatal) and 'nervous prostration' respectively and the third went temporarily out of his mind, they had not devoted much time to the consulate. It was a large rambling house right inside the city with a small stage and a picturesque garden. The living-rooms, however, 'were a nightmare ... damp streamed down them ... the staircase and floors of the upper rooms were rickety in the extreme. Rats flourished everywhere and it was no rare thing to find frogs in the dining-room.' Moreover, the local inhabitants, 'generally speaking, were very anti-foreign ... The mob in Hunan were always easily roused.'[47]

Subsequently posted to Chengtu in Szechwan in 1916, he had to face years of violence of a more modern sort, not the 'anti-foreign mob' but fighting between Szechwanese, Yunnanese and Kweichow warlord troops in the city. In Amoy, where he was posted between 1923 and 1927, he also faced student unrest and an anti-British boycott as well as the enduring problem of coolie emigration which had been a business in the Fukien treaty ports for almost a century. Hewlett actually enjoyed counting the coolies, though 'from the very beginning certain aspects of this emigration worried me intensely'. He found, however, that intervention in the trade led to major complications.

When children were rejected for emigration at the last minute because they had skin diseases, his attempts to reunite them with their families were often unsuccessful because, for financial reasons, parents would refuse to recognize a child rather than be put on shore themselves. He also had to contend with the problem of young girls who had been kidnapped in the interior for shipment to south-east Asia as concubines or prostitutes, a matter of concern to women like Stella Benson who campaigned against slavery in Hong Kong. Hewlett interfered where he could as 'Protector of the Girls'.

Though a consul had to send for gunboats for the protection of his community during riots or warlord battles, he now spent less time promoting British trade. The country was open, though dangerous: foreign firms had offices in the treaty ports and commercial travellers scattered over the country, so more consular time was taken up in attempting to understand and report on the complex political conditions in China. Though British efforts to maintain their traditional control over the Customs succession in 1926–7 revealed some high-handed imperialist attitudes, many of the younger consular officers took their duties very seriously. All were trained in Chinese and some retained a life-long love of the language and continued their researches in Chinese history and literature. Some twentieth-century consuls also developed friendships and contacts that survived the transition to Communism. In retirement, they taught Chinese, translated works from the Chinese and acted as unofficial ambassadors in the difficult years of the Cold War.

14

Maintaining Standards

In the twentieth century, China's treaty ports were not only centres of foreign business activity but also came to represent worldly pleasure and luxury, and to attract tourists. For those for whom the larger treaty ports were home, there was plenty of entertainment available and a pleasant life to be had in comfortably furnished Western-style homes, with a troop of servants and the convenience of instant tailors, shoe-menders and 'takeaway' cake shops outside the door. The Stead family lived for a while in the cotton-mill manager's house at 32 Pingliang Road in Yangtzepoo near the industrial district in north-eastern Shanghai. The house was enormous, with a tennis court and umpteen strawberry beds. There, on Saturdays, the Steads held tennis parties, and in the evenings they and their friends would sit down to play poker or mahjong: 'We had an account at the [German] Café Federal on Broadway so a standing order was placed for goodies to be sent each weekend.'[1]

For those who ventured out in the evenings, particularly tourists and visitors with no home to go to, there were restaurants, nightclubs, cabarets and brothels, though Edward Ward (later Lord Bangor, who worked for Reuters in Shanghai and Tientsin in the 1930s) found 'the nightlife of Shanghai ... on the whole, very over-rated. There were a few smart nightclubs for mixed company where you always saw the same people night after night. And there was a much larger number of cabarets essentially for men with Chinese or White Russian taxi-dancers.'[2]

Though home life in the treaty port cities varied according to the circumstances of each family or household, most tried to achieve the same

standards as 'at home'. Harry Franck, an American journalist, caricatured the Shanghai businessman who

> rents as nearly an American house or apartment as he can get, near a
> trolley-line if he is still below the automobile scale, and settles down into
> the narrow rut of Western existence amid the more or less Occidental
> comforts ... His office is as much like the offices of his homeland as he
> can make it; at noon, he gathers, almost exclusively with his own fellow-
> countrymen, in his club, an almost exact copy of similar gatherings at
> home ... except that the more or less slight sense of secrecy in the matter
> of strong drink is replaced by an almost ostentatious publicity ... When
> his business day is over he is trolleyed or chauffeured home, or out to
> the country club, plays a round of golf, or a set of tennis, or rides an hour
> on horse-back ... He dines, at home, club or foreign hotel, as nearly in
> the homeland style as carefully instructed Chinese cooks and 'boys' can
> accomplish, and settles down to the home newspapers and magazines,
> though they are seldom less than a month old.[3]

The foreign wife had the same ambitions but she had to deal more
directly with the servants. They were cheaper than 'at home' and were,
of course, Chinese. The Stead family in Shanghai had the typical
minimum household staff of 'Cookboy and his wife, Amah ...
Cookboy did all the shopping, cooking, saw to the fires (there was no
central heating) and generally kept the brasses polished. He was a very
good, economical cook and was quick to pick up special favourite
"English" recipes ... Amah looked after the clothes, bedrooms, washing
and ironing and, no doubt, endless tidying up.'[4]

In Tientsin, the Power family had three principal servants, Y Jieh, the
amah, Sung Ge-ge, the coolie, and Jieh-jieh (Y Jieh's daughter-in-law)
who also helped look after the children, as well as a cook and a gardener.
They did not, however, have a 'Number One Boy, a kind of butler', a
feature of wealthier households like that of their grandfather.[5]

Those who came out to China to work for long-established companies always inherited their servants and if they had to find a replacement
they would try to get one of the servants in the house to suggest and
recommend someone – 'otherwise if you brought a complete outsider
in it might upset the rest of your staff'. In larger households two servants in particular ruled their own separate domains: the head amah, in
charge of the nursery if there were children, with the wash amah under

her, but otherwise acting as a wash amah herself; and the Number One Boy, who 'opened the door to guests, waited at table and was responsible for overseeing all the other servants'.[6]

Not all servants worked within the house. In Hainan, the British consul E.T.C. Werner referred to his tennis coolies obliquely when he acquired a monkey,

> a fine specimen of the *hylobates hainanus*, a shorthaired, tailless ape, found only in the island – a gentle, gentlemanly, timid, friendly, philosophical creature, standing about two and a half feet high, with a short triangular tuft of hair above its forehead – quite unlike the mischievous little brown monkeys. It was so clever that it could be taught to field the balls for one at tennis, occasionally throwing them back to the server in imitation of the action of the tennis coolies, but at other times regarding them as good to eat.[7]

The 'ways' of Chinese servants continued to be the subject of repetitive stories which still revolved around the habit of borrowing from other households, the lack of hygiene and the custom of 'squeeze'. One Shanghai resident commented, 'I knew things were borrowed but I was very fierce ... you could go out to dinner and have your grandmother's dessert plate put in front of you but I wasn't going to allow any of that.' Another had a cook who was very good at icing cakes. His mistress fondly assumed that he used the icing bag with assorted funnels that she had acquired for the purpose in Whiteways of Shanghai, but he announced to her replete guests that for icing purposes, '"I used one old toothbrush." And when he saw the look of horror on their faces he went on, "Oh missee, not master's toothbrush, one old toothbrush of mine."'[8]

There were rare stories illustrating the good-hearted willingness of some servants. When Leila Burke, a missionary's wife, was teaching her servant to make French fried potatoes

> she happened to have a sore foot at the time and was wearing a bedroom slipper on it as she sat at the kitchen table peeling and slicing potatoes. She had a shoe on the other foot. Next day she came into the kitchen to watch the cook prepare the dish. He was sitting at the table peeling and slicing and he wore only one shoe. 'What is the matter with your foot?' Leila asked. 'This is the way to prepare the potato dish,' he said soberly.[9]

More common were the views expressed in Elsie McCormick's extended parody, 'The Diary of a Shanghai Baby' (1920), where every possible variation on the unhygienic, un-Western habits of amahs and servants was spelled out in detail: 'Watched coolie cleaning corners of washstand with mamma's toothbrush', 'Sat in kitchen and watched cook scrub potatoes with old hair brush', 'Saw new coolie mopping floor with mamma's sweater on broomstick.'

Not even the amah escaped the infant observer's eye:

mamma said, 'He's getting to be such a big baby that pretty soon we can give him solid food.' If she only knew what I had this morning! A piece of meat dumpling that Amah chewed for me and a water chestnut. Amah is a good sport . . . Went out this morning with amah and wooden elephant. Elephant very nice to bite tooth on but always falling out of perambulator into street. Amah very kind about picking it up and giving it back to me. Know taste of every street in Shanghai.[10]

Squeeze was an eternal source of humour: 'Sat on porch with wooden elephant and watched our coolie cut flowers from next-door garden. Later coolie came in and collected twenty cents from mamma to pay flower-man.' However, dishonesty was not always ignored. The missionary wife Grace Service, normally based in Chengtu, visited friends in Shanghai and came upon the Boy 'in the act of climbing out of the transom above the locked door of my friend's storeroom' with 'some tins in the front part of his gown held up like an apron'. Nothing was said although the next day, when the Boy embarrassed her with his attentions, she simply remarked to her friend that the transom should be nailed shut.[11]

Bad jokes aside, the relationship with an amah was one which many foreign children never forgot, for the amah was usually a patient and loving woman, often responsible for the child's first introduction to Chinese culture. Brian Power's Y Jieh took him further than Tientsin's manicured and regulated local park: they crossed the river on a 'long raft . . . packed with Chinese and . . . a few Russians who smelt of sour kaoliang wine' and walked past the old houses on Romanoff Avenue to the Russian park, a stretch of wild woodland where he could run barefoot and play hide-and-seek. She told him about ghosts and the local White Lotus secret society bandits and took him to the market place where he watched the local *ni ren* (mud figure) makers. 'You could ask for anything you wished, an opera singer, dancer, mandarin or warrior ... Once an old *ni ren* maker called out to me, "Ying-kuo ping ... English soldier." Then in two minutes, he made a figure of an officer with his hands behind his back. Over his khaki uniform the officer wore a Chinese yellow waistcoat.'[12]

For Pearl Buck, daughter of a missionary and brought up in China, her amah was 'one of two clear figures in the dimness of my early child-hood. Foremost stands my mother, but close beside her ... I see ... the blue-coated figure of my old Chinese nurse.' She made Pearl wear a Chinese cap with little Buddhas on it and fitting very closely 'so as to hide the unfortunate [fair] hair. My mother doubted the propriety of Buddhas on the cap of a missionary child, but she was too soft-hearted to say anything about it when she saw how seriously the old nurse felt about it. "We have lost those two [Pearl's elder siblings who had died at the age of 6 months and 4 years] ... It is all very well to trust in a foreign god, but how can we be sure he has power over a country not his own?"' Pearl remembered 'her hard brown hand, its forefinger very rough with needle pricks', her brown and wrinkled face, and her remedy for the thinness of her hair – 'she painted her scalp black ... She used our black shoe polish.' She remembered too being told stories of Chinese magic and dragons and of her amah's own life and how her feet were bound.

They lived in a small town on the Yangtze and the amah used to hatch chickens' eggs herself if the mother hen abandoned them.

> The old nurse would dispose the eggs carefully about her own capacious garments and hatch them with the warmth of her own body. At night she put the eggs under her quilt and slept half awake lest she lie on them. And what a moment it was when we caught the half-absorbed look on her face and saw her shrug herself gently and pull her hand up her wide sleeve and fumble in her depths somewhere! She would whisper in a hushed voice: 'Wait – a chick!' We waited breathless until she reached her hand out carefully with the little damp, new fowl in it.[13]

Unlike their parents who spoke English or pidgin to the servants, foreign children in the treaty ports learnt Chinese from their amahs, though in their recollections they rarely mention this but recount such conversations or repeat the stories they learnt as if there was no language barrier at all. John Espey and his sister, children of American missionaries in Shanghai, were sent to a local nursery school where John got into trouble for repeating a Chinese phrase he had often heard by which 'I had told my little neighbour to commit on a member of his family an act that neither he nor I was capable of performing at that unripe age'. He had to learn to be careful, for every time he opened his mouth to make a general observation on life, something went wrong. 'My idioms were all too highly flavoured. The alley brats would have loved them; the well-bred members of the kindergarten were not amused.' At Christmas, the kindergarten learnt new songs: 'the tune Miss Zung had chosen was a cheerful one but we found trouble with the words. In one of the pauses my sister whispered to me in awe: "It's in Mandarin!" [rather than the familiar Shanghai dialect] ... The song was called "Gau lei tzu" as far as we could tell ... the first line ran ... "Gao lei tzu mei li jen too meng".' When their mother turned up for the Christmas concert, John and his sister discovered that they had spent two earnest weeks memorizing Miss Zung's English version of 'God Rest You Merry Gentlemen'.[14]

Many missionary children mixed more with Chinese children than did those of other foreign residents, but their encounters were not always easy. The Espeys, resident in Chinese rather than 'foreign' Shanghai (just south of the walled Chinese city), were only too aware of the attitude of the local children to their privileged neighbours:

> When we rode unescorted in a rickshaw, they leapt up and pulled off my sister's hair-ribbons ... Or they would grab an end of my Windsor tie on gala days and pull out the bow and knot as the heavy silk scorched out through my Eton collar ... Our amah grew worried over my diminishing stock of cravats, so one day she tied a square knot in a new Windsor before she made the bow. I bore the scar of that encounter for months. We were occasionally spat upon, and more than one stone sailed over the bamboo fence.

Encounters with the local children reached a climax in about 1920 over their determined efforts to destroy the flowers in the Espey garden – the gate having been left open by the gate-keeper, asleep over his opium pipe. After an exchange of blows with the 'Lady Bandit' leader of the local children, parents were involved and John Espey's pious mother 'decided that the alley brats would make excellent subjects for her children's Christian zeal. She pointed out to us that the alley children were not really bad ... at all. They lived hard, meagre lives, barren of beauty. They did not really mean to ruin our flowers out of spite.' Instead, they should be provided with the generous gift of flowers of their own. Some thirty plants were grown, potted and presented. Returning across the canal bridge with her gifts, 'the Lady Bandit, without a flicker of hesitation, poised the flowerpots and shot out both her arms ... A dwarf rose soared over the left railing, a white geranium over the right, and both plants splashed into the yellow water of the canal.'[15]

When he went to school, John Espey's fellow-pupils were all, like him, foreign. He spent some time at the Shanghai American School, one of many in the city which served the considerable number of foreign children. The Stead sisters attended St Joseph's and later the Holy Family Convent, travelling the considerable distance by rickshaw and then by bus when they were old enough.

In Tientsin, the writer Mervyn Peake, son of a medical missionary, attended a British grammar school, which in retrospect he remembered as having 'nothing to do with China. It might have been flown over in a piece from Croydon. It faced the dusty street ... The rickshaws would rattle by in the sun while we tried to remember the name of the longest river in England, the date of Charles II's accession, or where one put the decimal point.' Mervyn Peake admired a one-eyed Russian boy who swung from the Venetian blinds and lived in a 'fantastic tawdry gaudy muddle of a flat'.[16]

In the same city, Brian Power and his brother attended various schools, each change being the result of the unruly behaviour of Brian's elder brother Patrick, who was friendly with some similarly wild Russians. First of these schools was the British Municipal Council's junior school in Gordon Road. The choice was made by their mother who was anxious, so Brian recorded, 'that our English should be improved. All Pat's friends were Siberians and I was nearly always downstairs with the servants, speaking Chinese.' When Pat began playing truant the boys were sent to a Marist Brothers' school in the French concession. There their schoolfellows numbered

Russians from Manchuria, Siberians, French, Belgians and a sprinkling of Turks, Armenians and Portuguese. We also had six or seven half-castes. Two of them sat on the same bench as me. Carlos Simões, a sad-looking boy, had a Portuguese father and a Chinese mother. Bobby Thomas had a Korean mother. His father, a Welsh seaman, worked on a passenger ship . . . A half-caste was the worst thing you could be and I used to feel sorry for them.[17]

It was not long before Pat was once again expelled for playing truant and drawing satirical cartoons and the two boys were next sent to the British School in Avon Road. On Sundays, Brian served as an altar boy in the Jesuit College, the Hautes Etudes Commerciales et Industrielles, in Racecourse Road, where he met Father Pierre Teilhard de Chardin who came to tea. Teilhard was a famous Jesuit theologian who had discovered the fossil remains of Peking Man in the Gobi desert (although he was later, less gloriously, involved in the Piltdown Man hoax), and his sister had been the Mother Superior of the convent of the Little Sisters of the Poor in Shanghai until her early death from smallpox.[18]

Though the Power boys attended day schools, some treaty port children were sent home to boarding school. As one woman explained, 'Climatically I think babies and young children did very well in China, but they became awfully leggy if they stayed out.'[19] Parents not worried by legginess could send their children to a boarding school in China itself, of which there were now an increasing number. The earliest were established in the seaside town of Chefoo in Shantung province. A guide of 1907 recorded, 'there are several well-conducted schools to which children are sent from all parts of the East, as much in the interest of their health [seaside Chefoo was bracing] as their education'.[20]

Ex-pupils seem to remember more of the exciting trips home than of the day-to-day routine of school life. Gren Wedderburn, the son of missionaries in Manchuria, was sent to school in Chefoo when he was 7.

Mainly because of the terrible winter, Chefoo School surrendered its pupils for a two-month winter holiday, a short Easter holiday and a one-month summer holiday. In winter our journey from Chao yang chun [Chaoyangzhen] to school took at least a week. In summer, by the time one got home one would have to leave the next day to be back in time for the new term, because the road from the railway to Chao became a sea of mud. The lead horse could easily be drowned in the mud ... My father and mother would come to stay in Chefoo for the summer or we would travel the short distance from school to Pei Tai Ho [Beidaihe], a resort on the coast connected by rail to Peking.[21]

Adrian Dansey Smith and his brother, sons of second-generation Wesleyan missionaries who were based up the Yangtze, travelled home for the holidays to the different medical missions at which their parents worked. This involved some long and complicated trips, sailing to Amoy by Japanese steamer via Port Arthur and Japan. On his journeys to and from school, Wedderburn remembered escorts, usually missionaries or businessmen, who were sent to keep an eye on the travelling schoolchildren. 'The missionary would try to achieve reasonable behaviour from his treasures by appealing to our Christian upbringing. The businessman adopted a more pragmatic approach – outright bribery ... handing out candies, ice cream and soft drinks.'[22]

John Espey was sent to board at the Kuling American School in January 1923. His journey from Shanghai was long, though not as long as that of some Chefoo schoolboys. First there was the Jardine steamer from Shanghai to Kiukiang, then a public bus to the foothills of the mountains where thick clothes were put on. 'I was wearing a brown corduroy suit, over it a green and red plaid mackinaw. I put on my heaviest gloves and a piece of knitted headgear modelled after a balaclava helmet.' He and his 'Courtesy Aunt', who was escorting him, 'carried rubber hot-water bottles which we filled at a tea shop, and we got into our sedan chairs, put the bottles next to our feet and wrapped our steamer rugs around our legs.' They were carried all day, up stepped paths through groves of bamboos 'weighted down with ice and snow', with two stops in the day for the chair coolies to eat and drink tea. Near the snowy summit in Kuling, John Espey was introduced to the American School, to dormitory life, to examinations of dirty fingernails, to making toast on bath night, and to running, football and French lessons from Madame Poliakoff who had 'been taught with the Czar's daughters'.[23]

When not confined in school or *en route* to it, children found much to do in China. In Tientsin, in winter, there was skating and ice-boat races on sledges with sails. In summer there were daily visits to the iron-railinged Victoria Park in the company of amahs, or donkey rides and bicycle trips. In Shanghai and other large ports, there were clubs and Boy Scout troops. Brian Power belonged to the Number One Troop Tientsin Boy Scouts. On Armistice Day he paraded in his uniform and wondered, 'Was it ever as cold as this in the South African veldt where Colonel Baden-Powell had invented this uniform?'[24] John Espey, enrolled in the Pine Tree Patrol in Kuling, went on camping trips. The Scouts sent semaphore messages with red and white flags – 'What hav Lnch?' 'Chs sanwch banas' – and had coolies to carry their bedding rolls, wood coolies to light the camp-fire and still others to bring in supplies of meat, eggs and milk, though the Scoutmaster liked to do most of the cooking.[25]

The solitary children of missionaries in small towns had to make their own amusements. Pearl Buck's family home in Yangchow stood on a hill covered in graves. Traditionally, Chinese did not hold funerals for very young children, for in the days of high infant mortality they were not considered real people until they had survived their first years. As a good Presbyterian missionary daughter, however, Pearl Buck was distressed by the little bodies lying on the hillside and the stray 'yellow curs' that sought them out, so she would wander over the hill and hold proper funerals with 'flowers, or if it were winter . . . a twig or evergreen or a bit of bright tile or a pretty pebble' as she buried the remains. She also began her literary career at the age of 6 in the same morbid vein by writing a letter about the deaths of her brothers and sisters which was published in the *Christian Observer* in Louisville, Kentucky, in April 1899: 'I have two little brothers in heaven, Maudie went first, then Edith and on the tenth of last month my brave little brother Clyde, left us to go to our real home in heaven.'[26]

Many such childhood deaths were still attributable to cholera or dysentery, despite the soaking, filtering and boiling that mothers organized and improvised. John Service's only sister Virginia died on a boat bound up-river on the Yangtze in 1906. On board the little boat, his mother had tried to boil everything that was needed for the six-month-old baby as they traversed the section of the river where the worst rapids occurred, but to no avail. She had also tried varying the child's diet, using the various infant foods they had brought with them, but this, too, proved useless.[27] One other threat, not restricted to China but shocking to children, was that of rabies. Several Shanghai schoolchildren died after contact with infected pets.

Under more settled conditions, apart from soaking vegetables and fruit in permanganate of potash (and then rinsing them in filtered water) as the Stead family did, all drinking water had to be 'boiled, filtered and then cooled in the ice-box'. This was a huge wooden case with two compartments lined with zinc: one at the top for food and ice and the lower one to collect the water as the ice melted. Even in Shanghai, the Western staple of milk was hard to find. The Stead sisters were brought up on Carnation milk and tinned butter. 'The Culty dairy was established in the 1930s. Our first drink of cold fresh milk didn't go down well – it had a completely different taste and we thought it was off!'[28]

Far from the conveniences of Shanghai, it was still difficult to maintain a Western household although, in the memories of some, it was possible. Whilst the Stead family made do with their ice-box, in 1923 the missionary Service family up the Yangtze in Chungking acquired a refrigerator. It ran on a small kerosene flame and, though it could not produce ice in hot weather, it kept drinks and jellies cold.[29] Their water, drawn from the Yangtze in which people washed, dropped their rubbish, defecated and died, was not only boiled but also strained through gravel, sand and, finally, charcoal in 'massive sand filters ... arranged in tiers' in the rat-proofed kitchen.

Sanitary arrangements remained primitive outside Shanghai and Tientsin. Baths were taken in Soochow tubs, huge ceramic pots filled with water by the servants. Stella Benson described the arrangements in her house in Nanking: 'I live in a very comfortable, largish house, rather modern, with wide cool verandas and electric light. There are three bathrooms in the house ... but (and I put this in deference to your known interest in such matters) wooden commodes instead of what are sometimes called flush toilets. At 9 a.m. the commodes are carried out and dropped in the river.'[30]

As well as being filthy, China's rivers regularly burst their banks. On the night Brian Power was born, in 1918, his mother was 'marooned by flood waters in our house on Meadows Road and Y Jieh ... acted as midwife', while the huge bronze bell from the Light of the Sea pagoda tolled 'all day long because the Sea River had burst its banks'.[31]

Such natural disasters were not uncommon and added to the difficulties of keeping a nice Western-style home. Even without disasters, life in southern China was uncomfortable enough and E.T.C. Werner determined to find a posting in the north as soon as possible to escape

being mildewed for three-quarters of the year; when the walls of one's rooms dripped with moisture, when one's skin did ditto, the pores never seeming to close, when one was constantly stung by mosquitoes and sand-flies, when ladies sitting at dinner had to put their feet and ankles into paper bags to prevent them being bitten, when steam-damp spoiled the pages and pictures of one's library books, cockroaches ate off the backs of the covers, and the borer beetle (*anobium striatum*) tunnelled through volume after volume from title-page to index, when swarms of flying ants, moths etc., cremated themselves in the lamps or dived into one's soup, white ants ate through the floors of the rooms and pillars of the house, when the atmosphere seemed almost too solid to breathe.[32]

In memory, at least, some appear to have managed to surmount the heat, and the self-cremating insects and the paper bags faded from recall. Pearl Buck wrote lyrically of her missionary mother's house-keeping in Chinkiang and Yangchow:

She made homes in China that were exquisite in taste. All my memories there are of quiet cool rooms, flowers everywhere, simple delicious meals and pervading order. Yes, she created every room except the room where my father lived, which was called his study. There he allowed no curtains or flowers, and the floor was bare. Books covered the walls and a vast desk stood in the middle of the room. His typewriter, which he took care of himself, though with difficulty, for he had no mechanical ability, was on a small separate table.

Mrs Buck must have been a strict manager: 'her Chinese servants had first of all to be clean in every way. Raw foods and salads she made herself, because she did not trust their hands, and although she taught her cook to make the lightest cakes that tongue ever tasted and his hot breads were delectable, she would not let him touch them with his hands.' Heaven knows how he made bread under these conditions, but Mrs Buck's hygienic practices extended further, for even when her small daughter helped her make coconut cake, 'The pieces of fresh white [coconut] meat were then ... grated by hand on an old-fashioned grater, for unless one were careful one scraped one's fingers, in which case my mother's sharp eyes always detected pink stains upon the snow-white coconut.'

As they grew up, those children not eventually sent home to boarding school could continue to enjoy home life and make many friends amongst the younger arrivals in the bigger treaty ports. Young men, sent out to work in Western business enterprises, still lived together in 'messes', as they had since the 1840s. There were, however, now more women to go round than there had been then. The four Stead sisters grew up in Shanghai and found their boyfriends there. 'The first crush Ivy had was on Tommy Buchanan and Mary thought Malcolm, his brother, was pretty nice too ... They met at one of the Saturday swimming parties at Hongkew Baths.' The sisters also joined the Junior Tennis Club at Wayside Park where 'their affections turned to Charlie and Jimmy Taylor ... both good tennis players but, more interestingly, they played the pipes in the Shanghai Volunteer Band and, wore KILTS! Also they attended the same Union Church.'[33]

While the bright and pretty Stead sisters with their attractive outfits (made to their own designs by the local tailor) had no trouble finding suitors in populous Shanghai, the eccentric E.T.C. Werner reported on different conditions in Canton. He described the consul, Sir Challoner Alabaster, 'an official of the old gunboat policy', as a 'physically insignificant and crippled dwarf' and expressed surprise that Lady Alabaster, daughter of the missionary Dr MacGowan (who had been so oddly dressed when Fortune and Hart met him in Foochow in the 1860s), 'had no less than fifty proposals of marriage' but actually accepted him. Alabaster was, said Werner, so small 'that the amah once went and tucked him up in bed, mistaking him for one of his children!' Werner, who took the prudent course of going home to find a spouse whom he married in 1911, reflected on the difficulties of finding a wife in the smaller treaty ports.

> Foreign spinsters were rare birds in China in those days, and what really constituted a proposal is, of course, a moot question, and would be quite differently defined by the proposer and the proposee. Desperate spinsters, clutching at straws, and confusing attention with intention, might consider being helped on with a cloak or an over-hearty shake of the

hand as coming within the definition, only to be disillusioned by the relentless march of time.[34]

For those in modern Shanghai, less likely to be confused by a hearty hand-shake, there were tea-rooms for decorous meetings, like Bianchi's on the Nanking Road, which was Italian, and where they had 'nice cakes, lovely little finger rolls with foie gras'. At the Chocolate Shop, which was run by an American, there was quite a large restaurant – 'you could get all the lovely things like cakes and ice creams, beautiful sundaes American style, hamburgers, club sandwiches – I've never had a club sandwich as good as I had there.'[35] Shanghai's eating establishments were as cosmopolitan as its inhabitants.

The Stead sisters enjoyed

> Marcel's, a French tea-room, [which] was pish-posh – with its cool decor of lilac and pale grey. They offered a delectable selection of dainty cakes … Didi's on Avenue Foch in the French Concession … was an Italian nightclub but on Sundays they served special teas. It had a rather gloomy atmosphere of black and silver furnishings and neon lights – their ice-cream cake compensated for the gloom … in the Bubbling Well area … there was a country tea-shack run by Scots. We would sit in the garden and enjoy home-baked scones and goats-milk cream cheese.[36]

The cinema was a source of much entertainment in twentieth-century China. At the Empire cinema in Tientsin, Herr Schneider – who looked like Charlie Chaplin and who normally played Viennese waltzes in a trio at Kiessling's restaurant in the centre of town – accompanied the showing of *Tarzan of the Apes* and Charlie Chaplin shorts to Saturday afternoon audiences of rowdy children. Herr Schneider had particular trouble with cowboy films which excited Pat Power and his Siberian friends Ibragimoff and Kravchuk so much that they took to throwing paper darts down from the front row of the gallery until caught and banned from the cinema. Herr Schneider, deprived of his Saturday afternoon job by the arrival of the 'talkies', was later spied in floods of appreciative tears at Chaliapin's concert in Gordon Hall.

Apart from special events like Chaliapin's concert, for ordinary recreation there were clubs of all sorts. Shanghai possessed 'a Cricket Club which everybody belonged to, even if you didn't play cricket', the American Columbia Country Club, and, more famously, the men-only

Shanghai Club on the Bund, 'very largely for luncheon' and known for its bar, the longest in the world, where the 'senior people ... were on the left as you go in ... and the more junior people in the middle and right'. The French Club had an Olympic-size swimming-pool – 'you could sit round and there was a lot of space to have snacks; there were lovely diving boards; a lot of super tennis courts, both hard and grass; a ballroom with a sprung floor ... a dining-room with marvellous food'.

In more remote treaty ports, the smaller number of foreign residents were still thrown upon each other's company. Stella Benson must have been a rather terrifying fellow-resident in Chungking. Already a well-known novelist when she arrived in 1920, she did not find many kindred spirits. At dinner she met Captain Hall, his wife and his sister-in-law, 'such fools that they amused me rather. Mrs Hall asked me in such an exasperating voice whether I didn't think people wasted their time reading novels when this wonderful scenery was around. I said no, I always read the most outrageous novels I could find when this wonderful scenery was around.' Mrs Hall's sister ('sillier still') repeatedly asked Stella how she liked Chungking. 'Every time she said that, I gave her a different opinion, always as if it were my first pronouncement on the subject.'

Bored stiff at another lunch, she asked her hostess,

'Do your visitors ever insist on climbing up the flagstaff between courses?' For it was just outside with a tantalizing wire-rope ladder. Mrs Toller said, 'Yes. Do please, our tiffin parties are always quite informal.' I was cold all over at this calling of my bluff so I toiled up in the rain. It is a very high flagstaff and the ladder is as limp in the air as a rag. I hadn't got more than 20 rungs up before I knew that my arms were not really strong enough ... However, Seamus shouted at me to come down at once, so of course I went on up, feeling very sick and certain that my head would burst like an egg when it hit that massive stone base of the mast ... the ladder was jerking and twisting around so that the river and the city and the hills were all confused in my eyes ... I was watching without realizing it a tethered goat on the lawn biting at a mocking white butterfly.

Stella Benson's husband was transferred in 1922 to Mengtse (Mengzi), near the border with Indo-China, where there were even fewer foreign residents to shock. Her neighbours, the Pritchards, 'took great trouble to discourage us about everything at Mengtse, there was not a single domestic or intellectual or social essential for our future about which they would allow us to harbour hope – again the lower middle class love of imparting bad news'. There was a Customs colleague in the throes of an excruciatingly long-drawn-out affair with the wife of a French official, given to 'amorous yap'. Though no woman thought of going out to tea without putting her gloves on, the French wives apparently took no baths but 'lounged in slovenly kimonos all day except when they expect company, in which case they appear in exquisite but unwashable satins and silks in sweltering heat – men playing tennis in coloured shirts, braces and stiff-trousers (non-washing) with glimpses of sky blue underwear at the ankles'.[37]

When her husband was transferred northwards to another Customs post, Stella Benson suffered most from having to leave her animals behind. Presumably the Customs were unwilling to bear the cost of moving horses and dogs. With more pathos than the average treaty port parent sending its offspring home to boarding school, she wrote, 'I can hardly bear to think of them, going through their lives, looking in vain for all the love and notice and talk that I have given them – and all the joy, the bouncing and whinnying that is lavished on us whenever we come in must be bottled up forever now. The little funny special voice that belonged to each dog will never be heard again.'[38]

For most, their dogs and horses were no more than sporting essentials, the horses, in particular, often sold off unsentimentally at the end of the season. Even in sybaritic Shanghai, sport and racing remained major preoccupations. The races, whether in Shanghai, Tientsin or at the smaller courses in Foochow or Hankow, were a great social event and a grand excuse for dressing up.

From the innocent owner-rider races of the mid-nineteenth century, the whole business had become far more complex as owners discovered cross-bred ponies that were taller and faster than the little Mongol ponies. These cross-breeds were produced by the Russians near Harbin from about 1915, and the introduction of some twenty of them by J.M. Dickinson to Tientsin in 1924 provoked a major crisis. Dickinson was well-liked but his action resulted in the disbarment of 'any animals superior to our own' in subsequent years. Zoologists, anatomists and veterinary surgeons attempted to decide what was a true Mongol pony and what was not, and whether cross-breeding was deliberate or accidental. In the end, all the race clubs made their own decisions. The problem was by no means settled, however, for a Z class pony in Tientsin remained a B class pony in Shanghai.[39]

Paper-hunts, not for betting but for fun, persisted in Shanghai and spread throughout China, but they were not without their own peculiar problems. On the outskirts of Shanghai, Edward Ward experienced little success at the sport. 'The first time out, I was chased by an enraged Chinese peasant wielding a formidable thornbush. The second time I fell off my pony miles out in the country and had to walk home. My pony was not found until the following day.' On another occasion he was charged by a water-buffalo.

> These ungainly, black beasts, with swept-back sabre-shaped horns, hated foreigners, though they could be controlled easily by a small Chinese child. Small Chinese children ... found it very profitable to ride buffaloes in places where foreigners were likely to be found on Sundays ... and let the buffalo chase the foreign devils up a tree ... Then they would demand a dollar to drive the animal away.[40]

As paper-chases had to be held after the harvest to prevent too much damage to crops, the cold of the winter in some parts of China brought its own problems. Mrs Giles, whose husband was with the Hongkong and Shanghai Bank in Mukden, won a paper-chase and the privilege of laying the trail for the next one. In the Mukden area, however, with its fierce winds, paper was impracticable, so whitewash was used instead. Wearing Russian boots and furs, she set out to lay the trail until, halfway through, the hunt mafoo announced that they had to go home. '"We can't! We must finish it!" "No can, missie," he answered. I said, "How say no can?" The mafoo ... proffered the bucket of whitewash. It was totally frozen.'[41]

In warmer Shanghai, though 'everybody' may have joined the Cricket Club, there were plenty of restrictions. 'Anybody' could go to the French Club although it actually had a quota for each nationality. Betty Welbelove was not allowed to join the Country Club because her father was 'in a Trade'; members had to be 'in a profession or an office'. Even if you were allowed in, distinctions were maintained: C.E.

Tremlett was 'cut dead in mid-dance when his partner discovered he was a Customs out-doorman, one of the dead-end boys'.[42]

Such class distinctions were strong. The greatest, of course, was that between foreigners and Chinese: apart from contact with servants, social interaction was generally restricted to formal lunches which seldom included women. When they did, the honour was rarely appreciated.

> My husband was asked out to dinner by some of the Chinese Chamber of Commerce ... but it wasn't usual really to ask a wife as well. So it was rather a special occasion when we were asked out by the chairman of the Electric Light Works ... My husband and I and ... two Germans were the only other Europeans ... The chairman of the Light Works didn't speak any English at all and I sat next to him and he kept putting nasty bits of food, which he thought were lovely bits of food, on my plate ... I wasn't very happy as I was having a rather dull time.[43]

H. Picard-Destelau, who worked in the Chinese postal service, simply stated that he 'found it a bore to maintain personal relations' with his Chinese colleagues.[44]

Along with Betty Welbelove and her father who was in trade, there were other lower orders. Despite the existence of two synagogues in Shanghai, Jewish businessmen were excluded from many clubs and social events and, in consequence, often formed better relationships with Chinese than with their fellow-Europeans. The ships' captains who commanded the merchant fleet on the Yangtze were similarly excluded from polite society although missionaries befriended them. Pearl Buck, with her little brother and their amah, visited Captain Swan, the river master who managed the movement of Jardine's ships on the Yangtze, and his wife on the Jardine 'hulk' at Chinkiang. It had a cosy cabin and a saloon 'that Mrs Swan had made over to look as much as possible like the parlour in a Scotch Presbyterian manse'. There they sat down to 'an enormous Scotch tea, with scones and jam and strong English tea and sweet biscuits and shortcakes and fine pound cake and fresh raisin cake'. Captain Swan drank 'out of an enormous moustache cup that said on one side "A Present From Glasgow" in gold letters mixed with pink roses ... The talk during tea was exactly as though we were not on a hulk in the Yangtze River, but in a respectable small home somewhere in Scotland. No mention was made of China or the Chinese.'[45]

By the beginning of the twentieth century, another precious feature of foreign residence had appeared in the growth of the 'hill-stations' or holiday resorts, similar to those in the Indian Himalayan foothills, where foreign residents of most classes could enjoy a cool summer holiday away from the terrible heat of the cities. Missionaries, too, made their way from distant stations to join their children released from Chefoo College for the summer. The most famous of these resorts was Kuling, established in the last years of the nineteenth century by Edward Selby Little, its name reputedly invented by Little and meant to be understood as 'cooling'.

E.T.C. Werner was less complimentary about the hill-station, referring to 'the deadly monotony of Kuling with its transferred pettiness',[46] for the story of a violent eruption in Foochow involving him had pursued him to the summer resort. It is hardly surprising that the gossip had travelled, for it involved consular officials and Customs officers, and both communities were spread wide across China only to gather and gossip in the hill-stations during the summer holidays. In his memoirs, Werner was circumspect about the origin of the problem. He wrote that he had received long letters of complaint, criticism and abuse, first from one disgruntled merchant and then, later, a stream of anonymous letters from, he believed, a number of people. Soon after the death of the disgruntled merchant in September 1913, the Werners' house at Foochow was broken into. Convinced that the miscreant (also suspected of writing anonymous letters) was a junior member of the Customs staff, Werner pursued him, according to some, armed with a horse-whip, to the Foochow Club where, Werner says, 'a foul epithet was hurled' at Mrs Werner. For Werner, the case was never satisfactorily resolved and in his memoirs he vented much fury on his enemy's superior, Paul King, the Customs commissioner. Werner never mentioned King's name but the description of a man devoted to sports and suffering from sprue and the after-effects of smallpox caught in Tientsin is easy to identify. Werner said that the smallpox still looked so horrible that 'when he called at the consulate ... my wife used to sit as far away from him as possible. This, I was afterwards informed, he regarded as an official slight!' Werner continued his pen-portrait, 'An interesting study for a psychoanalyst would be the fact that one of his sons later presented him with a Tibetan daughter-in-law and some half-baked grand-children.'[47] In his memoirs, Paul King makes no mention of this unpleasant scandal but concentrates on the (less) difficult character of his chief, Sir Robert Hart.

Provided no one was gossiping about him, there were times when Werner, stationed in the British consulate at Kiukiang, positively appreciated Kuling. Kiukiang was 'intolerably hot ... lying in a depression ... and shielded from the southern breeze (the only one which blows in summer)' so it was a relief in Kuling to 'enjoy respite from the stifling and enervating heat of the plains, with good tennis, walks, picnics and swimming in the pool'. Werner used to travel there by sedan chair but his last consular act in Kiukiang was to negotiate with the Taotai of the district an agreement for the building of a railway to the foot of the mountains. 'This, afterwards changed to a motor service, lessened the discomfort across the baking plain to about half an hour.'[48]

With such infrastructural support, Little acquired land in Kuling and sold lots on Cambridge Road, Oxford Road, Cardiff Road, Pennsylvania Road, Verdun Road and Highland Avenue. There was a cemetery, shops, a post office, a swimming-pool, tennis courts, the Fairy Glen Hotel, numerous churches and, eventually, boarding schools like the Redcroft School and the Kuling American School.[49] Villas, built out of local stone but with elaborate woodwork verandas and porches, perched on the mountainside, and were rented by the missionaries and businessmen who came up to join their children in the summer.

Kuling was not, however, the only summer resort established by foreigners. Mokanshan (Moganshan), some forty miles north of Hangchow, was another favourite. To reach it missionary families sailed along the Grand Canal: 'It was lovely and peaceful on the small deck in the evenings, our feet trailing in the canal, the green rice fields, the fishermen with cormorants on their wrists, the squeak of the oars as we slept under mosquito nets.' The family servants, together with bedding, pots, pans, dishes and baggage, were all then transferred to sedan chairs and carrying poles to ascend the mountain, away from the sultry plain. As in Kuling, families installed themselves in villas, some like stone

Swiss chalets, some Gothic miniatures, some Mediterranean in appearance with green-painted shutters and windows with leaded panes, filled with art deco and bamboo furniture. Whatever their source of inspiration, all had the inevitable veranda. And just as in Kuling, there was plenty to do – 'an annual tennis tournament, a field day, picnics, ball games, swimming and diving lessons, amateur dramatic productions and sing-alongs, boy-scout hiking and wilderness camping trips'.[50]

For residents of Peking and Tientsin, the nearest summer resort was Peitaiho, on the coast near the place where the Great Wall ran down into the sea. Ann Bridge, in her novel *Four-part Setting*, described the summer holiday of a Post Office superintendent and his sister and cousin there. They took a bungalow with french windows opening on to a long veranda and 'bathed in the mornings, sometimes from their own mat-shed at the foot of the green-clad bluff, sometimes from the ministerial bathing boat at Legation Point, which boasted a diving platform ... They sat about afterwards on the sand and drank cherry brandy and ate ginger snaps.' Returning to their bungalow, they found the amah waiting with cans of water beside a sitz-bath to rub her mistress down and powder her shoulders. In loose silk robes and espadrilles they drank cocktails on the veranda, lunched and then lay and sweated on their beds behind lowered blinds. After tea they played tennis or went for walks, and kissed (generally not each other although the Post Office superintendent and his cousin got perilously close).[51]

At Peitaiho, apart from bungalows with verandas and diving platforms, the most famous of the Tientsin shops and restaurants opened branches for the summer season where

> Europeans purchase such articles as cannot well be left to the discretion of their Number One boy – medicines and chemical supplies, tapes and buttons, fine groceries. The Number Ones make their purchases elsewhere, in the Chinese village ... [that] is not smart; the smart part is at West End, where there are villas standing amongst trees ... bungalows ... half-hidden in the native growth of bushes and small trees, mimosas and thorns.[52]

Kiessling's, whose main branch was in the centre of Tientsin, served ice cream with chocolate sauce, Chicken Kiev, caviare and pastries, whilst a Russian quartet played under the chandeliers. On the beach there were straw-matting bathing huts, and Chinese pedlars wandered along the sand selling straw sun-hats and sandals and also making spun-sugar silhouettes for children.

The end of the summer marked a return to the treaty ports: 'the first concern of those who return from a sojourn at Peitaiho is – in the case of the women at least – to get their hair set'.[53] Perhaps it was, but there were also children to return to school and control to be re-established over servant expenditure, as well as bread-making and the winter round of dinner parties and Christmas celebrations. Perhaps, too, there might be visitors from home to entertain.

15

Tourists and Aesthetes

Visitors to the treaty ports were numerous and varied. Some travelled in pursuit of professional interests. Others were drawn by China's ancient civilization, though more evidence of this was to be found beyond the treaty ports, notably in and around Peking. Many were attracted by the curious and convenient blend of East and West that Shanghai, in particular, offered. As travel beyond Europe became increasingly possible and popular from the 1920s, large numbers of tourists visited Shanghai and Tientsin for luxury shopping, rickshaw rides, temple visits and evenings in bars and cabarets.

Among the earliest visitors were the plant-hunters, drawn to China by the richness of her flora and responsible for the introduction of many new species to the West.[1] Robert Fortune's descriptions of the early treaty ports were the result of three plant-hunting trips made in 1843–6, 1848–51 and 1853–6. At the ports he collected cultivated plants but, as soon as he could manage it, he was off to the mountains and the tea-producing areas. Other plant-hunters, among them E.H. Wilson, Reginald Farrer and George Forrest, concentrated on Szechwan, the Tibetan foothills and Yunnan, far from the coastal and Yangtze ports. Farrer, in particular, disliked the smaller treaty ports, describing Ichang, through which he used to pass on his way home, as 'the saddest place on earth. Rounding a vast bend in the Yangtze it lies sad and flat and forbidding-looking, grey under a grey sky, with nothing but grey flatness filling all the world around and the mountains left behind for ever ... It may indeed be a delightful place to those who live there but to me it spells the close of everything.'

Further down the Yangtze, one treaty port did have its uses. In Hankow, Farrer paused to have a real bath, the first since he had left London. He was similarly appreciative of the comforts of Chungking in 1918 after two years plant-hunting in the north-western province of Kansu (Gansu) and in Szechwan.

> Chungking lies high and up and down above the curve of the river. In due course a brace of chairs came down for us and we were conveyed dizzyingly up flights of stairs into the town itself; and thence along its very narrow streets, very crowded, dark and dank and paved, to the narrow dark yard of what proved, however, an inn so foreign as to rightly justify its claim to be an hotel. For here, after two years of exile, I felt myself quite like a child come back to its doll's-house, revelling in the folly of white sheets and spring-mattresses and tables and chairs and cutlery and glasses ...
>
> Out in front was a big wooden loggia looking over the river far below to a range of peaked wooded hills with temples and pagodas on them and immediately in front of us, across the river, the name of that great nobleman Sir Alfred Mond [of the chemical company Brunner Mond] emblazoned across the frontal of a factory, to bring us once more in touch with the beloved benefits of British enterprise.

Farrer, however, soon tired of the 'civilization' of the treaty ports: 'Not even this happy home touch, however, not even the spectacle, one night, of a raging fire, devouring house after house in its maw, but not Sir Alfred Mond, could cheer the dark of our declining days, in this dark place where the air is always suggestive of a London fog.'[2]

The journalist and traveller Peter Fleming, who made several extensive trips to China in the 1930s, one a journey of 3,500 miles across mountain and desert from Peking to Kashmir in 1935, was most appreciative of British life in a Chinese outpost. One of the later chapters in his account of the 1935 trip is entitled 'Kashgar-les-Bains' in honour of the surprisingly homely comforts of the isolated British consulate there. 'After the rigours of the trip, sitting in comfortable armchairs with long drinks and illustrated papers and a gramophone playing ... was a heavenly experience ... We stayed a fortnight in Kashgar, leading a country-house life.'[3]

Rather against both their wills, Fleming had travelled with the attractive Swiss ski-champion and explorer Ella ('Kini') Maillart. In

Kashgar, 'very prone to spy-fever', on the night they arrived 'the bazaar rumour ran that a British agent had ridden in from Khotan, accompanied by a White Russian disguised as a woman. This was hard on Kini; but the next evening we both played Association Football with the consulate guard of Hunzas, so that rumour had a longer life than most.' When not playing football, there was tennis with the Russians and, twice a week, polo organized by the consul's wife, Mrs Thompson-Glover. Life in Kashgar was not always so enjoyable. The year before Mrs Thompson-Glover had been shot in the shoulder on the consulate terrace by a Chinese Muslim soldier.[4]

Like Reginald Farrer's, Peter Fleming's visits to the treaty ports were marked by baths, and by good food. He arrived in Changsha 'very tired', but thanks to the hospitality of the Commissioner of Customs, 'a delightful Pickwickian American in a bottle-green coat', he departed with a full stomach and very nearly clean.[5] Harbin in 1933 had proved less relaxing. The city was dangerous: 'few foreigners dared to walk abroad at night and none to walk unarmed'. On the golf course, 'a White Russian guard, armed to the teeth, was much more indispensable than a caddy'. Bandits still throve and the branch manager of a leading British firm entertained Fleming in a compound whose wall was crowned with electrified barbed wire.[6] His visit to Harbin was also enlivened by a swim with a legendary figure, One-Arm Sutton, the bodyguard of the local warlord Chang Tso-lin and, according to Fleming, the only Old Etonian claiming to hold the rank of General in the Chinese Army. Whilst Fleming and Sutton bathed under the eyes of soldiers and police armed with rifles and automatics, there was a bandit scare: 'the girls, who had withdrawn to undress behind some tombs, failed to reappear within the expected period ... soon it was apparent that a nice problem for the chivalrous had been raised. But in the end our anxious whistles were answered and everyone was reassured.'[7]

After the tense atmosphere of Harbin, Fleming went on to the calmer treaty port of Kiukiang. There he slept in the least repulsive of the Chinese hotels before proceeding up the mountain to Kuling. On the way he encountered 'a great globular European woman with a face like a boot. She was clad in dark blue shorts and a sorely tried blouse.' As she thundered past them – 'with heaving flanks and nostrils distended' –

Fleming's interpreter murmured, 'Jesus-man', for she was one of many missionaries leaving the hill-station to return to their missions at the end of the summer. 'A patriarchal Belgian priest sat in his chair nursing a bunch of red and yellow flowers, and smiling very sweetly. Behind him came an angry American, accompanied by two anaemic daughters in shorts. Then a German with a large square wife, both dressed for the Victorian tropics.' In Kuling itself (where Fleming hoped to interview Chiang Kai-shek), there were 'hawkers selling picture postcards, and notice-boards announcing whist-drives and church services, and shops selling tourist bric-à-brac and tennis balls'.

Fleming came across, not Chinese but European 'squeeze' in Kuling when, leaving his travelling companion in the Fairy Glen Hotel, he tried to get into the swimming-pool. He needed to obtain the signatures of two Kuling property-holders and a medical certificate. Mrs Gosfoot, 'a small, fat, fierce woman, signed twice in the space reserved for property-holders and offered to throw in a medical inspection as well'. For these services she charged him a dollar. 'It seemed a lot to pay for having one's word about one's feet taken by a woman; but it was a low price at which to buy an insight into such a demure little racket.'[8]

In 1938, on another trip to China, this time as a correspondent for *The Times*, Fleming was to encounter an unlikely pair of reporters, the novelist Christopher Isherwood and the poet W.H. Auden. Isherwood's account of their travels together emphasizes the brisk efficiency of Fleming: 'In his khaki shirt and shorts, complete with golf stockings, strong suede shoes, waterproof wristwatch and Leica camera, he might have stepped straight from a London tailor's window, advertising Gent's Tropical Exploration Kit.' In contrast, Isherwood sadly observed, his own trousers 'were still soaked, my shirt had a large burn on the front – it had lain too near the coals – my shoes were shrunken and stiff with mud'. Equally failing to keep the side up, Auden spent one meal with his handkerchief stuffed in his mouth, unable so much as to look at 'a dish of small blanched, slippery creatures'.[9]

Though Auden and Isherwood travelled briefly with Fleming and interviewed many of the same officials, the motives behind their visit and their account of China were very different. Fleming was a journalist and a traveller; Auden and Isherwood were travellers with a social conscience.

In Shanghai, they saw the darker side of China, in its factories and workshops. They were taken there by Rewi Alley, a New Zealander, who had come to China as a factory inspector to try and improve industrial conditions. (Alley was to spend the rest of his life in China, writing of the glories of Communism.) Shanghai's foreign residents lived in the suburbs and worked in the solid comfort of the International Settlement and the French Concession, but much of northern and eastern Shanghai was filled with factories, many of them foreign-owned and run, with working conditions that would no longer have been tolerated in the West.

> In the accumulator factories, half the children have already the blue line in their gums which is a symptom of lead-poisoning. Few of them will survive longer than a year or eighteen months. In scissors factories you can see arms and legs developing chromium holes. There are silk-winding mills so full of steam that the fingers of the mill-girls are white with fungus growths. If the children slacken in their work the over-seers often plunge their elbows into the boiling water as punishment. There is a cotton mill where the dust in the air makes TB almost a certainty.[10]

Shocking as such sights were, Auden and Isherwood were at least able to escape and return to the British ambassador's private villa in the French Concession for lunch. Yet even in this haven, the outside world intruded. At a garden party, where with 'the co-operation of the ladies of the British colony, the Seaforth Highlanders, the embassy staff ... the drinks and cold buffet are organized ... gaily as the charade-players laugh, and loudly as they chatter, they cannot altogether ignore those other, most undiplomatic sounds which reach us, at intervals, from beyond the garden trees. Somewhere out in the suburbs, machine-guns are rattling.'[11]

The mass of visitors to China at the time were unaware of the potential rattle of machine-guns in the suburbs for the treaty ports still remained curiously isolated from the turbulence of banditry and warlord rivalry that was affecting much of the rest of the country. With the development of turbine engines and the construction of large and comfortable ocean liners, cruises became popular amongst the rich in the late 1920s and early 1930s. The great ships docked at Shanghai. There, as Isherwood put it,

> the tired or lustful ... will find anything to gratify his desires. You can buy an electric razor, or a French dinner, or a well-cut suit. You can dance at the Tower Restaurant on the roof of the Cathay Hotel ... you can attend race meetings, baseball games, football matches ... If you want girls or boys, you can have them at all prices, in the bath-houses and the brothels. If you want opium you can smoke it in the best company, served on a tray, like afternoon tea ... The jeweller and the antique-dealer await your orders.[12]

Most tourists came to shop for silks (produced in the awful factories that Auden and Isherwood visited), satins, embroidered table- and bed-linen, tailor-made clothes run up in a day, beaded evening bags, screens, porcelain, carved hardwood furniture, and all sorts of knick-knacks – cunning silver name-card holders for the dining-table in the shape of tiny coolies with conical straw hats were popular.

They would have a drink in the Shanghai Club, at the longest bar in the world, though Auden and Isherwood drily observed that 'it proved to be far shorter than we had expected'.[13] Or they could, like André Malraux and his wife in 1931, visit the Great World Amusement Centre. The Great World was described in vivid detail by the film-maker Joseph von Sternberg who visited the city to make *Shanghai Express* (1932):

> The establishment had six floors ... that seethed with life and all the commotion and noise that go with it, studded with every variety of entertainment Chinese ingenuity had contrived ... On the first floor were gambling tables, sing-song girls, magicians, pick-pockets, slot machines, fireworks, bird-cages, fans, stick incense, acrobats and ginger. One flight up were the restaurants, a dozen different groups of actors, crickets in cages, pimps, midwives, barbers and earwax extractors. The third floor had jugglers, herb medicines, ice-cream parlours, photographers, a new bevy of girls, their high-collared gowns slit to reveal their hips, in case one had passed up the more modest ones below who merely flashed their thighs; and under the heading of novelty, several rows of exposed toilets, their impresarios instructing the amused patrons not to squat but to assume a position more in keeping with the imported plumbing. The fourth floor was crowded with shooting galleries, fan-tan tables, revolving wheels, massage benches, acupuncture and moxa cabinets, hot-towel counters, dried fish and intestines, and dance platforms

serviced by a horde of music makers competing with each other to see who could drown out the others. The fifth floor featured girls whose dresses were slit to the armpits, a stuffed whale, story-tellers, balloons, peep-shows, masks, a mirror maze, two love-letter booths with scribes who guaranteed results, 'rubber goods' and a temple filled with ferocious gods and joss-sticks. On the top floor and roof of that house of multiple joys a jumble of tight-rope walkers slithered back and forth, and there were see-saws, Chinese checkers, mahjong, strings of firecrackers going off, lottery tickets and marriage brokers.[14]

Thrilled by such exotic oriental scenes, many tourists then took a few days off to travel by train to Peking to see the more serious sites – the Great Wall, the no-longer Forbidden City and the Summer Palace – and do yet more shopping.

In 1929 Noël Coward travelled in the opposite direction on the slightly down-at-heel *Tenyo Maru* to Yokohama, crossing to Korea and thence to Mukden where he saw the New Year in with the British consul (whose brother was musical director of *Bitter Sweet*). The New Year's Eve party was fancy-dress. Coward found it a strange occasion, and, beneath its gaiety, exceedingly touching, for the oddly dressed Europeans were 'condemned to stay in that grim, remote place perhaps for years'.[15] Then he and his travelling companion, Jeffrey Amherst, 5th Baron Holmesdale, wrapped in fur coats and drinking brandy, surrounded by twenty-seven pieces of luggage and a gramophone, took a train down to Peking, and thence to Shanghai where Coward caught flu. There, confined to his bed in the Cathay Hotel on the Bund for four days, he wrote *Private Lives* with an Eversharp pencil.

Despite the flu, Coward and Amherst enjoyed Shanghai, though Coward described the city as 'a cross between Brussels and Huddersfield'.[16] Perhaps he was referring to the architecture.

There were lots of parties and Chinese dinners and cosmopolitan junketings which, while putting a slight strain on our lingual abilities, in no way dampened our spirits. We found some charming new friends, notably Madame Birt and her twin daughters who, apart from being extremely attractive, could quarrel with each other in six different languages without even realizing they were not sticking to one; and three English naval officers ... with whom we visited many of the lower and gayer haunts of the city.[17]

The lower and gayer haunts of the city were notorious. The Great World was an amusement palace but Shanghai also boasted famous brothels and, according to Christopher Isherwood and no doubt Noël Coward's naval friends, bath-houses where one could find male prostitutes. In Foochow Road (also famous for its herbalists) was a tea-house-cum-bordello noted for its Soochow sing-song girls. The higher-class brothels were all situated in the International Settlement. There were cheaper brothels in Hongkew for sailors on shore leave. Though most of the sing-song girls were Chinese, after 1917 White Russian girls, 'hairdressers, dance hostesses and whores', refugees from Soviet Russia, haunted the Avenue Joffre in 'Frenchtown'. The first brothel featuring foreign prostitutes had been opened in Shanghai in 1864, but Chinese were barred from it; the White Russian prostitutes provided Chinese residents with their first occidental erotic thrill, as they were also to do in Tientsin.[18]

Not all sing-song girls were prostitutes: hostesses, dancing partners or entertainers might be a better description. At the Wee Golf Club in Hankow (which boasted an indoor miniature golf-course), where the sing-song girls could be seen any evening dancing with their friends and customers, Christopher Isherwood discovered that they 'were not, as we had first imagined, professional prostitutes. Indeed, it is very difficult to start an affair with one of them. Introductions, and a period of courtship, are necessary; and if a girl doesn't like you, she won't have you.' They were there to spend the evening dancing, flirting and drinking tea ... and they wore 'sleeveless Chinese gowns of patterned silk, tight under the armpits, with a high collar clasped close around the throat. The gown falls to the ankles, but its sides are slashed, so that the wearer's legs when she moves are visible right up to the knee.'[19] In Shanghai in winter, when it was damp and chilly, nightclub hostesses carried rubber hot-water bottles which slip-slopped audibly as they approached customers.

For many short-stay visitors, the brothels and tea-houses were probably a voyeuristic experience. Wallis Simpson, later Duchess of Windsor, visited China in 1924 when her first husband, Win Spencer, was serving there in the US Navy. According to a sensational biography, she went to a brothel in Hong Kong, at Repulse Bay, the only one in the colony which allowed in foreign women.

As the visitor entered, a smiling male in a blue cotton robe would appear, bowing deeply. He ushered the visitor into an immense square room with green and white draperies covering the walls. Beyond the entrance hall was a long corridor which led to another hall fitted with sumptuously upholstered chairs and settees. Both doors and walls were decorated with lattice-work and scrolls in Chinese. There were cabinets of expensive mahogany, containing shelves of valuable china ornaments. The girls were customarily dressed in blue or red silk. The upper floor consisted of a series of tiny but elegantly furnished rooms where the prostitutes awaited their customers.[20]

Rumour, in the form of a 'substantial documentary file ... in the State Department', hinted that Mrs Simpson was 'taught perverse practices in these houses of prostitution' (she was also suspected of spying, 'attempting to obtain information concerning Naval secrets from the British officers she met').[21] When not spying or practising hot oil massage and 'delayed intromission', she travelled to Shanghai and stayed at the Astor House Hotel. There she was reputedly bankrolled by wealthy men as she played baccarat, roulette and blackjack, and engaged in extensive drug peddling, living the murkier side of Shanghai life to the full.[22] She also met a handsome Fascist, Count Galeazzo Ciano, Mussolini's son-in-law, who was serving in the Italian consulate in Shanghai, and scandalously spent time with him during a summer holiday at Chinwangtao (Qinhuangdao; a summer resort at the point where the Great Wall meets the sea). In Peking she is reported to have flirted with Alberto de Zara, naval attaché at the Italian embassy. She stayed first at the Grand Hotel de Pekin (now the Peking Hotel) and found time to visit the Forbidden City before moving into a courtyard house on Shih-chi hu-t'ung with Katherine and Herman Rogers (he was serving as an Intelligence officer at the American embassy). She had her own maid and rickshaw driver (until he got run over by a car) and joined the Rogers for weekends in a Buddhist temple in the surrounding hills where they rode and played mahjong, poker and contract bridge.

A more fleeting visit was paid by someone who was later to be a relation of Wallis's by marriage: Edwina Mountbatten, who was married to Edward VIII's cousin, Lord Louis Mountbatten. Whilst her husband was in the Navy, she travelled the world with her companion, Harold

'Bunny' Phillips. Setting her sights on China as a fashionable destination, she travelled across Russia and Manchuria by train accompanied by Bunny and a tortoise. After a fortnight on the train, they reached Peking. Edwina found it freezing, and the spring dust-storms gave her sinusitis. They left almost immediately for Shanghai where they took the first boat to the tropical Philippines.[23]

Edwina Mountbatten was unusual in not succumbing to the attractions of Peking. In the 1930s, it was still a walled city that had retained much of its traditional character, filled with elderly gentlemen in long silk robes and tiny silk skull-caps, with tranquil antique shops in Liu-li-ch'ang and the nearby Street of Extended Longevity. It was also a centre of learning, with several fine universities whose lecturers, both Chinese and foreign, provided stimulating company. For Laurence Binyon, poet and pioneer in the study of Chinese and Japanese painting, a ten-day visit to Peking (where he enjoyed an 'Arnold Bennett millionaire style of life') revealed 'a sort of legendary grandeur' which attracted longer-term residents,[24] among them Harold Acton who made his home in Peking from 1931 until 1937.

Acton's residence encouraged others. Osbert Sitwell and his friend David Horner arrived in 1934 and stayed for many months. Desmond Parsons, a rich young man who translated fairy stories from the Chinese, also arrived in the same year and when he went home, suffering from the cancer that was to kill him, the architectural historian Robert Byron came out to look after Parsons's house and keep the servants, and to write up his Persian travels. Byron, always perverse, did not share Binyon's impression of Peking's stupendous architecture, with its marvellous sense of scale: 'of architecture in the real sense of the word, there is nothing ... Cubically and intellectually it is all a vacuum.'[25]

At about the same time as Acton and Byron took up residence, a young American, Robert Winter, arrived in Peking to escape the respectability of Philadelphia and the expectations of his mother and numerous sisters that he should marry and have children. Bob Winter stayed until he died in his early nineties in 1986. He never married but taught English for decades at Peking University and the next-door establishment, Tsing-hua University. In his old age, he lived alone in a charming ex-hunting lodge in the grounds of Peking University, with only one of his paintings, of a bare-chested young fisherman from Chefoo, left to suggest a love-life that he could not have enjoyed in Philadelphia.

Similarly, Harold Acton never hinted in his memoirs that he went to China in search of love or uncomplicated masculine relationships, but stressed the aesthetic delights of Peking life. He stayed first in a court-yard house on Kan-yu hu-t'ung or Sweet Rain Lane, later moving into a house on Pei-ho-yen, a stream bordered with willows near the Forbidden City. There, 'everything was perfectly proportioned; every table, picture, vase and bowl fitted comfortably into the general design, and I had chosen these objects and bargained for them over innumer-able cups of tea, one by one'. Later, in 1936, he moved into a 'perfect' Chinese mansion with three successive courtyards and a side garden in Kung Hsien hu-t'ung off Wang-fu-ching (Hatamen Street).[26] In the inner garden, 'a modest *hortus conclusus* of lilacs and ornamental rocks', he built a swimming-pool.

> The vast front courtyard ... I carpeted with fresh green grass from the country ... Crab-apple trees grew in the last courtyard, the rooms of which I decorated with Chinese panels ... They were bounded by a brick trellis through which flowering creepers twined ... Here I had ample space to hang all my pictures and arrange the old furniture I had collected. A dozen long scrolls of birds in their arboreal or floral affinities, painted on silk in the eighteenth century ... A choice collec-tion of bronze ritual vessels ... vases and brush-pots carved of variously twisted, gnarled and knotted woods, fantastic specimens of fossilized fungi and roots like ancient Lohans meditating.[27]

Osbert Sitwell likewise found the traditional lifestyle of Peking entrancing. He had arrived from Nanking, of which, he said, he would not write save to 'place on record as a matter of interest, that when, in the chief hotel, organized by my fellow-countrymen, I asked for a cup of tea, they brought me something that reminded me of a wet Saturday afternoon in a Hindhead boarding-house; and that when, more expli-citly, I then indicated that I wanted *China* tea, the reply came, "We only supply Ceylon and Indian here."' Peking, by contrast, was filled with ancient temples, gardens of forsythia and 'agonized rocks', men wearing 'thick padded robes, sometimes with fur collars, surmounted in this season with triangular fur hats, similar to those in the portraits of

Flemish merchants by Van Eyck or his followers'; multi-coloured kites flew in the blue sky, flocks of pigeons wheeled overhead with whistles tied to their feathers to produce an eerie humming sound and, near the Hatamen Gate, tiny blossoming trees were for sale – 'apples and quinces, peaches and cherries with their heads in little rosy clouds or bowed under a load of snow, orange trees bearing at the same time their blossom and their fruit, some of these glowing like lamps, others green-bronze and nestling hidden in their glossy foliage, and little formal bushes of button roses, wisteria plants, about two or three feet high, coiled and serpentine, their drooping fragile clusters the colour of storm-clouds of an etiolate white'.[28]

Sitwell was a passer-by. Acton, however, as a permanent resident, needed occupation and, like Bob Winter after him, taught English literature at Peking University, then situated at the north-eastern corner of the Forbidden City in a grim, barrack-like structure of butcher-red brick. Built in the Western style in 1910, it still stands today. Visitors staying only a short time had no need to find employment. Desmond Parsons travelled, in some danger, to the Buddhist caves at Tunhuang (Dunhuang) in distant Kansu (though when in Peking, he liked to accompany Harold Acton to the Chinese theatre); Sitwell himself travelled south.[29]

Robert Byron, staying in Desmond Parsons's house, found it charming: 'a series of courtyards, with trees, bamboos etc., in them ... Three sides of every pavilion are made of brick, the rest of paper. It is curious how warm they keep.'[30] Though writing up his Persian travels, eventually published as *The Road to Oxiana*,[31] he found time to indulge 'in an orgy of clothes. A tweed suit costs 25/–, an evening suit 30/–, silk shirts 4/– ... a decent overcoat – very dark grey, almost black, with a pseudo-sable collar and lined with spotted cat – extremely smart I imagine myself to look – it all cost £4.10.0.'[32]

Byron was unwell in Peking; depressed by Parsons's fatal illness and worried about his book, he took to his bed and only rarely strolled out for a constitutional with Harold Acton, sometimes 'beaten back by the eddies of frozen dust'. He hated rickshaw travel – 'I think it is humiliating to feel one is humiliating someone else every time one goes out' – though he observed that everyone else seemed to adore it. Despite his reclusiveness, Byron seems to have met many of the foreign visitors to

Peking, dominated, in his view, by 'unemployed American women with large incomes [who] sail into one's life like bats into one's hair ... What is one to *do*?'[33]

A more welcome encounter was with Julian Bell, the elder son of Clive and Vanessa Bell, and nephew of Virginia Woolf, 'a pleasant half-fledged person with a most ridiculous Bloomsbury voice'.[34] In the summer of 1935, Julian Bell had applied for a job teaching in China and had been appointed to Wuhan University.[35] In January the following year, during the winter holidays, he travelled to Peking with Ch'en Shu-hua, wife of the dean of the university, with whom he was having an affair. (He used the alphabet to enumerate his lovers: Mrs Ch'en was K but by the autumn of 1936, 'possible candidates for L and M had appeared in Wuhan, one Chinese, the other English'.)[36] Ch'en Shu-hua was a skilled painter and poet. She had been one of the most popular female students at Peking University in the late 1920s but was somewhat bored in provincial Wuhan. Julian Bell described the Ch'ens on first meeting as 'extremely cultured: he a critic and translator of Turgenev . . . She a painter (Chinese style), writer of short stories and editor of a literary page in one of the big Hankow papers; I gather she's sometimes called the Chinese Katherine Mansfield, but I fancy there's more to her really.'[37]

Living out in the wooded hills of the university campus, Julian Bell was some distance from Hankow and its British residents on the other side of the Yangtze, and he left almost no mention of treaty port life, concentrating instead on the 'mediterranean Cambridge' atmosphere of the university itself and asking his mother, as he tried to organize his servants to manage dinner parties, 'How do you ever manage to work and keep house?'[38] For him, as for Harold Acton, Peking was the supreme Chinese city:

> incredibly beautiful, powder-coloured: pale blue sky, pale ochre earth, pale yellow trees: a grove of bamboos the colour of olives: Chinese pines ... fantastic ... Lovely Bactrian camels march the streets. Everyone wears furs ... the tiled roofs have rather satisfactory flat curves; the tiles are ... rich deep brownish and gold-deep yellows ... with very cold blues and greens.

Julian Bell also shopped in Peking, for 'enamel ear-rings, jade fragments ... A silk shop where I bought embroidery silks for Nessa until I had all the colours of a sunset, a phoenix's tail lying on the counter.'[39]

While in Peking he and Harold Acton were taken by Ch'en Shu-hua to meet Ch'i Pai-shih, probably the best known Chinese painter of the twentieth century. Ch'i, 'in a skull-cap and faded blue gown bespattered with paint and putty, received us in a studio ... the torn paper windows flapped in the breeze like imprisoned birds. A thick layer of Gobi dust had settled on everything. Ch'i Pai-shih himself looked as if he had been out in a dust-storm.'[40]

Although Bell's letters convey something of Peking's atmosphere, probably the best descriptions of the city by a foreigner were made by Ann Bridge, the pen-name of Mary O'Malley, wife of Owen O'Malley who served as counsellor at the British legation in Peking between 1925 and 1927. Despite her duties as a diplomatic wife and mother of children who managed to contract scarlet fever, diphtheria, dysentery and septic pneumonia during the two short years they spent in Peking, she gathered enough material to write three extremely successful novels about north China: *Peking Picnic*, *The Ginger Griffin* and *Four-part Setting*. The stories may now seem somewhat dated, their heroines suffering a great deal of unrequited temptation while being married to beasts whom they are too loyal to divorce. The tales are often dominated, too, by a tall, slim, fearfully intuitive, well-read and attractive (though slightly horse-faced) leading lady who bears a surely coincidental resemblance to the author's photograph. For all that, their descriptions of place and atmosphere are strikingly accurate and nostalgic.

Unlike Robert Byron, Ann Bridge obviously enjoyed rickshaw rides:

A rickshaw is the most delightfully civilized form of locomotion. Seated in a well-sprung bath-chair, the passenger bowls along on pneumatic tyres at surprising speed; he is alone, for it only holds one; his view is unimpeded by anything but the lowered head and shoulders of the trotting coolie; the air fans his face gently, and there is nothing to prevent his holding up a sunshade in comfort. The only drawback is that in order to reach any objective unfamiliar to the coolie, he must know, not only the way thither, but the points of the compass *en route* as well, for the Chinese do not use left and right as directions but north, south and so on. 'Wang tung' (turn east!) you cry at a corner ... (which is also, if you come to think of it, both a more civilized and a more intellectual way of giving directions than our own).[41]

Travel is a constant theme in her novels. Both *Peking Picnic* and *Four-part Setting* centre on a trip to the hills to the north of Peking, of the sort often made by diplomats and foreign residents in the summer when the city on the plain below was uncomfortably hot and humid. In *Peking Picnic* a diplomatic caravan moves off to the great temples of Chieh-t'ai ssu (Temple of the Ordination Platform) and T'an-che ssu (Temple of the Pool and the Zhe Tree), where they happen to be captured by bandits. The beauty and tranquillity of the two temples are lovingly described; so, too, though perhaps less lovably, is the way in which foreign visitors in the 1920s would take over a temple hall and set up their camp-beds whilst long Buddhist services were held nearby. Mrs Leroy, one of the novel's protagonists, makes herself comfortable in the Chieh-t'ai ssu with little concern for the temple's plasterwork.

> Taking a couple of nails from her trouser pocket, she drove them into the wall ... and hung her pocket mirror on one and her towel on the other. Her spare clothing was placed under the pillow of her camp-bed to heighten it, and the camp-bed itself shoved up against the *kang*, so that the latter served as a bed-table on which her book, chocolate, a box of cigarettes and a candle stuck in a tin saucer were neatly arranged.[42]

After settling these domestic arrangements, Mrs Leroy enjoys, not a picnic but dinner on the terrace 'at a table correctly spread with linen, glass, and a profusion of silver'. Sherry was served 'by a white-robed manservant, and clear soup with a pigeon's egg in it ... broiled crayfish with Hollandaise sauce, white wine ... grilled chicken à l'Americaine (with Russian salad) ... macedoine of fruit and cream mousse ... coffee and liqueurs'.[43]

In *Four-part Setting*, the weekend travellers, somewhat less well-supplied with culinary delicacies, are from 'the Posts' (Sir Robert Hart's Imperial Post Office which, like the Customs, was mainly staffed at the higher levels by foreigners) and the Diplomatic Service: though menaced by bandits, they escape to fall in love (and out, and in again) and discover deep truths about themselves at the Trappist monastery in the hills. *The Ginger Griffin* describes (in between exalted love affairs and dramatic illnesses based upon those suffered by some of the O'Malley children) another foreign passion in China – owning, training and riding Mongolian ponies.[44]

Ann Bridge's characters were to some extent based on Peking residents, visitors and diplomats whom she met. Somerset Maugham might
perhaps have wished he had drawn less on those he met. His collection
of short stories, *On a Chinese Screen*, published in 1922, is a series of
vignettes based upon a winter trip he made in China in 1919–20.
Satirical and bitter, and caricaturing 'types' – 'The Consul', 'The
Servants of God', 'Her Britannic Majesty's Representative', 'The
Sinologue', 'The Old-Timer' – they so outraged foreign residents that
Maugham was threatened with a horse-whipping should he ever dare
to set foot in Hong Kong again. The satire is heavy and the brevity of
the pieces is contrived; in 'Rain', the picture of little Elizabeth, dry and
warm after her bath, waiting for her bed-time story, who 'looks really
nice in her pyjamas with her hair done up in two plaits', is contrasted
with 'a string of coolies, lolloping along, bent forward ... under the
weight of the great bales of cotton that they carry. The rain plasters their
blue clothes, so thin and ragged, against their bodies.'[45] 'Fear' is the
ghastly portrait of the self-martyring missionary who devotes his whole
life to the conversion of the Chinese whom he hates and who physically
repel him, and 'The Vice-Consul' is the 'very young' representative of
the Foreign Office who participates in the trial of a young Chinese
charged with some offence against a foreigner. After the execution,
he chats in the Club over a drink and observes of the prisoner at his
execution, 'He wriggled a bit.'

Somerset Maugham may have been unwelcome in Hong Kong but
the rest of China had its share of foreign undesirables for whom China's
distance and size, and lack of visa requirements and a unified police
force, offered both escape and fresh potential. A figure whose name
crops up constantly in the British legation's list of 'Suspicious persons
in Peking' is that of Trebitsch Lincoln. Born in Hungary in 1879, after
a juvenile career as a petty thief in Montreal he had become a prominent member of the Montreal Branch of the London Society for the
Promotion of Christianity among the Jews and was elected Liberal
Member of Parliament for Darlington in 1910.[46] He resigned ten
months later just before being declared bankrupt. Thereafter he started
a fraudulent oil company and spent the First World War as a double
agent, trading secrets back and forth between England and Germany.

Following a spell in prison in America and involvement in a putsch in Germany in 1920, Trebitsch Lincoln arrived in China in 1922, 'one of the few places left for him to enter without fear of arrest. Britain and the entire British Empire were barred to him. In Germany he was still a wanted man. He could not be sure of a cordial reception in most of the other countries of western and central Europe. His recent experience in the United States did not suggest that he had much of a future there.'[47]

In China he appears to have fitted in rather well with warlord politics for a while, promising to arrange loans, offering anthracite against aeroplanes and, under a new name, announcing in the Nanking press, 'Mr H. Trautwein, accompanied by his wife and two sons, has recently come to Nanking as tutor to the son of General Wu ... They are living at Chen Hsien Chai. The youngest son, Clifford, will attend Hillcrest.'[48] The 'Trautweins' left China in 1924 (with Austrian passports made out in the name of Tandler), much to the relief of all British consulates, but Trebitsch Lincoln returned alone the following year and had a mystical experience in Tientsin. Subsequently, professing Buddhism, he turned up frequently in China where he was supported, to the intense irritation of British diplomats, by Peking's English Buddhists, led by Mr Basil Crump and the wealthy widow Mrs Leighton Cleather.[49] In 1930, he was ordained as a Buddhist monk in the Pao-hua monastery near Nanking.

After his ordination, Trebitsch Lincoln lived in Buddhist robes as 'the venerable Chao Kung', first in Shanghai and then in Tientsin. There he was constantly under the watchful eye of the British police who reported of the small group of Buddhists on 20 November 1936, 'All the inmates [of the house on the corner of Poppe Road and Romanoff Avenue] appear to be living a very quiet life: part of the morning is taken up with prayer, and at other times they are seen ... quietly sitting on a bench ... Occasionally they go for walks ... Some of them have been seen to visit the Post Office in Dickinson Road.'[50] Characteristically, Trebitsch Lincoln was to emerge from this quiet life to welcome the Japanese invasion of north China in July 1937. 'As a resident of Tientsin,' he wrote, 'I have never seen a better-behaved Army of Occupation ... they are kind and helpful ... chivalrous, well-intentioned and spiritually superior.' By now the British Foreign Office, though noting that Trebitsch Lincoln was presumably hoping for

Japanese Buddhist funds, was practically beyond words on the subject. 'A single official minute was recorded ... "I think the only comment I can make on this is ! ! ! "'[51]

Trebitsch Lincoln died in the Shanghai General Hospital in 1943. He had not been interned by the Japanese, presumably because of his Austrian passport, and had, indeed, offered to help the Japanese war effort in India and south-east Asia through his Buddhist connections.

Another character to figure in the British diplomatic list of 'Suspicious persons' (and to achieve a file all of his own) was Sir Edmund Trelawney Backhouse. Though his origins were far more distinguished than those of Trebitsch Lincoln, he exhibited some of the same characteristics, fleeing to China in 1898 when he had been declared bankrupt, after running up debts amounting to £23,000 during his three years at the University of Oxford. In Peking, he worked as a translator and collaborated with the journalist J.O.P. Bland on two historical works, *China under the Empress Dowager* (1910) and *Annals and Memoirs of the Court at Peking* (1914). Though these were generally well-received, one major source used by Backhouse, the diary of a high official, 'Ching-shan', was suspected by some of being a forgery; the argument over its authenticity rumbled on for nearly half a century amongst historians of China, the final consensus coming down against Backhouse.

Backhouse worked in Peking for forty-five years, somehow managing to stay out of jail despite selling imaginary battleships on behalf of the shipbuilders John Brown & Co., promising huge consignments of equally imaginary guns to the British government during the First World War, and defrauding (amongst many others) the American Bank Note Company.[52] He also acted as a benefactor to his alma mater, sending back valuable cases of palace editions of classical Chinese books in 1913 and 1915, perhaps in the hope of becoming Professor of Chinese at the university. These acts of generosity eventually turned sour for he subsequently demanded advances for further purchases and their dispatch. Though the Bodleian Library sent £2,495, quite against its normal practice of payment upon receipt, none of the promised treasures ever arrived.[53] Backhouse died in Peking in 1944, like Trebitsch Lincoln welcoming the Japanese invasion with his last breath: 'nobody in the Peking British community ... spoke so highly of Germany and Japan'.[54]

Yet even after his death, Backhouse continued to embarrass and shock. Among his papers were found two obscene manuscripts detailing his love affairs with both the British Foreign Secretary Lord Rosebery – 'a slow and protracted copulation ... gave equal pleasure to both parties' – and the extremely elderly dowager empress of China – 'Was I sexually adequate for Her Majesty's overflowing carnality?' Backhouse also claimed endless affairs with the eunuchs of the Imperial Palace (would they have been sexually adequate for him?) and close, loving friendships with the French poet Paul Verlaine, Aubrey Beardsley, la belle Otero, Herbert Spencer and Henry James (encountered in a male brothel in London), to name but a few.[55]

A far more respectable foreign resident of Peking, whose connections with the imperial family were genuinely close and not at all scandalous, was Reginald Johnston. Though they were photographed together with members of the court, Johnston always disclaimed any acquaintance with the disreputable Backhouse. After serving as a colonial officer in Weihaiwei between 1904 and 1918, Johnston was appointed English tutor to Aisin-Gioro Puyi, the last emperor of China, and lived in Peking until 1926. He did not have to borrow temple halls, like Ann Bridge and her characters, for he had a house and temple of his own in the Western Hills outside Peking which he called 'Cherry Glen'. Though he never married, Johnston had a series of lady visitors to Cherry Glen including the novelist Stella Benson and the medieval historian Eileen Power.

On her first visit to China in 1921, Eileen Power went to the T'an-che ssu, like the *Peking Picnic* travellers, and reported, 'I always look at monasteries with an eye trained in the English middle ages and T'an-che ssu struck me as having much the same atmosphere as a lax and worldly house towards the close of the fifteenth century. I hear that the abbot is an opium fiend, which is another illustration of the almost invariable rule in the middle ages that a bad abbot meant a bad house.' By contrast, Chieh-t'ai ssu, lower down in the valley, 'might have stood for the good monastery of medieval documents and true to analogy, it had a saintly abbot'.[56] In a more lyrical vein, she wrote of another temple, 'Someone brings you out a cup of tea, clear amber-coloured Chinese tea in a blue-grey handle-less cup; a dim gong sounds from the hidden temple above and a sudden puff of wind, the last breath of the expiring day, rustles the rose-leaves on their mats.'[57] Succumbing to the exotic charms of days expiring in quiet temples amidst the rustle of rose-leaves, Reginald Johnston proposed to Eileen Power in 1930 and, deeply impressed by his knowledge of China and Chinese history, she accepted (though somewhat to everyone's relief she eventually married someone else).

Whilst in Peking, she also met two other academic visitors, Bertrand Russell and Dora Black. Russell had been invited in 1920 by the progressive China Lecture Association to spend a year in China, an opportune invitation that came after a visit to Russia where he was seized by a mood of disenchantment with Western culture.[58] He was also desperate to become a father and 'fervently hoped' that Dora Black would become pregnant in China (as indeed she did). Russell was to spend the year at Peking University lecturing on philosophy and mathematical logic, but upon arrival in Shanghai in October, he and Dora were taken off on tours around the country, to Hangchow, Nanking and Changsha. The couple left, earlier than planned, after Russell had been taken seriously ill with pneumonia in the spring of 1921.

Working in the university, Russell and Black were able to make far better contact with Chinese intellectuals than the average Peking resident (let alone the average treaty port resident). He was delighted by the wit of Chao Yuan-ren (later to become a distinguished teacher of Chinese linguistics in America) and happy to be welcomed as 'Confucius the Second', though he later wrote, 'I would do anything in the world to help the Chinese but it is difficult. They are a nation of artists with all their good and bad points. Imagine the British Empire ruled by Augustus John and Lytton Strachey and you will have some idea how China has been governed for 2,000 years.'[59]

In 1933, another radical organization, the Chinese League for the Protection of Human Rights (founded by Madame Sun Yat-sen and the ex-Chancellor of Peking University, Tsai Yuan-p'ei), invited George Bernard Shaw to China during his world tour on the cruise ship *Empress of Britain* (where he took his own vegetarian menus and ate grapefruit, porridge and 'Instant Postum').[60] He called at Hong Kong as the guest of Sir Robert Ho Tung, the ex-comprador of Jardine's, and spent a single day in Shanghai, crammed with meetings with prominent left-wing Chinese intellectuals and sympathizers. He met Lu Hsun, the great essayist and short story writer, Lin Yu-tang (novelist and essayist), the Marxist poet Ch'u Ch'iu-pai and the American journalists Harold Isaacs and Agnes Smedley on a 'very jovial' visit where he made Madame Sun Yat-sen laugh so hard she cried. Calling at Peking for a few frozen February days, Shaw wrote after this extremely brief stay, 'I have fallen in love with China ... I felt at home there – I belonged there!'[61]

Shaw's reaction was a common one, particularly amongst intellectual visitors. They met charming and stimulating Chinese, many of whom had been educated abroad and spoke fluent English whilst still retaining their exotic Chinese dress and profound understanding of a very different traditional culture. Apart from Auden and Isherwood, few visitors raised political doubts as to the legitimacy of the treaty port system and the domination of treaty port Chinese by foreign masters. For cruise-ship tourists, China was only one stop in a whole world carved up into foreign empires.

16

The Chinese and the Treaty Ports

From the mid-nineteenth century onwards, as the treaty ports proliferated, many rich and powerful Chinese increasingly adopted Western ways. From the beginning, those Chinese that had the most to do with foreigners (apart from household servants) were the compradors. When the Cohong merchant monopoly was abolished after the First Opium War in 1843, compradors became the mercantile intermediaries. A comprador, the name deriving from the Portuguese for 'purchaser', was the Chinese manager of a foreign firm in China, serving as a middleman in the company's dealings with the Chinese.[1] The compradors were also wealthy merchants in their own right, their wealth, whether in tea, silk or (preferably) land, providing security for their foreign employers. Suffering cashflow crises in 1853 and 1863, the American China trader Augustine Heard wrote on one occasion, 'I must say the comprador has come out like a brick. I can count upon . . . $23,000.'[2] Besides possession of personal wealth, a comprador was required to know pidgin English for the purpose of communicating with his employers, to guarantee the Chinese banks and Chinese firms with which he arranged business, and to sort out the complexities of the varying systems of weights and measures in different parts of China and the varying silver taels, silver dollars, money certificates and credit bills issued by native banks. Indeed, so dependent were foreign merchants on their compradors during the early days that when, in Foochow, the local comprador of Augustine Heard & Co. fell ill in 1862, 'everything ground to a halt'.[3]

The majority of big firms employed a great many compradors, easily outnumbering their foreign employees, and they had to deal with a variety of business. The great house of Jardine Matheson was, by 1900, engaged in the export of tea, silk and other products, the import of timber, fertilizers, metals, liquor and food, shipping (running both docks and the China Coast Steam Navigation Co. and the Indochina Steam Navigation Co.), cold storage and ordinary storage godowns, insurance, banking and railway finance, export credit guarantees, silk filatures, cotton mills, a brewery, a dairy farm and sugar refinery, the Shanghai Electrical Co. and the Hong Kong tram system. All of these called for special comprador expertise.[4]

In the early days between 1843 and 1860, after which the interior of China was effectively opened to foreigners, the comprador's freedom to travel in the interior to buy tea and silk in the areas of their production reinforced his position. Compradors were also able to undertake their own business at the same time. Yakee, one of Jardine's Shanghai compradors, dealt very successfully in salt, and Hsu Chun, a Dent comprador in Shanghai, bought land near the International Settlement and built houses which provided an enormous rental income.[5] Sir Robert Ho Tung, Jardine's Hong Kong comprador, also acquired land in Hong Kong and Macao which added to his fortune and enabled him to become a considerable benefactor of the University of Hong Kong and other educational institutions as well as to establish the Hong Kong branch of the YMCA.

In the second half of the nineteenth century, the compradors, with decades of experience of dealing with foreigners and foreign firms, were instrumental in introducing Western methods to Chinese enterprises and in setting up modern industries: Chu Ta-chun, a Jardine comprador, invested in steamships in the 1880s, machinery companies (1883), a rice mill (1898), a flour mill (1900), a silk mill (1904) and electric light companies in Soochow (1908) and Yangchow (1913). In 1886, the Tientsin Chinese Match Co. (the first of its kind in China) was set up by Wu Mao-ting, comprador of the Hongkong and Shanghai Bank. Their investments, like those of the Western firms they served, were complex and interrelated. Tong King-sing, a Jardine comprador, was the manager of the China Merchants' Steam Navigation Co. Noting the lack of cargo in the boats returning from carrying rice from south China to Tientsin, he invested in the development of the Kaiping coal-mines in the north, China's first major modern mines, which filled the boats nicely.[6]

Though many compradors were quick to adapt to modern ways, some held to tradition. For hundreds of years, merchants had been a despised class in China and their wealth was eventually used to buy land or official titles in order to acquire respectability. Around 1900, of forty notable compradors in Shanghai, at least fifteen had purchased the official title of Taotai, and Hsu Chun had acquired the honorary title of 'department director of the Board of War'.[7]

Less respectable traditions also endured. Foreigners, already alerted to servant 'squeeze', were aware of corruption amongst the compradors but were unable to do very much about it. Compradors received small salaries and were responsible for their staff, so it was to be expected that they might 'supplement' their income in one way or another. Augustine Heard & Co.'s Hankow comprador in 1866 was responsible for twenty people: a 'shroff' (who collected chits), a godown man and two assistants, a tea office boy (not an office boy who made tea but a boy working in the tea office), three market men, a writer, two watchmen, two chair coolies, two porters (front door and street door), two table boys, a cook and two house coolies. Bills for their wages, suitably adjusted, were presented to the company. A further source of comprador income was commission, of anything from 1 to 5 per cent, paid by both Chinese and foreign firms, but it was assumed that the bulk of comprador wealth was acquired through squeeze, and the view in the 1880s was that compradorial 'opportunities for doing mischief were tenfold more numerous than those enjoyed by an ordinary Chinese or an ordinary European'.[8] The comprador's function as treasurer for a firm meant that he could place money where he wanted and make interest on it, and he could also play off the different currencies in circulation. One foreign trader reckoned in 1862 that a comprador could make perhaps twenty-five times his annual salary in this way.

By the turn of the century, the power of the comprador within the foreign firms was lessening. Though foreign firms were advised in a consular report as early as 1867 that the only way to reduce squeeze was for foreign traders to learn Chinese, they paid little attention to this advice for decades. By the time they did act on it Chinese companies had become more sophisticated. Various aspects of the traditional system were also disappearing: modern banks were making it easier to obtain reliable credit, and weights and measures and the currency were being standardized. The comprador's sources of squeeze and private profit were dying out, as was the need for his services as a middle-man.

Those compradors who were forward-looking, who adopted modern Western methods and who supported modern manufacturing enterprises, Western-style education and modern political causes, offer an all too rare example of the beneficial influence of the treaty ports. Robert Ho Tung was politically progressive, welcoming the reformer K'ang Yu-wei to Hong Kong where he took refuge after the failure of the Hundred Days Reform movement in 1898 and inviting George Bernard Shaw to Hong Kong in 1933. Some adopted foreign homes, foreign dress and foreign furnishings wholesale, but Ho Tung, who married an Englishwoman, took pains to stress the importance of both cultures. Despite such examples of compradors who rose above the primary task of getting rich, even at the turn of the century there were many who despised the whole class. The novelist Wu Chien-jen complained, 'To the comprador, even the foreigner's fart is fragrant.'[9]

Though the accumulated wealth of some comprador families was enormous, there were others who rose even more meteorically. Ken Cheang studied at Balliol College, Oxford, where he was described as 'an athletic though sometimes incomprehensible young man', and his elder brother went to Cambridge. Yet their grandfather and great-uncles had been poor, uneducated Macanese who had gone abroad as labourers to the Philippines, Peru and California. Their savings had been invested in Shanghai where the Cheang family acquired property, including two theatres, and worked as senior managers in the Nanyang Brothers Tobacco Co. ('3,000 women, 39 toilets, modern machinery, a 10 hour day ... but ... no great evils'). As a result of this enterprise the Cheangs now lived 'in a castle-like stone mansion equipped with a swimming-pool, tennis courts, one Daimler, two Isotta-Fraschinis and sundry smaller cars ... Ken was no longer a solitary, rather shy student in the damp chill of Oxford but part of a bustling crowd who enjoyed their worldly goods.'[10]

Compradors and Chinese businessmen learnt modern techniques and more liberal factory management from abroad; Chinese intellectuals adopted an even more significant Western development, the press. Though China had been a literary civilization for thousands of years, the immediacy and wide circulation of newspapers and journals had not formed part of that tradition and censorship had a long and effective history.[11] There was only one official Chinese publication, the *Peking Gazette*, 'traditionally dating from the end of the tenth century ... a daily metropolitan *affiche*, containing court gazette, decrees and memorials. Manuscript copies were sent to the high provincial authorities, and the printed form was sent to Canton, etc.'[12] In the treaty ports, newspapers were an early innovation.

It was the missionaries who, in their zeal to disseminate Christianity, had first brought modern Western printing methods to China, and with them, to a lesser degree – through the work of such as John Fryer who translated Western scientific works into Chinese – modernization. But the arrival also satisfied other needs. The newly settled merchants required business information and news. This was first supplied by broadsheets such as the *Canton Price Current* which detailed wholesale prices and ship departures. A more recognizable newspaper, the *North China Daily Herald*, was founded in Shanghai in 1850 by Henry Shearman. The *Peking and Tientsin Times* and the *North China Star* were later foundations, published in Tientsin. Other papers and journals soon proliferated for the benefit of foreign residents, and Shanghai, in particular, saw a great development in Chinese-language newspapers and periodicals in the early years of the twentieth century.

The Commercial Press was founded in Shanghai in 1897 by three young Chinese graduates, all practical printers and all of them Christians, the product of a Presbyterian Mission School in Shanghai.[13] Within a decade it had sixty modern presses imported from England, America and Germany and including off-set and three-colour printing machines, was using up to 25,000 reams of foreign paper and 3,400 reams of Chinese paper annually, and was publishing schoolbooks, literature, fiction, biography and travel books, including such titles (all in Chinese) as *Ready-made Speeches, Poultry and Profit, All about Railways* and a series called *Common Commodities of Commerce*. It was not only the content of the publications that was progressive. The Commercial Press had a trades union with meeting facilities and employed several deaf-mute boys and graduates of the Shanghai Reformatory, and a number of women (none under the age of 14). Two months' maternity leave on full pay, Sundays off and a profit-sharing scheme, as well as cheap accommodation, a hospital, a school and a kindergarten, were all offered to employees.

The Commercial Press was progressive but not revolutionary. However, radicals and revolutionaries also made use of the power of the press. Ch'en Tu-hsiu, dean of students at Peking National University and founder of the Chinese Communist Party in 1921, had set up the journal *New Youth* in Shanghai in 1915 with a group of like-minded intellectuals. It was to become one of the most influential of left-wing publications and its establishment in Shanghai was significant: censorship was less stringently applied by the non-Chinese-speaking administration there.

Though such intellectuals were unable to match the luxury of Western life in the treaty ports, seeking instead to raise the living standard of the workers, by the end of the nineteenth century rich local treaty port inhabitants had succumbed to the compradoric residential style. Cheong Chi Pio, ship's painter, decorator and contractor in Shanghai, founder of the Hongkew Iron Foundry and amazingly lucky in the local lottery, built Verdant Villa near North Honan Road with a domed tower and elaborate romanesque arches over the verandas. The grounds boasted an artificial lake and several excellent specimens of Chinese rockery against which Mr Cheong and his family were photographed in both Chinese and Western dress. His town residence on Haining Road was in the traditional treaty port style, with a veranda running all along the front, though the arches of the veranda were in romanesque style, emphasized by stripes of brick in alternating colours. Less imposing was the country house of S.K. Tong, son of the Hankow 'Tea King'. Built in the Shanghai suburb of Jessfield, it was a small and simple, vaguely Edwardian, villa set on a large flat lawn, with no sign of Chinese rockery.[14]

Whether the inhabitants of such houses in Shanghai were compradors or simply Chinese who had acquired their wealth by other means, their houses were generally replete with heavy furniture in dark wood, potted plants, huge Chinese pots in porcelain or cloisonné, and glass-fronted cupboards filled with curios. It was the same in Tientsin.

Brian Power, son of an employee of the Imperial Maritime Customs Service, was invited to dinner by the first Chinese boy to attend the Tientsin British School. James Ni's father was a 'retired' warlord with a car and a chauffeur; in the early 1930s, Brian Power had never been in a car before. Inside the house, the austere entrance hall was approached by a long paved courtyard bordered with flowering shrubs in earthenware pots. The entrance hall itself was paved with plum-coloured tiles. 'A lantern with silk tassels hung down from the ceiling. On each side of the hall was a line of ebony benches. A scroll depicting an ancient battle ran along the walls.' By contrast, upstairs there was a foreign-style living-room. 'All the furniture was European. Framed photographs stood on the many cabinets and tables. A piano and a gramophone were on one side of the fireplace. On the other side was a large cabinet filled with objects carved in ivory ... at dinner we had European-style food. The old servant filled our glasses with crème de menthe.' The only other exotic note was provided by a procession through the courtyard below.

> A giant wearing a black skull-cap walked in front. He carried a wooden frame in the shape of a cross and the bells rang. Behind him, in pairs, walked twelve young girls in bright pink gowns buttoned up to the neck. They seemed to be wearing white masks. As they drew nearer, shuffling along on their tiny bound feet, I saw that their faces were coated with white powder and that their cheeks had red spots painted on them.

These were General Ni's concubines going to supper; the bells were rung by his eunuch to warn the servants not to look at the girls.[15]

Such mixed lifestyles were not uncommon. The author Lynn Pan's grandfather went into partnership with Monsieur Minutti, 'a canny Swiss architect', who arrived in Shanghai in 1920. Mr Pan had contacts amongst Ningpo bankers and Monsieur Minutti was on friendly terms with the Frenchmen who ruled the Concession. Together they constructed Cubist houses and office buildings with metal-framed windows, 'a representation of the Bauhaus in China'. They also built the Chapoo Road bridge across Soochow Creek, the Canidrome (for greyhound racing), the Grand Auditorium (now the Luwan Sports Centre), the Hua-tung Hospital (as Lynn Pan was informed when rushed there with a serious chest infection) and the Messageries Maritimes building on the Quai de France.[16]

Mr Pan made an unusual marriage, marrying for love (rather than by arrangement through a match-maker) a woman who worked on one of his building sites and who bore him the required son. Nevertheless, as a rich Chinese man, he also acquired two concubines, Jade Peach Number Five and Pearl Number Six, from the sing-song houses that he frequented. His wife endured some years of argument over them (at one point he threw a teapot at her) before committing suicide when her son was only 4. In the time-honoured way of Chinese women she took opium. 'You swallowed two lumps of it, raw. You washed it down with a cup of brandy, neat. And there you were, dead.'[17]

Such a mixture of tradition and modernity, business success and tragedy was to persist in the Pan family and in others in Shanghai and Tientsin. Adeline Yen Mah's missionary-educated great-aunt founded the Shanghai Women's Bank in 1924, a progressive institution staffed by and for women, to enable them to save for themselves. Despite this progressive and very successful project, the superficially independent Aunt Baba responded to family demands in the traditional way, leaving her flat above the bank in Shanghai to take charge of the household when Adeline's mother died and supervise Adeline's three brothers who were at school in Shanghai. She used her bank salary for her own needs and collected the monthly rental income from their father's properties to run the household.

Adeline Yen Mah's father had started a company in Tientsin that exported Chinese medicines, walnut kernels, straw hats, candle wax, pig bristles and dried fruits, and imported bicycles and pharmaceutical products.[18] He made a traditional arranged marriage with a Shanghainese girl and they were happy until 1937 when the Japanese invasion made travel to hospital difficult and she died of puerperal fever two weeks after Adeline was born. As his second wife, her father chose a half-Chinese, half-French girl, for 'during the 1930s, in the treaty ports such as Tianjin [Tientsin] and Shanghai, everything Western was considered superior to anything Chinese'. He wooed her with meals at expensive hotel restaurants and at the Country Club and at the Gaiety, Empire and Capital cinemas, which showed romantic Hollywood films. At first he gave her flowers and chocolates. Pearls, jade, diamonds and a Russian sable coat soon followed.[19]

Though her childhood was to be made miserable by this wicked step-mother, Adeline Yen Mah's first memories of life in Tientsin were of going to St Joseph's School 'dressed in pretty Western frocks decorated with ribbons and bows'. When her grandmother died, there was a grand Buddhist funeral at which monks chanted as paper effigies of silver ingots, 'Father's Buick' and a mahjong set were burnt. Grandmother's favourite dinner was set out and her grandchildren wore 'white, with white headbands or pretty white ribbons' rather than the undyed calico traditionally worn by Chinese mourners.[20]

The family then moved to Shanghai, to a complex which might have been built by Pan & Minutti. With Bauhaus features and a simplicity which evoked art deco lines, the complex consisted of seventy closely packed residences built in the same style, surrounded by a communal wall. There was a roof terrace as well as a small garden in front, a small lawn, flowering camellia bushes and a magnolia tree, and against the wall was a well in which watermelons held in string baskets tied to a rope were cooled and stored in the summer.[21] Adeline's living-room had a parquet floor, velvet curtains, white lace antimacassars, a sideboard, a refrigerator and an imitation Louis XVI coffee table.

All the children were sent to Catholic schools but on Sundays they would go out to the Mandarin Gardens and to the Cathay Cinema, sustained by baguettes filled with 'layers of eggs flavoured with garlic, onions and Yunnan ham'. At 7.30 in the evening the family gathered together for a Chinese dinner, summoned by the dinner bell. They sat stiffly in their school uniforms, 'hair combed, bladders empty and hands washed', ready for 'six or seven tasty dishes ... pork loin, roasted chicken, steamed fish, Shanghai crabs, sauteed vegetables ... a steaming tureen of hot soup'. Adeline and her brother James hated fatty meat and, like children everywhere, 'developed ingenious methods of hoarding chunks of it in our pockets, socks, trouser cuffs or sticking it to the bottom of the table. Sometimes we would make a dash for the bathroom with our cheeks bulging with fatty meat which would be flushed down the toilet.'[22]

Within some Shanghai families, the influence of the West was less strongly felt. Tseng Chi-fen was married to Nieh Ch'i-kui who ran the modern Shanghai Arsenal. Though a friend of the wife of John Fryer, the missionary and translator who was based at the Arsenal and who translated Western scientific works into Chinese, Mrs Tseng led a traditional life.[23] When her husband, who had served the Ch'ing imperial house in various capacities, died in 1911, she went to live with her son, a modern entrepreneur, who ran a cotton mill in Shanghai. In 1915 she, her son and his wife were all baptized in the Methodist Episcopal Church on Kunshan Road in Shanghai. This conversion influenced her in the division of her husband's estate: she gave 10 per cent to charity and she also forbade the traditional ostentatious displays on birthdays.

During the 1920s she noted with some alarm the advent of bobbed hairstyles and, with greater horror, the rising of hemlines. Though aware of transport changes in Shanghai, she also eschewed automobiles in favour of a horse-drawn carriage. Her reasons were not purely conservative. 'The horse is natural power ... at present China has no prospect of opening oil wells. Why should we contribute great sums of money to the foreign powers to indulge personal tastes for travel? I am old. If I have occasion to travel, it is not urgent ... Furthermore, recently the traffic congestion in Shanghai is growing worse. There is not a single street that is entirely safe.'

Tseng Chi-fen died in 1942 at the age of 91 after passing her last years in Shanghai in a carefully regulated manner. For breakfast, she would eat 'leftovers from the evening meal' and afterwards read the Bible and pray. For the rest of the morning she wrote letters or read the newspaper. After lunch, she had a nap and then turned her attention to the distribution of medicine or made clothing for the poor on her sewing-machine. After dinner, she might play Chinese chess with someone from the family. She was (unusually for someone resident in gastronomic Shanghai) uninterested in food. Although her teeth were good, she often ate soft foods like millet gruel, and since her cook was old and lacked the art of seasoning food, members of her family were often reluctant to eat with her.[24]

Mrs Tseng chose to ignore much of what was changing around her in Shanghai. In the smaller treaty ports, many Chinese families lived as they always had done, taking very little from their foreign neighbours. In his recollections of his childhood in the treaty port of Kiukiang in the early years of the twentieth century, the writer and artist Chiang Yee only adverted on three occasions to the fact that Kiukiang was a treaty port. He noted that the city was hardly affected physically by this new status, 'except for some Western buildings erected along part of the riverfront'. Westerners, like the Chinese inhabitants of Kiukiang, appreciated the fine porcelain produced in nearby Ching-te-chen which was on sale in the shops; and, so he also noted, they tended to walk faster. As a child, Chiang often went down to the riverbank, a trip that took him a quarter of an hour, though 'if I walked in the English manner it would take five minutes exactly!'[25]

Chiang Yee's recollections present a charming picture of a traditional Chinese extended family, visiting together his mother's grave every year to sweep it clean and to make offerings amongst the red azaleas, enjoying four-day wedding ceremonies complete with bright red sedan-chairs and fireworks, carrying paper lanterns in the shape of goldfish and dragons through the dark streets in early February and playing with green-haired turtles.

His family, however, was not entirely immune to Western influence. His sister attended a mission school briefly: '[she was] the first of our family to learn the twenty-six letters of the English alphabet. I tried to curl my tongue around the strange sounds, imitating her, thinking she uttered them perfectly. And I also made circles and curves to represent English writing.'[26] Chiang Yee himself must have attended a similar school for he later studied chemistry at university. When he wrote about his childhood, he was living in exile in England, writing to remind Westerners of the plight of China under Japanese occupation during the Second World War. Though he was concerned to stress the Chinese-ness of his childhood and the simple family pleasures of a vanished world, clearly the Chiang family in Kiukiang were less affected by treaty port life than those who lived in the larger cities.

The Pan and Yen families were in the comprador tradition, living in Shanghai and making use of Western technology and Western methods. Residence in Shanghai notwithstanding, Tseng Chi-fen followed Chinese ways; but there were other families devoted to traditional Chinese pursuits who, nevertheless, found aspects of treaty port life attractive. The actress Tsai Chin's father Chou Hsin-fang had been trained from childhood in Peking Opera and when, in 1913, he moved to Shanghai as artistic director of the Tang-kui Theatre, he took the city by storm.[27] The move was significant for traditional opera in China is rooted in regionality. Shanghai had its own opera and Chou Hsin-fang's voice briefly failed him, but he began to create a more modern form, mixing realism with the extreme stylization of the tradition, providing more for the eye, so that 'before Hsin-fang, going to the opera was called *t'ing-hsi*, listening to a play; after him, the term changed to *k'an-hsi*, watching a play'.

Like the Yens the Chou family lived in a three-storey lane house that bore some resemblance to a London town house. A double iron gate led from the street to a small roofless porch which gave directly on to the main or 'guest' room, which was traditionally furnished, according to the pattern repeated in every Chinese guest room. 'A high and narrow altar table faced the french windows and the front door and sheltered a square table that seated eight at meal-times. Four identical redwood chairs were backed against either side wall, separated by small square tables with marble tops ... The french windows looked onto the skywell that separated ours from our neighbour's house.'[28]

The male servants slept in a box-room under the stairs. On the upper floor, in a similar arrangement to James Ni's house in Tientsin, Chinese formality gave way to Western decoration. Tsai Chin's parents' bedroom was furnished with a 'Western bedroom suite in the dark wood that was fashionable then, ornately carved with fruits'; her mother wore 'silk chiffon dresses, her jade in diamond jewel settings'.

Most of the children were looked after as babies by wet-nurses although they acquired 'Banana (from the shape of his nose) ... to cook Western food for the family, a great catch for Mother since he came straight from the French consulate'. He was followed by Mao Sheng, also from the French consulate, who joined Banana as butler. Such changes in the kitchen required adjustments in the dining-room where 'The traditional redwood table ... was replaced by a long mahogany table complete with high-backed Edwardian chairs that Mother picked up at auction. She began to brief us on the use of a knife and fork, which seemed to me a very clumsy way of eating with two hands rather than one.'[29]

The wet-nurses came and went, leaving the Chou family with the normal complement of servants: 'a well-to-do family in Shanghai normally had four or five servants, including a cook and several maids. A chauffeur was essential if a family could afford a motor car and wanted to be fashionable. Otherwise a private rickshaw puller was engaged to ferry the family about.' The Chous had Fu Sheng who had fallen in love with cars. 'He was a born mechanic, which was just as well since the sort of second-hand cars Mother bought from foreign brokers, after much haggling, needed all the love and patience they could get to keep going.' The servants hated the family pets, two dogs and five cats. When the Alsatian bitch had puppies, Chou Hsin-fang fed them meat and eggs himself – an act particularly resented by the women servants whose children in the countryside were probably not half as well fed. Chou Hsin-fang's indulgence towards his dogs contrasted with his memories of childhood poverty. ' "In my childhood," said Father, "we had to make do with cold tea." "Cold tea still needs hot water to make it in the first place," my mother retorted. "These days we buy a refrigerator to keep tea cold," she added, making a face at me. Father gave up and left the room.'[30]

Just like the foreign children who learned Chinese folklore from their amahs, the Chou children were put to bed by servants who told them traditional ghost stories. On hot, sultry summer nights, the servants moved their little stools outside into the lane:

> constantly plying their fans, the women gossiped amongst themselves. The men in vests played cards, or maybe Chinese chess ... Under the night sky, the servants taught us to make friends with the stars. They told us that the Milky Way was really a heavenly bridge for the Celestial Weaving Girl to meet her cowherd husband on the seventh day of the seventh moon. And it was very important to pray to the Weaving Girl for a good husband.[31]

Chinese children from bourgeois homes were often sent to foreign schools although some, like the Chou family, had after-school tutors to teach them Chinese calligraphy. Tsai Chin started at the Sacred Heart Primary School, a co-educational establishment with a Chinese curriculum, which was across the road from her home. She was always taken there by a servant. Adeline Yen Mah, who attended the same school, lived a mile and a half away. On her first day, the cook took her on the handlebars of his bicycle on the way to market but no one thought to collect her. She wandered through unfamiliar streets (she had only just arrived from Tientsin) until a restaurant-keeper took pity on her. She did not know her address but had fortunately been taught the telephone number by her elder brother. Eventually her father arrived in his big black car. 'You wouldn't be lost if you had taken a map with you and studied the location of the school and your home,' he told the 6-year-old.[32]

Though Tsai Chin's mother was infinitely more protective, she did move her daughter to a convent attended by European girls when she was still far from bilingual. The first day was not a success.

> During play with other girls, I was driven to fury by the constant bully-ing of my foreign classmates and jabbed a pen nib into a little girl's arm. She screamed loudly ... Mother Robert wanted me to apologize to my victim, but I felt only a sense of injustice. Incapable of expressing this in a foreign language I merely refused to say sorry ... I found myself cling-ing to doorknobs for what felt like hours, resisting all attempts to send me home to face my mother's wrath.[33]

Eventually, she found herself protecting a Eurasian fellow-student: 'Half-Chinese, half-Scottish, she was prey to racial taunts on every front.'

Well-to-do Chinese often chose to live in the French Concession in Shanghai with its wide, quiet, tree-lined residential streets. In contrast, the central districts of the International Settlement were given over to office and bank buildings, with smaller, meaner lanes of houses cluster-ing in between. Their inhabitants were crammed even closer: it was not unusual for people to rent half a room, with only a curtain as a divider, or, for even less money, a sort of shelf built over the stairwell.

It was also true that the feared Sikh policemen were restricted to the International Settlement, as Tsai Chin observed.

> In the crowded thoroughfare of the Bund in the British zone ... I tried hard to be immune to the aggressive way the Sikh policemen directed the traffic, leaping from their rostrums to beat defenceless Chinese rick-shaw pullers whenever it suited them. These hated subjects of the British Raj had been imported from India, like opium, but as slaves to control slaves.[34]

There were other reminders of foreign rule in the International Settlement: Chinese who crossed Garden Bridge over Soochow Creek paid the toll in cash whilst Europeans generally crossed it on credit,

The Chinese and the Treaty Ports

which caused much bad feeling.[35] There was also the disputed garden on the Bund which excluded Chinese, dogs, flower-picking, ball games and bicycling and where, to add insult to injury, a Sikh was posted at the gate to enforce the regulations.[36] Chinese wives of British subjects were given entry passes to the garden and since Japanese and overseas Chinese were also admitted, local Chinese visitors wearing Western dress (as the overseas Chinese and many Japanese usually did) were not challenged for fear of upsetting Japanese sensibilities.[37]

The International Settlement was also better policed than the French Concession. Revolutionary activities were ruthlessly put down. On 17 January 1931, a group of young Communist writers met in the Eastern Hotel on Avenue Edward VII only to be seized by the British police and handed over to the Kuomintang authorities. As a result, on 7 February five of them, all aged between 21 and 29, were executed by firing squad in the suburb of Longhua, together with eighteen other suspected Communists.[38]

The authorities in the French Concession were more tolerant, or perhaps simply less efficient. The Chinese Communist Party, proscribed by Chiang Kai-shek and feared by foreign residents, held its founding meeting there in July 1921. Mao Tse-tung and other secret delegates were staying at the Po Wen Girls' School on Rue Auguste Boppe and they began their meeting in a small house at 106 Rue Wantz. The French police did turn up and search the house but no arrests followed (although the delegates thought it prudent to move to a houseboat on a lake outside Shanghai).[39]

For some, the inefficiency and corruptibility of elements among the Shanghai police provided a perfect background for illicit activity. One of the owners of the Great World Amusement centre, Huang Chin-jung or 'Pockmarked Huang', fostered the career of Shanghai's most notorious gangster Tu Yueh-sheng. Busy Pockmarked Huang also held a high rank in the French police force and was, simultaneously, one of the biggest opium dealers in the city. His protégé Tu Yueh-sheng, born into extreme poverty on the Pootung side of the river, made Shanghai safe for opium dealers through a profit-sharing scheme that put an end to the frequent hi-jacks of valuable shipments. Like Huang with his respected position in the French police force, Tu Yueh-sheng also gained a respectable front. He was elected to the French Municipal

Council in 1931 and his positions, listed in the Shanghai *Who's Who* for 1933, included, 'President, Chung Wai Bank and Tung Wai Bank, Shanghai. Founder and Chairman, Cheng Shih Middle School. President, Shanghai Emergency Hospital. Member, supervisory committee, General Chamber of Commerce. Well-known public welfare worker...'[40]

Tu and Huang were unusual, covering their illegal work with a French veneer. The vast majority of the treaty port inhabitants were ordinary Chinese and for almost all of them, apart from occasional brushes with violent traffic policemen, the foreign way of life meant little or nothing. The only city in China where foreign residence and enterprise met something like its modern Chinese equivalent was in forward-thinking Shanghai. It was, particularly, the Chinese publishing industry that drew modern Chinese writers of all sorts to the city where Chinese intellectual life flourished in the 1920s and 1930s.

Foreign residents were almost entirely ignorant of the fact that most of the progressive Chinese intellectuals of the period were living among them. There was Lu Hsun and his young wife and child who lived on Shanyin Road from 1927 until he died of tuberculosis in 1936. He sympathized with student radicals (and married one), and to some extent with the Communists, although he satirized their poetry.

> 'Oh steam whistle!
> Oh Lenin!'[41]

The woman writer Ting Ling – whose best-known story, 'The Diary of Miss Sophie', records the thoughts of a self-pitying, self-indulgent hysterical girl in the manner of a Chinese 'stream of consciousness' – also lived in Shanghai, as did Ch'ien Chung-shu who was later to devote himself to the study of ancient Chinese bronzes, and who wrote a tragicomic novel, *Fortress Besieged*,[42] about young Chinese intellectuals on their return from study abroad struggling to find love and secure academic jobs in Shanghai and further afield. Another major writer was Mao Tun whose novel *Midnight*, published in 1933, focused on the new Chinese business class.

The novel, according to Mao Tun's introduction to the book, was intended to describe how the new Chinese industrialists, hampered by feudalism and threatened by the compradors who controlled the financial institutions, were compelled to intensify their brutal exploitation of the working class in order to save themselves; faced with these circumstances, the working class was obliged to put up a violent resistance, and the new Chinese industrialists, opposing the people and opposing the Communists, were compelled to submit to the imperialist lackeys, the compradors, or become compradors themselves.[43]

His use of literature as polemic was also favoured by other modern Shanghai intellectuals, particularly during the Japanese occupation, when the theatre became especially lively as a form of political protest (although many nationalistic works were banned by Japanese censors).[44]

Young Chinese intellectuals, their sense of nationalism heightened by the existence of the treaty ports on Chinese soil, also took practical steps to preserve China from foreign depredations. From the earliest years of the twentieth century, Western archaeologists and explorers had been travelling across the Taklamakan desert, acquiring ancient manuscripts, paintings and antiques for Western museums. The Germans Albert Von le Coq and Albert Grunwedel, the Swede Sven Hedin, Paul Pelliot from Paris, Sir Aurel Stein, supported by the British Museum and the Government of India, and American art historians like Langdon Warner had acquired masterpieces for their museums in Europe and America in the face of complaisance from local Chinese officials. When Sir Aurel Stein planned his fourth expedition to the Taklamakan in 1929, this time with financial support from Harvard and enthusiastic support from the British legation in Nanking, he found that the Chinese authorities in Nanking had been tipped off by a patriotic young student in America, William Hung, who felt strongly that Chinese works of art should stay in China. Unlike his previous triumphant expeditions, Stein's fourth (and last) trip to China was a disaster and marked the end of the antiquities free-for-all in China's western provinces.[45]

William Hung's warnings were not publicly known for seventy years and the political activities of radical Chinese also went unnoticed by treaty port residents, unless they were policemen. Though Western material goods and styles were taken up by young Chinese, it was in the end Russian Communism rather than Western consumerism that, combined with the Japanese internment of most Western inhabitants of the treaty ports in 1943, led to the end of the treaty port system in China.

17

The Rising Sun

Japan's determination to acquire a sphere of influence in China had been apparent since she had seized the German concessions in Shantung at the outbreak of the First World War. In 1919, despite protest from the Chinese government, she had been formally granted all Germany's Chinese territory by the post-war peace settlement, an action that provoked the May Fourth movement (a student protest with far-reaching cultural influence) and a widespread boycott in China of Japanese goods. The German concessions were eventually returned to China as a result of the Washington Conference of 1921–2, but Japanese ambitions in China remained undiminished and they were soon to acquire a useful figurehead in the shape of the last emperor of China, Puyi.

Puyi had been living in the Forbidden City in Peking since his abdication in 1912. On 3 November 1924, the warlord Feng Yu-hsiang seized the city and forced the emperor to flee. Puyi's tutor, Reginald Johnston, who had been seconded to the post from the Consular Service, arranged for the young emperor and empress to take refuge in the Legation Quarter, at the Japanese legation. Some months later, they left for the Japanese concession in Tientsin where they were to stay for twenty-seven years. They lived in the Chang garden on Asahi Street, in a two-storey mansion with a garden that had a pond and a cage for Manchurian cranes (and a houseful of Japanese Secret Service agents just over the road).[1] Reginald Johnston was careful to avoid any sugges-tion that the Japanese had masterminded these moves – 'Japanese imperialism had nothing whatsoever to do with "the flight of the dragon"[2] – but the choice was significant and a propaganda coup for the Japanese.

When, in 1928, the Nationalist Army approached Shantung province on its Northern Expedition, whose aim was the recapture of warlord territory, the Japanese reacted (as other foreign powers had done) by bringing in naval forces. Though the German concessions had officially been returned to China, Japanese residence in Shantung had increased dramatically and the area was still considered to 'belong' to Japan. On 20 April 1928, Japan notified the Chinese Foreign Ministry that three companies of Japanese infantry were being sent to Tsinan in Shantung from Tientsin and that a further 5,000 troops were arriving by sea. Battle between the Nationalist Army and these Japanese forces was inevitable. In order to view the action, the journalist Hallett Abend travelled to Tsinan by Japanese troop train. He had been warned of the dangers. 'The telegraph is broken, the track is often torn up, bridges have been exploded ... When they tell you to lie down you must lie down and be very flat in the train.'[3]

Arriving in the aftermath of what became known as the May Third Incident (one in a long list of dated outrages remembered by the Chinese today), Abend found that 'the streets of this city, then with a population of 400,000, were entirely deserted except for an occasional Japanese military patrol. No Chinese were to be seen – that is no live Chinese ... On the sidewalks, in the doorways, and often in the middle of the thoroughfare, lay Chinese dead, in uniforms and civilian clothes, of all ages and both sexes. Most of the corpses were already bloated and discoloured.' More than 7,000 Chinese had died but no foreigner – apart from the invading Japanese – was killed or even molested during the disorders, though Herr Schad, proprietor of the Stein Hotel, had forty-one suits ruined when a bullet went straight through his wardrobe.[4]

In September 1931, the Japanese finally moved on Manchuria, the great north-eastern province of China. The treaty ports were pre-occupied with the arrival of the flyer Charles Lindbergh and his wife on a round-the-world trip. There had been disastrous floods in the Yangtze basin. In Nanking, the lower floor of the Bridge House Hotel was still under water and the Lindberghs offered their services to China to survey the flooded regions from the air and even to land food and medical supplies in isolated walled towns and cities. In October, as they took off from the river in their sea-plane, 'a wingtip touched the water and the plane all but turned over. Colonel and Mrs Lindbergh were dumped into the dirty, swift river and the plane was badly bashed.'[5] Pearl Buck recalled that the Chinese believed 'the river reached up and pulled at the plane in revenge' and that 'by all Chinese experience and belief they should have been drowned, but they kept up till they were rescued, to the awe and astonishment of everyone and most of all the Chinese'.[6] Their plane, however, was so badly damaged that their round-the-world trip ended in Hankow.

By the time the Lindberghs left, Japan was in control of Manchuria. In defiance of the League of Nations, the Japanese proceeded to establish the puppet state of Manchukuo, inaugurated in a ceremony on 9 March 1932 attended by the last emperor, Puyi, wearing a dress suit made by Whiteway & Laidlaw of Tientsin. Two years later, on 1 March, Puyi donned yellow imperial robes and made a dawn sacrifice to a hastily erected wooden Altar of Heaven. He then put on

a grey double-breasted Napoleonic coat which reached to his knees. Gilt epaulettes hung from each shoulder. His dark blue trousers were much too long for him. Attached to the white belt around his waist was a curved sword. On his right arm he carried a large gilt helmet. Dark red feathers hung down from the crown and there was a chin-strap in the form of a chain. The whole headpiece looked as if it had been designed for a centurion in a Hollywood film about Ancient Rome.[7]

In this uniform of Generalissimo of the Land, Sea and Air Forces, he was enthroned as emperor of Manchukuo.

Chinese students reacted violently to the capture of Manchuria. Demonstrations took place in Nanking in December 1931, demanding that the government declare war. Once again, Japanese goods were boycotted, student pickets standing guard to prevent people from entering Japanese shops and hotels, and seizing and burning Japanese goods. One Western observer in Shanghai expressed the prescient view that the 'lawless activities of the local boycott committees ... seizing cargo alleged to be of Japanese origin in warehouses and shops ... [and] arresting the owners' was likely to lead to a local Sino-Japanese conflict.[8]

The Japanese Minister in China and the admiral on board the

Japanese flag-ship anchored at Shanghai viewed such protests as provocation and decided to act. On 28 January 1932, Admiral Shiozawa offered cocktails and caviare to the *New York Times* correspondents and announced:

> There are 600,000 excited Chinese in the Chapei district of Shanghai, and most of them are violently anti-Japanese. About 6,000 helpless Japanese civilians have their homes and shops in Chapei. I hear a rumour that the Chinese policemen are deserting their posts, and that there is danger of rioting and looting. At eleven o'clock tonight I am sending my marines into Chapei, to protect our nationals and to preserve order.[9]

That night, Japanese marines with machine-guns mounted on their motorcycles roared 'up and down most of North Szechuen Road and its tributary streets shooting out all lights and spraying bullets into even second- and third-storey windows of the buildings on all sides'. Such was the separation of Shanghai, Chapei being largely populated by Chinese and Japanese, that Western men and women in evening clothes came to watch. 'These people had come from theatres, from hotels and from private dinner parties ... they stood around ... smoking cigarettes, occasionally drinking liquor from bottles and enjoying sandwiches and hot coffee procured from nearby cafés.' Early next morning, Chapei was bombed by Japanese planes. The bombardment of the densely populated area continued for weeks but on the other side of the city H.G.W. Woodhead reported: 'The foreign Municipalities, backed up by the reinforced foreign garrisons, and assisted by the local volunteers and police reserves, once more demonstrated their ability to maintain internal order during a period of intense crisis.' At the same time, Woodhead deplored the fact that newspapers unaccountably lost their most lucrative advertising during this local difficulty.[10] A local difficulty it may have been, but around 35,000 Chinese and Japanese soldiers and, above all, Chinese civilians died within the next two months.

For the next four years, largely ignoring such aggression, Chiang Kai-shek concentrated the efforts of the Nationalist government and its army on the elimination of the Communist Party in its rural bases. This policy increasingly alienated students, intellectuals and all Chinese concerned with the gathering Japanese threat. Such was the feeling against his policies that in December 1936, Chiang Kai-shek was taken prisoner in Sian (Xi'an) by the local warlord Chang Hsueh-liang. Madame Chiang Kai-shek, the glamorous Mei-ling Soong, who since she had been educated in America at Wellesley College, translated for her husband in interviews with foreign journalists, added sartorial details to his description of the event.

> I was asleep in one of the northern pavilions near the back wall of the temple compound ... when I was awakened about four o'clock in the morning by the sound of shooting and shouting ... I suspected an attempt at assassination. I've never liked pyjamas, but prefer what you Americans call the old-fashioned nightshirt as a sleeping garment. I jumped out of bed, and did not stop to dress but stepped into loose Chinese cloth slippers, and thrust my arms into a lightly padded robe of dark-gray silk.[11]

Captured on the hillside (and later caricatured by the Communists as bare-bottomed in his 'old-fashioned nightshirt'), Chiang was presented with Chang Hsueh-liang's eight demands which called for unity against Japan. Chou En-lai, a leading Communist, mediated in the negotiations to seek a national front against the common enemy. The alliance proved short-lived.

On 7 July 1937, Japanese troops on night manoeuvres near the little walled town of Wanping on the outskirts of Peking demanded that the town be searched on the pretext that a soldier was missing and then bombarded it, thus marking the beginning of the Japanese invasion of north China. Unusually, this incident did not go down in China's history as the 'July Seventh Incident', joining the May Fourth Movement, the May Thirtieth Incident and the May Third Incident, but was named after the local bridge, Lugou bridge in Chinese, Marco Polo bridge in European parlance. By the end of July, Peking and Tientsin had been taken by Japanese forces. Foreign residents were not threatened, as George Kates reflected later: 'For a long while, during the years of the Japanese occupation of Peking, the Westerner there had been untouched and unharmed. Nevertheless he did live more and more like a man who, although physically comfortable, knows that he has a fatal disease.'[12]

Many, however, did leave; among them the painter Sir Francis Rose, who had been staying in a courtyard house like that of his friend, Harold Acton. As coloured leaflets dropped by Japanese planes fluttered into his garden on 26 July, announcing the imminent arrival of troops in the city, the British embassy telephoned him, advising that he move into the Legation Quarter for safety. When he discovered that his telephone line to the New York Stock Exchange was cut and that he could not contact his yacht in Hong Kong either, he decided to abandon his courtyard and his temple in the hills.[13]

Shanghai residents were worried by the Japanese advance and occupation of Peking and there was evidence of panic as thousands of Chinese refugees tried to make their way into the safety of the International Settlement (as they had done for almost a century whenever danger threatened) but many foreign residents displayed almost the same spectator spirit as they had done during the attack on Chapei five years earlier, gathering on apartment balconies and roof terraces to see what was going on.

On the morning of Saturday 14 August, the Stead girls followed their usual routine. 'Mary left for work, Ivy for her office at Sassoon's in the Cathay Hotel building on the Bund, Nellie for her lessons at Mrs Corneck's.' At eleven in the morning, Ivy saw from her office window a Chinese plane trying to drop bombs on the Japanese destroyer *Idzumo* anchored nearby. The office was closed and the staff sent home, whereupon Ivy suggested that the family move to what she thought was the safety of the Cathay Hotel. Two or more bombs were dropped on Nanking Road, Shanghai's busiest shopping street. Mary Stead, who had nipped out to buy books and sweets 'as well as knitting wool (if possible)', had been pushed into the shelter of a doorway by a man who was killed in front of her; her sisters were waiting in the Cathay Hotel which was also hit. 'Our hotel room filled with concrete dust from the falling debris ... We huddled together on the stairs.'[14]

Over the next few weeks, battles were fought over Shanghai between Japanese and Chinese bombers, anti-aircraft guns and naval guns. On 23 August, Anthony Billingham went to the Wing On department store to order a pair of field-glasses (the better to watch the action). Wing On was hit by a bomb which once again left Nanking Road 'almost carpeted with the dead for a block in each direction'. Billingham had been in the lift: 'Of the eleven people in the elevator, nine were killed and Billingham and the little 12-year-old elevator boy were the only survivors.'[15]

The Stead sisters took refuge with friends during the weeks that followed the first bomb. 'One night, as we were assembled around the dining table, Uncle Jack looked (to Nellie at least) angry.' They heard a plane circling and all crouched under the dining table for safety.

> Later, we were told by Georgina that the reason Uncle had stared at Nellie was that he had to make a snap decision if the aeroplane came over again. The decision he had made – a dreadful one – was that he would have to shoot us all rather than let us go through the atrocities and rape which the enemy had warned him about – who to shoot first? Nellie, as she was the youngest at the table.[16]

For a while, unless they were hit by bombs, the Stead sisters and other foreign residents of Shanghai were fairly safe, since though the Japanese now occupied Chinese Shanghai, they did not enter the International Settlement or the French Concession.

It was in Nanking in December 1937 that the worst atrocities of the Sino-Japanese War occurred. One commentator has called the Rape of Nanking 'a storm of violence and cruelty that has few parallels ... The female rape victims, many of whom died after repeated assaults, were estimated by foreign observers at 20,000; the fugitive [Chinese] soldiers killed were estimated at 30,000; murdered civilians at 12,000. Robbery, wanton destruction and arson left much of the city in ruins.'[17] The smaller incidents in Shanghai had been watched by foreign journalists from the rooftops but the Rape of Nanking was not recorded by many eyewitnesses. Judging from some contemporary accounts, many Western residents of China expressed far greater outrage over the Japanese bombing of the American gunboat *Panay* which was carrying refugees from Nanking (and of the British river gunboat *Ladybird* at Wuhu on the same day).

Some foreigners, at least, were to discover what had happened at Nanking. An Australian journalist, Rhodes Farmer, was given photographs of schoolboys being hanged, blood-soaked execution yards, 'a group of Japanese posing behind the body of a dead Chinese girl', one of them 'wiping his bayonet on her dress', Japanese soldiers 'in the act of raping Chinese women', 'Japanese soldiers revoltingly examining the bodies of Chinese women'. The photographs 'were taken by the Japanese themselves ... Every Japanese carried a camera in those days' and, he added with prescient understatement,

> They may do so still. They sent their pictures for developing and print-ing to the Japanese photographic shops in the heart of the International Settlement of Shanghai. The staffs invariably contained a few Chinese. These men, at the risk of their lives, made additional prints and for-warded them to the Chinese Ministry of Information at Hankow.[18]

In the extreme south of the country, in Pakhoi and Kongmoon, the greatest danger remained that of violent smugglers who regularly attacked or killed Customs officials. In Wuchow (Wuzhou) near Hong Kong, by 1938, there was sufficient awareness of the potential danger from the Japanese advance in the north for most wives and children to be evacuated to Hong Kong, but there were still bachelors working for the major oil companies and a new (British) Commissioner of Customs with 'a twinkling eye, a partiality for good wine and cigars' and an animal-loving wife. Apart from the rabbits in the drawing-room and a drooling Great Dane, the beasts that most bothered Richard Dobson (of British-American Tobacco) when he called in search of convivial company were the family of doves that roosted above his head on the veranda. They were not house-trained so the Customs commissioner had a 'sanitary squad' in permanent attendance with warm water, mops and cloths.[19]

In Changsha in 1938, there was still a 'big weekly do' at the Club on Saturday nights when 'everybody turned up to dance to the gramo-phone and eat buffet supper'. This was followed by 'morning gin on any British gunboat that happened to be in' before Sunday lunch. There was a weekly musical evening at the British consulate when local business representatives scraped away at their violins.[20] Such cultural activities ended abruptly on 12 November 1938 when the city was set ablaze and almost completely destroyed. As the Japanese forces moved southwards through China, it was Nationalist policy to burst dykes or set fire to cities before abandoning them to the Japanese. In late October, both Canton and Wuhan had been set on fire by retreating Nationalist troops, with scant concern for the Chinese inhabitants. The Japanese had not actually reached Changsha when it was set on fire, but the result was the same. The British ambassador, Sir Archibald Clark-Kerr, called at Changsha when 'smoke was still rising from the collective pyre' because 'in spite of indifferent health, Sir Archibald insisted on being on hand when anything was going on'.[21] He found a depleted foreign community gathered on the island in the middle of the river surrounded by what belongings they had been able to carry but still able to set up a four for bridge.[22]

In the same year, as the Japanese army continued to move inexorably through China, Chiang Kai-shek retreated to Chungking, the treaty port deep in the western province of Szechwan, on the upper reaches of the Yangtze. Chungking now became China's wartime capital, protected to some extent by its distance from the Japanese-controlled east and also by the relentless blanket of low cloud that hung over the city almost all year round. Even in the 1980s, air transport to Chungking was fraught with delays due to cloud; in the 1930s, the difficulties of blind flying were greater, but in the summer months 'the sun brought bombs' and what one journalist described as 'the worst instantaneous killing in the history of aerial warfare'.[23]

As Chungking began to fill with refugees from eastern China, the writer Robert Payne, who taught English literature at the refugee Chinese University just outside the city, found that

the values of Shanghai have been transplanted to Chungking. It is curious to notice how many of the shops describe themselves as coming from Shanghai ... To get rich quickly, to have a beautiful mistress ... to be able to give dinners in which shark's fin, already almost unobtainable, will be served as a delicacy, to ride in motor cars and be able to say your income can be measured in millions are the hallmarks of the most exquisite taste. The old Chinese scholars have temporarily vanished, or they are hiding in small hotel bedrooms no larger than a cupboard.[24]

Foreigners, too, came with their old habits, gathering in the Chungking Club.

Sitting among the black leather armchairs, uncomfortably manoeuvring against the broken springs, you can watch the foreign population off their guard. There are the fanatical bridge-players, two young Jews whispering in a corner, the wife of an insurance agent, three or four Customs officials, the soldiers and the sailors ... Missionaries who have taken to business, armament vendors, dope-smugglers ... You come upon a man who is white-haired and holds himself stiffly as he drinks his last glass of the extremely potent drink which is known as 'Chungking Gin'.[25]

Once Chiang Kai-shek's government had moved to Chungking, Sir Archibald Clark-Kerr, the British ambassador, also moved his embassy there, into a house that had once belonged to a Chinese general but where, in the winter of 1938–9, Robert Payne found a blazing log fire, photographs, enormous bookcases, a collie dog, comfortable armchairs, a mahogany radio and pipes on the mantelpiece. At this crucial period in China's history, Sir Archibald was reading Joyce's *Finnegans Wake*.[26]

Back in Shanghai, as Chinese residents tried to make their way westwards to Chungking, an increasing stream of refugees began to arrive in China as Germany threatened their survival in Europe. The first Jewish refugees had reached Shanghai in 1933 and gradually established businesses in the French Concession but it was in 1938 that the greatest numbers began to arrive. Coming on Italian boats they saw China as a safe haven where, whilst Europe had begun to close its doors, no visa was required. The Chinese government may have been otherwise occupied but the Shanghai Municipal Council was soon alert to the influx. In December 1938, when there were still only about 1,000 Jewish refugees in Shanghai, a telegram was sent to the American Jewish Joint Distribution Committee expressing grave perturbation at the 'abnormal influx of Jewish refugees ... Council may be compelled to prevent further refugees landing in International Settlement'.

By June 1939, nearly 10,000 European Jewish refugees had reached Shanghai and liners from Genoa and Trieste continued to bring in thousands more who eventually settled in squalid, overcrowded conditions, in a 'ghetto' designated by the Japanese in the run-down district of Hongkew.

The municipal council continued to object. Before the 1939 council elections, the Japanese, anxious to increase their seats on the British- and American-dominated council, tried to get the Jewish Relief Committee to support Japanese candidates. The British hit back: 'Do you wish this International Settlement to be ruled by the Japanese and German Jews or by the British and Americans?'[27] The Japanese effort failed, though another Japanese council seat was gained in 1940 after an enraged Japanese ratepayer took a shot at a British councillor during a meeting.[28]

Though many of the old-established Jewish families in Shanghai, the Sassoons, Kadoories and Hardoons, offered help to the refugees, their growing numbers, together with the Japanese invasion of China and tighter Japanese control of Shanghai, made assistance difficult. Sir Victor Sassoon allocated two floors in his Embankment Building near Garden Bridge as a refugee reception centre where, in 1938, the stream of new arrivals could stay for a couple of weeks. They were given 'a blanket and bedsheets, a tin dish, cup and a spoon'. A small boy disembarking from the *Potsdam* found the contrast amusing. 'This morning we ate breakfast in the dining-room of the *Potsdam*, served by uniformed stewards, at a properly set table with the silverware laid out, and now we were queuing up in a soup kitchen.'[29]

In Hongkew, Jewish families settled in poky rooms in houses built for low-income families. 'Whole families lived in a single room ... the walls were paper-thin ... standards of etiquette were impossible to maintain when men and women were forced to meet in the narrow hallways at all hours of the day or night in all stages of undress on their way to or from the "honey bucket".' Refugee children played in the narrow lanes with Chinese children, picking up pidgin English and Chinese, for until Sir Horace Kadoorie opened the first school for refugee children in 1939, they had little else to do, although some joined the 'Thirteenth Rovers' of the British Boy Scout Association. The Thirteenth Rovers was led by Fred Mittler, an old Scout from Vienna, whilst the Jewish troop of Russian refugees was led by Captain Noel Jacobs, for the Shanghai Scout troops were organized by country of origin (forty-two nations were represented).[30]

In 1939, when the Second World War broke out, Japan was not, at first, directly involved. Nonetheless, the Japanese occupying army began to take measures against the British and French in China. They had closed the Yangtze (once Britain's 'sphere of influence') to all but Japanese ships in 1938, which was a serious blow to British trade, and now they began to put pressure on the foreign concessions in areas controlled by the Japanese army. There was a long and bitter negotiation about the activities of anti-Japanese Chinese Nationalists in Tientsin in 1938–9. The Japanese felt that the British tacitly allowed such 'terrorists' to operate from the British concession, and when first Ssu Ching-wu, leader of the North China National Anti-Japanese Army, and later four terrorist suspects were arrested by concession police in September 1938 and April 1939 respectively, the Japanese demanded that they be handed over. The British authorities in Tientsin, at the Foreign Office and in Chungking were divided. The British consul in Tientsin felt that in the interests of British trade and the residents of the British concession the men should be handed over to the Japanese, whilst the British ambassador in Chungking, Sir Archibald Clark-Kerr, did not agree, remarking that 'the mere fact that he [Ssu Ching-wu] was fighting against the Japanese was not a crime in English law'. Faced with a Japanese blockade of the British concession, the guerrillas were handed over to the (Japanese-controlled) Peking 'authorities' but the blockade of Tientsin continued, and was made worse by severe flooding.

In 1939, during the blockade and flood, Margaret Mackay, an American writer normally resident in Tientsin, was visiting friends back home. On 21 October, her friend Augusta Mullikin wrote to her, not from 397 Elgin Avenue in Tientsin as the letter-head suggests but from Peking where she had taken refuge:

> the flood water rose to 18 inches in our first floor and I hate to think what it may have done to your bungalow. I hope someone has been able to salvage your things, but ... it is almost impossible to get boats. I can report that my brave sister has survived all the hardships and appears to be no worse for the experience, though we are far from normal life as yet. While the water was actually in the house, the stench and pest of mosquitoes were really appalling. After two weeks, the water had lowered so that it was out of the house, but at the end of the month when I left, to come to Peking, I had to take a boat at our front door and ride to Woodrow Wilson St, before transferring to a rickshaw. I left at the time that Lesbia returned from two months in Tsingtao, as there was not room for both of us. All the furniture from the first floor was somehow crowded into the second, while the servants and an improvised kitchen occupied the third floor. As the servants' families all took refuge with us we had twenty-five Chinese on the premises, eleven of them on the second floor of the garage and the rest in the house. Mr P.J. Liang told us that in the course of a few days 240,000 entered the two concessions, after which our ever thoughtful protectors closed the barricades once more. The efforts to house and feed these poor folk is proof that the

goodness of the human heart is not exhausted yet. The volunteers saved countless lives and the Salvation Army and other agencies have worked under the B[ritish] M[unicipal] C[ouncil] making use of more than $200,000 contributed locally. The K[ailan] M[ining] A[dministration] and French Club were made into emergency hospitals, the schools into emergency living quarters ... there was a colony of rickshaw men living on the roof of the public lavatory opposite the post office, who somehow built themselves tents, collected a stove and a few pans and even retrieved three pots of flowers to ornament their terrace!

A few days later she wrote again from Peking.

Things are still bad ... although the furnace room was pumped out, the water has seeped in again and the furnace can not yet be repaired. Meanwhile there is an unseasonable cold spell and coal is short, while kindling is almost non-existent. The contents of lumber yards floated away during the floods and was appropriated by the finders. The barricades are also in full force, so that my niece goes to the Italian market and I am commissioned to carry all the foodstuffs I can when I return to Tientsin. There is a coal shortage in Peking, too. I believe that, and much else, is being shipped to certain islands [Japan]. Coal is real, if money is not. The invaders are undoubtedly having a hard, possibly even a serious time. It is likely that we Yankees will soon have our names on the blacklist, too, so altogether it is not a cheerful picture I am painting you.

My niece writes that mushrooms are growing on the first floor walls and I fear this is literally true. I hope that someone is doing what must be done for your house.[31]

The calm shown by Miss Mullikin was echoed elsewhere. The American ambassador, who visited Tientsin just before Christmas 1939, reported:

Getting in and out of the British concession is like going in and out of a beleaguered city. Crowds of Chinese stand for hours at the barriers ... when a truck loaded with goods ... is permitted to proceed, it is stopped halfway through the barrier and required to unload its entire contents ... The British community apparently is resigned to its situation and asks little and receives little.[32]

Dismal though things were, they were soon to get very much worse.

18

Internment

As Japanese troops moved through China establishing their empire, mis-leadingly termed the Greater East Asian Co-Prosperity Sphere, foreign residents of the treaty ports found it increasingly difficult to work and survive. Japan held Manchuria, north China down to the Yellow River, and the Yangtze up to the Gorges, and she was fighting to expand her territory on all fronts. And on all these fronts, she set up blockades which prevented the movement of goods. In 1940, she blockaded the Burma Road, the main source of supply for the wartime capital of Chungking in the far south-west, and encircled Hong Kong, not only cutting it off from the rest of China but also, by burning and looting all the villages on the Chinese side of the border, increasing the influx of refugees into the tiny enclave. Foreign wives and children were evacuated from the smaller treaty ports and businessmen retreated as their work became impossible. All over China, refugees were on the move, most trying to travel westwards to the provinces of Szechwan and Yunnan.

An American artist and journalist, Graham Peck, who had visited China in 1935 and had fallen in love with the place, had been dislodged from Peking by the Japanese in 1937. In 1940, he returned to China, hoping to find work in one of the relief or propaganda bureaux that welcomed foreigners.[1] Getting back was not easy, as all points of entry had been closed by the Japanese. But he met a party in Hong Kong who planned to have themselves smuggled through the Japanese-held sections of the West River delta.

The leader of the party was an elderly Texan missionary from Kwangsi province, who spoke rapid Cantonese with a high Panhandle accent and

284

had made the trip several times before, running church literature and canned goods through the blockade. This trip, he was escorting half a dozen Chinese Christian virgins whose families had decided they would be safer in the interior even though they weren't pretty. Also with him were an English girl, an Austrian doctor, a German doctor: all in the Chinese Red Cross.[2]

Though he managed to reach Chungking two months later, Peck and his fellow-travellers were attacked by pirates on the West River and intimidated by Japanese patrols, by Chinese working for the Japanese and, finally, by Nationalist soldiers, all of whom were bent on extorting money. However, the difficulties encountered by this mixed group were as nothing compared with what was about to happen.

On 8 December 1941, the day after the Japanese attack on the American fleet at Pearl Harbor, Japan declared war on Britain and America and the World War came to China. The British and American troops stationed in Shanghai had been moved away in 1940 and the Japanese now seized control of the International Settlement and French Concession. Previously they had left foreigners largely alone. Now, overnight, they went on to the offensive. In a move presumably copied from Hitler, Western residents in Shanghai and throughout China were ordered to wear red armbands at all times: those for the British had a large 'B' on them, followed by a personal number. In early 1942, the leaders of the business community in Shanghai, and those working in 'political' areas like the telephone company, were rounded up and imprisoned in a makeshift interrogation centre at 42 Haiphong Road.

Already cramped in their ghetto in Shanghai, the Jewish refugees likewise suffered from the changed nature of relations with the Japanese. The Kadoorie school was closed down, rations were cut and houses were ransacked in the search for short-wave radios. The popular football referee Herman Natovic was accused of spying, arrested and tortured.

In Peking, the Talati family had missed the BBC broadcast on 7 December 1941 with its announcement of the attack on Pearl Harbor because they were having a dinner party.[3] When one visitor tried to leave, he found the front gate locked. Mrs Talati put on her fur-lined jacket and said she would 'get the Japs to open the gate', for up until then their local street patrol had been on its best behaviour. That evening, however, she was greeted by an irate gendarme who bellowed at her in Japanese and finally reversed his bayonet and hit her over the head with the butt end. On 11 December, Mr Talati, whose family owned a lot of valuable property in Tientsin, was taken away by the Japanese who wanted the Talati family to sign over all their property in the city. He was held in prison in Tientsin and his family in Peking moved, like most of the British community, into the spacious quarters of the British legation. There they enjoyed tea parties, a communal mess, conversations with the elderly Sir Edmund Backhouse and, wearing the appropriate armbands, trips into the city for painting lessons from the emperor Puyi's brother.

In other parts of China, those foreign residents who had not already left gathered together. In Shanghai, larger apartments were occupied by groups of friends who pooled their meagre resources as food and other essentials became increasingly expensive in the wake of the Japanese blockades. It was easier to stay cheerful during this anxious time if there were friends close by.

On 25 March 1943 in Peking, the interlude in the British legation ended when all were ordered to prepare to march to an internment camp 200 miles away at Weihsien (Weixian), in Shantung province. The Japanese had prepared this camp for British and American 'enemy' residents of north China, while several others were established in the Yangtze delta for those from the south. Missionaries were brought in from their outposts. In many of the northern provinces, they left their possessions and their churches in the care of Scandinavian missionaries who, coming from neutral countries, were not liable to be interned.

Each internee was allowed only one suitcase and promised that a trunk, with bedroll and bedding, would follow immediately. Having always had rickshaws or cars at their disposal, none were accustomed to walking, let alone to carrying or dragging a suitcase the few miles to Peking's railway station. After a journey of twenty-four hours, in over-crowded third-class carriages where many had to stand all the way, they were transferred by army truck to the derelict American mission at Weihsien. There they found that the European inhabitants of Tientsin, Tsingtao and other places in north China had already been assembled some ten days before. Their bedding, however, had not arrived and in the freezing March nights they had to sleep on bare concrete floors.

In Chefoo School in December 1941, David Michell's Latin teacher, Gordon Martin, affectionately known as Goopy, had seen some figures in military uniform crossing the playing-field as he taught his class. 'Our new rulers have arrived,' he announced to the boys.[4] By February 1942, many of the Chinese servants had gone, so the boys and girls had to set the tables and clean the rooms. Food now became scarce and the children subsisted largely on bean curd, raw cabbage and slices of bread. In November, the children were transferred with their teachers to a transit camp at the Temple Hill Mission compound. David's only prized personal possession from that moment was his set of dominoes which he carried in his pocket. Several months later, they were moved once again, to Weihsien.

The sanitary arrangements at Temple Hill had been bad, the outside latrines 'a seething sea of maggots'. At Weihsien they were equally primitive: the worst work detail was to clean out the frozen latrines with pickaxes. The dormitories were routinely infested with bedbugs and occasionally visited by scorpions. Camp inmates ate unleavened bread, baked by Catholic priests, with millet porridge for breakfast, aubergine stew for lunch (known as SOS or 'same old stew') and soup ('watered-down SOS') for supper, washed down with 'tea-leaves' wrapped in muslin and brewed *en masse* in cauldrons of boiling water.[5]

Ingenious camp inmates constructed their own stoves out of Jacobs' cracker tins (with chimneys made from cylindrical food tins) and, under the leadership of the six-foot platinum blonde who, in better times, had run a souvenir shop called 'The Camel's Bell' in Peking, they set up 'The White Elephant Bell' to exchange such articles as they had been able to pack in their single suitcases.

Red Cross parcels were the subject of fierce national dispute, the Americans claiming that American Red Cross parcels were intended solely for Americans, until the Allied camp commanders decreed otherwise. Communication with the outside world was achieved by a redoubtable Catholic priest who assisted the coolies who came in to collect the nightsoil from the disgusting latrines. The smell was such that the Japanese guards stayed outside during the operation. Inside, the priest would remonstrate with the coolies for not doing their job properly and they would spit at him, showering him with tiny messages written on silk that they had concealed in their mouths.

Schoolchildren were given lessons every day although French had to be abandoned when the French teacher died of typhoid. David Michell recalled the stress laid on good behaviour, but relations were difficult in such cramped conditions. When Italy surrendered to the Allies in 1943 and Italians were interned by the Japanese, British and American internees listened with some horror to the clamour set up by the ebullient new arrivals. Then there was the sad case of the retired consul E.T.C. Werner. He had left the service in 1914 and after the death of his wife had retired to Peking where he continued his researches into Chinese history and culture and where his adopted daughter was the victim of a horrible and unsolved sex murder. Interned at Weihsien, 'his doubtless quite unfounded belief that a fellow-internee was the murderer added to the strains of internment camp life'.[6]

A very different long-term China resident who was interned in Weihsien was Eric Liddell, 'the Flying Scotsman', who had refused to participate in the 100-metre race at the Paris Olympics in 1924 because it took place on a Sunday when his Scottish missionary conscience would not allow him to run. Most unexpectedly, he did win the 400 metres, which was not held on the Sabbath. His parents had married in Holy Trinity Cathedral in Shanghai in 1899 and then moved to a mission at Hsiao-ch'ang (Xiaochang) in Mongolia. Eric was born in Tientsin in 1902 and spent much of his early childhood in China. He returned as a missionary teacher in 1925, joining the staff of the London Missionary Society's Anglo-Chinese College in Taku Road, Tientsin, which had 500 Chinese pupils. As well as taking academic classes, he used his considerable physical skills in teaching football.

While in Tientsin, Liddell married Florence Mackenzie, the daughter of a Canadian missionary, after courting her in Kiessling's. In 1937, they joined his brother at their parents' old mission in Hsiao-ch'ang. Florence and their young daughters went to Canada when war broke out so it was only Eric who was interned at Weihsien. There, he taught schoolchildren and gave intensive coaching to pre-university student internees until his sudden but swift death from a brain tumour on 21 February 1945.

Though the Japanese had begun to intern members of the Shanghai business community in 1942, the majority of the foreign civilian population were interned from February 1943. Shanghai residents were ordered to prepare four pieces of luggage: a bed and bedroll (to be transported later as the Peking internees had been promised) and three suitcases to include food for four days as well as clothing. They were then sent to one of the numerous camps in and around Shanghai.

A 12-year-old Shanghai schoolgirl, Fay Angus, had just been operated on for appendicitis when ordered to prepare for evacuation and internment. Though the doctor had 'assured my mother that all was well and that I would be strong and hearty again in a matter of weeks', the pressing question was '"How much will she be able to carry into camp?" His unfortunate answer was, "Practically nothing."'[7]

Nevertheless, Mrs Angus made her preparations. A crystal vase was bartered in exchange for two tins of butter. These, and all the tinned fish, meat and milk that she could buy (and carry single-handed) were put into her suitcase, along with vitamins. She and Fay sewed all their remaining money into Fay's knitted toy, 'Dog Toby', who thus became 'a multi-thousand dollar dog'. The Steads packed wellingtons and sou'westers, salt and yeast tablets and made their way, as ordered, to Holy Trinity Cathedral to be labelled and sorted. Together with Fay Angus and her mother and hundreds of others, they were then taken by boat to a China Inland Mission hospital in Yangchow. Fay's friends, the Bradley boys, had brought a gramophone: 'as our ship churned the muddy waters of the Whangpoo out into the Yellow Sea, I sat clutching Dog Toby, reassured by the hard crinkle of his monetary skeleton, listening to Glenn Miller, Artie Shaw and Benny Goodman'.[8]

Many internees assumed that the war would be over in a matter of months, but as it turned out, the Bradley boys' six records eventually served as their sole supply of music, 'growing fainter and fainter as needles and grooves wore down over the years'.

The China Inland Mission at Yangchow had been established in 1868 and had witnessed a major riot when the missionaries were accused of collecting foundlings in order to eat them. One inmate of the camp there noted that 'Christian missionary compounds throughout China with their protective walls, dormitory facilities, large chapel buildings, dining halls and kitchens were ideally suited for internment camps'.[9] The dormitories at Yangchow were divided: families shared the smaller rooms on the lower floor and dormitories for men or women only were on the second floor. Fay Angus and her mother were not quick enough to secure a space by a window or a wall but had to make do with their allocation of six and a half feet each into which a bed and mosquito net had to be fitted. For Fay, this space 'was my cave, my castle, my secret garden'.[10]

Ivy Stead and her husband shared a tiny room at Yangchow with another couple and soon realized that they 'were in for a long stretch of no secrets, no privacy and, in fact, no anything'. The lack of privacy (even the latrines were communal) was particularly trying, one inmate reckoning that she regretted its lack even more than that of some fondly remembered meals. As the Peking internees at Weihsien had discovered, the promised bedding took days to arrive so those at Yangchow had to sleep on bare boards. Washing was no easier. Each inmate was restricted to a bucket of cold canal water per day (reduced to three cups per person in the summer) and that had to serve for clothes washing as well. For the adolescent Fay Angus, menstruation under such circumstances was a nightmare, for she was forced to wash 'each sodden rag in limited water with no soap'. In winter, when snow covered the ground, chilblains were common.

> In bed at night, snuggled under a covering of practically all my cloth-
> ing, piled up for warmth, I would feel the chilblains heat up and start
> itching madly. I would thrust my hands and feet out from under the
> covers to cool them down, and then as they lost the itch they would ache
> with cold. In and out my feet would go all night and the trick was to try
> and get to sleep in between the itching and the aching.

Food was rationed to 900 calories a day in the form of watery rice congee in the morning 'complete with weevils or maggot-like worms . . . the evening meal brought us SOS [in Yangchow, SOS apparently meant 'Same old slop'], a watery stew with a tiny fragment of pork or turnip for the lucky ones'.[11] There was a bakery, whose products appealed to Fay Angus, although they were not to Ivy Stead's taste: she described the black bread as turning green overnight. As in Weihsien, chores were rotated, 'kitchen duty meant nibbling an extra carrot or slipping one into a pocket for later'.[12] Food became an obsession. Katy Talati in Weihsien dreamed of pineapple ice-cream cake. In Yangchow conversation revolved round the same subject and, on 'single turnip' days, Fay Angus would imagine herself 'at one of our family banquets at Sun Ya's, my teeth crunching into bamboo shoots and Peking duck'.

Children attended school every day and the curriculum included French, Latin, arithmetic, algebra, geometry, history, geography, science (with an emphasis on botany due to the lack of equipment), English composition, dictation and literature. Fay Angus recalled that 'a prominent businessman and accountant taught higher mathematics to the upper grades ... Our geography lessons, taught by a Canadian, took us twice around Canada.' There were no textbooks and there was a serious shortage of copybooks and paper, 'even the coarse brown toilet paper the Japanese sent in was used for schoolwork towards the end of our internment ... Eventually our pencils became stubs and a lost pencil became a disaster.'[13]

When Ivy Stead's husband Donald had dysentery, she nursed him. Though there was a camp hospital, medicines were in short supply and all she could do was bathe him with cool water to reduce his temperature and feed him the slippery, horseradish-like 'mountain potatoes', supplied by the Japanese. She herself had given birth to a still-born child while in the camp and, deprived of a visit from her husband, had been offered a single egg to build up her strength after the birth.[14] For those who were well, hospital duties were 'a coveted chore, as it meant access to the leftovers of the specially prepared foods ... The better, leaner sides of pork were always removed for the sick before the camp cooking was done.'[15] The internees were plagued by 'stink-bugs' in the summer and by bedbugs which would only be tackled when there was water to spare that could be boiled and poured over them.

During the enforced 'quiet time' from 2 to 4 every afternoon, Ivy Stead and her husband played bridge by sign language with their fellow-internees – a fist for clubs, the ring finger for diamonds, the heart for hearts and a digging motion for spades. 'Passing your hand quickly from left to right under your chin meant no trumps.' Organized entertainment included softball and sports, camp concerts and dances.

While the inmates of Weihsien had to put up with E.T.C. Werner, in the Yangchow camp, 'women of ill repute rubbed shoulders with the aristocracy, taipans [company directors], doctors and other professional men stood in the food queues with gamblers, knaves, clergymen and children'.[16] A well-known judge from Shanghai had a nervous breakdown and was found standing in an empty enamel basin, stark naked.

He was transferred to another camp where he took a dislike to buttons and cut them off all his clothes.

Ivy Stead and her husband, together with their fellow-prisoners, were moved back to Shanghai in September 1943, to the Yu Yuen Road camp where they were given tea, bread and margarine. They had not seen margarine since they had first been interned. Ivy 'wolfed everything down until I saw Doreen, a friend of mine, watching us with tears in her eyes'. Yu Yuen Road was a great improvement on Yangchow, with chlorinated water, flushing lavatories and electricity. In early 1945, they were transferred yet again, to a military camp in the Yangtzepoo district where Ivy Stead had grown up. In this move, at the end of the war when the Japanese were preparing for air attacks, Japanese soldiers were housed in the civilian camps whilst civilian internees were placed in the Japanese military camps. There, prisoners were confined in very large numbers, 'twenty couples to a large ward, families of three in another ward', and the lack of privacy was worse than elsewhere although Ivy still managed to find pleasure in meeting prisoners from the other camps.

Among those incarcerated in Shanghai was the Reverend D.E. Hoste, director of the China Inland Mission, who had come to China with six others, famous in missionary circles as the 'Cambridge Seven' – the original muscular Christians, who included the captain of the Cambridge University cricket eleven, the stroke of the Cambridge eight of 1882 and two vigorous ex-Army officers.[17] Hoste, then aged 82, and his frail wife were imprisoned with forty others (all but three of them over 60) in the Missionary Home on Tifang Street in Shanghai. There, in 1944, his wife died. Her funeral was held at the Bubbling Well Church, attended by neutral Swiss officials with a choir formed by German missionaries who had not, of course, been interned. Hoste's son and his family were brought under armed guard from their camp. Two months later, compassion for the elderly ran out and all the inhabitants of the Missionary Home were sent to an internment camp established in former residences of the staff of the Bank of China. Hoste was confined to bed most of the time and was to die in London seven months after his release from internment.[18]

Probably the most famous camp in Shanghai was Lunghwa (Longhua) which formed the background for much of J.G. Ballard's novel, *Empire of the Sun*.[19] Ballard himself was interned with his parents and small sister although his novel describes the camp through the eyes of a young English boy who has become separated from his parents. Among his characters is the Japanese wife of a Methodist missionary who reports daily to the Japanese – 'No one criticized Mrs Pearce for this and, in fact, most of the prisoners in Lunghwa were only too keen to collaborate.' The fictional Jim shares his room with a young English couple, Mr and Mrs Vincent, and their 6-year-old son. 'He had lived within inches of the Vincents for two and a half years ... he still liked Mrs Vincent, although her nerves were always overstretched and she had never made the slightest attempt to care for him. During the first years in Lunghwa, the few single children were neglected unless they were prepared to let themselves be used as servants.'[20] Whether or not such fictional elements had any basis in truth, the novel's portrayal of British internees as less than selflessly generous shocked many ex-inmates of the camp.

Peggy Abkhazi taught French to J.G. Ballard at the Lunghwa camp school. 'I love teaching the seven year olds and those in their late teens, but for sheer unmitigated gangsterism, commend me to Form IIB!'[21] She also kept a diary of life in Lunghwa which, for Ballard, was like 'a window suddenly opened in the small room that I shared with my father, mother and sister in G Block ... the stench, the boredom, the fierce winter cold, the stifling summers, the moody Japanese guards and equally unpredictable fellow-internees'.[22]

Unmarried at the time, Peggy Abkhazi was housed in a wooden hut, B West, for 'loose women'. In it there were fifty-one beds, electric light, coal stoves and a washroom with cold running water. Though the water was so brackish that no soap would lather, it was still an unexpected blessing. Peggy established herself in the corner next to the door to the washroom which, though it meant a certain amount of disruption, gave her eighteen inches of extra wall space. She put up

> hooks for my clothes, a small shelf above which holds books, and a curtain made from my kimono ... which helps to keep the clothes slightly protected from the eternal dust. My corner window just permits of my chair being placed so that I can put my feet up on the window ledge. One small trunk and three suitcases and the bed occupy the remaining floor space. The bucket, 'iron rations' of tinned food, odd-

ments of wire, wood, glass and other trifles which one picks up because they may come in handy some day – and the day always comes, all live under the bed, along with anything else that you simply can't bear to look at for another moment ... the folding table, washboard and deckchair rest against the wall at the bed's head, and above them a shoe-bag arrangement with compartments to hold toilet articles. On the lower shelf stand my two thermos flasks, two saucepans, frying pan, coffee pot, tea pot, plates and mug, kettle and mirror. On a tiny extra shelf – also my own erection (and our pride over any bit of handiwork or display of ingenuity is really pathetic) stand writing things, ink, soap and manicure case ... The topmost shelf holds gumboots, small medicine chest, dustpan and brush, scrubbing brush, tool basket, shoe cleaning and sewing kits, sun hat, cardboard box with stores for immediate use, tin of biscuits, tray, jars with tea, honey, sugar, peanut butter, milk and egg powder, and that is a catalogue of all my possessions, excepting for a change of underwear and sheets which recline under the mattress. I have the misguided notion that they may possibly air there and so feel less like death warmed up when I next have to use them.[23]

Further home improvements were soon reported:

My 6′ × 4′ is looking as pleasant as possible under difficulties since the completion and installation of blue and white check gingham curtains at the windows, and as for my bed, since its adornment with blue sheets and pillow cases, it is the admiration of the whole dormitory and the added effect of blue pyjamas calls forth much good-humoured chaff from the passers-by on the way to the washroom. It is something new for me to be a leader of fashion.[24]

Below her window, she cultivated a small garden with snapdragons, melons and a rose found elsewhere in the camp and she acquired a series of cats (all experienced ratters). These required a change of occupation. Abandoning school-teaching, she became quartermaster in the hospital kitchen: 'The grandeur of my title conceals the fact that actually one is a glorified coolie with a bunch of keys, a pencil and scraps of paper, and that one requires the tact usually associated with the doyen of the diplomatic corps ... the Cat family has made it plain to me that I must hang on to this job for evermore – the scrapings from the plates are such a great consideration.'[25]

Peggy endured cold winters when there was not enough coal for the stoves and, like the Yangchow internees, suffered from chilblains. In winter, she reported,

> I never change my underclothes unless there is a gleam of sunshine light-ing up my corner. And except that the topmost layer of fur jacket is exchanged for a padded dressing gown, I wear the same garments night and day. And as it is sometimes even colder inside the hut than it is outside, we wear the same clothes inside and out. But how many layers? Thick knitted vest and pants, woollen combinations, angora sweater, woollen ditto, flannel blouse, pyjamas under slacks, long cotton stock-ings, woollen socks with gaiters on top, leather waistcoat, and either a padded jacket or a fur jacket, head tied up in a scarf. It is tiring and tire-some to be so bundled up, I am just like a Chinese baby, if I fell down, I'd certainly need someone to help me up, being so padded out.[26]

Her possessions and clothes thus enumerated were considerable but ingenuity was still required. Peggy's clothes-washing bucket was volun-teered for chicken-bone soup. The chamber pots or 'Jeremiahs' were indeed sometimes used as intended – she watched 'staid Taipans of former days, stalking majestically to their respective washrooms, each bearing as company, Jeremiah Esq.' – but they might also serve as a makeshift refrigerator, filled with salt water. Makeshift stoves ('chatties') were constructed out of biscuit tins just as at Weihsien, a skill learnt at beach picnics at Peitaiho before the war. Ironing was also contrived: 'our champion ironer ... achieves miracles of smoothness upon our blouses, even pleated fronts undertaken, by a series of astounding evolutions around the stove pipe'. One aspect of life mentioned by all female internees was the levelling effect on the hair. Permanent waves grew out and 'as to dyed hair, once a makeshift turban is arranged around the coiffure, we judge that the worst is beginning to happen'.[27]

Life in the camps was not without humour. Writing to friends, Peggy reported a conversation overheard between two boys: '"What was your report like?" "Awful, and yours?" "Rotten." "And Jack's?" "Rotten. I know what it is, the masters here aren't paid, so they tell the truth."' But she wrote too of how quickly the veneer of a lifetime peels off. She developed an extraordinarily efficient 'boarding house reach' and 'In the absence of table napkin, I find that I wipe my fingers on my bare knees ... all crumbs are flicked off my plate onto the floor ... I wonder whether these ghastly habits will trip one up, during a fit of absent-mindedness, after one returns to civilization, or will one, on the contrary, develop an ultra-gentility of manner, just to be on the safe side.'[28]

Peggy Abkhazi and those fellow-internees who had survived did return to civilization when the war ended in August 1945, but not to the world of the treaty ports that they had known for so long. Shortly before they had been rounded up and sent to the internment camps, on 11 January 1943 in the wartime capital of Chungking, the British ambassador had signed a Sino-British treaty which abolished extraterritoriality and returned the remaining concessions and foreign settlements to China. Simultaneously in Washington, a Sino-American treaty with the same stipulations was signed by the Chinese ambassador and the US Secretary of State.

In March 1946, Ivy Stead and her husband left Shanghai for ever.[29] David Michell sailed for Australia to be reunited with his missionary parents after two years' separation. Peggy Pemberton-Carter (as she was then) left Shanghai in the autumn of 1945 for Canada where she married Nicholas Abkhazi (whom she had first encountered in Paris before the war). Fay Angus, the granddaughter of China missionaries, who had been born and brought up in Shanghai, sailed for America and a new life.

J.G. Ballard revisited Lunghwa camp in 1992. 'To my surprise, everything was as I remembered it, though the barrack huts had gone and the former camp was now a Chinese high school.' Provocative still, he reflected: 'Standing between the bunks in my old room, I knew that this was where I had been happiest and most at home, despite being a prisoner living under the threat of an early death.'[30]

19

The Legacy of the Treaty Ports

Paradoxically, the institution of the treaty port had eventually been accepted by the Chinese government – which had unilaterally declared several further ports open to foreign trade, such as Nanning in the far south-west in 1907, Pukou in 1915 and Hsuchow in 1922 – at a time when the announcement was of little further interest to foreign traders. As the *Encyclopaedia Sinica* (1917) noted of Nanning, although 'Land has been set apart by the Chinese and bunded, and some roads macadamized . . . with a view to making a foreign settlement . . . the regulations have not however been accepted by the foreign powers'.[1] During the twentieth century, the treaty ports had become less and less necessary as bases for business and as havens for foreigners. China, despite civil war and banditry, was now more open and many felt that there were greater opportunities for business outside the foreign enclaves.

The treaty ports were also expensive to maintain and, in the face of Chinese nationalism and Japanese aggression, they had become a political embarrassment. The return of the concessions in Hankow and Kiukiang was the result of local riots led by nationalist Chinese. There was disagreement between the British Minister in Peking and the Admiral of the China Fleet over their defence and it was the view of the latter, that defence would be ruinously expensive and politically provocative, that had prevailed in London. The return of Hankow and Kiukiang had not immediately led to the wholesale abandonment of the treaty ports but it had signalled the increasing reluctance of the British government to maintain the institution. The problem of the defence of the treaty ports had grown more acute during the Second

World War when troops were withdrawn to European and other theatres of war. Now the treaty ports were gone – abandoned, as they had been founded, by treaty.

At the end of the Second World War, foreign residents left China in their thousands, anxious to get away from the memories of internment and the destruction of their homes. For some long-term residents, escape was not so easy, for China had been their home for generations. European Jewish refugees, anxious to avoid returning to their place of persecution, had to undergo agonizing periods of waiting before they were accepted elsewhere. In the end, it was not the abolition of extraterritoriality or the abandonment of the concessions that drove foreign residents away but the establishment of the new Communist government in 1949. Though some businessmen stayed on in the hope of remaining in business, they soon found conditions impossible. By 1950, the British Chamber of Commerce in Shanghai acknowledged that it was all over. Not only were firms facing bankruptcy but the lack of regulation made it dangerous even to attempt transactions.[2]

Many Chinese also left. Some of them were not only wealthy but had absorbed much of the Western lifestyle of the treaty ports. It was just as difficult for them to conduct business in China. Moreover, their possessions, their Western furniture, clothes and education were all looked upon with suspicion or worse by the Communists. For those, like the Shanghai gangster Tu Yueh-sheng, who lived and worked outside the law, the *laissez-faire* treaty ports had offered a haven: the same treatment could not be expected from the Chinese Communist police.

Hong Kong filled with refugees. Sikhs who had served in the police force for generations joined the Indian community there. White Russians who had fled one Communist regime now fled another. Wealthy Chinese sought to re-establish themselves in a tiny corner of China that was still ruled by the British.

The treaty ports had been symbols of foreign imperialism and a constant and humiliating reminder of past weakness. Communist China's attitude to the treaty ports was, and still is, one of outright condemnation. In 1992, the Institute of History of the Shanghai Academy of Social Sciences produced a sensational but well-researched book on 'old' Shanghai, *Jiu Shanghai de yan, du, chang* (*Opium, Gambling and*

Prostitution in Old Shanghai) in which two of these vices were blamed on foreign residents. Trade in opium, 'this foreign chemical', was 'accepted as legal by the Ch'ing government in an agreement signed in 1858 with Britain, France and the United States . . . From then on, Shanghai became a paradise on earth for foreign traffickers whilst, for the Chinese, it marked the beginning of the descent into hell.'[3] Dozens of cases involving foreigners and opium were listed, such as that of an American, Tracy Woodward, arrested in 1925 for importing 265 chests of opium to Shanghai, despite current American attempts to end the trade at that late date. According to the Institute of History, Woodward's opium 'disappeared' with the connivance of the British consul.[4]

Similarly, gambling was said to have been 'largely sustained by the British, who built . . . the first racecourse'. Only prostitution was recognized as growing 'not out of the opening of the city to foreign trade and the creation of the concessions but from the economic development of the city'. Prostitution was different because it was recognized that prostitutes of various sorts had existed in Shanghai before the foreigners arrived, and 'it was rare for Westerners and Chinese to frequent the same establishments'.[5]

Shanghai's recreational history as set out by the Academy of Social Sciences presents the other side of the Shanghai Recreation Fund's version. Acquiring land for a cricket pitch in 1860, the Recreation Fund paid a small sum to the inhabitants of sixty houses, who worked the surrounding 70 acres which were dotted with the tombs of their ancestors. Though the villagers were eventually driven off their land to make way for cricket, baseball and horse-racing, the human cost of these developments was not stressed by the benevolent members of the Shanghai Recreation Fund.

During the Cultural Revolution (1966–76), even the possible benefits attributable to the introduction of Western medicine through the treaty ports were dismissed out of hand: students in Peking University were taught, in an echo of the rumours that led to the Tientsin massacre in 1870, that foreign doctors were interested only in vivisection. The nationalistic rejection of every aspect of foreign influence was also complicated, even in the late nineteenth century, by problems relating to the shipping of coolie labour from China's coastal ports. Coolies who escaped from appalling conditions in Peru and

Cuba, to which they had been transported, made their way to the United States, provoking furious and often murderous hostility from American workers and a series of Acts designed to keep out the Chinese.

Though the treaty ports were abandoned over fifty years ago, and though the opium wars were fought a century and a half ago, these humiliations are still felt by the Chinese and still colour their attitude towards the West. In 1997 a film about the opium wars was released to coincide with the handover of Hong Kong. It portrays Westerners as out-and-out villains and is typical of the rhetoric current in the People's Republic of China. The attitude may best be summed up by a line in a song from the Cultural Revolution: 'The lessons of history cannot be forgotten, Class struggle is the key ...' Modern China has had its fine historians, but the torture and death of elderly scholars during the Cultural Revolution only emphasizes the prevailing view of history as a political weapon.[6]

Not all pronouncements on foreigners and their activities in China have been wholly condemnatory. Alfred Bosshardt, a missionary from Manchester, was captured by the Red Army in Kwangsi in 1934 and compelled to join the Long March for nearly two years. His memoirs, stressing the hand of God in this extraordinary event, were published in China in 1989. General Xiao Ke, Bosshardt's captor, wrote a preface for the Chinese edition in which he stressed the importance of using the full range of historical materials available, including those such as Bosshardt's memoirs which were not necessarily written in praise of Communist China. 'History is history and cannot be unilaterally distorted to serve politics,' wrote Xiao Ke.[7]

Nevertheless, General Xiao Ke's ideal of history as being above politics is unusual. Such an emollient approach to the presence of the treaty ports is not evident in the nationalistic and anti-Western rhetoric of China today. Though the Cultural Revolution is now officially condemned in China, the attitude to history and use of anti-missionary propaganda prevalent then unfortunately still hold sway. That views about imperialism might have changed, that the Western nations who insisted upon the treaty port system as a way of obtaining a foothold in China might today use other, less invasive methods, are concepts alien to the present line of historical interpretation.

A more balanced view of the treaty ports might allow for some achievements. There is, however, almost no official recognition in China of their role as a conduit for those Western ideas and Western methods that were to play an important part in the country's modernization. Western armaments and industrial methods were enthusiastically adopted by its modernizers, and the modern weaponry in use in China today owes its development to foreign ingenuity. The fact that the commercial city of Shanghai and the industrial complexes around Hankow still lead the field in China owes much to the earlier Western presence. Many of their elderly industrialists, enjoying a second lease of productive life after the difficulties of the early decades of Communist rule and the Cultural Revolution, were educated in universities such as St John's in Shanghai and grew up amid Western institutions in a Western industrialized city.

Western medicine, introduced by missionary doctors, is now firmly established in China and is used alongside Chinese traditional medicine. Western attitudes towards the education of women have also been adopted, proclaimed in a political rhetoric of equality that portrays women as holding up half the sky.

Though the foreign residents of the treaty ports have departed, physical reminders of their presence endure. For decades, Tientsin, Shanghai, Amoy and other Chinese towns and cities were dominated by huge bank buildings, mansion blocks, offices and railway stations all built by foreigners. Even now, though new Chinese skyscrapers soar above the skyline, many of the old buildings remain, so solid that they would be difficult to demolish, though now occupied by very different residents. Tientsin's grand houses are no longer lived in by a single Western family with servants but house a number of families, crowded together. Chinese washing on bamboo poles bristles from the houses on the outskirts of Shanghai, and a grand bank building in what was Hankow is now home to the Children's Palace where schoolchildren learn calligraphy after school and read comics and watch Fernandel films on wet Saturday afternoons.

Less tangible evidence of the treaty ports' influence also endures. In the 1970s, it was not uncommon to find elderly waiters in Shanghai hotels who, when asked in halting Chinese for mineral water, would reply in perfect English, proffering a bottle of Laoshan water, 'Madame would like some Vichy water?' Serving coffee in the old German Club, one elderly waiter combined Western and Chinese manners for his favourites, pouring until the coffee overflowed into the saucer – for an excess signifies warmth and welcome to the Chinese. Now the old waiters have finally retired and Chinese businesses flourish where the old foreign firms once ruled, but the young wear Western clothes, listen to Western pop music and curl their hair, Western-style. Despite official condemnation of treaty port influence and of their very existence, the Western style of life that they introduced is immovably established.

In the West, many of the younger ex-inhabitants of the treaty ports are still alive. Some now return to China to look for their old homes, their old schools and their holiday resorts. Bright young taxi-drivers in Wuhan have quickly learnt the favoured routes through Hankow and away to the hill-stations of Kuling and Mokanshan. The ex-alumni of Chefoo School publish a newsletter and organize tours to China, and the China Society's members, many of whom grew up in China and are the descendants of several generations of foreign residents, are still actively interested both in the China they knew and China today.

The treaty ports were established to promote trade but trade, eventually, had to find its own way. Despite the irritation of their presence, the Chinese often managed to control the excessive ambitions of foreign traders. This was partly due to the self-sufficient economy that Mitchell had noted in his dismal report on British trade prospects in 1852. It was also partly due to a greater intelligence than most merchants would have credited to the Chinese governments of the period. The development of the railway system was an object lesson in 'divide and rule'. No one power was allowed to hold a monopoly but, aware of the potential for rivalry between them, the Chinese government allocated different concessions to different powers. The same rivalry, and the same view of China as one single vast market, today leads companies to compete for such concessions as off-shore oil exploration or the provision of telecommunications, but monopolies remain as elusive as ever.

The pioneer inhabitants of the treaty ports struggled to break into the Chinese market, facing infinitely greater difficulties than today's businessmen. Battling against an uncomfortable and unfamiliar climate, against unfamiliar local conditions, against isolation and disease, the new arrivals attempted to create the secure conditions with which they were familiar. Water-buffalo milk and rice soup were a barely adequate substitute for porridge; paper bags on the feet to guard against mosquitoes did not help to create a sophisticated dinner-party atmosphere; and the difficulties of making decent bread without wheat flour or yeast in a recognizable form were enough to make any house-wife weep: yet they continued to try. Full as they are of politically incor-rect descriptions of dishonest servants and untrustworthy underlings, the memoirs of early residents demonstrate the determination of the pioneers to survive as best they could and to transform their surround-ings into what they knew, and they record what was sometimes a heroic struggle.

That they rarely got to know any Chinese, except by way of domes-tic service or in the course of business, may be unacceptable as an atti-tude today, but that was how it was. Those who lived in the treaty ports and wrote about their experiences reflected contemporary views and the vision they had of themselves as upstanding and superior citizens.

Twentieth-century memoirs are more informed. Left-wing journal-ists like Arthur Ransome deplored 'the Shanghai mind'. Auden and Isherwood contrasted foreigners' cocktail parties and the ghastly condi-tions in the nearby factories. But they were visitors: there were many who spent their whole lives in China generally unaware of what hap-pened in Chinese quarters. The treaty port was their home and they had to make the best of it.

Glossary of Place-names

Post-office form	Wade-Giles	Pinyin
Amoy	Hsia-men	Xiamen
Anhwei province	An-hui	Anhui
Antung	An-tung	Andong
Canton	Kuang-chou	Guangzhou
Changsha	Ch'ang-sha	Changsha
Chaochow	Ch'ao-chou	Chaozhou
Chaoyangchen	Ch'ao-yang chen	Chaoyangzhen
Chefoo		Yantai
Chekiang province		Zhejiang
Chengchow	Cheng-chou	Zhengzhou
Chengtu	Ch'eng-tu	Chengdu
	Ch'ien-ching	Qianjing
Chihli province	Chih-li	Zhili
[Kingtehchen]	Ching-te-chen	Jingdezhen
Chinkiang	Chin-chiang	Zhenjiang
Chinwangtao	Ch'in-huang-tao	Qinhuangdao
[Kufow]	Ch'u-fu	Qufu
Chungking	Ch'ung-ch'ing	Chongqing
Chusan archipelago	Chou-shan tao	Zhoushan dao
Dairen	[Ta-lien]	Luda (Dalian)
	Fan-ch'eng	Fancheng
Fengtai	Feng-t'ai	Fengtai
Foochow	Fu-chou	Fuzhou
Fukien province	Fu-chien	Fujian

Post-office form	Wade-Giles	Pinyin
Fushan	Fu-shan	Fushan
Hainan	Hai-nan	Hainan
Hangchow	Hang-chou	Hangzhou
Hankow	Han-k'ou	Hankou (Wuhan)
Hanyang	Han-yang	Hanyang
Harbin	Ha-erh-pin	Haerbin
Hoihow	Hai-k'ou	Haikou
Honan province	He-nan	Henan
Hongkew	Hung-ch'iu	Hongqu
Hong Kong		Xianggang
	Hsiao-ch'ang	Xiaochang
Hsuchow	Hsu-chou	Xuzhou
Hupeh	Hu-pei	Hubei
Ichang	I-ch'ang	Yichang
I-li	I-li	Yili
Jehol	Re-he	Chengde
	Jui-ch'ang	Ruichang
Kalgan	Chahar	Zhangjiakou
Kansu province	Kan-su	Gansu
Kashgar		Kashi
Keelung	Ch'i-lung	Qilong
Kiangsi province	[Chiang-hsi]	Jiangxi
Kiangsu province	[Chiang-su]	Jiangsu
Kiaochow Bay	Ch'iao-chou wan	Jiaozhou Wan
Kiukiang	Chiu-chiang	Jiujiang
Kiungchow		Qiongzhou
Kongmoon	Chiang-men	Jiangmen
Kuangchow Bay	Kuang-chou wan	Guangzhou wan
	Kuan-hsien	Guanxian
	Ku-ch'eng	Gucheng
Kulangsu Island	Ku-lang-su	Gulangsu
Kunming	K'un-ming	Kunming
Kwangsi province	[Kuang-hsi]	Guangxi
Kweichow province	Kuei-chou	Guizhou
Liaotung	Liao-tung	Liaodong
	Lin-ch'eng	Lincheng

Post-office form	Wade-Giles	Pinyin
Lintin Island	Ling-ting	Lingding
Lungchow	Lung-chou	Longzhou
Lunghwa	Lung-hua	Longhua
Lushan	Lu-shan	Lushan
Macao	Ao-men	Aomen
	Ma-ch'eng	Macheng
Mengtse	Meng-tse	Mengzi
Mokanshan	Mo-kan shan	Moganshan
Mukden	Feng-t'ien	Shenyang
Nanchang	Nan-ch'ang	Nanchang
Nanking	Nan-ching	Nanjing
Nanning	Nan-ning	Nanning
Newchwang	Ying-k'ou	Yingkou
Ningpo	Ning-po	Ningbo
Pagoda Island		Luoxing
Pakhoi	Pei-hai	Beihai
Paoting	Pao-ting	Baoding
Peitaiho	Pei-tai-ho	Beidaihe
Peking	Pei-ching	Beijing
Pichieh	Pi-chieh	Bijie
Port Arthur	Lu-shun	Lushun
Samshui	San-shui	Sanshui
Sanmen Bay	San-men wan	Sanmen wan
Shameen	Sha-mien	Shamian
Shanghai	Shang-hai	Shanghai
Shansi province	Shan-hsi	Shanxi
Shantung province	Shan-tung	Shandong
Shasi	Sha-ssu	Shasi
Shensi province	Shan-hsi	Shaanxi
Sian	[Hsi-an]	Xi'an
Siccawei		Xujiahui
Sinkiang province	Hsin-chiang	Xinjiang
Soochow	Su-chou	Suzhou
Ssumao	Ssu-mao	Simao
Swatow	Shan-t'ou	Shantou
Szechwan province	Ssu-ch'uan	Sichuan

Post-office form	*Wade-Giles*	*Pinyin*
Tachienlu	Ta-chien-lu	Dajianlu
Tainan	T'ai-nan	Tainan
Taitsang	Tai-ts'ang	Taicang
Taiwan	T'ai-wan	Taiwan
Taiyuan	T'ai-yuan	Taiyuan
Takow	Ta-kou	Dagou
Taku	Ta-ku	Dagu
Tamsui	Tan-shui	Danshui
	Ta-tz'u	Dazu
Tengyueh (Momein)	T'eng-yueh	Tengyue
Tientsin	T'ien-chin	Tianjin
Tinghae	Ting-hai	Dinghai
Tsinan	Chi-nan	Jinan
Tsingtao	Ts'ing-tao	Qingdao
Tunhuang	Tun-huang	Dunhuang
Wanching	Wan-ching	Wanjing
Wanghsia	Wang-hsia	Wangxia
Wanhsien	Wan-hsien	Wanxian
Wanping	Wan-p'ing	Wanping
Weihaiwei	Wei-hai-wei	Weihaiwei
Weihsien	Wei-hsien	Weixian
Wenchow	Wen-chou	Wenzhou
Whampoa	Huang-p'u	Huangpu
Woosung	Wu-sung	Wusong
Wuchang	Wu-ch'ang	Wuchang
Wuchow	Wu-chou	Wuzhou
Wuhan	Wu-han	Wuhan
Wuhsi	Wu-hsi	Wuxi
Wuhu	Wu-hu	Wuhu
Yangchow	Yang-chou	Yangzhou
Yingkow	Ying-k'ou	Yingkou
Yochow	Yueh-chou	Yuezhou
Yunnan province	Yun-nan	Yunnan

Chronology

1636   Captain John Weddell arrives in Macao to explore the possibilities of trade with China but finds the Portuguese well ensconced and neither they nor the Chinese particularly welcoming.

1684   The British East India Company establishes a factory in Canton for trade under terms of considerable restriction.

1769   William Hickey visits Canton and the factory.

1787   Colonel Cathcart embarks on the first official 'embassy' to the Chinese government to try and improve trading conditions. He dies in 1788 without ever reaching China.

1792   Lord Macartney heads a second embassy to China to secure a
−4   British ambassador resident in Peking, to improve trading conditions at Canton, to open other ports to British traders and to acquire 'an island base' in China. He is unsuccessful on all counts.

1816   With the ever-increasing shipment of opium from India to China, Lord Amherst leads another embassy to China to try and improve trading conditions. The embassy stays only one day in Peking.

1838   Lin Tse-hsu is appointed Imperial Commissioner with plenipotentiary powers to investigate and put a stop to the illegal opium trade.

1839   In March, Lin orders a blockade of the foreign factories in Canton after the traders' refusal to hand over their opium. At the beginning of May, the blockade is ended and in June, Lin reports to the imperial throne on the destruction of nearly 20,000 chests of opium. Relations between China and Britain deteriorate: British citizens leave Canton for Hong Kong. In September, refused permission to buy food in Canton, a British ship fires on Chinese junks and the First Opium War breaks out.

1840   British troops move north along the Chinese coast and occupy Tinghae on the Chusan archipelago. They reach Tientsin in August, but are persuaded to return to Canton for negotiations.

1841   In January, tiring of negotiation, British troops occupy Hong Kong and on 1 February declare it part of the British Empire. Palmerston dispatches Sir Henry Pottinger in an attempt to negotiate directly with the emperor.

1842   British troops take more coastal towns and move inland along the Yangtze, pillaging Shanghai on 19 June and reaching Nanking at the beginning of August. There, Pottinger signs the Treaty of Nanking, ending the First Opium War and opening Shanghai, Ningpo, Foochow, Amoy and Canton to foreign trade, on largely foreign terms.

1843   Shanghai, Amoy, Ningpo and Foochow are opened to foreign trade and residence. In Canton, there is greater resistance to change.

1845   Foreigners are still restricted in Canton, contrary to the provisions of the Treaty of Nanking. The United States signs a Sino-American Treaty of Wanghsia in Macao on 3 July. This extends the privileges accorded in the Treaty of Nanking to American citizens and further allows for the purchase of land for Protestant churches and missionary establishments. It also establishes the principle of 'extraterritoriality' by which Americans committing crimes in China (other than those related to opium) are to be tried only by their own consuls. In October, the Sino-French Treaty of Whampoa reinforces the principle of extraterritoriality.

1846   Throughout the year there are anti-British disturbances in Canton; in October, Lord Palmerston orders a British warship to the city.

1847   After British naval bombardments, foreigners are allowed into the walled city of Canton but not for long. In spring, the first shipload of Chinese coolie labourers leaves Amoy for Havana.

1850   The British make a formal protest at the Chinese failure fully to open Canton.

1852   Taiping rebels, led by the Christian-inspired Hung Hsiu-ch'uan, take several cities in Fukien province and along the Yangtze.

1853   The Taiping rebels take Nanking and establish their capital there. In May, another group of rebels, known as the Small Swords, seize and briefly occupy the treaty port of Amoy (with no loss of foreign life). In September, they take Shanghai.

1854   As a result of the Small Sword uprising and the destruction of the Chinese Customs House, the local consuls collect customs duties on foreign ships until the formation of the Chinese Imperial Maritime Customs in June. Though run by the Chinese government, all senior officials and most juniors are foreign.
        An attempt by British, American and French envoys to revise the Treaties of Nanking, Wanghsia and Whampoa is rebuffed by the court.

1856   The *Arrow*, flying the British flag, is boarded and all crew-members arrested on suspicion of piracy. Yeh Ming-ch'en, Viceroy of Canton, refuses to apologize for the incident and British warships shell Canton. This marks the beginning of the 'Arrow' or Second Opium War.

1857   French troops join a blockade of Canton and the city is taken.

1858   Lord Elgin, British High Commissioner and Plenipotentiary, the French Baron Gros and American and Russian envoys arrive at Tientsin and demand treaty negotiations. Their rebuff leads to the seizure of the Taku forts in May. By the end of June, all have signed Treaties of Tientsin permitting foreign ambassadors to reside in Peking and opening more cities, particularly along the Yangtze in the interior of China, to trade and foreign residence.

1859   Against the court's wishes, British, French and American Ministers arrive at the Taku forts, intending to go to Peking for the exchange and ratification of the Treaties of Tientsin. The Chinese garrison repels the British and French warships.

1860   The British and French demand apologies and reparation for their defeat at Taku; when this is refused, they occupy Peking in October and sack and destroy the Imperial Summer Palace. The Sino-British and Sino-French Treaties of Tientsin and Conventions of Peking are signed, marking the end of the Second Opium War.

1861   Hankow, Chinkiang and Kiukiang on the Yangtze, Swatow, Taiwan, Pagoda Island and Hoihow in the south and Chefoo and Newchwang in the north are opened as treaty ports.

1863   French and British troops join the battle against the Taiping rebels. Under the overall leadership of Li Hung-chang, General Gordon takes charge of the foreign Ever Victorious Army against the Taipings. Gordon promises the Taiping leaders in Soochow that their lives will be spared if they surrender the city. To Gordon's horror and eternal remorse, Li Hung-chang overrules him and has them executed.

   In Shanghai, the British and American concessions merge to form the International Settlement; the Mixed Court, a police court dealing with foreigners where a Chinese magistrate sits with a (foreign) consular assessor, is established; and the Shanghai Club is founded. Sir Robert Hart is appointed Inspector-General of the Chinese Imperial Maritime Customs.

1864   The Taiping capital at Nanking is retaken.

1865   As a result of his experience in the joint effort to defeat the Taipings, Tseng Kuo-fan sets up outside Shanghai the first

Western-style arsenal to produce modern weapons. Her Britannic Majesty's Supreme Court for China and Japan is established in Shanghai.

1866 A modern (Western) shipyard is set up in Foochow.

1870 In June, the Tientsin massacre causes the death of 17 French citizens, mainly missionaries but including the French consul, and over 30 Chinese converts and 100 Chinese orphans.

In the same month, London is connected to Shanghai by undersea electric cable.

1875 The British diplomat Augustus Raymond Margary is murdered in Yunnan near the Burma border.

1876 Under the Chefoo Agreement, signed as a result of Margary's murder, Ichang and Wuhu on the Yangtze and Wenchow and Pakhoi are opened to trade.

The Shanghai–Woosung railway line opens in July. When a man is crushed to death on the line in August, the line is closed.

In December, the first Chinese ambassador to Britain, Kuo Sung-t'ao, leaves to take up his post.

1877 The Shanghai–Woosung railway line is torn up. Pakhoi is officially opened as a treaty port by the first British consul.

1878 Li Hung-chang sets up the first modern, Western-style Shanghai cotton cloth mill.

1881 The first telephones are installed in the concessions in Shanghai. A water company is also established there. Shanghai and Tientsin are joined by telegraph.

1882 French troops take Hanoi. Chinese troops are sent over the border but withdrawn.

1884 The Sino-French War breaks out over French actions in Indo-China.

1885 France blockades Taiwan but in June signs a treaty with China confirming the French protectorate in Indo-China.

In Shanghai, the British missionary John Fryer and Chinese

colleagues found the Shanghai Polytechnic Institute to teach modern science and technology to Chinese students.

1890   In an Additional Article to the Chefoo Agreement of 1876, Chungking in Szechwan, high up the Yangtze River, is opened to trade.

1894   China and Japan go to war over Korea. Tengyueh on the Yunnan–Burma border is opened as a treaty port.

1895   Defeated, China cedes the Liaotung peninsula and Taiwan to Japan in perpetuity and Japanese are allowed to reside and trade in China. Though the Liaotung peninsula is returned against an enormous indemnity later in the year, the shock of this defeat provokes young radicals in China to form 'Self-Strengthening' and 'Revive China' societies which are proscribed by the court.

   Ssumao in Yunnan is opened as a treaty port.

1896   The German Minister in China demands a 50-year lease on Kiaochow Bay in Shantung province.

   The first film is shown in Shanghai.

   The Tientsin–Peking railway line is built and Sir Robert Hart (Commissioner of Customs) also takes on the reorganization and direction of the Chinese Post Office.

1897   The Germans seize Kiaochow Bay. Russian warships enter Lu-shun (Port Arthur) on the Liaotung peninsula, explaining that this is to protect the Chinese from the German invasion. The French are granted rights to build a railway from Yunnan to Indo-China.

   Two German Catholic missionaries are killed in Shantung.

   Shasi, on the Yangtze, Samshui in the far south and Soochow and Hangchow in the Yangtze delta are opened as treaty ports following the Sino-Japanese War.

1898   In response to Russian demands a 25-year lease on Port Arthur and the neighbouring port of Dairen is granted them. China accedes to German demands over Kiaochow Bay. The French demand a lease on Kuangchow Bay and Britain obtains a lease for Weihaiwei for as long as the Russians remain in Port Arthur.

   In an attempt to strengthen China the Kuang-hsu emperor

embarks on a programme of reform but the 'Hundred Days Reform' is effectively ended when the empress dowager places him under arrest in the New Summer Palace.

Archibald Little takes the first steamer up the Yangtze, through the gorges to Chungking. Floods submerge more than 400 villages in Shantung province; the harvest fails.

1899   Italy demands a naval station on Sanmen Bay, but unlike everyone else, withdraws three months later. Railway concessions are granted to the Russians in the north and north-east, and to the Germans in Shantung; Kuangchow Bay is ceded to France for 99 years.

Attacks by Boxers on Christians and foreign institutions begin in Shantung.

In north-west China, a series of Buddhist cave temples filled with frescos and manuscripts from the fifth to the tenth centuries is rediscovered at Tunhuang.

Yochow in Hunan opens as a treaty port.

1900   Boxers attack telegraphs, railways and stations on the outskirts of Peking, and in Taiyuan, with official support from the local provincial governor, murder 44 missionaries. Foreigners are also murdered in several northern and eastern provinces. Foreigners in Tientsin are cut off in their concessions. In June, Boxers enter Peking and kill the chancellor of the Japanese legation and the German Minister. On 20 June, all foreigners withdraw to the Legation Quarter where they are beseiged for nearly two months. A composite force of foreigners finally takes the Taku forts, relieves Tientsin and marches on Peking. The empress dowager and court flee to Sian. Russia takes advantage of the moment to move troops into Manchuria.

1901   The Boxer Protocol is signed with Germany, Britain, Austria, Belgium, Spain, the USA, France, Italy, Japan, Holland and Russia. China is required to pay 450 million taels in indemnity.

China abolishes the traditional examinations for entry into government service.

Yochow, Shasi and Soochow are given up as treaty ports.

1902   Motor cars are imported into Shanghai.
        Russian troops still occupy Manchuria.

1904   Japan attacks Port Arthur and defeats the Russian fleet. The
        Russo-Japanese War is fought over Chinese territory. Three
        Japanese armies move into the Liaotung peninsula and occupy
        its coastal cities, then the provincial capital.

1905   The Japanese defeat the Russians at Mukden. President
        Roosevelt proposes peace talks. China's sovereignty over the
        Liaotung peninsula is recognized, although Japan takes over the
        Russian lease and railway concessions there.

1907   Nanning is opened as a treaty port by the Chinese.

1908   The empress dowager dies and the 2-year-old Prince Puyi is pro-
        claimed emperor.
        The first trams appear in Shanghai.

1911   As the result of an uprising begun in Hankow the imperial
        house is overthrown, and Nanking proclaimed the national
        capital.

1912   On 1 January the Republic of China is proclaimed with Sun Yat-
        sen as provisional president; in March, Yuan Shih-k'ai, a general,
        takes over.

1914   China declares herself neutral in the First World War but Japan
        demands the handover of all German concessions in China.
        Japan invades the German areas of Shantung. In November
        Germany formally hands over Tsingtao to the Japanese.

1916   In response to President Yuan Shih-k'ai's proposal to restore the
        monarchy, generals of provincial armies declare their independ-
        ence as local warlords. Yuan Shih-k'ai dies in June.

1917   Sun Yat-sen's Nationalist party sets up a military government in
        Canton.

1918   Workers in the British-American Tobacco Company factory in
        Shanghai go on strike.

1919   At the Paris Peace Conference following the end of the First World War, Japan's demands for control of all former German territories in China are accepted by the Powers. Students in Peking organize a strike and boycott of Japanese goods which spreads to Shantung, Hankow and Amoy.

1920   Bertrand Russell arrives to spend a year lecturing in China.

1921   The northern warlords declare war on Sun Yat-sen's Canton government. Wuchow and Nanking are taken by the Canton army. 10,000 workers in the British-American Tobacco Company factory in Shanghai go on strike again. The Chinese Communist Party holds its first Congress in the French Concession in Shanghai but for fear of the police has to withdraw from the city.

1922   Sun Yat-sen launches the Northern Expedition: the Canton army marches towards Hunan. Hsuchow is opened (by the Peking government) as a treaty port. Japan hands back the former German territories to China.

1923   Bandits wreck an express train in Shantung and take 300 prisoners, killing one foreign passenger.

1924   The new Soviet government hands back the Russian concession in Tientsin. Puyi leaves the Forbidden City in Peking at the order of the local warlord.

1925   Puyi moves to Tientsin; Sun Yat-sen dies. A demonstration in Shanghai is fired on at the order of a British police inspector: 9 students are killed. A general strike is called in Shanghai; 4 more protestors are shot by British police. Anti-British demonstrations follow in Peking, Hankow (8 deaths) and Canton (52 demonstrators shot). A strike and boycott of British goods begins and lasts for 16 months.

1926   Chiang Kai-shek assumes leadership of the Nationalist armies, relaunches the Northern Expedition and takes Hankow.

1927   The Nationalist government's capital is transferred to Hankow. Chinese crowds demonstrate against the British presence and concession. In March, the British concessions at Hankow and Kiukiang are handed back to China. 8,000 workers in the BAT factory in Shanghai go on strike.

1928   Japanese troops land in Shantung. On 3 May a confrontation between the Japanese and the Nationalist Army causes great loss of life and destruction in Tsinan.

1929   Japanese troops withdraw from Shantung. In November, the Soviet army attacks and invades Manchuria; troops are withdrawn in late December. Britain returns Amoy.

1930   Britain returns Weihaiwei and Chinkiang to China.

1931   Japan invades Manchuria. The Yangtze bursts its banks at Hankow and floods along 1,000 miles.

1932   The Japanese attack Shanghai in January but withdraw troops in May.

1933   Japanese troops move closer to Peking.

1934   Puyi is enthroned as Emperor of Manchukuo.

1936   Chiang Kai-shek is briefly kidnapped in Sian in an attempt to force him to end the civil war between the Nationalists, Communists and warlords, and to devote his attention to resisting Japan.

1937   Japan takes Peking and Taku (July), and attacks Shanghai (August) and Nanking (December).

1938   Japan takes most of eastern China, including the treaty ports such as Changsha and Canton. Nationalist troops burn cities as they abandon them. The Yellow River dykes are breached to prevent the Japanese advance but thousands are killed in the ensuing floods. The Nationalist government moves the capital to Chungking (December).

1939   The Second World War breaks out in Europe. Japan continues the invasion of China and bombs Chungking. Thousands of Jewish refugees arrive in Shanghai.

Chronology

1940   Britain withdraws all its troops from Shanghai and north China.

1941   After the attack on Pearl Harbor, Japan bombs Hong Kong and declares war on Britain and America. Japanese troops occupy the International Settlement in Shanghai and British concessions in Tientsin and Amoy. Treaty port residents are compelled to wear armbands denoting their nationality.

1942   The first foreign residents are interned in camps: those from the north in Weihsien, Shantung, those from the south in several camps in Yangchow and around Shanghai.

1943   In January, Britain and America sign treaties with the Chinese, ending extraterritorial privileges and returning all concessions to China. From February, the remaining foreign civilian population is interned by the Japanese.

Notes

INTRODUCTION: DEFINITIONS

1. Martyn Atkins, *Informal Empire in Crisis: British Diplomacy and the Chinese Customs Succession, 1927–1929* (New York, Cornell University, 1955), Cornell East Asian Series, 74.
2. Samuel Couling, *Encyclopaedia Sinica* (London, Humphrey Milford, 1917: reprinted Hong Kong, Oxford University Press, 1983), p.171.
3. Arnold Wright (ed.), *Twentieth-century Impressions of Hong Kong, Shanghai and Other Treaty Ports in China* (London, Lloyd's Greater Britain Publishing Company, 1908), p.401.
4. Maurice Dekobra, *Confucius en pull-over*, translated (very badly) and re-titled *Confucius in a Tail-coat* (London, T. Werner Laurie, 1935).
5. Hope Danby, *My Boy Chang* (London, Gollancz, 1955), pp.7–8, 16–17, 37 and 85–7.
6. Harry Franck, *Roving through Southern China* (London, Appleton-Century, 1925), pp.3–5.

I: THE CHINA TRADE

1. P.D. Coates, *The China Consuls: British Consular Officers, 1843–1943* (Hong Kong, Oxford University Press, 1988), p.1.
2. Otherwise *gonghang*, or merchant guild.
3. An inappropriate mistranslation of *Hu Bu*, or Board of Finance.
4. William Hickey, *Memoirs of William Hickey*, ed. Peter Quennell (London, Century, 1975), pp.125, 129–30 and 133.
5. Michael Greenberg, *British Trade and the Opening of China 1800–1842* (Cambridge, Cambridge University Press, 1951), p.3.
6. Greenberg, p.8.

7. For the Cathcart and Macartney embassies, see Aubrey Singer, *The Lion and the Dragon: The Story of the First British Embassy to the Court of the Emperor Qianlong at Peking, 1792–1794* (London, Barrie & Jenkins, 1992).

8. Singer, p.5.

9. See George Leonard Staunton, *An Authentic Account of an Embassy from the King of Great Britain to the Emperor of China* (London, J. Nicol, 1797; also translated into French, German and Dutch).

10. See James Hevia, *Cherishing Men from Afar: Qing Guest Ritual and the Macartney Embassy of 1793* (Durham and London, Duke University Press, 1995).

11. John Keay, *The Honourable Company: A History of the English East India Company* (London, Harper Collins, 1991), p.21. For the widespread cultivation of opium in China, see G.E. Morrison, *An Australian in China* (London, H. Cox, 1895), p.5.

12. Jonathan Spence, *The Search for Modern China* (New York and London, Norton, 1990), p.129.

13. Couling, p.24.

14. Spence, *The Search for Modern China*, p.149.

15. On Lin Tse-hsu, see Arthur Waley, *The Opium War Through Chinese Eyes* (London, Allen & Unwin, 1958).

16. In June 1997, just before Hong Kong was returned to China, the People's Liberation Army supervised the burning of a huge quantity of heroin, the opium of the twentieth century, on the same site, at Humen, as a reminder to the British that their Far Eastern empire was based on trade in an illegal drug.

17. Bob Whyte, *Unfinished Encounter: China and Christianity* (London, Fount Paperbacks, 1988), p.79.

18. Spence, *The Search for Modern China*, pp.161–2.

2: EARLY DAYS IN SHANGHAI

1. Couling, p.507; and Spence, *The Search for Modern China*, p.162.

2. Quoted in Frances Wood, *Blue Guide to China* (London, A. & C. Black, 1992), p.205.

3. Alexander Wylie, *Memorials of the Protestant Missions to the Chinese, giving a list of their publications and obituary notices of the deceased with copious indexes* (Shanghai, American Presbyterian Mission Press, 1867), p.26.

4. W.H. Medhurst, 'Reminiscences of the opening of Shanghai to foreign Trade', *Chinese and Japanese Repository*, 12 October 1864.

5. Robert Fortune, *Three Years' Wandering in China* (London, John Murray, 1847: reprinted London, Mildmay Books, 1987), pp.119–20 and 125.

6. Fortune, p.116.
7. F.L. Hawks Pott, *A Short History of Shanghai* (Shanghai, Kelly & Walsh, 1928), p.18.
8. Hawks Pott, pp.35–6.
9. Charles M. Dyce, *Personal Reminiscences of Thirty Years' Residence in the Model Settlement Shanghai, 1870–1900* (London, Chapman & Hall, 1906), pp.32–5.
10. Although, according to Coates, the name was first applied to new (human) arrivals in India and thence transferred to (humans first) in China. See Austin Coates, *China Races* (Hong Kong, Oxford University Press, 1983), p.29.
11. Kerrie L. MacPherson, *A Wilderness of Marshes: The Origins of Public Health in Shanghai, 1843–1893* (Hong Kong, Oxford University Press, 1987), p.15.
12. See G. Lanning and S. Couling, *The History of Shanghai* (Shanghai, Kelly & Walsh for the Shanghai Municipal Council, 1921), pp.393 *et seq.*
13. Maurice Collis, *Wayfoong: The Hongkong and Shanghai Banking Corporation* (London, Faber & Faber, 1965), p.21.
14. Alexander Mitchie, *The Englishman in China during the Victorian Era as illustrated in the career of Sir Rutherford Alcock KCB, DCL, many years Consul and Minister in China and Japan* (London, Blackwood, 1900), p.127.
15. Lanning and Couling, p.429.
16. R.J. Smith, J.K. Fairbank and K. Bruner (eds.), *Robert Hart and China's Early Modernization* (Cambridge and London, Harvard University Press, 1991), pp.231 and 237.
17. Lanning and Couling, pp.440 and 430.
18. Austin Coates, p.26.
19. *Anecdotes of Old Shanghai* (Shanghai, Shanghai Cultural Publishing House, 1985), p.2.
20. *History of the Shanghai Recreation Fund from 1860 to 1906* (Shanghai, North China Daily News and Herald, 1907), p.11.
21. Austin Coates, pp.22–5.
22. C. Noel Davis, *History of the Shanghai Paper Hunt Club 1863–1930* ((Shanghai, Kelly & Walsh, 1930), p.3.
23. Davis, pp.5 and 14.
24. Lanning and Couling, p.436.
25. Wylie's *Memorials of the Protestant Missions* (1867) makes depressing reading at first because of the extraordinarily high death-rate, but Victorians in China seem to have been quick to pick up the pieces for remarriages were remarkably common.
26. Hawks Pott, p.81.

27. James Henderson, *Shanghai Hygiene or Hints for the Preservation of Health in China* (Shanghai, Presbyterian Mission Press, 1863).
28. John Gavin, Letterbook, British Library.
29. K. Bruner, J.K. Fairbank and R.J. Smith (eds.), *Entering China's Service: Robert Hart's Journals, 1854–1863* (Cambridge and London, Harvard University Press, 1986), pp.14, 71 and 151–3.
30. MacPherson, p.75. According to S.J. Perelman ('No starch in the dhoti *s'il vous plaît*'), Nehru's father used to send his washing to Paris.
31. MacPherson, pp. 83, 96, 118–20, 149, 172–4 and 209.
32. Hawks Pott, p.72.

3: THE SMALLER PORTS

1. See the Ningpo correspondence in Chang Hsiu-jung, Anthony Farrington, Huang Fu-san *et al.* (eds.), *The English Factory in Taiwan, 1670–1685* (Taipei, National Taiwan University, 1995).
2. Fortune, pp.82–3.
3. Fortune, pp.84–5.
4. Wright, p.814.
5. P.D.Coates, p.20.
6. P.D.Coates, p.59.
7. Bruner *et al.*, p.30.
8. Bruner *et al.*, pp.61–3.
9. Bruner *et al.*, p.64.
10. Philip Wilson Pitcher, *In and About Amoy: some historical and other facts connected with one of the first open ports in China* (Shanghai and Foochow, Methodist Publishing House in China, 1912: reprinted Taipei, 1972), pp.16–18.
11. Fortune, pp.35–42.
12. Russell & Co.'s involvement in the opium trade worried Eleanor Roosevelt, for her husband's grandfather and two uncles were partners in the company. She took the opportunity of questioning a smooth descendant of one of the other major opium-trading firms, John Keswick, when on a visit to Hong Kong. She told him, 'Certain newspaper writers who were opposed to the administration often liked to assert that Franklin's family made money in the opium trade in the days when the clipper ships sailed to China.' Keswick, with scant regard for the truth, reassured her: 'all foreign merchants trading in tea in China in those days were required to obtain special permits. And one of the requirements for getting a permit was that they agree to take a small amount of opium when they

were purchasing tea and other goods.' See Carroll Lunt, *Some Builders of Treaty Port China* (Los Angeles, privately published, 1965), p.49.

13. Wylie, pp.72–5 and 105; and Pitcher, p.235.
14. Wylie, p.97.
15. P.D. Coates, p.18.
16. Fortune, pp.368 and 371–3.
17. P.D. Coates, p.161.
18. Fortune, pp.370–1.
19. P.D.Coates, p.191.
20. P.G.L., *A Reminiscence of Canton 1863* (London, Harrison & Sons, 1866), bound together with R.H. Graves in the British Library's Topographical Tracts 1846–84; and Jean-Jacques Matignon, *Superstition, Crime and Misery in China* (Lyons, 1899).
21. R.H. Graves, 'Report of the Medical Missionary Society's Dispensary . . . for 1863' (n.p., n.d., in British Library, Topographical Tracts 1846–84, 10058.cc.8).

4: CONSULS AND MERCHANTS

1. P.D. Coates, p.87.
2. John K. Fairbank (ed.), *The Cambridge History of China: vol. 10, Late Ch'ing, 1800–1911, Part I* (Cambridge, Cambridge University Press, 1978), pp.189–90.
3. P.D. Coates, p.24.
4. P.D. Coates, pp.50–3.
5. Bruner *et al.*, p.370 note 141.
6. P.D. Coates, p.53.
7. P.D. Coates, p.67.
8. P.D. Coates, p.61.
9. Bruner *et al.*, p.111.
10. P.D. Coates, p.62.
11. Wylie, p.131.
12. P.D. Coates, pp.60 and 63–5.
13. Bruner *et al.*, p.76.
14. P.D. Coates, p.59.
15. Bruner *et al.*, p.72.
16. Bruner *et al.*, pp.104–6, 109 and 125.
17. Quoted in Douglas Hurd, *The Arrow War: An Anglo-Chinese Confusion* (London, Collins, 1967), p.54.
18. Exhibition 1850–1, vol. 5 (on permanent loan from the Royal Archives,

Windsor Castle), and Great Exhibition, Box 4, Royal Commission Archive for the Exhibition of 1851, quoted with permission.

19. Coloured lithograph, *The Living Chinese Family*, published by C. Hancock, London, n.d., *c.* 1851.
20. Nathan A. Pelcovits, *Old China Hands and the Foreign Office* (New York, American Institute of Pacific Relations, 1948), pp.15–17.
21. Hawks Pott, p.37.
22. Wright, p.399.
23. Mary Ninde Gamewell, *The Gateway to China: Pictures of Shanghai* (1916: reprinted Taipei, Cheng-wen, 1972), p.21.
24. Wright, pp.400 and 414.
25. Wright, p.813.

5: SMALL SWORDS AND IMPERIAL CHINESE CUSTOMS

1. John K. Fairbank, *Trade and Diplomacy on the China Coast* (Cambridge, Harvard University Press, 1953), vol. 1, p.410.
2. P.D. Coates, p.24.
3. Lanning and Couling, p.316.
4. Fairbank, *Trade and Diplomacy*, p.143.
5. Lanning and Couling, pp.296–7.
6. Smith *et al.*, *Robert Hart*, p.416.
7. This saintly activity is listed in A. Hummel (ed.), *Eminent Chinese of the Ch'ing Period* (Washington DC, United States Government Printing Office, 1943), p.118.
8. Lanning and Couling, p.300.
9. Smith *et al.*, *Robert Hart*, pp.406–9.
10. Lanning and Couling, p.302.
11. Lanning and Couling, p.306.
12. Lanning and Couling, pp.311–12.
13. Fairbank (ed.), vol. 10, p.359.
14. Couling, p.328.
15. Couling, p.328.

6: THE TAIPING REBELLION

1. Couling, p.382.
2. Jonathan Spence, *God's Chinese Son: The Taiping Heavenly Kingdom of Hong Xiuquan* (London, Harper Collins, 1996), p.93.
3. Bruner *et al.*, pp.133–4.

4. Couling, p.53; and Colin Mackerras and Robert Chan, *Modern China: A Chronology from 1842 to the Present* (London, Thames & Hudson, 1982), pp.52–80.

5. Spence, *God's Chinese Son,* p.203.

6. Blakiston, 1862, quoted in Spence, p.276.

7. Spence, *God's Chinese Son,* p.289.

8. John Gavin, Letterbook, British Library.

9. Couling, p.593.

10. Spence, *God's Chinese Son,* p.311.

11. John Gavin, Letterbook, British Library.

12. John Pollock, *Gordon: The Man Behind the Legend* (London, Constable, 1993), p.58.

13. Quoted in Pollock, pp.55–8.

14. Pollock, p.59.

15. Pollock, p.66.

16. John Gavin, Letterbook, British Library.

17. Pollock, p.82. Halliday Macartney's son George was to become a very successful consul in Kashgar from 1890 to 1918: see C.P. and P.M. Skrine, *Macartney at Kashgar: New Light on British, Chinese and Russian Activities in Sinkiang, 1890–1918* (London, Methuen, 1973) and Lady Macartney, *An English Lady in Chinese Turkestan* (London, Benn, 1931; reprinted Hong Kong, Oxford University Press, 1985).

18. Demetrious C. Boulger, *The Life of Sir Halliday Macartney KCMB, Commander of Li Hungchang's Trained Force in the Taeping Rebellion, Founder of the First Chinese Arsenal, for Thirty years Councillor and Secretary to the Chinese Legation in London* (London, Bodley Head, n.d. but c. 1910), p.106.

19. Pollock, p.83.

20. Pollock, p.67.

7: THE SECOND OPIUM WAR

1. Pelcovits, pp.14–15.

2. Spence, *The Search for Modern China,* p.179.

3. Couling, p.316.

4. Chronology from Mackerras and Chan.

5. Hurd, p.34.

6. Hurd, p.35.

7. Susanna Hoe, *The Private Life of Old Hong Kong* (Hong Kong, Oxford University Press, 1991), p.55.

8. Theodore Walrond (ed.), *The Letters and Journals of James, Eighth Earl of Elgin* (London, John Murray, 1873), pp.184 and 188.

9. Walrond, p.206.
10. Walrond, pp.226–30.
11. Hurd, p.134.
12. Walrond, pp.253–4.
13. Walrond, p.317.
14. Walrond, p.333.
15. Walrond, p.361.
16. Walrond, pp.376–7.
17. Couling, p.536.

8: MORE TREATY PORTS

1. Isabella Bird, *The Yangtze Valley and Beyond* (London, John Murray, 1899: reprinted London, Virago, 1985), p.59.
2. Imperial Japanese Government Railways, *Guide to China* (Tokyo, 1915: reprinted Tokyo, 1923), p.114.
3. Bird, p.59.
4. Imperial Japanese Government Railways, pp.122 and 125.
5. P.D. Coates, pp.263 and 268.
6. Bird, p.57.
7. P.D. Coates, pp.259–63.
8. Bird, pp.54–5.
9. P.D. Coates, p.255.
10. P.D. Coates, pp.256–7.
11. P.D. Coates, pp.257–8.
12. Imperial Japanese Railways, p.346.
13. P.D. Coates, pp.228–9.
14. P.D. Coates, pp.233–4.
15. Couling, p.537.
16. P.D. Coates, pp.319–20.
17. P.D. Coates, p.323.
18. P.D. Coates, pp.236–8.
19. Wright, p.767.
20. P.D. Coates, pp.289–90.
21. P.D. Coates, pp.292–30.
22. P.D. Coates, p.295.
23. P.D. Coates, p.298.
24. Wright, p.724.
25. P.D. Coates, p.187.
26. Bird, p.91.

27. Bird, p.92.
28. Couling, p.597.
29. P.D. Coates, pp.305–7.
30. Bird, pp.127–8.
31. W.E. Smith, *A Canadian Doctor in West China: Forty Years under Three Flags* (Toronto, The Ryerson Press, 1939), pp.73–5.
32. 'Charon', *Excelsior: being an inadequate description of the Upper Yangtze* (Shanghai, North China Daily News and Herald, 1934), pp.49–50.
33. Mackerras and Chan, p.186.
34. Shiona Airlie, *Thistle and Bamboo: The Life and Times of Sir James Stewart Lockhart* (Hong Kong, Oxford University Press, 1989), p.111.
35. Wright, p.733.
36. Wright, p.774.

9: PRIVATE LIFE AND THE SOCIAL ROUND

1. John Gavin, Letterbook, British Library: two accounts of the trip are given, to his mother, on 2 June 1863, and to Mr Miller, on 14 August 1863. I have combined them.
2. Charles Drage, *Servants of the Dragon Throne: Being the Lives of Edward and Cecil Bowra* (London, Peter Dawnay, 1966), p.59. Oddly enough, Garibaldi himself also went to China sometime between 1850 and 1853, during his second period of exile from Italy. There, he was interviewed by Samuel William Bonney, an American missionary who 'interested himself especially in the welfare of seamen' (see Wylie, p.150). Garibaldi held a master's certificate as a merchant captain and often resorted to seafaring at times of difficulty. In 1842 he was in command of the (very small) Uruguayan navy.
3. Gilbert Gadoffre, *Cahiers Paul Claudel 8: Claudel et l'Univers Chinois* (Paris, Gallimard, 1968), p.127, my translation.
4. Drage, pp.67–8.
5. Drage, pp.70–1 and 78.
6. Oliver G. Ready, *Life and Sport in China* (London, Chapman & Hall, 1903).
7. J. Wong Quincy, *Chinese Hunter* (London, Robert Hale, 1939), p.57.
8. Bruner *et al.*, pp.68–9 and 73.
9. J.O.P. Bland, *Houseboat Days in China* (London, Edward Arnold, 1909), p.41.
10. Lunt, pp.100–1.
11. Paul King, *In the Chinese Customs Service: a personal record of forty-seven years* (London, Heath Cranton, 1924), p.82.
12. King, p.187.
13. Ready, pp.90–1.

14. Ready, pp.126–9.
15. Dyce, pp.201–2 and 205.
16. Bruner *et al.*, p.231.
17. Ready, pp.19–20.
18. King, pp.178–80.
19. Couling, p.75.
20. Ready, p.26.
21. Ready, p.32.
22. Ready, pp.40–1.
23. Bruner *et al.*, pp.68 and 73.
24. Ready, pp.43–5.
25. W.T.A. Barber, *David Hill: Missionary and Saint* (London, Charles H. Kelly, 1899), p.43.
26. Elisabeth Croll, *Wise Daughters from Foreign Lands* (London, Pandora, 1989), p.48.
27. Bruner *et al.*, p.109.
28. Marshall Broomhall, *Martyred Missionaries of the China Inland Mission with a Record of the Perils and Sufferings of Some who Escaped* (London, China Inland Mission, 1901).
29. Wylie, pp.152 *et seq.*
30. Lucy Soothill, *A Passport to China: being the Tale of Her Long and Friendly Sojourning amongst a Strangely Interesting People* (London, Hodder & Stoughton, 1931), pp.34–5; and Barber, p.56.
31. P.D. Coates, p.307.
32. D.M. Berry, *The Sister Martyrs of Ku Cheng: Memoir and Letters of Eleanor and Elizabeth Saunders ('Nellie' and 'Topsy') of Melbourne* (London and Melbourne, James Nisbet & Co., n.d. but *c.* 1898), p.97.
33. Soothill, p.102.
34. P.D. Coates, p.294.
35. P.D. Coates, p.211.
36. P.D. Coates, p.294.
37. William Ferdinand Tyler, *Pulling Strings in China* (London, Constable, 1929), pp.34–5.
38. King, p.34.

10: CONFLICTING LOYALTIES: THE IMPERIAL MARITIME CUSTOMS SERVICE

1. Couling, p.294.
2. Bruner *et al.*, p.84.
3. Jack G. Gerson, *Horatio Nelson Lay and Sino-British Relations, 1854–1864*

(Cambridge, Mass., Harvard University Press, 1972), Harvard East Asian Monographs 47, pp.60 and 67.

4. Couling, p.294.
5. J.K. Fairbank, M.H. Coolidge and R.J. Smith, *H.B. Morse: Customs Commissioner and Historian of China* (Lexington, University Press of Kentucky, 1995), p.28.
6. Gerson, p.79.
7. Bruner *et al.*, pp.317–18.
8. John Gavin, Letterbook (27 February 1863), British Library.
9. Couling, pp.327–33.
10. Jacqueline Scipion, *La Famille Li* (Virton, privately published, 1996), pp.24 and 52–7.
11. J.K. Fairbank, *Chinabound: A Fifty-year Memoir* (New York, Harper & Row, 1982), p.102.
12. King, p.17.
13. King, pp.181–2 and 113–14.
14. Fairbank *et al.*, *H.B. Morse*, pp.150–2.
15. Drage, pp.144–6 and 191–2.
16. Fairbank *et al.*, *H.B. Morse*, p.80.
17. Fairbank *et al.*, *H.B. Morse*, pp.38 and 46–7.
18. King, pp.80–5. Ice boats and *pai-tzu* were ice sledges propelled in different ways and used in winter on the many frozen rivers and canals of the Tientsin delta.
19. Fairbank *et al.*, *H.B. Morse*, pp.100, 143–4, 116–17, 134, 160, 173, 195 and 138–9.
20. Tyler, pp.141 and 143–4.

II: A MISSION TO CONVERT

1. Whyte, p.108.
2. Whyte, p.110.
3. Whyte, p.110.
4. Berry, p.40.
5. P.D. Coates, p.194. According to a Chinese anti-Christian tract, Chinese eyes were needed to extract silver (to make mirrors) from Chinese lead. European eyes did not work. See *A Death Blow to Corrupt Doctrines* (Shanghai, 1870), p.15.
6. FO 228/500, 1871.
7. Berry, pp.301–2.
8. Chester Ronning, *A Memoir of China in Revolution: From the Boxer*

Rebellion to the People's Republic (New York, Pantheon Books, 1974), p.7.

9. The list of attacks on foreigners culminating in the Boxer rebellion was compiled from Mackerras and Chan.

10. Paul A. Cohen, *History in Three Keys: The Boxers, as Event, Experience and Myth* (New York, Columbia University Press, 1997), p.16.

11. Cohen, p.100.

12. Kong Demao and Ke Lan, *The House of Confucius* (London, Hodder & Stoughton, 1988), p.122.

13. E.H. Edwards, *Fire and Sword in Shansi: The Story of the Martyrdom of Foreign and Chinese Christians* (Edinburgh, Oliphant, Anderson & Ferrier, 1903); and Archibald E. Glover, *A Thousand Miles of Miracles in China* (London, Hodder & Stoughton, 1904).

14. Cohen, pp.50–1.

15. Cohen, p.346 note 46.

16. Cohen, p.195.

17. Cohen, pp.134–5.

18. Cohen, pp.179, 183 and 208.

19. Robert Hart, 'The Peking Legations' in *These from the Land of Sinim* (London, Chapman & Hall, 1901), pp.1 and 11.

20. Mary Hooker, *Behind the Scenes in Peking* (London, John Murray, 1910; reprinted Hong Kong, Oxford University Press, 1987), pp.81, 108–9, 124–5 and 160–1.

21. Couling, p.63.

12: FROM BOXERS TO WARLORDS

1. For attempts at modernization, see Jonathan Spence, *The Gate of Heavenly Peace* (London, Faber, 1982).

2. P.D. Coates, p.392.

3. P.D. Coates, pp.419–21.

4. See Peter Hopkirk, *Foreign Devils on the Silk Road* (London, John Murray, 1980).

5. See Wright, pp.454–82 and 724–54.

6. Eric Teichman, *Affairs of China: A Survey of the Recent History, and Present Circumstances of the Republic of China* (London, Methuen, 1938), p.293.

7. S.J. Perelman, *Crazy Like a Fox* (New York, Random House, c. 1944), pp.109–11.

8. Drage, p.255.

9. Danby, p.97.

10. John S. Service (ed.), *Golden Inches: The China Memoir of Grace Service* (Berkeley, University of California Press, 1989), pp.125–6.
11. Scipion, p.124.
12. H.G.W. Woodhead, *A Journalist in China* (London, Hurst & Blackett, 1934), p.76.
13. Shanghai, 27 March 1916.
14. Shanghai, 27 February 1917.
15. Woodhead, p.59.
16. Woodhead, p.69.
17. Scipion, p.129.
18. Mackerras and Chan, p.252.
19. Fairbank *et al.*, *H.B. Morse*, pp.183–4.
20. Woodhead, pp.132–44.
21. Meyrick Hewlett, *Forty Years in China* (London, Macmillan, 1943), p.155.
22. Hewlett, pp.167–9.
23. P.D. Coates, pp.459–61.
24. P.D. Coates, p.462.
25. Hallett Abend, *My Years in China, 1926–1941* (London, John Lane The Bodley Head, 1944), p.13.
26. Abend, pp.11, 17 and 26.
27. Arthur Ransome, *The Chinese Puzzle* (London, George Allen & Unwin, 1927), p.45.
28. Ransome, pp.51–5.
29. Hewlett, pp.59–71.
30. Alice Tisdale Hobart, *Within the Walls of Nanking* (London, Jonathan Cape, 1928), pp.200–1.
31. P.D. Coates, p.474.
32. Hobart, p.225.
33. Betty Peh-t'i Wei, *Shanghai: Crucible of Modern China* (Hong Kong, Oxford University Press, 1990), pp.231–2.
34. Teichman, pp.146–7.
35. Woodhead, p.65.
36. Atkins, p.107.
37. Ransome, p.17.
38. Ransome, pp.28–30.
39. Woodhead, pp.23–35.
40. Woodhead, pp.181–5.
41. Atkins, p.7.
42. Atkins, pp.33 and 94–5. Atkins assumes that 'the great Englishman' was a

reference to the great Ulsterman, Sir Robert Hart, but perhaps the thunderer was thinking of Hart's gung-ho predecessor Horatio Nelson Lay.
43. Atkins, pp.52, 84, 93 and 108.

13: FOUR HUNDRED MILLION CUSTOMERS

1. Owen Lattimore, *China Memories* (Tokyo, University of Tokyo Press, 1990), p.11.
2. Wright, p.726.
3. Brian Power, *The Ford of Heaven* (London, Peter Owen, 1984), p.21.
4. Thorsten Warner, *Deutsche Architektur in China: Architekturtransfer* (Berlin, Ernst & Sohn, 1994), p.90 *et seq.*
5. Hawks Pott, pp.306–7.
6. Carl Crow, *Foreign Devils in the Flowery Kingdom* (London, 1943), p.63.
7. Edward Ward, *Number One Boy* (London, Michael Joseph, 1969), p.42.
8. Lattimore, pp.14–15.
9. Crow, pp.30–1.
10. Elsie McCormick, *Audacious Angles on China* (New York and London, Appleton, 1928), pp.15–18.
11. Ward, pp.59–61.
12. Wright, p.666.
13. Couling, p.470.
14. Wright, p.666.
15. Wright, p.673.
16. Richard P. Dobson, *China Cycle* (London, Macmillan, 1946), p.18.
17. Christopher Cook, *The Lion and the Dragon: British Voices from the China Coast* (London, Elm Tree Books, 1985), pp.39–40.
18. Cook, p.41.
19. Dobson, p.33.
20. Cook, p.42.
21. Dobson, pp.76–80.
22. Cook, p.43.
23. FO 228/1885, 1914.
24. Sigurd Eliasson, *Dragon Wang's River* (London, Methuen, 1957).
25. 'Tinko' Pawley, *My Bandit Hosts* (London, Stanley Paul, *c.* 1934), p.20.
26. Joy Grant, *Stella Benson: A Biography* (London, Macmillan, 1987).
27. Dobson, p.23.
28. Cook, p.47.
29. Cook, p.44.
30. Lunt, p.42.

31. Lunt, pp.43–4.
32. Bernard Llewellyn, *I Left My Roots in China* (London, Allen & Unwin, 1953), pp.133–4.
33. Cook, p.37.
34. Lunt, p.44.
35. Lunt, p.141.
36. Cook, p.44.
37. Grant, p.228.
38. Llewellyn, pp.58–63.
39. Patrick Brodie, *Crescent over Cathay: China and ICI, 1898 to 1956* (Hong Kong, Oxford University Press, 1990), p.8.
40. Tess Johnston and Deke Erh, *Near to Heaven: Western Architecture in China's Old Summer Resorts* (Hong Kong, Old China Hand Press, 1994), pp.55–6.
41. Power, *Ford of Heaven*, pp.53–4.
42. Hewlett, p.214.
43. E.T.C. Werner, *Autumn Leaves: An Autobiography with a Sheaf of Papers, Sociological, Sinological, Philosophical and Metaphysical* (Shanghai, Hong Kong and Singapore, Kelly & Walsh, 1928), pp.583–9.
44. R.F. Johnston, *Lion and Dragon in Northern China* (London, John Murray, 1910), p.105.
45. Hewlett, p.42.
46. Airlie, pp.113 and 140.
47. Hewlett, pp.50–5.

14: MAINTAINING STANDARDS

1. The Stead sisters, *Stone–Paper–Scissors: Shanghai, 1921–1945: An Autobiography* (Deddington, Oxon Publishing, 1991), pp.23–4.
2. Ward, p.43.
3. Franck, p.4.
4. Stead sisters, p.4.
5. Power, *Ford of Heaven*, p.46.
6. Cook, pp.53–4.
7. Werner, p.571.
8. Cook, p.55.
9. James Burke, *My Father in China* (London, Michael Joseph, 1945), p.172.
10. 'The unexpurgated diary of a Shanghai baby', in McCormick, *Audacious Angles on China*, pp.209–302.
11. Service, p.229.
12. Power, *Ford of Heaven*, pp.61 and 24.

13. Theodore Harris, *Pearl S. Buck: A Biography* (London, Methuen, 1970), pp.31 and 39–40.
14. John Espey, *Minor Heresies, Major Departures: A China Mission Boyhood* (Berkeley, University of California Press, 1994), pp.35–7.
15. Espey, pp.11 and 17–18.
16. John Watney, *Mervyn Peake* (London, Michael Joseph, 1976), pp. 26–7.
17. Power, *Ford of Heaven*, pp.62 and 67.
18. Power, *Ford of Heaven*, p.159.
19. Cook, p.62.
20. Wright, p.676.
21. Gren Wedderburn, *No Lotus Garden* (Hong Kong, Gulliver Books, 1979), pp.2–3.
22. Wedderburn, p.3.
23. Espey, pp.146–239.
24. Power, *Ford of Heaven*, p.162.
25. Espey, pp.187–91.
26. Harris, pp.74–5 and 86.
27. Service, pp.26–8.
28. Stead sisters, p.24.
29. Service, p.270.
30. Grant, p.264.
31. Power, *Ford of Heaven*, pp. 23 and 34.
32. Werner, p.556.
33. Stead sisters, p.30.
34. Werner, pp.550–1.
35. Cook, p.30.
36. Stead sisters, p.40.
37. Grant, pp.197–212.
38. Grant, p.212.
39. Austin Coates, p.206.
40. Ward, pp.45–6.
41. Austin Coates, pp.227–8.
42. Robert Bickers, 'Changing British Attitudes to China and the Chinese, 1928–1931', unpublished PhD thesis, University of London, 1992, p.113.
43. Cook, pp.66–7.
44. Quoted in Robert Bickers, 'Changing British Attitudes', p.144.
45. Harris, pp.60–1.
46. Werner, p.692.
47. Werner, pp.659–78, where he goes into considerable detail about the affair.
48. Werner, pp.580–1.

49. Johnston and Erh, pp.56–97.
50. Johnston and Erh, pp.12–13.
51. Ann Bridge, *Four-part Setting* (London, World Books, 1941), pp.17 and 33.
52. Bridge, p.6.
53. Bridge, p.55.

15: TOURISTS AND AESTHETES

1. See E.H.M. Cox, *Plant-hunting in China* (London, Collins 1945; reprinted Hong Kong, Oxford University Press, 1986), and for many travellers' accounts see A.C. Grayling and Susan Whitfield, *A Literary Companion to China* (London, John Murray, 1994).
2. Reginald Farrer, *Rainbow Bridge* (London, Edward Arnold, 1921; reprinted 1986), pp.397, 380 and 373.
3. Peter Fleming, *News from Tartary* (London, Jonathan Cape, 1936), in *Travels in Tartary and News from Tartary* (London, The Reprint Society, 1941), p.539.
4. Fleming, *News from Tartary*, pp.539–41.
5. Peter Fleming, *One's Company* (London, Jonathan Cape, 1934; reprinted London, The Reprint Society, 1941), pp.222–3.
6. Fleming, *One's Company*, p.31.
7. Fleming, *One's Company*, p.52.
8. Fleming, *One's Company*, pp.170–4.
9. W.H. Auden and Christopher Isherwood, *Journey to a War* (London, Faber, 1939; reprinted London, Faber, 1973), pp.197, 206 and 212–13.
10. Auden and Isherwood, pp.236–43.
11. Auden and Isherwood, p.229.
12. Auden and Isherwood, pp.227–8.
13. Auden and Isherwood, p.233.
14. Joseph von Sternberg, *Fun in a Chinese Laundry* (New York, Macmillan, 1955).
15. Quoted in Phillip Hoare, *Noël Coward: A Biography* (London, Mandarin, 1996), p.214.
16. Hoare, p.215.
17. From Noël Coward's *Present Indicative*, quoted in Lynn Pan, *In Search of Old Shanghai* (Hong Kong, Joint Publishing Company, 1982), p.42.
18. Wei, pp.140–1.
19. Auden and Isherwood, pp.147–8.
20. Charles Higham, *Wallis: Secret Lives of the Duchess of Windsor* (London, Pan Books, 1989), p.65.
21. Higham, pp.66 and 69.

22. Higham, p.69.
23. Janet Morgan, *Edwina Mountbatten: A Life of Her Own* (London, Fontana, 1992), p.248.
24. John Hatcher, *Laurence Binyon: Poet, Scholar of East and West* (Oxford, Oxford University Press, 1995), p.245.
25. Lucy Butler (ed.), *Robert Byron: Letters Home* (London, John Murray, 1991), p.258.
26. Harold Acton, *Memoirs of an Aesthete* (London, Hamish Hamilton, 1984), p.362.
27. Acton, pp.362–3.
28. Osbert Sitwell, *Escape with Me!: An Oriental Sketchbook* (London, Macmillan, 1949), pp. 171, 230.
29. Acton, pp.353–4.
30. Butler, p.257.
31. Robert Byron, *The Road to Oxiana* (London, Macmillan, 1937).
32. Butler, pp.257 and 262.
33. Butler, p.267.
34. Butler, p.267.
35. Peter Stansky and William Abrahams, *Journey to the Frontier: Two Roads to the Spanish Civil War* (London, Constable, 1994), pp.249–50.
36. Stansky and Abrahams, p.290.
37. Julian Bell, *Essays, Poems and Letters*, ed. Quentin Bell (London, Hogarth Press, 1938), p.42.
38. Bell, pp.50 and 52.
39. Bell, p.80.
40. Acton, p.377.
41. Ann Bridge, *Peking Picnic* (London, Chatto & Windus, 1937; reprinted Harmondsworth, Penguin, 1938), pp.21–2.
42. Bridge, *Peking Picnic*, pp.105–6.
43. Bridge, *Peking Picnic*, pp.110–11.
44. Ann Bridge, *Four-part Setting* (London, Chatto & Windus, 1939) and *The Ginger Griffin* (Boston, Little Brown, 1934; reprinted Harmondsworth, Penguin Books, 1951).
45. W. Somerset Maugham, *On a Chinese Screen* (London, Heinemann, 1922; reprinted London, Mandarin, 1997), p.64.
46. Bernard Wasserstein, *The Secret Lives of Trebitsch Lincoln* (Harmondsworth, Penguin, 1989), pp.98 *et seq.*
47. Wasserstein, p.232.
48. Wasserstein, p.242.
49. Wasserstein, p.267.

50. Wasserstein, p.300.
51. Wasserstein, pp.302–3.
52. Hugh Trevor-Roper, *Hermit of Peking: The Hidden Life of Sir Edmund Backhouse* (London, Macmillan, 1976; reprinted London, Eland, 1993), pp.216–19 and 162–87.
53. Trevor-Roper, p.144.
54. Trevor-Roper, p.282.
55. Trevor-Roper, pp.294–311. One typescript of the memoirs was placed in the British Library. I once planned to display it as part of an exhibition of curiosities in the Chinese collections. There was not, however, a single page that could have been decently shown in public so we used the box in which the memoirs had been placed and a photograph of Backhouse instead.
56. Maxine Berg, *A Woman in History: Eileen Power, 1889–1940* (Cambridge, Cambridge University Press, 1996), pp.100–1.
57. Berg, p.100.
58. Ray Monk, *Bertrand Russell: The Spirit of Solitude* (London, Vintage, 1997), p.584.
59. Monk, p.593.
60. Michael Holroyd, *Bernard Shaw: The One-Volume Definitive Edition* (London, Chatto & Windus, 1997), pp.648 and 653.
61. Holroyd, pp.654–6.

16: THE CHINESE AND THE TREATY PORTS

1. Hao Yen-p'ing, *The Comprador in Nineteenth-century China: Bridge between East and West* (Cambridge, Mass., Harvard University Press, 1970), p.1.
2. Hao, p.40.
3. Hao, p.68.
4. Hao, p.23.
5. Hao, p.113.
6. Hao, p.147.
7. Hao, p.184.
8. Hao, pp.91 and 93, quoting the *North China Herald*, 22 September 1882.
9. Lynn Pan, *Tracing It Home: Journeys Around a Chinese Family* (London, Secker & Warburg, 1992), p.68. Lynn Pan's earliest book, *In Search of Old Shanghai*, was published under the name Pan Ling.
10. Fairbank, *Chinabound*, p.64.
11. See L.C. Goodrich, *The Literary Inquisition of Ch'ien-lung* (Baltimore, Waverley Press, 1935; New York, Paragon Reprints, 1996) for a spine-chilling introduction to the difficulties of the literati in traditional China.

12. Couling, p.429.
13. Gamewell, p.128.
14. Wright, pp.516–36.
15. Power, *Ford of Heaven*, p.149.
16. Lynn Pan, *Tracing It Home*, pp.145, 35 and 41–5.
17. Lynn Pan, *Tracing It Home*, p.50.
18. Adeline Yen Mah, *Falling Leaves: The True Story of an Unwanted Chinese Daughter* (London, Michael Joseph, 1997), pp.9 and 16.
19. Mah, p.27.
20. Mah, p.39.
21. Jia You, 'General Aspects of Street Lanes in Shanghai', in *Anecdotes of Old Shanghai* (Shanghai, Shanghai Cultural Publishing House, 1985), pp.128–49.
22. Mah, p.48.
23. Thomas L. Kennedy (ed.), *Testimony of a Confucian Woman: The Autobiography of Mrs Nie Zeng Jifen, 1852–1942* (Athens, Georgia, and London, University of Georgia Press, 1993), p.61. For Fryer, see Adrian Arthur Bennett, *John Fryer: The Introduction of Western Science and Technology into Nineteenth-century China* (Cambridge, Mass., Harvard University Press, 1967).
24. Kennedy, pp.64, 95 and 97–102.
25. Chiang Yee, *A Chinese Childhood* (London, Methuen, 1940), p.6.
26. Chiang Yee, p.109.
27. Tsai Chin, *Daughter of Shanghai* (London, Chatto & Windus, 1988), pp.9–10.
28. Tsai Chin, p.21.
29. Tsai Chin, p.52.
30. Tsai Chin, pp.38 and 35.
31. Tsai Chin, p.36.
32. Mah, p.45.
33. Tsai Chin, p.53.
34. Tsai Chin, p.34.
35. Pan Ling, *In Search of Old Shanghai*, p.35.
36. Pan Ling, *In Search of Old Shanghai*, pp.37–8.
37. Robert Bickers and Jeffrey Wasserstrom, 'Shanghai's "Dogs and Chinese Not Admitted" Sign', in *China Quarterly*, 142, 1995, pp.444–66.
38. Spence, *The Gate of Heavenly Peace*, pp.221–3.
39. Pan Ling, *In Search of Old Shanghai*, p.88.
40. Pan Ling, *In Search of Old Shanghai*, pp. 94–9.
41. Quoted in Spence, *The Gate of Heavenly Peace*, p.215.

42. Ch'ien Chung-shu, *Fortress Besieged*, trans. Jeanne Kelly and Nathan Mao (Bloomington, Indiana University Press, 1979).
43. Mao Tun, *Minuit* (Paris, Robert Laffont, 1972), p.10; my translation of Mao Tun's introduction.
44. See Poshek Fu, *Passivity, Resistance and Collaboration: Intellectual Choices in Occupied Shanghai, 1937–1945* (Stanford, Stanford University Press, 1993), Chapters 2 and 3.
45. Annabel Walker, *Aurel Stein, Pioneer of the Silk Road* (London, John Murray, 1995), pp.263–87; and N. Shareen Blair Bryson, 'Last of the Foreign Devils', *Archaeology*, New York, vol. 50, no. 6, 1997, pp.53–9.

17: THE RISING SUN

1. Brian Power, *The Puppet Emperor: The Life of Pu Yi, Last Emperor of China* (London, Peter Owen, 1986), p.88.
2. Reginald F. Johnston, *Twilight in the Forbidden City* (London, Gollancz, 1934; reprinted Hong Kong, Oxford University Press, 1987), p.433.
3. Abend, p.77.
4. Abend, pp.80–2.
5. Abend, pp.155–6.
6. Harris, pp.64–5.
7. Power, *Puppet Emperor*, p.173.
8. Woodhead, p.247.
9. Abend, p.187.
10. Woodhead, p.248.
11. Abend, p.233.
12. George Kates, *The Years that Were Fat: Peking, 1933–1940* (New York, Harper, 1952; reprinted Hong Kong, Oxford University Press, 1988), p.258.
13. Sir Frances Rose, *Saying Life: The Memoirs of Sir Francis Rose* (London, Cassell, 1961), p. 298.
14. Stead sisters, pp.95–101.
15. Abend, pp.259–60.
16. Stead sisters, p.106.
17. Spence, *The Search for Modern China*, p.448.
18. Rhodes Farmer, *Shanghai Harvest: A Diary of Three Years in the China War* (London, Museum Press, 1945), pp.100–1.
19. Dobson, p.69.
20. Dobson, pp.26–7.
21. Dobson, p.106.

22. Dobson, p.135.
23. Farmer, p.206.
24. Robert Payne, *Chungking Diary* (London, Heinemann, 1945), p.99.
25. Payne, p.17.
26. Payne, pp.32–3.
27. Ernest G. Heppner, *Shanghai Refugee: A Memoir of the World War II Jewish Ghetto* (Lincoln, University of Nebraska Press, 1993), pp.51 and 107.
28. D. Franzler, *Japanese, Nazis and Jews* (New York, Yeshiva University, 1976), p.107.
29. Heppner, p.40.
30. Heppner, p.74.
31. Manuscript, British Library Oriental and India Office Collections.
32. Nicholas R. Clifford, *Retreat from China: British Policy in the Far East, 1937–1941* (New York, Da Capo Press, 1976), p.125.

18: INTERNMENT

1. Graham Peck, *Two Kinds of Time* (Boston, Houghton Mifflin), 1950, p.4.
2. Peck, pp.11–12.
3. Katy Talati's experiences in Peking and Weihsien are recounted in an unpublished manuscript. I am very grateful to her for showing it to me and allowing me to use the material.
4. David Michell, *A Boy's War* (Singapore, Overseas Missionary Fellowship, 1988), p.23.
5. Michell, p.71.
6. P.D. Coates, p.441.
7. Fay Angus, *The White Pagoda* (Wheaton, Illinois, Tyndale House, 1978), p.101.
8. Angus, pp.103 and 107.
9. Angus, p.109.
10. Angus, p.116.
11. Angus, p.117.
12. Angus, p.118.
13. Angus, pp.126–7.
14. Stead sisters, p.154.
15. Angus, p.134.
16. Angus, p.133.
17. Phyllis Thompson, *D.E. Hoste, 'A Prince with God'. Hudson Taylor's Successor as General Director of the China Inland Mission 1900–1935* (London, China Inland Mission, 1947), pp.35–6.

18. Thompson, pp.147–51.
19. First published in 1985.
20. J.G. Ballard, *Empire of the Sun* (London, Gollancz, 1984), p.169.
21. Peggy Abkhazi, *Enemy Subject: Life in a Japanese Internment Camp, 1943–5* (Stroud, Allan Sutton, 1995), p.93.
22. Preface to Abkhazi, p.7.
23. Abkhazi, pp.60–1.
24. Abkhazi, p.68.
25. Abkhazi, p.109.
26. Abkhazi, p.97.
27. Abkhazi, pp.95, 83, 58 and 63.
28. Abkhazi, pp.95, 57, 85 and 69.
29. Stead sisters, pp.145–59.
30. J.G. Ballard, 'The End of My War', *Sunday Times* (News Review section), 20 August 1992, p.2.

19: THE LEGACY OF THE TREATY PORTS

1. Couling, p.392.
2. Aron Shai, *The Fate of British and French Firms in China, 1949–1954: Imperialism Imprisoned* (Basingstoke and London, Macmillan, 1996), pp. 24–7.
3. Nadine Perront (trans.), *Shanghai: opium, jeu, prostitution* (Arles, Philippe Picquier, 1992), p. 21.
4. Perront, p. 45.
5. Perront, pp. 79, 152, 171.
6. Wu Han (1909–69) was one of the greatest historians of modern China whose work on the Ming dynasty is outstanding. He was a patriot and a liberal but became a member of the Communist Party. His work was viciously attacked during the Cultural Revolution, and he died, deprived of medical care, after suffering a series of beatings. See History Department of Peking University, *Wu Han jinian wenji* (Peking, Beijing chubanshe, 1984).
7. Jean Watson, *Bosshardt: A Biography. The Story of a Christian Missionary Caught up in Mao's Long March* (Crowborough, Overseas Missionary Fellowship, 1995), p.240.

Bibliography

Abend, Hallett, *My Years in China, 1926–1941* (London, John Lane The Bodley Head, 1944).

Abkhazi, Peggy, *Enemy Subject: Life in a Japanese Internment Camp 1943–5* (Stroud, Allan Sutton, 1995).

Acton, Harold, *Memoirs of an Aesthete* (London, Hamish Hamilton, 1984).

Airlie, Shiona, *Thistle and Bamboo: The Life and Times of Sir James Stewart Lockhart* (Hong Kong, Oxford University Press, 1989).

Anecdotes of Old Shanghai (Shanghai, Shanghai Cultural Publishing House, 1985).

Angus, Fay, *The White Pagoda* (Wheaton, Illinois, Tyndale House, 1978).

Atkins, Martyn, *Informal Empire in Crisis: British Diplomacy and the Chinese Customs Succession, 1927–1929* (New York, Cornell University, 1995), Cornell East Asian Series, 74.

Auden, W.H., and Isherwood, Christopher, *Journey to a War* (London, Faber, 1939; reprinted London, Faber, 1973).

Ballard, J.G., 'The End of My War', *Sunday Times* (News Review Section), 20 August 1992.

Barber, W.T.A., *David Hill: Missionary and Saint* (London, Charles H. Kelly, 1899).

Bell, Julian, *Essays, Poems and Letters*, ed. Quentin Bell (London, Hogarth Press, 1938).

Bennett, Adrian Arthur, *John Fryer: The Introduction of Western Science and Technology into Nineteenth-century China* (Cambridge, Mass., Harvard University Press, 1967).

Berg, Maxine, *A Woman in History: Eileen Power 1889–1940* (Cambridge, Cambridge University Press, 1996).

Berry, D.M., *The Sister Martyrs of Ku Cheng: Memoir and Letters of Eleanor and Elizabeth Saunders ('Nellie' and 'Topsy') of Melbourne* (London and Melbourne, James Nisbet & Co., n.d. but *c.* 1898).

Bickers, Robert, 'Changing British Attitudes to China and the Chinese, 1928–1931', unpublished PhD thesis, University of London School of Oriental and African Studies, 1992.

Bickers, Robert, and Wasserstrom, Jeffrey, 'Shanghai's "Dogs and Chinese Not Admitted" Sign', in *China Quarterly*, 142, 1995, pp. 444–66.

Bird, Isabella, *The Yangtze Valley and Beyond* (London, John Murray, 1899: reprinted London, Virago, 1985).

Bland, J.O.P., *Houseboat Days in China* (London, Edward Arnold, 1909).

Boulger, Demetrious C., *The Life of Sir Halliday Macartney KCMB, Commander of Li Hungchang's Trained Force in the Taeping Rebellion, Founder of the First Chinese Arsenal, for Thirty years Councillor and Secretary to the Chinese Legation in London* (London, Bodley Head, n.d. but *c.* 1910).

Bridge, Ann, *The Ginger Griffin* (Boston, Little Brown, 1934; reprinted Harmondsworth, Penguin, 1951).

——*Peking Picnic* (London, Chatto & Windus, 1937; reprinted Harmondsworth, Penguin, 1938).

——*Four-part Setting* (London, World Books, 1941).

Brodie, Patrick, *Crescent over Cathay: China and ICI, 1898 to 1956* (Hong Kong, Oxford University Press, 1990).

Broomhall, Marshall, *Martyred Missionaries of the China Inland Mission with a Record of the Perils and Sufferings of Some who Escaped* (London, China Inland Mission, 1901).

Bruner, K., Fairbank, J.K., and Smith, R.J. (eds.), *Entering China's Service: Robert Hart's Journals 1854–1863* (Cambridge and London, Harvard University Press, 1986).

Bryson, N. Shareen Blair, 'Last of the Foreign Devils', in *Archaeology*, New York, vol. 50, no. 6, 1997, pp. 53–9.

Burke, James, *My Father in China* (London, Michael Joseph, 1945).

Butler, Lucy (ed.), *Robert Byron: Letters Home* (London, John Murray, 1991).

Byron, Robert, *The Road to Oxiana* (London, Macmillan, 1937).

Chang Hsiu-jung, Farrington, Anthony, Huang Fu-san *et al.* (eds.), *The English Factory in Taiwan, 1670–1685* (Taipei, National Taiwan University, 1995).

'Charon', *Excelsior: being an inadequate description of the Upper Yangtze* (Shanghai, North China Daily News and Herald, 1934).

Chiang Yee, *A Chinese Childhood* (London, Methuen, 1940).

Ch'ien Chung-shu, *Fortress Besieged*, trans. Jeanne Kelly and Nathan Mao (Bloomington, Indiana University Press, 1979).

Clifford, Nicholas R., *Retreat from China: British Policy in the Far East, 1937–1941* (New York, Da Capo Press, 1976).

Coates, Austin, *China Races* (Hong Kong, Oxford University Press, 1983).

Coates, P.D., *The China Consuls: British Consular Officers, 1843–1943* (Hong Kong, Oxford University Press, 1988).

Cohen, Paul A., *History in Three Keys: The Boxers as Event, Experience and Myth* (New York, Columbia University Press, 1997).

Collis, Maurice, *Wayfoong: The Hongkong and Shanghai Banking Corporation* (London, Faber & Faber, 1965).

Cook, Christopher, *The Lion and the Dragon: British Voices from the China Coast* (London, Elm Tree Books, 1985).

Couling, Samuel, *Encyclopaedia Sinica* (London, Humphrey Milford, 1917: reprinted Hong Kong, Oxford University Press, 1983).

Cox, E.H.M., *Plant-hunting in China* (London, Collins, 1945; reprinted Hong Kong, Oxford University Press, 1986).

Croll, Elisabeth, *Wise Daughters from Foreign Lands* (London, Pandora, 1989).

Crow, Carl, *Foreign Devils in the Flowery Kingdom* (London and New York, Harper, 1940).

Danby, Hope, *My Boy Chang* (London, Gollancz, 1955).

Davis, C. Noel, *History of the Shanghai Paper Hunt Club 1863–1930* (Shanghai, Kelly & Walsh, 1930).

Dekobra, Maurice, *Confucius en pull-over*, translated (very badly) and retitled *Confucius in a Tail-coat* (London, T. Werner Laurie, 1935).

Dobson, Richard P., *China Cycle* (London, Macmillan, 1946).

Drage, Charles, *Servants of the Dragon Throne: Being the Lives of Edward and Cecil Bowra* (London, Peter Dawnay, 1966).

Dyce, Charles M., *Personal Reminiscences of Thirty Years' Residence in the Model Settlement Shanghai, 1870–1900* (London, Chapman & Hall, 1906).

Edwards, E.H., *Fire and Sword in Shansi: The Story of the Martyrdom of Foreign and Chinese Christians* (Edinburgh, Oliphant, Anderson & Ferrier, 1903).

Eliasson, Sigurd, *Dragon Wang's River* (London, Methuen, 1957).

Espey, John, *Minor Heresies, Major Departures: A China Mission Boyhood* (Berkeley, University of California Press, 1994).

Fairbank, J.K., *Trade and Diplomacy on the China Coast* (Cambridge, Harvard University Press, 1953).

——(ed.), *The Cambridge History of China: vol. 10, Late Ch'ing, 1800–1911, Part I* (Cambridge, Cambridge University Press, 1978).

——*Chinabound: A Fifty-year Memoir* (New York, Harper & Row, 1982).

Fairbank, J.K., Coolidge, M.H., and Smith, R.J., *H.B. Morse: Customs Commissioner and Historian of China* (Lexington, University Press of Kentucky, 1995).

Farmer, Rhodes, *Shanghai Harvest: A Diary of Three Years in the China War* (London, Museum Press, 1945).

Farrer, Reginald, *Rainbow Bridge* (London, Edward Arnold, 1921; reprinted 1986).

Fleming, Peter, *News from Tartary* (London, Jonathan Cape, 1936), in *Travels in Tartary and News from Tartary* (London, The Reprint Society, 1941).

——*One's Company* (London, Jonathan Cape, 1934; reprinted London, The Reprint Society, 1941).

Fortune, Robert, *Three Years' Wandering in China* (London, John Murray, 1847: reprinted London, Mildmay Books, 1987).

Franck, Harry, *Roving through Southern China* (London, Appleton-Century, 1925).

Franzler, D., *Japanese, Nazis and Jews* (New York, Yeshiva University, 1976).

Fu, Poshek, *Passivity, Resistance and Collaboration: Intellectual Choices in Occupied Shanghai, 1937–1945* (Stanford, Stanford University Press, 1993).

Gadoffre, Gilbert (ed.), *Cahiers Paul Claudel 8: Claudel et l'Univers Chinois* (Paris, Gallimard, 1968).

Gamewell, Mary Ninde, *The Gateway to China: Pictures of Shanghai* (New York, Revell, 1916: reprinted Taipei, Ch'eng-wen, 1972).

Gavin, John, Letterbook, British Library.

Gerson, Jack G., *Horatio Nelson Lay and Sino-British Relations, 1854–1864* (Cambridge, Mass., Harvard University Press, 1972), Harvard East Asian Monographs 47.

Glover, Archibald E., *A Thousand Miles of Miracles in China* (London, Hodder & Stoughton, 1904).

Goodrich, L.C., *The Literary Inquisition of Ch'ien-lung* (Baltimore, Waverley Press, 1935; New York, Paragon Reprints, 1996).

Grant, Joy, *Stella Benson: A Biography* (London, Macmillan, 1987).

Graves, R.H., 'Report of the Medical Missionary Society's Dispensary ... for 1863', (n.p., n.d., in British Library, Topographical Tracts 1846–84, 10058.cc.8).

Grayling, A.C., and Whitfield, Susan, *A Literary Companion to China* (London, John Murray, 1994).

Greenberg, Michael, *British Trade and the Opening of China, 1800–1842* (Cambridge, Cambridge University Press, 1951).

Hao Yen-p'ing, *The Comprador in Nineteenth-century China: Bridge between East and West* (Cambridge, Mass., Harvard University Press, 1970).

Harris, Theodore, *Pearl S. Buck: A Biography* (London, Methuen, 1970).

Hart, Robert, 'The Peking Legations', in Robert Hart, *These from the Land of Sinim* (London, Chapman & Hall, 1901).

Hatcher, John, *Laurence Binyon: Poet, Scholar of East and West* (Oxford, Oxford University Press, 1995).

Henderson, James, *Shanghai Hygiene or Hints for the Preservation of Health in China* (Shanghai, Presbyterian Mission Press, 1863).

Heppner, Ernest G., *Shanghai Refugee: A Memoir of the World War II Jewish Ghetto* (Lincoln, University of Nebraska Press, 1993).

Hevia, James, *Cherishing Men from Afar: Qing Guest Ritual and the Macartney Embassy of 1793* (Durham and London, Duke University Press, 1995).

Hewlett, Meyrick, *Forty Years in China* (London, Macmillan, 1943).

Hickey, William, *Memoirs of William Hickey*, ed. Peter Quennell (London, Century, 1975).

Higham, Charles, *Wallis: Secret Lives of the Duchess of Windsor* (London, Pan Books, 1989).

History Department of Peking University, *Wu Han jinianji* (Peking, Beijing Chubanshe, 1984).

History of the Shanghai Recreation Fund from 1860 to 1906 (Shanghai, North China Daily News and Herald, 1907).

Hoare, Philip, *Noël Coward: A Biography* (London, Mandarin, 1996).

Hobart, Alice Tisdale, *Within the Walls of Nanking* (London, Jonathan Cape, 1928).

Hoe, Susanna, *The Private Life of Old Hong Kong* (Hong Kong, Oxford University Press, 1991).

Holroyd, Michael, *Bernard Shaw: The One-Volume Definitive Edition* (London, Chatto & Windus, 1997).

Hooker, Mary, *Behind the Scenes in Peking* (London, John Murray, 1910; reprinted Hong Kong, Oxford University Press, 1987).

Hopkirk, Peter, *Foreign Devils on the Silk Road* (London, John Murray, 1980).

Hummel, A. (ed.), *Eminent Chinese of the Ch'ing Period* (Washington DC, United States Government Printing Office, 1943).

Hurd, Douglas, *The Arrow War: An Anglo-Chinese Confusion* (London, Collins, 1967).

Imperial Japanese Government Railways, *Guide to China* (Tokyo, 1915; reprinted Tokyo, 1923).

Jia You, 'General Aspects of Street Lanes in Shanghai', in *Anecdotes of Old Shanghai* (Shanghai, Shanghai Cultural Publishing House, 1985), pp. 128–49.

Johnston, R.F., *Lion and Dragon in Northern China* (London, John Murray, 1910).

——*Twilight in the Forbidden City* (London, Gollancz, 1934; reprinted Hong Kong, Oxford University Press, 1987).

Johnston, Tess, and Erh, Deke, *Near to Heaven: Western Architecture in China's Old Summer Resorts* (Hong Kong, Old China Hand Press, 1994).

Kates, George, *The Years that Were Fat: Peking, 1933–1940* (New York, Harper, 1952; reprinted Hong Kong, Oxford University Press, 1988).

Keay, John, *The Honourable Company: A History of the English East India Company* (London, Harper Collins, 1991).

Kennedy, Thomas L. (ed.), *Testimony of a Confucian Woman: The Autobiography of Mrs Nie Zeng Jifen, 1852–1942* (Athens, Georgia and London, University of Georgia Press, 1993).

King, Paul, *In the Chinese Customs Service: a personal record of forty-seven years* (London, Heath Cranton, 1924).

Kong Demao and Ke Lan, *The House of Confucius* (London, Hodder & Stoughton, 1988).

Lanning, G., and Couling, S., *The History of Shanghai* (Shanghai, Kelly & Walsh for the Shanghai Municipal Council, 1921).

Lattimore, Owen, *China Memories* (Tokyo, University of Tokyo Press, 1990).

Llewellyn, Bernard, *I Left My Roots in China* (London, Allen & Unwin, 1953).

Lunt, Carroll, *Some Builders of Treaty Port China* (Los Angeles, privately printed, 1965).

McCormick, Elsie, *Audacious Angles on China* (New York and London, Appleton, 1928).

Mackerras, Colin, and Chan, Robert, *Modern China: A Chronology from 1842 to the Present* (London, Thames & Hudson, 1982).

MacPherson, Kerrie L., *A Wilderness of Marshes: The Origins of Public Health in Shanghai, 1843–1893* (Hong Kong, Oxford University Press, 1987).

Mah, Adeline Yen, *Falling Leaves: The True Story of an Unwanted Chinese Daughter* (London, Michael Joseph, 1997).

Mao Tun, *Minuit* (Paris, Robert Laffont, 1972).

Matignon, Jean-Jacques, *Superstition, Crime and Misery in China* (Lyons, 1899).

Maugham, W. Somerset, *On a Chinese Screen* (London, Heinemann, 1922; reprinted London, Mandarin, 1997).

Medhurst, W.H., 'Reminiscences of the opening of Shanghai to foreign trade', *Chinese and Japanese Repository*, 12 October 1864.

Michell, David, *A Boy's War* (Singapore, Overseas Missionary Fellowship, 1988).

Mitchie, Alexander, *The Englishman in China during the Victorian Era as illustrated in the career of Sir Rutherford Alcock KCB, DCL, many years Consul and Minister in China and Japan* (London, Blackwood, 1900).

Monk, Ray, *Bertrand Russell: The Spirit of Solitude* (London, Vintage, 1997).

Morgan, Janet, *Edwina Mountbatten: A Life of Her Own* (London, Fontana, 1992).

Morrison, G.E., *An Australian in China* (London, H. Cox, 1895).

Pan, Lynn/Pan Ling, *In Search of Old Shanghai* (Hong Kong, Joint Publishing Company, 1982).

——*Tracing It Home: Journeys Around a Chinese Family* (London, Secker & Warburg, 1992).

Pawley, 'Tinko', *My Bandit Hosts* (London, Stanley Paul, *c.* 1934).

Payne, Robert, *Chungking Diary* (London, Heinemann, 1945).

Peck, Graham, *Two Kinds of Time* (Boston, Houghton Mifflin, 1950).

Pelcovits, Nathan A., *Old China Hands and the Foreign Office* (New York, American Institute of Pacific Relations, 1948).

Perelman, S.J., *Crazy like a Fox* (New York, Random House, *c.* 1944).

Perront, Nadine (trans.), *Shanghai: opium, jeu, prostitution* (Arles, Philippe Picquier, 1992).

P.G.L., *A Reminiscence of Canton 1863* (London, Harrison & Sons, 1866).

Pitcher, Philip Wilson, *In and About Amoy: some historical and other facts connected with one of the first open ports of China* (Shanghai and Foochow, Methodist Publishing House in China, 1912, reprinted Taipei, 1972).

Pollock, John, *Gordon: The Man Behind the Legend* (London, Constable, 1993).

Pott, F.L. Hawks, *A Short History of Shanghai* (Shanghai, Kelly & Walsh, 1928).

Power, Brian, *The Ford of Heaven* (London, Peter Owen, 1984).

——*The Puppet Emperor: The Life of Pu Yi, Last Emperor of China* (London, Peter Owen, 1986).

Quincy, J. Wong, *Chinese Hunter* (London, Robert Hale, 1939).

Ransome, Arthur, *The Chinese Puzzle* (London, George Allen & Unwin, 1927).

Ready, Oliver G., *Life and Sport in China* (London, Chapman & Hall, 1903).

Ronning, Chester, *A Memoir of China in Revolution: From the Boxer Rebellion to the People's Republic* (New York, Pantheon Books, 1974).

Rose, Sir Francis, *Saying Life: The Memoirs of Sir Francis Rose* (London, Cassell, 1961).

Scipion, Jacqueline, *La Famille Li* (Virton, privately printed, 1996).

Service, John S. (ed.), *Golden Inches: The China Memoir of Grace Service* (Berkeley, University of California Press, 1989).

Shai, Aron, *The Fate of British and French Firms in China, 1949–1954: Imperialism Imprisoned* (Basingstoke and London, Macmillan, 1996).

Singer, Aubrey, *The Lion and the Dragon: The Story of the First British Embassy to the Court of the Emperor Qianlong at Peking, 1792–1794* (London, Barrie & Jenkins, 1992).

Sitwell, Osbert, *Escape with Me!: An Oriental Sketchbook* (London, Macmillan, 1949).

Skrine, C.P. and P.M., *Macartney at Kashgar: New Light on British, Chinese and Russian Activities in Sinkiang, 1890–1918* (London, Methuen, 1973).

Smith, R.J., Fairbank, J.K., and Bruner, K. (eds.), *Robert Hart and China's Early Modernization* (Cambridge and London, Harvard University Press, 1991).

Smith, W.E., *A Canadian Doctor in West China: Forty Years under Three Flags* (Toronto, The Ryerson Press, 1939).

Soothill, Lucy, *A Passport to China: being the Tale of Her Long and Friendly Sojourning amongst a Strangely Interesting People* (London, Hodder & Stoughton, 1931).

Spence, Jonathan, *The Gate of Heavenly Peace: The Chinese and Their Revolution, 1895–1980* (London, Faber, 1982).

—— *God's Chinese Son: The Taiping Heavenly Kingdom of Hong Xiuquan* (London, Harper Collins, 1996).

—— *The Search for Modern China* (New York and London, Norton, 1990).

Stansky, Peter, and Abrahams, William, *Journey to the Frontier: Two Roads to the Spanish Civil War* (London, Constable, 1994).

Staunton, George Leonard, *An Authentic Account of an Embassy from the King of Great Britain to the Emperor of China . . .* (London, J. Nicol, 1797).

Bibliography

The Stead sisters, *Stone–Paper–Scissors: Shanghai 1921–1945: An Autobiography* (Deddington, Oxon Publishing, 1991).

Sternberg, Joseph von, *Fun in a Chinese Laundry* (New York, Macmillan, 1955).

Teichman, Eric, *Affairs of China: A Survey of the Recent History, and Present Circumstances of the Republic of China* (London, Methuen, 1938).

Thompson, Phyllis, *D.E. Hoste, 'a Prince with God'. Hudson Taylor's Successor as General Director of the China Inland Mission 1900–1935* (London, China Inland Mission, 1947).

Trevor-Roper, Hugh, *Hermit of Peking: The Hidden Life of Sir Edmund Trelawney Backhouse* (London, Macmillan, 1976; reprinted London, Eland, 1993).

Tsai Chin, *Daughter of Shanghai* (London, Chatto & Windus, 1988).

Tyler, William Ferdinand, *Pulling Strings in China* (London, Constable, 1929).

Waley, Arthur, *The Opium War Through Chinese Eyes* (London, Allen & Unwin, 1958).

Walker, Annabel, *Aurel Stein, Pioneer of the Silk Road* (London, John Muray, 1995).

Walrond, Theodore (ed.), *The Letters and Journals of James, Eighth Earl of Elgin* (London, John Murray, 1873).

Ward, Edward, *Number One Boy* (London, Michael Joseph, 1969).

Warner, Thorsten, *Deutsche Architektur in China: Architekturtransfer* (Berlin, Ernst & Sohn, 1994).

Wasserstein, Bernard, *The Secret Lives of Trebitsch Lincoln* (Harmondsworth, Penguin, 1989).

Watney, John, *Mervyn Peake* (London, Michael Joseph, 1976).

Watson, Jean, *Bosshardt: A Biography. The Story of a Christian Missionary Caught up in Mao's Long March* (Crowborough, Overseas Missionary Fellowship, 1995).

Wedderburn, Gren, *No Lotus Garden* (Hong Kong, Gulliver Books, 1979).

Wei, Betty Peh-t'i, *Shanghai: Crucible of Modern China* (Hong Kong, Oxford University Press, 1990).

Werner, E.T.C., *Autumn Leaves: An Autobiography with a Sheaf of*

Papers, Sociological, Sinological, Philosophical and Metaphysical (Shanghai, Hong Kong and Singapore, Kelly & Walsh, 1928).

Whyte, Bob, *Unfinished Encounter: China and Christianity* (London, Fount Paperbacks, 1988).

Woodhead, H.G.W., *A Journalist in China* (London, Hurst & Blackett, 1934).

Wright, Arnold (ed.), *Twentieth-century Impressions of Hong Kong, Shanghai and Other Treaty Ports of China* (London, Lloyd's Greater Britain Publishing Company, 1908).

Wylie, Alexander, *Memorials of the Protestant Missions to the Chinese, giving a list of their publications and obituary notices of the deceased with copious indexes* (Shanghai, American Presbyterian Mission Press, 1867).

Index

354

Index

Sassoon family, 281
Saunders, Nellie, 155–6, 158
Schad, Herr, 272
Schneider, Herr, 223
schools, 216–18, 265–6, 291
Schultz, H.M. & Co., 172
Scott, Sir Gilbert, 28
Second World War, 263, 281, 284–96, 297
Seitz, Carl, 194
servants, 131–3, 150–1, 211–15
Service, Grace, 174, 213
Service, John S., 219
Service family, 219–20
settlements, 1, 42–3
Seymour, Admiral Sir Michael, 83, 84, 85
Shaanxi province see Shensi province
Sha-li-pu, 117
Shandong see Shantung
Shanghai, 1, 3, 86; abolition of
   concessions, 297; anti-Japanese
   demonstrations, 273, 274; buildings,
   129, 192–4, 258, 259, 261, 299, 301;
   businessmen, 4, 205, 206; children's
   amusements, 219; Chinese families,
   263–8; Communist attitudes to, 298–9;
   compradors, 255; customs service,
   67–8, 142, 152; early history, 18–33; First
   World War, 175, 177; French
   Concession, 21, 32, 59–60, 80, 236, 266,
   267, 277, 280, 285; horse racing, 225–6;
   International Settlement, 60, 80, 175,
   179, 185, 193, 236, 239, 254, 266–7, 276,
   277, 280, 285; Jewish refugees, 280–1;
   Kuomintang seizes, 181, 185, 186, 189;
   law courts, 2, 80, 187–8; Mixed Court
   Riots, 177–8; municipal council, 21,
   59–60; newspapers, 257, 258; 1911
   revolution, 174–5; opera, 263–4; opium
   trade, 87; paper-chases, 27, 123;
   schools, 216; Second World War, 285,
   286, 288–9, 292–6; Sino-Japanese War,
   276–7, 278, 280; Small Sword
   rebellion, 61, 63–8; social and private
   life, 194–5, 210, 211, 222, 223–4, 226–7,
   261–2; strikes, 179; Taiping rebellion,
   73–7, 80; Treaty of Nanking, 16;
   visitors, 232, 236, 237–9, 251

Shanghai Academy of Social Sciences,
   298–9
Shanghai Club, 80
Shanghai Electrical Co., 254
Shanghai Fire Service, 60
Shanghai–Nanking railway, 196
Shanghai Paper Hunt, 27
Shanghai Recreation Fund, 26, 299
Shanghai Volunteer Force, 60, 66–7
Shanghai Women's Bank, 260–1
Shanghai–Woosung railway, 196
Shantou see Swatow
Shantung (Shandong) province, 89, 109,
   161, 170, 177, 178, 196, 271, 272
Shanxi province see Shansi province
Shasi, 107
Shaw, George Bernard, 251–2, 256
Shearman, Henry, 257
Shensi (Shaanxi) province, 154
Shenyang see Mukden
Shiozawa, Admiral, 274
shooting trips, 120–3
Sian (Xi'an), 275
Siccawei (Xujiahui), 28, 154
Sichuan province see Szechwan province
Siege of the Legations, Peking, 161, 163,
   164–5
Sikhs, 60, 94, 266, 267, 298
Silk Road, 171
silk trade, 22
silver, 23–4
Simao see Ssumao
Simpson, Wallis (later Duchess of
   Windsor), 239–40
Sinclair, C.A., 43
Singapore, 84
Sinkiang (Xinjiang) province, 174
Sino-French War (1884), 147
Sino-Japanese War (1894–5), 98, 106–7,
   275–80, 281, 284
Sisters of St Vincent de Paul, 32
Sitwell, Osbert, 241, 242–3
Skinner, Mr, 65
Small Sword rebellion, 21, 60, 61–8, 69, 81
Smedley, Agnes, 252
Smith, Alfred, 150